THE I TATTI
RENAISSANCE LIBRARY

James Hankins, General Editor

FLAVIO
ROME IN TRIUMPH

VOLUME I

ITRL 74

LATIN TEXT EDITED BY

MARIA AGATA PINCELLI

INTRODUCTION,
ENGLISH TRANSLATION,
AND NOTES BY

FRANCES MUECKE

THE I TATTI RENAISSANCE LIBRARY
HARVARD UNIVERSITY PRESS
CAMBRIDGE, MASSACHUSETTS
LONDON, ENGLAND
2016

Printed in the United States of America

Series design by Dean Bornstein

Library of Congress Cataloging-in-Publication Data

Names: Biondo Flavio, 1392–1463, author. | Pincelli, Maria Agata, editor. |
Muecke, Frances, writer of introduction,
translator, writer of supplementary textual content. |
Biondo Flavio, 1392–1463.
Roma triumphans. Container of (expression): |
Biondo Flavio, 1392–1463.
Roma triumphans. English. Container of (expression):
Title: Rome in triumph / Biondo Flavio ;
Latin text edited by Maria Agata Pincelli ; introduction,
English translation, and notes by Frances Muecke.
Other titles: I Tatti Renaissance library ; 74.
Description: Cambridge, Massachusetts : Harvard University Press, 2016. |
Series: The I Tatti Renaissance library ; 74 |
English translations on rectos with Latin originals on versos.
Identifiers: LCCN 2015037411 | ISBN 9780674055049 (alk. paper)
Subjects: LCSH: Rome (Italy) — Antiquities — Early works to 1800. |
Rome — Civilization — Early works to 1800.
Classification: LCC DG65 .B56 2016 |
DDC 945 — dc23
LC record available at http://lccn.loc.gov/2015037411

Contents

Introduction

Non possim non clamare plurimum Blondo secula nostra,
plurimum doctos, plurimum indoctos, plurimum posteritatem debere.

—Jacopo Bracelli, 1447

Toward the end of 1459, Biondo Flavio (1392–1463) was in Mantua. In his role as Apostolic Secretary he had accompanied the curia to the Congress of Mantua (May 27, 1459—January 19, 1460), at which the ailing Pope Pius II (1405–64) hoped to rally support for a crusade against the Turks, one of his main concerns since taking office in 1458. It was from here that on December 12, 1458, Biondo wrote the letter to Galeazzo Sforza, which gives the earliest extant news of the book with the title *Rome in Triumph* (*Roma triumphans*), the first attempt at a comprehensive exposition of Roman civilization, and it was here that he completed it before his return to Rome.[1]

Born in Forlì, Biondo was educated in Cremona, where he took lessons in grammar, poetry, and rhetoric with Giovanni Balestrieri.[2] Subsequently, he trained as a notary. His early life was spent in the north of Italy, where he made important contacts at the courts of Milan and Mantua and in the republic of Venice. His meeting with the humanist educator Guarino in Verona in 1420 was highly significant for his development as a scholar. A longstanding friendship ensued, which involved the discussion of and exchange of texts. Another important early friendship was with his contemporary, the Venetian patrician Francesco Barbaro (1390–1454), whom he assisted in the latter's magistracy at Vicenza in 1424–25. From 1432, Biondo rose through temporary positions of this nature to a more stable role in the curia of Eugenius IV, whose trusted officer he became. The absence of the pope from

Rome (from May 1434 to September 1443) gave the curia extended stays at Florence and Ferrara and gave Biondo more opportunities for discussion with other humanists and their elite patrons, the young Leonello d'Este, Marquis of Ferrara from 1441, for example. Having fallen out of favor with the next pope, Nicholas V, a few years earlier, Biondo returned to his curial position in 1453.

By this time Biondo had become well known for his humanist writings and historical research, both deeply affected by his involvement in political life at a time of major cultural and institutional change.[3] Among other works, he had just completed his ambitious history (begun in 1439) of the period from the sack of Rome in 412 CE to 1441, *Three Decades on the History of the Romans Beginning with the Decline of Their Empire* (*Historiarum ab inclinatione Romani imperii decades III*).[4]

The threat of the Turks to the West dominated the period of the conception and writing of *Rome in Triumph*. The Fall of Constantinople (1453) has been emphasized as an important factor in Biondo's advocacy of Roman civilization in this work.[5] Its framing certainly sets it in the context of resistance to Turkish encroachments, now threateningly close to Italy. In his dedication to Pius II, Biondo speaks of an alliance of Italy, France, Spain, and Germany for "the liberation of Europe" and of the role his work might play in stimulating such an enterprise. In the light of the lack of real success achieved by the Congress of Mantua, he concludes the whole work with a disillusioned warning that if Western Christians do not fight they will eventually suffer the fate of the Greeks.[6] Two of the longer digressions concerned with contemporary events are more or less connected with the Turkish threat: the description of the victory celebration (March 1457) for the battle at Belgrade on July 21–22, 1456, in Book 2 (§51), and, in Book 5 (pp. 117d–18b), the commendation of Isabel of Burgundy's support (in 1454?) of a crusade against the Turks.[7]

Overt endorsement of Pius II's campaign follows from the main idea that drives *Rome in Triumph*, that is, that the Roman state in its totality presents a high-point of human civilization that has not been surpassed. Through conquest and the resulting spread of a common language, the Romans had brought long-lasting peace to their empire, which they ruled with good laws and practices, disseminating beneficent ethical, civil and political values. For this reason Rome is a compelling subject, which Biondo explicitly presents as exemplary for human life. In this last of his major works, his purpose is to show his contemporaries how and why the Roman system worked well. Nevertheless, the historian's eyes are not dimmed by his rose-colored spectacles. Most important of all is to understand and show, in as concrete and accurate a way as possible, the facts, whether positive or negative, about particular aspects of Roman institutions.

In his Proem, Biondo divides the work into five parts: religion (Books 1–2); government of the state, first within Rome and then without (*externum regimen*) (Books 3–5); military organization (Books 6–7); the customs and institutions of everyday life (Books 8–9); and the triumph itself (Book 10). Further subdivisions are introduced where necessary. The more important are Books 1–2: gods, priesthoods, cult and sacrifice, ceremonies and festivals; Books 3–5: public magistrates, provincial government, elections, the senate, administrative functions, law and the penal code, citizenship, the treatment of slaves, fiscal arrangements, monetary values, the grain dole and largess, debt and interest, the old virtues of moderation, integrity and continence; Books 6–7: formations and ranks of the army, military discipline, pay and privileges of soldiers, their retirement, order of battle, insignia, the fleet, Rome's military history, and the ideal general; Books 8–9: marriage, divorce, education, agriculture, food, drink and parties, country villas and town houses, furniture, clothes, roads, means of

transport.[8] In reality, the organization is flexible and Biondo allows himself detours.

One of the longest detours is in Book 4, where, in the middle of a discussion of trials, Biondo has an extensive treatment of slaves and freedmen and turns from this to an excursion, acknowledged as such, on the status, prestige, and role of literature and learning in the Roman state (pp. 96–100). The discussion of buildings in Book 9 incorporates a more relevant collection of passages on the history of luxury (pp. 184e–87a), which itself includes a section on medicine (p. 186), and ends with the apology: "We have given enough rein to our indignation in this description."

Methodologically, Book 7 and Book 10 do not fit the general pattern of composition of the whole work, for in them there is a marked separation of the historical and exemplificatory strands, which are elsewhere woven together.[9] Book 7's first part consists of a severely abbreviated (*strictissima brevitate*) history of Rome's wars, including the civil, from Pyrrhus' invasion to Rome's fall to the Goths (which Biondo notoriously dates April 412 CE).[10] The purpose of this is to illustrate, in a historical perspective, the efficacy of Roman military science as well as "the greatness, importance, and variety of Roman military affairs" (p. 152g). A substantial portion of the chronicle is intended to fill in minimally the gaps caused by the missing decades of Livy, something that Leonardo Bruni had already done, at least for the second decade, in *De primo bello punico* (1422), as Biondo knew.[11] The second part of Book 7 (pp. 152g–59d) contains sections selected and transcribed from the recent (*proximis temporibus*, 1456?) translation of Onasander's *Strategikos* (*De optimo imperatore*) by his friend and former curial colleague under Eugenius IV, Niccolò Sagundino (1402–64).[12] Similarly, in Book 10 a historical survey of the triumph from beginning to end precedes the template for a Christian triumph abstracted from a number of historical examples.

Toward the end of the work a second address to Pius II, written perhaps soon after his election in 1458, reveals something about the genesis of the work. At the beginning of Book 9 Biondo tells Pius II about a disagreement he had had with their mutual friend Francesco Barbaro shortly before the latter's death (January 1454).[13] During a discussion of other aspects of Rome's former glory (*priscae felicitatis*) as well as matters to do with buildings, which lasted for some days, he had not been able to convince Barbaro that not even one magnate of their own time in Italy could, in the luxury and splendor of his private furnishings and dwelling, equal that of any number of ancient Romans. The resolution of the dispute was put off until Biondo had completed "this work determined on with his advice and encouragement," and now its judgment is delegated to Pius. This shows that by 1453 Biondo was planning to write a work that illustrated and accounted for Rome's long-standing success. We do not know when he began to compose it or when it acquired its special focus on institutions.[14]

For Biondo himself, "the matter of Rome," the city and the ideal, ramified through his major works.[15] It is not surprising that he returned to it after finishing the second recension of *Italy Illuminated* (*Italia illustrata*) in 1453. His earlier works, especially *Rome Restored* (*De Roma instaurata libri tres*, 1446), three books on the topography of ancient Rome, had stimulated, not satisfied, the interests of his friends in Roman matters.[16] In a letter to Leonello d'Este of February 1, 1446, we glimpse him called in to perform as an expert at a dinner party given by Cardinal Prospero Colonna (a fellow *antiquitatis investigator*) and informing the guests about the Roman treasury.[17] A query of Colonna's quoted in Book 4 illustrates the sort of questions Biondo got from his friends and that he attempted to answer in *Rome in Triumph*: Colonna wanted to know what pay the senators had to live on.[18] Elsewhere Biondo refers to his readers' interests and sometimes explains why he cannot fully satisfy them.[19] Allied to this is Biondo's concern to point

out particular Roman practices that he thinks worthy of imitation by his contemporaries, in keeping with the declaration of intent in his proem:

> Therefore I have begun the attempt to see if I can bring forward and set before the eyes and minds of the intellectually gifted and learned people of our time, a mirror, model, image, and lesson of all moral excellence and of the way of living well, religiously and happily, the City of Rome when it flourished and triumphed as St. Augustine wished to see it.

What makes *Rome in Triumph* unique in its time is the ambitious scope and detail of its coverage of Roman public and private institutions and its tenacious and painstaking research. There was no comparable precedent for its scale and combination of topics in the post-antique world, but a few previous or contemporaneous works give evidence of parallel interests.[20] The most influential and important of these for our purposes, since Biondo used it, is Andrea Fiocchi's *De potestatibus Romanis* (ca. 1425).[21] This is a historico-antiquarian treatise focusing on the republican period in two parts, the first on priests, the second on magistrates.[22] Similarly, Biondo's friend Pier Candido Decembrio, a humanist from Milan, included in his *Historia peregrina* (ca. 1430–33) a brief treatment of the *mores et instituta* of the Roman state, that this time began with civic magistracies and moved on to priesthoods.[23] This remained in manuscript, as did Gasparino Barzizza's earlier work of the same kind.[24] As to treatises on the state, Biondo claims at the beginning of Book 3 that his own treatment will exceed any previous ones, ancient or modern, in inclusiveness.[25]

Another key topic that had already been treated by another was military organization. We know that in 1422 Biondo made a manuscript copy of Leonardo Bruni's *De militia* (ca. 1420), a humanist treatment mainly based on ancient sources.[26] Also known to

Biondo in person was Roberto Valturio, but possibly not his twelve-book *De re militari*, as it was written in the 1450s, at about the same time as *Rome in Triumph*.[27] Other works can be mentioned that did not focus primarily on the ancient world but still collected evidence about it, which their authors regarded as relevant to their contemporary world. Francesco Barbaro's precocious *De re uxoria* (1416) presents ancient customs to do with marriage and the family, but not as its main *raison d'être*. Likewise, Leon Battista Alberti's *De re aedificatoria* (conventionally dated 1443–52) has a great deal of material from ancient sources on topics that go beyond architecture strictly conceived.

Biondo's *Rome in Triumph* should be recognized as belonging to the long-established late-antique and medieval genre of the "compilation," with the proviso that compilation of knowledge also means creation of knowledge. As such, it is primarily made up of excerpts from ancient literary texts, the author's main task being their selection and purposeful organization.[28] Unlike medieval compilators, however, Biondo is not self-effacing. He often reaches out to involve the reader in his questions and conclusions and brings up a number of contemporary analogies to reinforce his descriptions.[29]

Biondo's sources are too many and various to be surveyed here with any completeness.[30] His great strength lies not only in the number of works he used but in his ability to find highly relevant material in so many different places. The chronological scope ranges from early Latin literature (Ennius and Cato) through to later antiquity and the Christian fathers (Augustine, Lactantius, Jerome, Cassiodorus) and to contemporaries (Fiocchi). He draws on historians (Livy above all), biographers (*Scriptores Historiae Augustae* stands out), and poets, on oratory and letters (Cicero is the most represented here), on technical works (the *Digest*,[31] Frontinus, Varro, Vegetius), on glossaries and lexicography (Festus,[32] Nonius Marcellus, Placidus), and on ancient encyclopedic and

miscellaneous works (Pliny the Elder, Aulus Gellius, Macrobius). Philosophical texts as such present little attraction for our author. Sources drawn on particularly in *Rome in Triumph,* apart from those Biondo used regularly, such as Livy, are Festus, Plutarch, Aulus Gellius, Asconius Pedianus, Vergil, Pliny the Younger, Seneca, and the *Digest*.[33]

Biondo was working at a time when he was able to take advantage of the important discoveries made by Poggio Bracciolini, such as Asconius, Cicero (especially *Brutus* and *On the Laws*), Quintilian, Frontinus, and other recent acquisitions in Italy, such as Pliny the Younger's *Epistles* and Tacitus *Annals* 11–16.[34] However, perhaps owing to his estrangement from the curia in the time of Nicholas V, Biondo did not have translations of Polybius (Niccolò Perotti, ca. 1454), or Diodorus Siculus (Poggio Bracciolini, 1449). That of Dionysius of Halicarnassus (Lampugnino Birago, 1468–69) came too late.

Nevertheless, absence from Rome did not prevent Biondo from obtaining George of Trebizond's translation (1448), commissioned by Pope Nicholas V, of Eusebius' *Preparation for the Gospel*. Among much else that it contains are sizable excerpts from Diodorus and Dionysius (see Book 1, §25; and §9, where Diodorus is the real source, not Porphyry). Eusebius' *Preparation for the Gospel* underlies §§4–25 of Book 1. The translator's name is never acknowledged, nor is that of Gian Pietro d'Avenza, who translated Plutarch's antiquarian miscellany *Roman Questions* (1453) just in time for it to become Biondo's most important Greek source.[35] In contrast are the emphatic introductions of the extract from Herodian (*History of the Empire after Marcus,* 4.2–3) supplied by Marco Barbo from Ognibene da Lonigo[36] and of the many pages from Niccolò Sagundino's *Strategikos* in Book 7. Similarly, Biondo silently incorporates a few snippets from Pier Candido Decembrio's translation of Appian's *Roman History* (1450–54).[37]

It is comparatively rare for ancient sources not to be acknowledged. Medieval and contemporary ones are another matter.[38] One instance is the "concealed" passage based on Fiocchi in Book 4, and another is much of the first part of Book 7. From the beginning of the historical narrative until it reaches the end of the Republic, the unmentioned underlying source, supplemented mainly from the *Periochae* of Livy and occasionally elsewhere, is a version of Paul the Deacon's *Roman History,* interestingly recast in a more classical style.[39] Some absences may be noted. Very few inscriptions are cited.[40] Authors whom one might expect to meet more often are Caesar and Sallust, both of whom provide very few citations, though their works are praised, Sallust's *Catilinarian War* as a "very fine history" (Book 7, p. 148h), and Caesar's *Gallic Wars* in the same place for the elegance of its writing.

Cappelletto's observations on the different ways in which Biondo quotes his sources in *Italy Illuminated* apply equally to *Rome in Triumph.* His procedures range from exact word-for-word citation, a mixture of abridgment and quotation, paraphrase with some verbal echoes, to fairly free rewriting.[41] In very many places Biondo's text is different from that of modern critical editions of the ancient authors, but it can generally be shown that he is reproducing readings from the manuscripts he has in hand. Occasional lapses in attribution or in understanding betray haste or misrepresentation by what Jeffrey White nicely terms "strenuous customization."[42] Biondo's usual method of presenting evidence is to collect and put together excerpts from different genres and historical periods,[43] but occasionally, as in the pages in Book 1 from Eusebius, *Preparation for the Gospel* and Augustine, *City of God,* and, as already mentioned, in the case of Book 7, there are places where a single source dominates, without however excluding other relevant information.

The reforming zeal that Biondo expresses clearly at the end of *Borsus* (January 16, 1460) surfaces, but only rarely, in *Rome in*

Triumph.[44] This coheres with the author's stated reluctance to express value judgments on particular aspects of Roman history. In the face of the contemporary controversy over the merits of Julius Caesar, he declines to take a position on whether his *opinio principatus* (expectation of gaining supremacy) brought more harm or good to the Roman state.[45] Though it is inevitable that Biondo at times reflects the political views expressed in his sources ("liberty" versus "tyranny"), generally he steers clear of political history for its own sake. As Fubini says, the nature of the work does not permit a coherent interpretation of either the republican or the imperial eras.[46] Two matters draw his particular criticism, the civil wars of the late republic (Book 7, §38, Capra; compare pp. 148h–49a) and the unconstitutional role of the praetorian guard after it was stationed in the city (Book 6, p. 131a).[47] He expresses open admiration of Roman constitutional arrangements and methods of government (beginning and end of Book 5), and of their old-fashioned integrity, moderation, and frugality (last part of Book 5). He praises equality before the law ("The true excellence of Rome lies in the fact that no one could be exempted from a trial," Book 4, p. 91c), and recommends (imperial) measures taken against corruption in provincial administration (Book 4, p. 87d). Good emperors, such as Augustus, Vespasian, Trajan, Antoninus Pius, and Marcus Aurelius, are praised, while bad emperors receive due criticism.

Biondo's time frame, which he treats as a single historical period, is from the foundation of Rome to its sack by the Goths—more than a thousand years.[48] For him this is a cultural continuum in which institutions and customs persist, but not a time-free zone. It manifests both stability and innovation. The main historical eras—those of the kings, the republic, and the empire, each of which had their own form of government (*formas gubernationis*, Book 3, p. 54h)—are naturally referred to most often in the books on government. Here Biondo notes constitutional developments

over time and the innovations, some good, made in the imperial period (Book 3, p. 59d; Book 4, p. 87c). Customs evolve too, and Biondo observes changes over time in such matters as food and drink (Book 8, pp. 176–78) and modes of transport, as far as he is able, while marshaling sixteen different kinds of wheeled vehicles (Book 9, pp. 199–202).

The triumph was a highly suitable topic to conclude a celebration of Roman imperialism. Despite its putative origins in Greek mythology, the triumph became a quintessentially Roman institution. It was almost as old as Rome itself and, for Biondo, a gauge of Rome's growing power, lasting for almost the whole period he treats, from Titus Tatius (*sic*) to Probus (late third century CE).[49] By calling his work *Rome in Triumph*, Biondo highlights, as Tomassini says, not so much the work's historical investigations and the topics it treats, as Rome as a symbol of glory and victory and promise of future success.[50] The triumph was a spectacular visual display, embedded in Roman sacral topography, with which the route of modern papal processions, in Biondo's eyes, showed remarkable parallelism.[51] Accounts of and references to the triumph were ubiquitous in Roman literature and historical texts, lending themselves to literary *imitatio* and providing the scripts for the celebrations of real-life reenactments. Petrarch, for example, makes his epic *Africa* culminate with a long and vivid description of Scipio's triumph (9.322–99).

When Biondo wrote, the recasting of celebratory processions as "triumphs" *all'antica* in political and civic spectacle had already begun. Not long before there had been the spectacular triumphal entry of Alfonso of Aragon into Naples, on February 26, 1443, celebrated in art and architecture as well as in prose and verse (see *Italy Illuminated*, pp. 393d, 417d).[52] Soon after, in 1448, Sigismondo Pandolfo Malatesta of Rimini held a triumphal entry in Florence.[53] He was the dedicatee of Valturio's *De re militari*, which culminates in Book 12 with description of the Roman triumph and

other military rewards. Biondo's aim is less partisan. By his vivid description of the sights and the sounds of the ancient triumph as it might be celebrated by a Christian leader in the streets of his own Rome, he wishes to kindle enthusiasm, not only for victory over the Turks but also for the restoration of a world empire as admirably governed as that of the Romans.

These clues to the contemporary dimension of Biondo's work bring us back to the proem and, with that, the circumstances of the work's completion at the Congress of Mantua. Biondo's presence at the Gonzaga court had a lasting impact there and beyond, arousing interest in *Rome in Triumph* among the eminent figures gathered for the Congress from Italy and abroad.[54] Their curiosity piqued, no doubt, by conversations about *Rome in Triumph*, members of the Gonzaga family acquired early copies of the work. Similarly, another early copy was carried back to Portugal, by the ambassador Giovanni Fernandez, who had discussed it en route with Biondo and "seen it completed at Mantua."[55] Some years later (1473), Mantua too saw the first printing of *Rome in Triumph*.[56]

Memories of Biondo's stay and interest in *Rome in Triumph* would have been alive when in 1460 the artist Mantegna, famous for his "Triumphs of Caesar," arrived in Mantua.[57] The *Triumphs*, his "most ambitious project as an archaeological painter," were painted from an uncertain date until about 1495.[58] Art historians concur that *Rome in Triumph* was probably one of Mantegna's written sources, and Biondo's self-conscious visualization of a triumph happening before his eyes could well have inspired an artist already interested in visual reconstruction of the Roman past. A connection was discerned and disseminated in the early 1500s, when snippets of Biondo's text accompanied some editions of a monumental print of a triumph of Caesar made in Venice by Benedetto Bordon and Jacobus Argentoratensis.[59]

After its first printing in Mantua, *Rome in Triumph* went though four more editions, until 1533, as well as being included in the

Opera Omnia put out by Froben in Basel (1531, 1559). Our edition is the first since 1559. Despite this lacuna, Biondo's legacy was long lasting. He initiated the study of Roman civilization as a unified whole, establishing a division of the main categories (religion, government, the army, daily life), which remained fundamental for many centuries.[60] From the 1550s on, *Rome in Triumph* began to be displaced by a series of single-topic treatises on aspects of Roman cultural and institutional history, but in the later fifteenth and early sixteenth centuries it was still a much-used reference work, especially by the authors of the spate of printed commentaries on ancient texts that began to appear and circulate throughout Europe.[61] A vivid indication of the spread of its fame is the request from the Cistercian monk and scholar Conrad Leontorius to the printer Johannes Amerbach in a letter written from the hermitage of Engental (March 4, 1504): "Then too there is a book I am looking for everywhere, for which I have been crying out for so long, for want of which I disturb the heavens, the seas, and the earth. The book in question is *De Roma triumphans* (*sic*) by Biondo of Forlì. . . . Price and money are no object. I want it so much I will pay whatever it takes."[62]

This volume initiates the series devoted to *Rome in Triumph*. Though their responsibilities have been divided, the two authors have worked closely together.

The project would not have reached its present stage without the support of Australian Research Council's Discovery Project Scheme (DP130102112) from 2013 to 2015. The University of Sydney also provided generous financial and other support, for which we are grateful.

In 2006 Maria Agata Pincelli was able to begin her research on Biondo in congenial surroundings as a Villa I Tatti Fellow. She would like particularly to thank the Director, Joseph Connors, and

all the staff, then and subsequently. Frances Muecke has benefited from valuable periods of work in the Library of American Academy in Rome, the Library of the Institute of Classical Studies, London, and the Warburg Institute, London.

People who have helped us in various ways and whom we are delighted to thank here are our research assistants Mary Jane Cuyler, Michelle McVeigh, and Kit Morrell. Maurizio Campanelli and Robert Ulery have willingly responded to requests for help. Albertus Horsting read the Latin text and translation meticulously and suggested numerous improvements. Throughout a rather extended gestation period, James Hankins has been ready with enthusiastic encouragement. We thank him for his patience, confidence in us, and belief in Biondo.

Sydney, November 2015

NOTES

1. The letter, which incorporates parts of *Rome in Triumph* (hereafter *R.T.*) Book 5, is printed in Nogara, *Scritti*, pp. 178–89. Biondo is sure his addressee will look at *R.T.* with great pleasure and profit (p. 186). (Full citations of works cited briefly in this Introduction may be found in the Bibliography or in the Abbreviations in the Notes to the Translation.)

2. *Italy Illuminated* (hereafter *I.I.*), Lombardy §23.

3. See Gary Ianziti, *Humanistic Historiography under the Sforzas: Politics and Propaganda in Fifteenth-Century Milan* (Oxford: Clarendon Press, 1988), pp. 1–19.

4. For more detailed accounts of the life, see Nogara, *Scritti;* Fubini, "Biondo Flavio"; and Masius, *Flavio Biondo*.

5. See Mazzocco, "Rome and the Humanists," p. 195 and n. 37; Tomassini, "Per una lettura," p. 50; Miller, *Roman Triumphs*, pp. 44–55. In 1452–53 Biondo had written *Oratio coram serenissimo imperatore Frederico et Alphonso, Aragonum rege* (text in Nogara, *Scritti*, pp. 107–14) and *Ad Alphonsum Aragonensem de expeditione in Turchos* (Nogara, *Scritti*, pp. 52–

58). See G. Rossi, "Reazioni umanistiche all'avanzata turca: l'appello di Biondo Flavio ad Alfonso d'Aragona (1453)," in *Oriente e Occidente nel Rinascimento*. Atti del XIX Convegno Internazionale (Chianciano Terme-Pienza, 16–19 luglio 2007), ed. L. Secchi Tarugi (Florence: Franco Cesati Editore, 2009), pp. 669–79.

6. See Mazzocco, "*Urbem Romam florentem*," pp. 138f.

7. See Marcellino, "Lo studio delle antichità romane." The defeat inflicted on the Turks at Belgrade (and subsequent death of John Hunyadi in the same year) is mentioned again in Book 7, pp. 150h–51a. (For Books 1 and 2 we refer to the sections of this edition; for the later books, to the page numbers and sections of the Basel 1559 edition.)

8. A fuller summary of the ten books may be found in Nogara, *Scritti*, pp. cli–cliv.

9. Ingo Herklotz, *La Roma degli Antiquari. Cultura e erudizione tra Cinquecento e Settecento* (Rome: De Luca editore d'arte, 2012), pp. 192f., recognizes Book 10 as a precedent for the compromise between the chronological and descriptive approaches evinced by later antiquarianism but not the extent to which the whole of *R.T.* is permeated by chronological awareness.

10. Book 7, pp. 145c–52g must be supplemented by the portion published by Capra, "Un tratto di *Roma triumphans* omesso dagli stampatori."

11. Nogara, *Scritti*, pp. 115f.; Gary Ianziti, *Writing History in Renaissance Italy: Leonardo Bruni and the Uses of the Past* (Cambridge, MA: Harvard University Press, 2012), pp. 61–88. Incidentally, in this part of Book 7, Biondo provides "an appraisal of the sources available on Roman History"; see Mazzocco, "Some Philological Aspects," p. 18.

12. Nogara, *Scritti*, p. cliii n. 186.

13. Biondo returns to this discussion on p. 193b. The friendship with Barbaro was an important and long-lasting one.

14. Mazzocco, "Some Philological Aspects," pp. 2–4, against Nogara, *Scritti*, p. cli. Mazzocco points out that the wager with Barbaro sits uneasily with Biondo's praise of Cosimo de Medici's residence in Florence as equaling that of any Roman potentate (*I.I.*, Tuscany §31).

15. Both *Roma instaurata* (hereafter *R.I.*) and *I.I.* were drawn on in later antiquarian treatments of Rome, such as Andrea Fulvio's *Antiquitates urbis* (Rome: [M. Silber], 1527), and Bartolomeo Marliani's *Topographia antiquae Romae* (Lugduni: S. Gryphius, 1534).

16. See Mazzocco, "Some Philological Aspects," pp. 10–15, on the complementarity of *R.I.* and *R.T.*

17. The letter is printed in Nogara, *Scritti*, pp. 159f.

18. Book 4, p. 85a, where Biondo calls him "a very important man and very assiduous (*diligentissimus*) investigator of Roman matters." Compare Tomassini, "Per una lettura," p. 47.

19. Similarly, in *Borsus* (1460) §§30–33, Biondo refers to the reaction of a reader of *R.T.*, Iacopo Zeno, to what Biondo said was the role of the *equites* in tax collecting (Book 5, p. 108); compare Blondus Flavius, *Borsus*, ed. Maria Agata Pincelli (Roma: Istituto Storico Italiano per il Medio Evo, 2009), p. xx. *Borsus* itself arises from just such a query (§5).

20. Giovanni Cavallini's *Polistoria de virtutibus et dotibus Romanorum*, ed. M. Laureys (Stuttgart: Teubner, 1995) is a precedent more for *R.I.*, though in Book 3 it treats some civic matters and in Book 5 the games. See M. Laureys, "Between *Mirabilia* and *Roma Instaurata*: Giovanni Cavallini's *Polistoria*," in *Avignon & Naples: Italy in France—France in Italy in the Fourteenth Century*, ed. Marianne Pade, Hannemarie Ragn Jensen, and Lene Waage Petersen (Rome: "L'Erma" di Bretschneider, 1997), pp. 101–15.

21. Fubini, "Biondo Flavio," p. 552, points out the degree to which Biondo surpasses Fiocchi. Andrea Fiocchi (Andreas Florentinus), a curial colleague, is one of the participants in Biondo's treatise *De verbis Romanae locutionis* (1435); for the text, see Nogara, *Scritti*, pp. 115–30. Biondo mentions *De potestatibus Romanis* in *I.I.*, Tuscany §32 and draws on it in Book 4, pp. 87a–b.

22. M. Laureys, "At the Threshold of Humanist Jurisprudence: Andrea Fiocchi's *De potestatibus Romanis*," *Bulletin de l'Institut Historique Belge de Rome* 65 (1995): 25–42, at pp. 34f., comments on the importance of the *Digest* (1.2.2) for its organization of material, and on other sources; see E. Spagnesi, "Andrea Fiocchi, il 'Fenestella' e la storia del diritto," in *Capitolo*

di San Lorenzo nel Quattrocento. Convegno di studi (Firenze, 26–29 marzo 2003), ed. P. Viti (Florence: L. S. Olschki, 2006), pp. 145–83.

23. Ernst Ditt, "Pier Candido Decembrio, Contributo allo studio dell'umanesimo italiano (con una nota di R. Sabbadini)," *Memorie del Reale Istituto lombardo di scienze e lettere* 24 (1931): 21–106, at pp. 56–58; Paolo Viti, "Decembrio, Pier Candido," *DBI* 33 (1987): 488–98.

24. For Gasparino Barzizza (1360–1431) and his *Epilogus de magistratibus Romanis*, see A. Azzoni, "Ricerche barzizziane," *Bergomum* 54.2 (1960): 15–26; G. Martellotti, "Barzizza, Gasparino," *DBI* 7 (1965): 34–39; L. Bertalot, *Studien zum italienichen und deutschen Humanismus*, ed. P. O. Kristeller, 2 vols. (Rome: Edizioni di storia e letteratura, 1975), 2:285–300; W. McCuaig, "On a Treatise Ascribed to Bernardo Rucellai," in *Florence and Italy. Renaissance Studies in Honour of Nicolai Rubinstein*, ed. P. Denley and C. Elam (London: Committee for Medieval Studies, Westfield College, 1988), pp. 335–43. Sicco Polenton, possibly inspired by Barzizza, included in his literary history (1437) a chronological excursus on magistrates of the republic; see Sicco Polenton, *Scriptorum illustrium Latinae linguae libri XVIII*, ed. B. L. Ullman (Rome: American Academy in Rome, 1928), pp. 97–107, with p. xiii n. 3.

25. Pages 54e–f. Biondo could not read Polybius in the original and, apart from the *Somnium Scipionis*, preserved by Macrobius, had only those parts of Cicero's *De re publica* quoted by Augustine. Leonardo Bruni translated Aristotle's *Politics* and in 1437 corresponded with Biondo about presenting it to Eugenius IV; see Nogara, *Scritti*, pp. lxxx–lxxxii, 93–97. Bruni's compilation based on Polybius, the *De bello punico* (1420) and the later translation by Niccolò Perotti (1454) did not contain Book 6, the only part of Polybius' work containing formal political theory. For circulation of Book 6 in the fifteenth century, see James Hankins, "Europe's First Democrat? Cyriac of Ancona and Book 6 of Polybius," forthcoming in a Festschrift for Anthony Grafton, ed. Ann M. Blair, Anja Goeing, and Urs Leu (Leiden: E. J. Brill).

26. *I.I.*, Romagna §29 (BAV Ottob. lat. 1592). For comparisons with *Borsus*, see C. C. Bayley, *War and Society in Renaissance Florence. The* De Militia *of Leonardo Bruni* (Toronto: University of Toronto Press, 1961),

pp. 219–25, with his text and notes pp. 360–97; *Borsus*, pp. xiv–xix. On Bruni's use of ancient sources in this text, see James Hankins, "Civic Knighthood in the Early Renaissance: Leonardo Bruni's *De militia* (ca. 1420)," *Noctua: International On-line Journal on the History of Philosophy* 1.2 (2014): 260–82.

27. *I.I.*, Romagna §10. They were colleagues in Eugenius IV's curia. See Miller, *Roman Triumphs*, pp. 39–42. Valturio's *De re militari* cannot be dated precisely and is conventionally put between 1446 and 1455.

28. For the "rules" of the compilation, see Laureys, "Between *Mirabilia* and *Roma Instaurata*."

29. Tomassini, "Per una lettura," p. 25; Muecke, "*Ante oculos ponere*."

30. We signal them in the Notes to the Translation. Catalogs of sources may be found in Mazzocco, "Some Philological Aspects," pp. 18–25, with discussion, pp. 15–18; Tomassini, "Per una lettura," pp. 79f., with discussion, pp. 31–39. Clavuot, *Biondos Italia illustrata*, pp. 163f., provides a comparison with the other major works. On the sources of *R.I.*, see also Raffarin, *R.I.*, 1:l–lxiv.

31. Fabio Della Schiava, "Biondo Flavio, il *Digesto* e il *De verborum significatione* di Maffeo Vegio," *Studi e problemi di critica testuale* 89 (2014): 163–84, has shown that in *R.I.* and, probably, *R.T.* Biondo's citations of the *Digest* come from Vegio's alphabetical anthology of about 850 terms from it (1433).

32. Biondo did not realize that Paul the Deacon (Petrus Diaconus) was the later epitomator of Sextus Pompeius Festus' *De verborum significatu*. He writes that Festus was a Christian, Book 2, §39.

33. Clavuot, *Biondos Italia Illustrata*, p. 164.

34. It is important to realize that Biondo wrote before Tacitus *Annals* 1–6 came to Rome (in 1506) and that he did not have Velleius Paterculus (rediscovered 1515).

35. *Roman Questions* is used *passim* but especially in Books 1–2 and 8–9. See Muecke, "From Francesco Barbaro to Angelo Poliziano."

36. D. Gionta, "Storia di una citazione erodiana nella *Roma triumphans*: da Ognibene da Lonigo a Poliziano," in *Vetustatis Indagator. Scritti offerti a*

Filippo di Benedetto, ed. V. Fera and A. Guida (Messina: Università degli studi di Messina, 1999), pp. 129–53.

37. Book 7, p. 148h; Book 10, p. 206h; compare p. 213d.

38. Clavuot, *Biondos Italia Illustrata*, pp. 158f., suggests some reasons why later sources are not named.

39. Most of the solecisms listed by Capra, "Un tratto di *Roma triumphans* omesso dagli stampatori," on p. 312, come from Biondo's version of Paul the Deacon.

40. At *R.T.*, pp. 213b–c, Biondo cites a recently discovered inscription that he has seen *in situ*, prominently displayed on the corner of Andrea Santacroce's palazzo near Piazza Giudea.

41. Cappelletto, "*Italia illustrata* di Biondo Flavio," p. 706.

42. J. White, *Italy Illuminated* (Cambridge, MA: Harvard University Press, 2005), 1:xv.

43. He occasionally draws the reader's attention to this procedure. Compare Book 4, pp. 82h, 95b.

44. Bayley, *War*, pp. 219–22; *Borsus*, pp. xiv–xix; G. Rossi, "Il *Borsus* di Biondo Flavio: militia e iurisprudentia a confronto dall'antica Roma all'Italia delle corti rinascimentali," *Historia et ius* [www.historiaetius.eu] 4 (2013): 1–26.

45. Book 7, p. 148h. See Fubini, "Biondo Flavio," p. 553. Biondo alludes to the severe criticism expressed in Cicero, *On Duties* 1.26, a passage well known in this debate, and which he probably recalls precisely for this reason. See Peter Stacey, *Roman Monarchy and the Renaissance Prince* (Cambridge: Cambridge University Press, 2007), pp. 23–30, 188f.

46. Fubini, "Biondo Flavio," p. 553. See T. J. Dandelet, *The Renaissance of Empire in Early Modern Europe* (Cambridge: Cambridge University Press, 2014), pp. 54f.

47. Biondo expresses this criticism more forcefully in *R.I.* 2.87–89.

48. This innovative periodization is justified in the Preface to Book 1 of *Decades*. See Mazzocco, "Decline and Rebirth in Bruni and Biondo."

49. Book 10, p. 212f., based on Orosius 7.9. Orosius reckons 320 from Romulus to Vespasian.

50. Tomassini, "Per una lettura," p. 19. Compare Book 10, p. 205d: "We shall keep to the temporal order so that it may become evident that the splendor of the triumphs mirrored the power of the Roman people as it grew."

51. Book 10, p. 214h. See M. Beard, *The Roman Triumph* (Cambridge, MA: Harvard University Press, 2007), pp. 54f. On papal processions of the Renaissance as triumphs, see Charles L. Stinger, "*Roma triumphans:* Triumphs in the Thought and Ceremonies of Renaissance Rome," *Medievalia et Humanistica* 10 (1981): 189–201; and A. Dupuis-Raffarin, "La célébration des triomphes de Rome dans la *Roma instaurata* et la *Roma triumphans* de Flavio Biondo," in *Grecs et Romains aux prises avec l'histoire. Représentations, récits et idéologie*, ed. Guy Lachenaud and Dominique Longrée, 2 vols. (Rennes: Presses Universitaires de Rennes, 2003), 2:643–54.

52. Margaret Ann Zaho, *Imago Triumphalis: The Function and Significance of Triumphal Imagery for Italian Renaissance Rulers* (New York: Peter Lang Publishing, 2004), pp. 49–64.

53. Ibid., pp. 65–82.

54. On historiographical projects fostered at the Congress, see Ianziti, *Humanistic Historiography under the Sforzas*, pp. 202f.

55. Nogara, *Scritti*, pp. 192f.

56. Mazzocco, "Some Philological Aspects," pp. 4–7.

57. See Pincelli, "La *Roma triumphans* e la nascita dell'antiquaria"; Georgia Clarke, *Roman House—Renaissance Palaces. Inventing Antiquity in Fifteenth-Century Italy* (Cambridge: Cambridge University Press, 2003), pp. 97f. There is speculation that the origins of Mantegna's *Triumphs* date to the 1460s: Dandelet, *The Renaissance of Empire*, p. 38 with n. 58.

58. Francis Ames-Lewis, *The Intellectual Life of the Early Renaissance Artist* (New Haven: Yale University Press, 2000), p. 126.

59. J. M. Massing, "'The Triumph of Caesar' by Benedetto Bordon and Jacobus Argentoratensis. Its Iconography and Influence," *Print Quarterly* 7 (1990): 2–21.

60. See Mazzocco, "Biondo Flavio and the Antiquarian tradition."

61. See Muecke, "*Fama superstes?*"

62. Barbara C. Halporn, *The Correspondence of Johann Amerbach. Early Printing in Its Social Context* (Ann Arbor: University of Michigan, 2000), pp. 119f.

SANCTISSIMO DOMINO
PIO SECUNDO
ROMANO PONTIFICI
CELEBERRIMO
BLONDUS FLAVIUS
FORLIVIENSIS
ROMAE TRIUMPHANTIS
LIBRI DECEM

BIONDO FLAVIO OF FORLI
ROME IN TRIUMPH
IN TEN BOOKS
TO OUR MOST HOLY LORD,
PIUS II
THE CELEBRATED ROMAN
PONTIFF

[Volume I: Books I–II]

[EPISTOLA DEDICATORIA]

1 Quotquot hactenus scriptores et vates opera sua principibus inscripsere id solum, Beatissime Pater, quaesivere, ut ab illorum potentatu et magnitudine laboribus suis apud omnes auctoritatem et ab invidis tutelam munimenque pararent. Prudenter id quidem quando ita veteri consuetudine fieri videmus ut omni in re, sed in litteraria in primis minus vulgo cognita, quod princeps probat gratum habet, ceteri etiam laudent, cupiant, tueantur. Ego autem, etsi meae *Triumphanti Romae,* multarum lucubrationum operi tuo nomini dicato, tibi inscripto, auctoritatem a tuo pontificatu, a tuoque potentatu protectionem non renuo, aliud tamen et quaero et expecto, quod plurimi sum facturus. Eo, Pater Sanctissime, post Leonem utrumque primum et secundum pontifices Romanos, dicendi et scribendi ornatu polles, ut, quales post illorum tempora non vidit Ecclesia, apostolicas denuo litteras, Romano principatu Romana dignitate dignas, iam tandem orbis Christianus accipiat, quique ad tuum veniunt conspectum oratores et omnium gentium, nationum, urbium viri praestantiores sedere in Petri sede vicarium Iesu Christi intelligant, orationis verborum et sententiarum dignitate ac gravitate ostendentem se unum esse cuius eloquentia omnium maximam aequet muneris pontificii amplitudinem. Si itaque meum opus accipis et probasse videris, abesse non poterit quin a tam eloquente laudatum Summo Pontifice, laudandum quoque ceteri omnes existiment.

2 Qua fretus confidentia non verebor facere editionem multis hoc tempore, ut mea fert opinio, profuturam. Exciti enim a te ingentes

[DEDICATORY LETTER]

All writers and poets who have hitherto dedicated their works to princes had, Most Holy Father,[1] one aim in mind. They sought to derive from those men's great power and stature universal esteem for the products of their labors, and protection and defense from ill will. This was indeed wisely done since experience of age-old custom shows us that in all matters, but especially in the sphere of literature that is less generally understood, when something wins the prince's approval and favor, all others too praise it, want to have it and defend it. My *Rome in Triumph* is a work I have labored over with much study, and it bears your name in the dedication: although I do not decline the influence and protection deriving from your papal power, yet I seek and anticipate something else, on which I will put the highest value. You, Most Holy Father, next after the two Roman Pontiffs named Leo, the first and the second,[2] have such distinction in your command of speaking and writing that the Christian world at long last receives once more apostolic letters of a quality that the Church has not seen since their time, letters worthy of Rome's sovereignty and dignity. The ambassadors and the very distinguished men of all races, nations and cities who come into your presence realize that there sits on Peter's throne a vicar of Christ who displays by the dignity and weight of his speech, words and opinions that he is one whose eloquence matches the eminence of the office of Pontiff, which is greatest of all. If therefore you accept my work and are seen to think well of it, the result must be that when it has been praised by so eloquent a Supreme Pontiff, everyone else too will consider that it is praiseworthy. 1

Confidently trusting in this, I shall not fear to publish a work that in my opinion will be of benefit to many at this time. In it the 2

Italiae, Galliarum, Hispaniarum et Germaniae populi in magnam praeclaramque expeditionem quam paras in Turchos, Graeciam, Constantinopolim, Moesiasque dura et crudeli tirannide prementes, nonnulla in ipso opere edocebuntur, aliquando alias simili in rerum difficultate gesta, ut ipsa priscorum virtutis imitatio generosi quibusque animi sit ad rem capessendam stimulos additura. Tuque interea, dum priscae urbis Romae triumphos lectitabis, clarissimum, quem Pio tibi optimus pientissimusque Deus noster ex deletis inanitis Turchorum opibus, ex liberataque primum omnium Europa post Hierosolima et terra illi adiacente sancta daturus est, triumphum expectabis brevi, ut auguror et confido, cum summo applausu, summa omnium gloria ducendum. Vale.

mighty peoples of Italy, France, Spain and Germany whom you have roused to join the great and glorious expedition that you are preparing against the Turks, cruel and tyrannical oppressors of Greece, Constantinople and the Moesias,[3] will learn of deeds performed in earlier times in other places in similarly difficult circumstances, so that imitation of the prowess of the ancients is itself another factor likely to stimulate all noble spirits eagerly to undertake the enterprise. You, meanwhile, while you read again and again of the triumphs of the ancient city of Rome, will anticipate the splendid triumph that our God in his goodness and piety will give you, Pius, first of all for the destruction and annihilation of the Turks' power and the liberation of Europe, after that the liberation of Jerusalem and the Holy Land adjoining it, a triumph that shortly, I confidently predict, must be held with the utmost praise and glory of all. Farewell.

PROOEMIUM

1 Ardenti virtute praestantique ingenio ferme omnes, quos de gestis rebus deque ceteris mortalium vitae partibus Latine scribendi libido cepit, ut ad urbem sese verterint gentemque Romanam factum videmus probabili id certe ac necessaria ratione. Ea enim fuit civitas, ut Cicero inquit, 'ex nationum conventu constituta,' 'quae propter virtutem omnibus nationibus imperavit'; peculiaris cuius fuit dignitatis, ut reges, ut nationes exterae, ut gentes ultimae non minus eam amaverint quam timuerint; quae firmissimum vel ea ratione habuit imperium, quod ei oboedientes gavisi sunt, Romanis magistratibus sua consilia, sua studia in id maiori ex parte conferentibus ut hi, qui in eorum imperio erant, quam beatissimi essent.

2 Qua ratione Cicero ipse non indigne eam urbem 'terrarum orbis atque omnium gentium arcem' appellavit. Et Plinius proprie scripsit Romam 'terrarum commercio patentem undique et tanquam ad mortales adiuvandos' natam esse, quod imperii maiestate orbi terrarum communicata societas festae pacis omniumque etiam, quae prius occulta fuerant, promiscuus usus sit effectus.[1] Romani enim maximam orbis partem suae subactam dictioni ita pacaverunt cultamque bonis moribus et artibus reddiderunt, ut disiunctae mari montibusque et fluminibus separatae gentes ac linguis litteraturaque differentes populi per Latinae linguae communionem perque communes omnibus Romanos magistratus una eademque civitas sint effecti; quod quidem maximum humani generis beneficium Dei potius quam hominum opus fuisse videtur. Licetque dicere quod Cicero *De haruspicum responsis* disserens inquit: 'Debere qui

PROEM

Nearly all those men of passion, vigor and outstanding intellect who have been seized by a desire to write in Latin about history and the other aspects of human life have turned to the City and people of Rome. This happened, we see, for good and necessary reasons. Rome was a state, as Cicero says, "established from an assemblage of nations,"[1] "that ruled all the nations because of its moral excellence."[2] Its special distinction was that kings, that foreign nations and that the most far away races loved it no less than they feared it. To be sure, the reason why its empire was exceedingly stable was that its subjects rejoiced in it, since the Roman magistrates for the most part devoted their deliberations and efforts to ensuring that those who were under their dominion were as happy as possible.[3] 1

This is why Cicero himself fittingly called this city "the citadel of the world and all nations"[4] and Pliny was right when he wrote that Rome "is accessible on all sides for the world's commerce and was brought into being to aid mortals, as it were,"[5] because by the greatness of its empire the world has come to share in joyful peace and general use even of all that had been hidden before has been made available. After the Romans had brought the largest part of the world under their sway, they made it so peaceful and so civilized it with good customs and conduct that races divided by sea and mountain and kept apart by rivers and peoples who had different languages and ways of writing were made one and the same state, through sharing the Latin language and all having the Roman magistrates in common.[6] Indeed this benefit, one of the greatest bestowed on the human race, seems to have been the work of God rather than of men. One may say, as Cicero in his speech *On the Responses of the Haruspices* says, that "those who have 2

deos esse intellexerint etiam intelligere eorum numine hoc tantum imperium esse natum et auctum et retentum.'

3 Nam, ut ab Italia incipiam, Roma annis iam trecentis condita, Etrusci Romanique silva intercedente Cimina, nunc Viterbio imminente, paulo plus minus triginta milibus ab urbe distante, nullum inter se commercium habuerunt. Livius enim Patavinus sic habet in nono: 'Silva erat Cimina magis tum invia atque horrenda quam nuper fuere Germanici saltus, nullus ad eam diem ne mercatorum quidem, abdita[2] ea intrare aut ferre quicquam praeter ducem ipsum audebat.' Et proximos Romae ad tertium lapidem Sabinos lingua, moribus et institutis differentes a Romanis fuisse eodem docente Livio constat; qui pariter ostendit circa Mutinam Bononiamque et proxima loca nunc totius Italiae amoenissima silvas omnia obtinuisse; remotiores vero ab urbe regiones, Campaniam, Lucaniam, Appuliam, Calabros et Brutios, maiori ex parte Graecis subditas, nec Latinis, nec Sabinis, neque etiam Etruscis per linguarum diversitatem satis communicasse nulli dubium videri credimus, cum ceterae omnes praesentis Italiae regiones quae ultra Bononiam et Mutinam sunt, Roma ab inicio crescente, Gallorum fuerint, quam gentem—auctor est in *Commentariis* G. Caesar—priusquam Romano subicerentur imperio nullas scivisse aut vidisse litteras, nisi quas Graeci advenae, pro miraculo habiti, vel pauculas ostendissent; pariter de Hispanis, pariter de Britannis nunc Anglicis, pariter de omnibus Germanis licet asserere.

4 Eas vero omnes maximas praeclarissimasque totius Europae gentes Romani litteris moribusque et omni virtutum munere ita

grasped that the gods exist must also understand that it is by their power that this great empire was created, extended and preserved."[7]

3 To begin with Italy, for example. At a time already three hundred years after Rome's foundation there was no trade between the Romans and the Etruscans because of the intervening Ciminian forest. This is now near Viterbo, at a distance of roughly thirty miles from Rome. Livy of Padua puts it like this in Book IX: "At that time the Ciminian forest was more impenetrable and dreadful than were found to be in recent times the forest passes in Germany, and up to that time no one, not even a trader, dared to go into those hidden depths or take anything in except the general himself."[8] As Livy again informs us, the Sabines, Rome's nearest neighbors, who were three miles away, differed from the Romans in language, customs and institutions.[9] Likewise Livy reveals that around Modena and Bologna and their environs, which are now the most beautiful places in the whole of Italy, everything was covered by forests.[10] In fact I believe it is obvious to all that the regions further away from the city, Campania, Lucania, Apulia, Calabria, and the land of the Brutii, which were for the most part under the sway of Greeks, did not interact much with the Latins and Sabines, let alone the Etruscans, because they spoke different languages. All the other regions of present-day Italy to the north of Bologna and Modena belonged to the Gauls in the early phase of Rome's growth. This race, as Caesar attests in his *Commentaries*, knew or saw no letters before they came under Rome's sway, except those very few which Greek strangers, regarded as a marvel, had shown them.[11] One may make the same claim in the case of the Spanish, the British (now the English) and all the Germanic peoples.

4 In fact, through their literature, customs and every endowment of excellence the Romans have made all these very important and illustrious peoples of the whole of Europe so civilized that they

cultas reddidere, ut nullis post Italiam dignitate et gloria unquam postea cesserint. Et omnis Africa, Romano subdita populo, per quingentos ferme annos litteris moribusque Romanis effloruit, adeo ut per tempora beati Aurelii Augustini, gente Afri, concilia ibi ecclesiae habita ab octingentis episcopis litteras edoctis Latinas celebrata fuerint. Nec minus Asia quam Africa Romanis litteris moribusque institutisque ornata atque pacata fuit, adeo ut plures in ea viros virtutum fama celebres quingenti Romanorum dictionis anni genuerint iis omnibus quos prius a condito orbe aut postea a mille iam et centum annis natos in ipsa aut nutritos fuisse possint ostendere. Romanae igitur gentis et urbis laudes, Romanorum instituta et vitae exempla non Italae magis quam externae gentes litteris utentes Latinis, haud secus quam parentum et progenitorum gesta, et legunt avide et attentissima exaudiunt diligentia, ut idoneos ad scribendum invitare ac impellere videantur.

5 Qua nos adducti ratione Romanorum inclinationis imperii historia duobus iam et triginta libris digesta, urbis Romae aedificia tercio volumine reddidimus instaurata, Italiamque facta priscorum novis urbium et locorum omnium nominibus collatione, quantum octo libris fieri potuit, illustravimus, et demum 'senectutis nostrae non inhertis grato atque honesto munere' cum ipso Cicerone in *Legibus* fungi voluimus. Neque passi sumus, sicut Varro *De agricultura* scripturus sese non passurum est professus, Sibyllam solam ea quae se viva et se demum mortua prodessent hominibus cecinisse; et, quando videmus Ciceronem *Plancium* defendentem dicere Marcum Catonem in *Originibus* scripsisse 'semper se praeclarum ac magnificum putavisse clarorum virorum atque magnorum non minus otii quam negotii rationem extare oportere', operam hanc

have never afterward yielded in dignity and glory to any bar Italy. In the whole of Africa, too, after it came under the Roman people, Roman literature and customs flourished for about five hundred years, so much so that in the time of St. Augustine (who was of African origin) the church councils held there were attended by eight hundred bishops trained in Latin.[12] Asia no less than Africa was adorned and made peaceful by the Romans' literature, customs and institutions, to such an extent that five hundred years of Roman rule produced more men there renowned for excellence than all those she could exhibit as born and brought up there previously after the creation of the world or in the subsequent 1,100 years. Accordingly, no less than the Italians, foreign peoples literate in Latin both eagerly read, and listen with the greatest of attention to, the glorious merits of the City and people of Rome, the Romans' institutions and models for living, no differently from the deeds of their own parents and forefathers. Thus they seem to invite and stimulate to write those with the capacity to do so.

This was the reason that induced me, after I had set out in 5
thirty-two books the history of the Romans beginning with the decline of their empire, to restore the buildings of the City of Rome in three volumes, to illuminate Italy as far as it was possible in eight books by comparing all the ancient cities and places with their new names.[13] After this I wanted, as Cicero himself says in *On the Laws*, to perform "the pleasant and honorable function of my not inactive old age"[14] and I did not allow, as Varro at the beginning of *On Agriculture* avowed that he would not allow, the Sibyl to be the only one whose prophetic utterances benefited mankind both while she lived and eventually after her death.[15] Further, we see that Cicero in his *Defense of Plancius* says that Marcus Cato wrote in his *Origins* that he always thought it was fine and noble "that illustrious and great men must always be able to render an account for their leisure no less than for their occupation."[16] So I shall devote this labor of my old age to that "great service, deserv-

nostrae senectutis magnae illi et gratae hominibus laudi praestabimus, quam idem Cicero *Murenam* item defendens esse dixit 'unum hominem elaborare in ea scientia quae sit multis profutura.'

6 Itaque coepimus tentare si speculum, exemplar, imaginem, doctrinam omnis virtutis et bene, sancte ac feliciter vivendi rationis, urbem Romam florentem ac qualem beatus Aurelius Augustinus triumphantem videre desideravit, nostrorum hominum ingenio et doctrina valentium oculis et menti subiicere ac proponere poterimus. Idque immensum opus quinque partita distributione tractabimus, ut quae ad religionem spectavere primum, quae rei publicae administrationis fuerunt secundum, tercium militiae disciplina; mores vero ac vitae instituta quartum; et triumphi ipsius ratio quintum obtineat locum. Praefari tamen hoc inicio libet nos de Romanorum gentiliumque aliorum religione ea ratione ac intentione dicturos, ut deorum appellationes cum templorum, aedium phanorumque vocabulis edocentes, simul loca urbis Romae in quibus ea fuere ostendamus; inde rituum quos dii gentium, sicut propheta inquit, daemonia suis sacrificiis adhiberi iusserunt spurcitia, impietate atque etiam maxima levitate ostensa Christianae religionis sanctimoniam bonae voluntatis hominibus gratiorem faciamus esse. Sed iam nostrae divisionis executioni partium incumbamus.

ing recognition from mankind," which Cicero, again, said in *Defense of Murena* consists in "one man taking pains over that science which will be to the benefit of many."[17]

Therefore I have begun the attempt to see if I can bring for- 6
ward and set before the eyes and minds of the intellectually gifted and learned people of our time, a mirror, model, image, and lesson of all moral excellence and of the way of living well, religiously and happily, the City of Rome when it flourished and triumphed as St. Augustine wished to see it.[18] I shall manage this immense work by dividing it into five parts. The first place will be held by matters pertaining to religion, the second by those belonging to administration of the state, the third military discipline, the fourth customs and institutions of daily life, and the fifth an account of the triumph itself. Before I begin I would like to state, however, that in speaking about the Romans' religion and that of other Gentiles, when I impart information about the names of the gods along with the words for their temples, temple buildings (*aedes*) and holy precincts (*fana*), I have the intention, [first], of indicating at the same time the places in the City of Rome where they were situated, then, by demonstrating the foulness, impiety and also the utter levity of the rites that the gods of the nations — demons,[19] as the prophet says — required to be employed in their sacrifices, of making the sanctity of the Christian religion more welcome to men of good will. But now let us press on to the treatment of the parts of our division.

LIBER PRIMUS[1]

1 Religionem 'deorum culturam' esse Nonius Marcellus scribit. Eandem 'divinarum rerum scientiam' a philosophis maioribusque ceteris appellatam fuisse Plutarchus in *Pauli Aemilii vita* est auctor; et Aulus Gelius M. Ciceronem dicit in oratione de accusatore constituendo asserere 'religiosa dici delubra maiestatis venerationisque plena'; et Massurium Sabinum velle 'religiosum esse id quod propter sanctitatem aliquam remotum ac sepositum sit a nobis a relinquendo' dictum. Serviusque Sulpicius religiosum esse voluit 'propter sanctitatem aliquam a relegando' appellatum, et Pompeius Festus 'religiosos' dicit 'qui facienda et vitanda discernunt.'

2 Qualis vero fuerit religio Romanorum, si hoc inicio passis, ut aiunt, velis nararre pergemus, eorum potius fatuitatem notare quam celebris famae populi virtutes, sicut profitemur, laudare voluisse videbimur. Hinc duximus paululum a proposito diggrediendum et gentium fama notissimarum, quae ante conditam urbem Romam fuerunt, religio qualis erat ostendendum, quo pateat prudentissimos tantae urbis ac rei publicae fundatores, si traditos in tam necessaria re mores secuti sunt, magis quod nullam habuerint meliorem propositam miseratione prosequendos, quam quod talem acceperint religionem culpandos esse. Ne etiam ignominiae, quam a Romanis avertere cupimus, notam ceteris inuramus gentium populis, quorum plerosque constat ingenio, doctrina et bonis vitae ac morum institutis excelluisse, nonnulla religionis et theologiae gentilium rudimenta partim ab ipsis gentilibus, partim

BOOK I

Religio, Nonius Marcellus writes, "is worship of the gods."[1] According to Plutarch in the *Life of Aemilius Paulus* the philosophers and all the other ancestors defined it as "knowledge of divine matters."[2] Aulus Gellius says that Marcus Cicero in a speech on the appointing of a prosecutor maintains that "shrines full of majesty and awe are called *religiosa.*" And Masurius Sabinus thinks that "*religiosus* is that which because of some quality of holiness has been removed and set apart from us, the term being derived from 'leaving behind' (*relinquere*)."[3] Servius Sulpicius thought that "*religiosus* is that which, because of some quality of holiness, has derived its name from 'to remove' (*relegare*),"[4] and Pompeius Festus says "*religiosi* are those who distinguish between the things that are to be done and the things that are to be avoided."[5] 1

If right at the beginning I launch under full sail, as they say, into an exposition of the nature of the Romans' religion, I shall give the impression of having intended to criticize their folly, rather than to praise, as I profess to do, the virtues of a people of a distinguished reputation. Hence I have concluded that I must digress a little from the main subject and demonstrate the nature of the religion of the best-known peoples who existed before the foundation of the City of Rome. From this it will become apparent that, if in so vital a matter the wisest founders of so great a city and republic followed traditional customs, they are more to be pitied because they had no better course than to be blamed because they accepted such a religion. But in order not to mark all the other pagan peoples, many of whom excelled in intelligence, learning, and good manners and morals, with the brand of shame I wish to keep away from the Romans, I shall review a little more deeply some basic principles of pagan religion and theology, partly 2

a doctissimo Christianae religionis theologo Eusebio Pamphili relata altiuscule repetemus.

3 Ex quibus id in primis multifaciendum apparebit nullas fuisse barbaras etiam gentes, nullos vel moribus et vita efferatissimos populos, qui non de Deo bene senserint, et, quod fuit consequens, immortalitatem non crediderint animarum. Cui sententiae Cicero in *Legibus* concordat 'animum esse ingeneratum a deo asserens, ex quo vel agnatio nobis cum caelestibus, vel genus, vel stirps appellari potest.' 'Nullam enim gentem esse' dicit 'neque tam immansuetam,[2] neque tam feram quae, etiam si ignoret qualiter habere[3] deum deceat, tamen habendum non[4] sciat.' Unde idem *De haruspicum responsis* orationem habens sic inquit: 'Quis autem, cum suspexerit in caelum, deos esse non sentiat et ea, quae tanta mente fiunt ut vix quisquam arte ulla ordinem rerum ac vicissitudinem persequi possit, casu fieri putet?' Tribuitque eam vim Cicero in *Legibus* huic opinioni ut dicat 'illud bene dictum a Pythagora doctissimo viro, quia maxime et pietas et religio versentur in animis, ideo nos rebus divinis operam dare.' Augustinus autem in *Dei civitate* Platonicos dicit affirmare 'animas hominum daemones esse, et ex hominibus fieri putare Lares si meriti boni sunt, Lemures si mali, seu Larvas. Manes autem incertum utrum boni vel mali.'

4 'Divinitus itaque insitum esse' inquit Eusebius 'non solum utile atque conducibile quid Dei nomine significatum, verum etiam rerum omnium creatorem sic appellari. Cum tamen verbo ita omnes natura duce conveniant, re autem creaturas pro creatore coluerunt,

related by the peoples themselves, partly by Eusebius Pamphili,[6] that very learned Christian theologian.

From what follows it must especially be emphasized that there 3
were no barbarian races, no peoples even the most savage in their customs and way of life who did not have a proper opinion concerning God and, consequently, did not believe in the immortality of the soul. Cicero is in accord with this judgment in *On the Laws* where he maintains that "the mind is implanted by god. Hence we have what can be called a relationship, descent, or stock in common with the gods." For he says "there is no race so uncivilized or so savage as not to know they must believe in god even if they do not know what kind of god they should believe in."[7] For this reason the same writer in his speech *On the Responses of the Haruspices* says as follows: "Who would not realize that the gods exist when he gazed up into heaven, and who would suppose that there could come about by chance those things that are created by so great an intelligence that it is almost beyond the ability of anyone to describe the order and change of the universe, whatever their artistic powers."[8] In *On the Laws* Cicero attributes so much force to this view that he writes that "that very learned man, Pythagoras, was right to say that we attend to divine matters because both piety and religion dwell in our minds in the highest degree."[9] Augustine in *City of God*, however, says that the Platonists assert "that the souls of men are demons and they think that when they cease to be men they become *lares* if they have deserved this by being good, if they have been wicked they become *lemures* or *larvae*. If it is uncertain whether they were good or evil they become *manes*."[10]

Accordingly Eusebius says that "it was implanted by divine 4
providence that not only anything useful and profitable be denoted by the name of God but also the creator of all things be so called. Yet though under the guidance of nature all concur in the word, in reality they worshipped the creation instead of the creator with the

praeter populum unum aut admodum paucos, sicut verissimis Hebraeorum litteris ostenditur, qui a rebus visibilibus ad intelligibilia oculos mentis sanctae reducentes, non creaturae alicui, sed ipsi rerum omnium creatori, cunctorumque largitori bonorum, Dei appellationem attribuerunt. Ceteri autem omnes tenebris animos involuti ad tantam impiet-atem deducti sunt, ut pecudum more honestum et conducibile bonorumque omnium supremum voluptate corporis terminarent. Qua ratione eos, qui genera voluptatum vel adinvenerunt, vel auxerunt amplificaveruntque, et hos quidem maleficos ac mortales viros, quasi bonorum largitores, salvatores ac deos suos appellaverunt, piam huius nominis notionem natura eis insitam ad eos transferentes quos bonorum inventores putabant. Tantumque ea mentis insania valuit, ut nec peccare se arbitrarentur, nec erubescerent divinis honoribus maleficos atque potentes propter regna tunc primum constituta colere et admirari; cumque mores hominum legibus stabiliti non essent, nec supplicia peccatoribus imminerent, adulteria, nefanda matrimonia, maribus ereptam pudiciciam, homicidia, parricidia, confecta scelere bella, quasi res pulcherrime gestas diis suis attribuebant, et earum rerum memoriam posteris suis quasi perutilem relinquere studebant.'

5 'Alii postea sensim virorum mulierumque membris et inexpertae rationis ferarum natura sanctissimam Dei appellationem inquinarunt, deoque talia attribuerunt, quae si de hominum aliquo dicantur, legibus et consuetudine civitatum gravissimo supplicio punirentur.' 'Alii argutiores doctrina habiti theologiam excogitarunt quadripartitam, in qua Deum patrem omnium atque regem in primis locandum putarunt, deinde aliorum deorum multitudinem, tertio loco daemones, quarto heroas deputantes, quos omnes

exception of one people or a very few, as is demonstrated by the true writings of the Hebrews. They turned the eyes of a pure mind from visible things back to the realm of the understanding and assigned the name of God, not to a created thing, but to the very Creator of all things and the Giver of all good gifts. All the rest, their minds clouded by darkness, were brought to such a pitch of ungodliness that like beasts of the herd they defined the beautiful and useful and the highest good of all as physical pleasure. For this reason, men called those who either discovered kinds of pleasures or increased and enlarged them, though they were in fact evil doers and mortals, their saviors and gods as if they were givers of good things, and transferred the holy conception of this name, which was implanted in them by nature, to those whom they supposed discoverers of benefits. This mental insanity had so powerful an influence on them that they did not consider they were sinning nor did they blush to honor, worship, and admire evil doers and men who had power because of the kingdoms which were then established for the first time. Since human behavior had not been put on a sound footing by laws, and no threat of punishment hung over sinners, they attributed to their gods, as the finest of achievements, adulteries, incestuous marriages, sodomy, murders, parricides, and wars provoked by crime, and they took pains to bequeath to their descendants a record of these deeds as if it would be of great utility."[11]

5 "Later on some gradually polluted the most holy name of God with the genitalia of men and women and the irrational nature of brute beasts and they attributed to God acts of such a kind as would be punished most severely by the laws and customs of human society if any human being were said to have committed them."[12] "Others, men very accurate in their learning, have discussed theology in a fourfold division, in which they considered God, the father and king of all, to be set in the first place, next the throng of other gods, classing demons in the third place and

lucem esse dicunt praeter malignos daemonas qui tenebrae appellantur. Daemones enim alios bonos, alios pravos arbitrati sunt, et bonis quidem regionem lunae atque aeris, pravis vero infernae[5] habitationis locum attribuerunt, quos Empedocles poenas peccatorum dare confirmat, quoniam aether eos et pontus expellat, terra nullo modo suscipiat, sicque ab alio in aliud depulsi elementum atrociter vexentur.' 'Bonos vero daemonas non deos, sed deorum ministros ea ratione dixerunt, quod oraculis praesint et magicam homines artem docuerint, per quam a maleficis hominibus ita illigentur, ut neque recedere quidem possint cum voluerint. Quorum aliquos Pythagoras dixit non sponte invitatos, sed necessitate quadam carminum impulsos accedere, alios quadam accedendi consuetudine et maxime si natura boni sunt facilius accedere, alios si negligentius quispiam in ea re se habuerit, cum inviti advenerint, ut noceant adniti.'

6 His praemissis, ex quibus apparet cupivisse et pro viribus quaesivisse barbaras etiam gentes aliquam Dei creatoris sui notitiam habere, ad particularem singulorum ex ipsis theologiae et religionis historiam veniamus. Eruntque primi Aegyptii, quos 'constat omnium primos, cum in caelum oculos sustulissent, motum, ordinem et quantitatem caelestium admiratos, Solem et Lunam deos putasse. Soli vero Osyris, id est multi oculi, Lunae Isidis tanquam priscae, quoniam sempiterna priscaque sit, nomina indidisse. Ritus vero qui his adhibebatur colendis, castus primo purusque fuisse videtur, nullam habens admixtam crudelitatem, quod nulla tunc, sicut postea factitatum est, caedebantur animalia, nullus effundebatur in sacrificio sanguis innoxius, sed fruges terrae, quibus ipsi

heroes in the fourth. All of these they say are light except the evil demons, who are called darkness. Some demons they considered good, others bad, and they assigned as a dwelling place the area around the moon and the atmosphere to the good demons, and the underworld to the bad.[13] Empedocles asserts that these suffer the punishments of sinners, 'since the air and sea cast them out, the earth in no wise receives them and in this way, cast out by one element to another, they are hideously tortured.'"[14] "Indeed they said that good demons were not gods, but servants of gods for the reason that they preside over oracles[15] and have taught men the art of magic, by means of which they are in such a way held bound by evildoers that though they may wish to they cannot even get away."[16] "Pythagoras said some of these did not come of their free will when they had been invoked, but by spells that forced them to come; but some, by a habit as it were of being present, come more readily, especially if they are of a good nature, while others strive to do harm when they have come against their will, especially if anyone has behaved rather carelessly in this affair."[17]

After these preliminary remarks, from which it is clear that 6
even the barbarian races desired and sought with all their might to have some conception of God[18] their maker, let us come to a specific account of the theology and religion of some of these peoples taken one by one. The Egyptians will be first. "It is well known that when they raised their eyes to the sky and were struck with wonder at the motion, regularity and size of the heavenly bodies, they were the first of all to suppose that the sun and moon were gods. They named the sun Osiris, that is, 'many-eyed' and the moon Isis, 'ancient' as it were, since she is eternal and ancient. The rite which was used in their worship seems at first to have been chaste and pure, with no element of cruelty involved, because at that time no animals were slaughtered, as was frequently done later on, no innocent blood was shed in sacrifice, but they gave as offerings the fruits of the earth on which they

vescerentur, offerebant. Herbas enim integras quasdam cum radicibus et foliis ac fructibus sumentes simul concremabant, ex qua fumigatione halationeque antedictis caelestibus litabant.'

7 Unde asserit Macrobius Aegyptios Saturno et Serapi ampla extra urbes constituisse templa, in quibus solis pecudum sanguine imolabant, cum ceteris in civitate thure et precibus. 'In templis vero ignem perpetuum tanquam diis simillimum servabant. Ab eaque exhalatione, quam Graeci "thamasin"[6] appellant, thisia quoque est dicta,' quod Latine sacrificium appellamus; parvo deinde post tempore alius adolendi modus per myrrae, cassiae, croci, primitiarum oblationem inventus est. 'Cui foedissimus et crudelitatis plenus surrepsit modus occisis animalibus eorum sanguine deorum aras cruentandi. Huiusmodi autem primos et antiquissimos hominum constat nec templorum extruendis molibus, nec simulachrorum dedicationibus operam dedisse, quippe qui nec pingere, nec fingere aut celare, sed nec aedificare scirent.'

8 Qui vero in Aegypto procedente tempore coaluerunt doctrina et litteris cultiores, cum theologiam, id est divinarum rerum scientiam, et sermonem tractare coepissent, maioribus homines erroribus intricare coeperunt, 'deos asserentes suos mortales homines fuisse, sed virtute ac beneficiis, quibus vitam communem excoluerunt, immortalitatem consecutos. Quorum nonnulli reges fuerint nominaque habuerint, alii nova quaedam, alii a caelestibus translata. Solem enim dixerunt primum omnium apud Aegyptum regnasse Solis caelestis[7] cognomine, deinde Saturnum qui, sorore[8] Cybele in uxorem ducta, Osyrim et Isidem, aut, ut plurimi dixerunt, Iovem et Iunonem, genuerit, eosque universum orbem imperio subiugasse, ac quinque deos procreasse: Osyrim, Isidem, Typhona, Apollinem et Venerem; Isidemque Cererem esse, quae

themselves fed. For taking certain plants complete with their roots, leaves, and fruit, they burned them all together; and from the fumes and vapor they made offerings to the heavenly beings I have mentioned."[19]

7 For this reason Macrobius asserts that the Egyptians set up large temples to Saturn and Serapis outside the cities, and only in these did they make offerings with the blood of animals, whereas within the city they made offerings of incense and prayers to all the other gods.[20] "In their temples they kept an undying fire as being especially like the gods. From this vapor, which the Greeks call *thymiasis,* comes the word *thysia* too,"[21] for which the Latin name is *sacrificium* (sacrifice). Next, not long after, another way of honoring the gods was discovered, through the offering of myrrh, casia, saffron, and firstfruits. "This was gradually overtaken by a most revolting and cruel way of killing animals and staining the gods' altars with their blood. It is well known that the first and most ancient people of mankind did not apply themselves either to building massive temples or the setting up of statues, since they did not know how to paint, mold or carve, or indeed build."[22]

8 With the passage of time there arose in Egypt men who grew better educated in learning and writing; and when they began to deal with theology, that is, the scientific discourse pertaining to divine matters, they began to entangle mankind in greater error. "They asserted that their gods had been mortals but had attained immortality by their virtue and from the improvements they bestowed on human life. Some of these were kings and had names, others had invented names, others names borrowed from the heavenly bodies. Sol, they said was the first king of the Egyptians and had the name of the heavenly sun; next reigned Saturn, who married his sister Cybele and begat Osiris and Isis, or as the majority have stated, Jupiter and Juno, to whose rule the whole world was subjugated. They gave birth to five gods: Osiris, Isis, Typhon, Apollo and Venus. Isis is Ceres, who was married to Osiris, that

Osyri, id est Dionysio,[9] coniuncta est, qui, cum regno successissent, plurimum humano generi contulerint; condidisse enim in tractu Thebaico centum portarum urbem, quam alii Iovis urbem, alii Thebas dixerint.' Fuit vero haec Thebana centum portarum civitas, de qua Ammianus Marcellinus scribit Gallum poetam, in patria nostra Forolivio genitum, praetorem Aegypti ab Augusto Caesare constitutum, abstulisse obeliscos conchasque peregrini marmoris, quibus etiam nunc urbs Roma et Italia est ornata.

9 Prosequiturque Eusebius ex Porphyrio 'erexisse Osyrim diis omnibus aurea templa, quorum singulis certas statuerit caerimonias, et proprios qui earum curam haberent consecraverit sacerdotes.' Unde profectum sit ut diversis distincti honoribus homines alii colerent, alii colerentur. Paulo post, Osyride insidiis laniato, alia quidem 'eius membra ab Iside uxore non mediocri labore inventa divinis honoribus sepulta, penis vero virilis membri in Nilum ab insidiatoribus proiecti constituto idolo, sacra ac caerimonias maioris aliquanto cultus statuta fuisse. Unde Graeci primum, post Romani acceperint ut Dionysii orgia et dies festi cum honore virilis membri fierent, cuius simulachrum in mysteriis ferentes "Phallum" Graeci,' Priapum nostri appellaverunt.

10 Multa hic omittimus superflua de aliorum deorum origine. Simulachrorum autem originem hanc Aegyptii fuisse perhibent: 'Cadmum enim ferunt ex Thebis Aegyptiis in Boeciam profectum Semelem aliosque filios procreasse Semelemque, ab ignoto pressam, septimo mense puerum peperisse; hunc mortuum a Cadmo deauratum et quasi deum ingenti cultu et sacrificiis decoratum

is, Dionysus.[23] When they succeeded to the kingdom, they bestowed great benefits on the human race. For they founded in the Thebaid a city of a hundred gates which some called the City of Jupiter (Diospolis), some Thebes."[24] In fact this was that hundred-gated city of Thebes from which Ammianus Marcellinus writes that the poet Gallus, who sprang from my native Forlì and was appointed praetor of Egypt by Augustus, removed the obelisks and basins of exotic marble that even now adorn the City of Rome and Italy.[25]

Eusebius, drawing on Porphyry, goes on to say that Osiris 9
"erected golden temples to all the gods, established particular ceremonies for each of them and appointed them priests of their own to take care of these."[26] So it has come about that men have been distinguished with different honors: some worship, while others are worshipped. Soon afterward, when there was a plot against Osiris and he was dismembered, "the other parts of him that had been found with much effort by his wife Isis were buried with divine honors. But as the penis, the male member, had been thrown into the Nile by the plotters, she set up an image of it and instituted especially honorable rites and ceremonies. From this, first the Greeks and later the Romans have taken over the practice that the orgiastic rites and festivals of Dionysus include worship of the male member. The image of it that they carry in their mysteries the Greeks called 'Phallus'"[27] and the Romans "Priapus."

Here I omit much on the origins of the other gods which it is 10
unnecessary to recount. The Egyptians say the origin of statues was as follows. "Cadmus, they say, went from Thebes in Egypt to Boeotia and begat Semele and some other children. Semele was raped by an unknown person and after six months gave birth to a boy. Cadmus covered this dead child with gold and honored him like a god with great reverence and sacrifices, and it was put out

fuisse parentemque eius praedicatum Iovem, ut stuprum Semelis leniretur.'

11 Adorationis vero animalium origo quam fecerunt Aegyptii causam hanc afferunt: 'effigies animalium ab Aegyptiis imperatoribus ducibusque in galeis sculptas ferri solitas in proelio, quibus principes insigniores forent; parta deinde victoria, ea animalia, quorum imaginem duces gestassent, quasi offensionem belli ipsa ad hostes reppulissent, in deos relata fuisse. Alia quoque affertur cultus animalium causa: bovem enim adorari ferunt, quod partu et arandi opera conducat; ovem, quod pariat et tegumentorum materiam praebeat ac lacte et caseo nutriat; canem, quia una cum hominibus venetur et ad custodiendos homines sit natus, quapropter deus qui apud eos Anubis vocetur caninum habet caput. Feles apud eos colitur, quia ad scuta facienda conducit. Ex avibus ibis apud eos utilis dicitur ad serpentum, locustarum et erucarum interitum. Aquila quia est regia. Hircusque eadem ratione in divinis suscipitur, qua et Priapus apud Graecos, quia per genitalis membri instrumentum species animalium conservetur; quapropter sacerdotes omnes Aegyptiorum huius dei mysteriis iniciantur. Unde Panas aiunt et Satyros huius rei causa cunctis hominibus esse venerandos, quia simulachra eorum in templis membra in morem hircorum habent, quod animal sua tentigine perpetua semper ad coniunctionem est promptum. Lupi etiam apud eos sunt sacri, quia canibus sunt simillimi. Cocodrilli Aegyptiis honori sunt, quia eorum terrore ab Arabia atque Libya latrones in Aegyptum natare non audent. Praedicta autem animalia quando obierint Aegyptii linteamine contegentes plangentesque et pectora cum gemitu tundentes in sacris sepeliunt condiuntque loculis, quorum si quis sponte aliquod interfecerit morte mulctatur. Felim autem et ibidem seu sponte, seu invitus quisquam necaverit, morte punitur. In

that the father was Jupiter in order to smooth over Semele's dishonor."[28]

The reason they adduce for the Egyptians' worship of animals is this: "It was the custom that Egyptian commanders and generals wore in battle carved images of animals on their helmets as a way of marking out the leading men. Subsequently when a victory had been won, they deified those animals whose images the leaders had worn, as though it had been they who had cast the misfortune of war onto the enemy. Another reason too is given for animal worship. They say the cow is honored because it is useful by bearing calves and plowing, the sheep because it bears lambs, furnishes stuff for clothes and provides food by its milk and cheese, the dog because it joins men in hunting and is fitted by nature to guard them; for this reason the god whom they call Anubis has a dog's head. They worship the cat because it is useful for making shields.[29] From among the birds, the ibis is said to be useful for killing snakes, locusts and caterpillars, the eagle because it is a royal bird. The he-goat has been deified for the same reason as Priapus among the Greeks, because the animal species is preserved by means of the generative member. For this reason, all the Egyptians' priests are initiated into the mysteries of this god. And so the Pans and the Satyrs, they say, must be honored by all men for this reason, because the statues of them in temples have genitalia similar to those of he-goats, this animal being always ready to mate because of its constant arousal. Wolves too are sacred among them because they are very like dogs. Crocodiles are honored by the Egyptians because robbers do not dare to swim across to Egypt from Arabia and Libya out of fear of them. When these animals die, the Egyptians wrap them in linen, and wail and beat their breasts in lamentation, bury them in shrines, and place them in caskets. Anyone who voluntarily kills one of these animals is condemned to death, but if anyone kills a cat or an ibis, whether voluntarily or not, his pun- 11

quacumque autem domo canis mortuus fuerit, omnes qui eam inhabitant universo capite raso luctu maximo afficiuntur, nec vino aut tritico ceterisque ad victum necessariis, quae in ea domo recondita fuerant, uti amplius licet.'

12 Unde Aelius Lampridius[10] scripsit Commodum Antoninum imperatorem Romanum Isidis sacra Romae raso capite coluisse. Et Aelius Spartianus[11] dicit 'in Commodianis hortis in porticu Posceninum Nigrum imperatorem Romanum cum turba pictum fuisse de musivo sacra Isidis facientem, quibus Commodus adeo deditus fuerit ut et caput raderet et Anubim portaret.' Et Antoninum Caracallum imperatorem Romanum—idem scribit Aelius Spartianus—cum habitaret Edissae atque inde Charras Luni dei gratia venisset, interfectum fuisse. Per cuius imperatoris narrandae mortis occasionem idem Spartianus ridiculam rem narrat Carretiis[12] civibus inoluisse opinionem femineo nomine Lunam qui nuncupassent 'addictos mulieribus semper servire, qui vero marem deum esse crediderit, eum uxori semper dominari neque ullas muliebres insidias pati.'

13 Prosequitur vero Eusebius: 'Api[13] deo bove albo naturaliter mortuo et magnifice sepulto, Aegyptii quousque alium invenerint similem in perpetuo luctu sunt, quem simul ac invenerint ad urbem Nili statim adducunt, quo solo tempore mulieribus ipsum videre conceditur. Obviam namque prodeuntes sublatis vestibus genitales partes ei ostendunt, nec unquam postea hunc deum mulieribus videre licet.' Cuius bovis adorandi insania Romanos etiam tenuit. Nam scribit Lampridius Titum Vespasianum imperatorem optimum 'in consecrando apud Memphim bove Api diadema gestasse de more priscae religionis.' Et gloriosus Ecclesiae doctor Hieronimus

ishment is death. Moreover if a dog has died in a house, all who live there shave their whole head and are greatly afflicted with mourning and they may not make any further use of the wine, grain or other necessities of life which had been stored in this house."[30]

12 This is why Aelius Lampridius wrote that the Roman emperor Commodus Antoninus participated in the rites of Isis at Rome with his head shaved.[31] Aelius Spartianus says that the Roman emperor Pescennius Niger was "depicted in a mosaic sacrificing to Isis among a crowd in a colonnade in Commodus' gardens. Commodus was so devoted to her worship that he both shaved his head and carried a statue of Anubis."[32] Aelius Spartianus writes again that the Roman emperor Antoninus Caracalla was killed when he was living at Edessa and went from there to Carrhae for the sake of worshipping the Moon god.[33] In connection with his account of this emperor's death the same Spartianus tells of an absurdity. The citizens of Carrhae had an ingrained view that those who called the moon by a name with the feminine form would always be "the devoted slaves of women whereas he who believed the moon a male god would always be master of his wife and never succumb to any female wiles."[34]

13 Eusebius continues saying that "when the white bull god Apis has died of natural causes and has been magnificently buried, the Egyptians are in continual mourning until they have found another like him. As soon as they have found him they immediately bring him to Nilopolis. This is the only time women are allowed to see him. As they go out to meet him they lift up their clothes and show him their genitals and never again are women allowed to see this god."[35] The Romans too were possessed by the mad worship of this bull. Lampridius writes that the excellent emperor Titus Vespasian "wore a diadem after the fashion and custom of the ancient religion at the consecration of the Apis bull at Memphis,"[36] and Jerome, the renowned Doctor of the Church, in a

ad Silvinam scribens: 'Ad tauri — inquit — Aegyptii sacra semel maritum admitti.' Et idem doctor ad Pamachium exclamat: 'ut sciremus quales deos semper Aegyptus recepisset nuper ab Hadriani amasio urbs eorum Antenous appellata est.'

14 Sed iam Phoenicum, quos primos litteras invenisse constat, theologiam videamus. 'Hi, chaos nescio quid turbidum principio rerum fuisse asserentes, spiritum dicunt sua principia concupiscentem fecisse connexionem, qui Cupido sit appellatus, et ex aquosae mixtura putredinis semina creaturarum omnium generationemque prodisse, ac in primis animalia sensu carentia, ex quibus facta sint animalia intellectualia, quae nominentur "Theophasumini," id est caeli conspectores, post efulxisse Moth id est Solem et Stellas et caeli astra. Mundo talibus inchoato principiis dicunt aerem igneum emisisse fulgorem, ex quo mare, terra, venti nubesque prodierint; paulo post Sole omnia suo calore separante, ex conflictu qui factus sit in aere, tonitrua et fulgura emanasse. Quo sonitu animalia ex limo quasi ex somno, tam ex terra quam ex mari, mas et femina eruperint, et ventos, cum per nomina essent discreti atque recogniti, deos fuisse habitos, quibus adorationes infusionibus atque fumigationibus factae fuerint, ex ventoque Colpia[14] et Nocte muliere Saeculum et Primogenium viros fuisse progenitos, quorum primus alimenta ex arboribus primum docuerit homines ex eisque natos, virum item et mulierem, Genus et Generationem dictos, Phoenicem habitasse. Cum vero aestus esset factus, Phoenices palmam ad Solem extendisse, quem nomine Beelsemon, id est caeli dominum, et deum vocant, isque sit quem Graeci Iovem postea appellarunt.'

letter to Silvina, says that "only those married once are allowed to share in the sacred rites of the Egyptian bull"[37] and the same Doctor exclaims to Pammachius: "So that we may know what kind of gods the Egyptians had always accepted, not long ago one of their cities was named Antinous after Hadrian's lover."[38]

But let us now consider the theology of the Phoenicians, the inventors of the alphabet, as is well known. "They assert that at the beginning of the universe there was a sort of confused chaos and they say that breath, lusting after its own first principles, made a connection, which was called Desire, and from a compound of watery putrescence there emerged the seeds of all creatures and generation, first of all the beings which had no sensation, and out of them were made intelligent beings, which were called 'Zophasemin,' that is 'observers of heaven.' Afterward Moth, that is the sun and stars and the constellations, burst forth into light. When the world had been begun by such principles, they say air sent forth a fiery brightness from which sea, earth, the winds and the clouds arose. A little later as the sun separated them all by its heat, thunder and lightning were produced by the collision that happened in the air. At the sound of this the animals burst forth from the mud, as if from a sleep, both from land and sea, male and female. When the winds had been recognized and distinguished by name, they were held to be gods and they were worshipped with drink offerings and sacrificial burning. From the wind, Colpias, and his wife, Night, were born the men Era and Firstborn. The first of these first taught mankind how to get nourishment from trees. From these again were born a man and a woman called Offspring and Generation, and they lived in Phoenicia. When there was a drought, the Phoenicians stretched out their hands toward the sun, which they call Beelsamen, that is, lord and god of heaven. He is the one whom the Greeks later called Jupiter."[39] 14

15 Et cum post haec multa habeat Phoenicum theologia parvi nunc faciunda. Additur in illa 'Misonem Taantuum elementa litterarum primum omnium conscripsisse esseque illum quem Aegyptii Thor, Alexandrenses Thot, Graeci Mercurium vocant, et ab Aelio muliereque Beruth vocata, Bibli habitantibus, natum esse Terrenium aut Indigenam, cui Coelus postea cognomen fuerit. A cuius nomine supremum corpus mira varietate formosissimum Coelum fuerit appellatum, cuius soror fuerit Terra. Hique patri suo altissimo a bestiis devorato sacra et caerimonias instituerunt. Coelusque patris regnum possidens terram sororem duxit uxorem, quae ei tres peperit filios: Betillum, quem et Saturnum dicunt, Dagona, qui et Frumentarius appellatur, ac postremo Athlanta.' Saturno autem, in sidus caeleste mutato, simulachrum Aegyptii facientes, quatuor oculos, in posterioribus duos, et alios in anterioribus posuerunt, qui vicissim contracti quiescebant. Alas quoque quatuor in humeris fixerunt, duas extensas quasi volaret, duas remissas quasi staret, significabaturque ipsum dormientem vigilare et vigilantem dormire, pariter per alas quiescentem volare et volantem quiescere; ceteris etiam diis Phoenices duas fecerunt alas in humeris, quasi Saturno convolarent. Vana vero atque ridicula Phoenicum theologia fuisse unica arguitur levitate, quod serpentum illi divinam esse naturam dixerunt, quoniam absque manuum ac pedum ac omnino alicuius organi exterioris adiumento eximiam celeritatem exaequantur, variasque figuras et formas gradientes, involuto revolutoque ad quam velint celeritatem gressu, facillime praestent. Longaevi etiam sint, nec solum senectam cum pelle deponentes revirescant, sed crescant etiam in adolescentiam redeuntes; ita nisi percussi pereant, vix naturali nece confici. Unde felicem daemona appellant serpentem, cui divinissimo, ut dicunt,

Though the Phoenicians' theology contains much besides this, 15
little weight need be given to it now. Included in it is "that Misor Taautos invented the first written alphabet. He is the one the Egyptians call Thor, the Alexandrians Thot and the Greeks Mercury. From Elioum and a woman called Beruth, who dwelt at Byblos, was born Earthborn or Native, who afterward was given the name Coelus. From him the highest body was named, the heaven (*coelum*), most beautiful in its marvelous variety. His sister was Earth. They established sacrifices and ceremonies for their father, the Most High, after he had been devoured by wild beasts. Coelus came into possession of his father's kingdom and took his sister Earth as wife. She bore him three sons: Betillus whom they also call Saturn, Dagon, who is also called Supplier of Grain, and finally Atlas."[40] Saturn was transformed into a heavenly constellation and the Egyptians, making a likeness of him, put on it four eyes that close and rest in turn, two in front and two behind. They also attached four wings to his shoulders, two spread as if he were flying, two folded, as if he were standing still. This signified that while sleeping he was alert, and while awake he was asleep. Similarly in the case of the wings, that he flew while at rest and was at rest when flying. The Phoenicians put two wings on the shoulders of all their other gods, as though they accompanied Saturn on his flight. A single instance of frivolity proves that the Phoenicians' theology was groundless and absurd, for they said that snakes have a divine nature, the reason being that without the aid of hands and feet or any external members whatsoever, they attain an extraordinary speed. Executing as they go various shapes and figures and winding and unwinding in their progress they very easily achieve the speed they choose. They are also long-lived and, not only do they grow young again sloughing old age with their skin, but also grow larger as they return to youth. So unless they die struck by violent blows, they are barely consumed by a natural death. For this reason the Phoenicians call the snake a "Propitious Demon"

animali Ophioni appellato sicut ceteris diis imolabant. Quam admiratus insaniam beatus Ecclesiae doctor Ambrosius, ut sacratissimam Dei nostri Iesu Christi religionem Christianis hominibus redderet gratiorem, hunc Ophionem, qui et Latine serpens dicitur, qualis a gentilibus Italicis Phoenices imitatis colebatur, in sua Mediolanensi ecclesia conservari voluit, qui etiam nunc integer conspicitur.

16 Graecorum vero facile omnium totius orbis sapientissimorum doctissimorumque theologia non multo minores praedictis habuit fatuitates. 'Cadmum ferunt, Agenoris filium, ex Phoenicia ad quaerendum Europam, quae fuerat a Iove rapta, a rege missum fuisse, nec invenientem in Boetiam tandem pervenisse, ac Thebas ibi aedificasse, cumque Hermionem, Veneris filiam, uxorem duxisset, Semelem et sorores eius ex ea genuisse. Postea ex Iove et Semele natum esse Dionysium, qui vitis et vini usum homines docuerit atque invenerit coctionem ex aqua et ordeo confectam, quam appellaverit cervisiam. Huncque cum exercitu non solum virorum, sed mulierum quoque orbem lustrasse, iniquis iniustisque hominibus ubique punitis; eius vero exercitus mulieres hastis tyrso ornatis armatae fuerunt, et Musae omnes deum hunc secutae, virginitate atque omni genere doctrinae florentes, tripudiis et cantu eum permulcebant. Paedagogum is habuit Silenum, cuius virtutem fuit consecutus. Mitra huic deo ligabatur caput propter dolores qui effumante vino caput aggrediuntur. Ferula ei in manibus est quia, cum non permixtum aqua vinum bibunt homines, in furorem versi alter alterum baculis caederent unde aliqui moriebantur. Itaque pro lignis ferula uti persuasit. Bachus a Bachis mulieribus est vocatus; Lenaeus quia lenus Graece, torcular Latine appellatur; Bromius a bromo, id est ignis sonitu, qui cum ille aborsu ederetur

and they used to sacrifice to this most divine, as they say, animal called Ophion, just as they did to all the other gods.[41] Marveling at this madness, Ambrose, the holy Doctor of the Church, decided to keep this Ophion, later called Serpens in Latin, in which state it was worshipped by the Italic Gentiles in imitation of the Phoenicians, in his church in Milan[42]—even now it is seen quite intact—in order to make the most holy religion of our God Jesus Christ more welcome to Christians.

The theology of the Greeks, easily the wisest and most learned 16 of men in the whole world, contained follies not much smaller than the ones I have mentioned. "They tell that Cadmus, Agenor's son, was sent from Phoenicia by the king to search for Europa who had been carried off by Jupiter. Failing to find her he arrived at last in Boeotia and there built Thebes, and, after marrying Hermione, Venus' daughter, he fathered from her Semele and her sisters. Afterward Dionysus, who taught men the use of the vine and wine, was born from Jupiter and Semele. He also invented a brew made of water and barley, which he called beer. He traversed the globe with an army not only of men but also of women, punishing everywhere the unjust and the wrong doers. The women in this army were armed with spears fitted with a thyrsus. All the Muses, virgins and distinguished for learning of every kind, followed this god and they delighted him with their singing and dancing. He had a tutor, Silenus, whose excellence he attained. This god's head is tied up with a headband, on account of the headaches that attack him from the wine fumes. He also has a fennel stalk in his hands, because when men drink unwatered wine, they become maddened and beat each other with their staves, and some used to die as a result. So he persuaded them to use a fennel stalk in place of clubs. He was called Bacchus after the Bacchants, and Lenaeus because the Latin *torcular* (winepress) is *lenos* (wine vat) in Greek, and Bromius from *bromos*, that is the sound of the lightning bolt which thundered when he was born prematurely.

insonuit. Satyri eum secuti sunt, qui saltando et tragice canendo voluptatem ei afferebant. Ab hoc ferunt theatrum primo et musicam fuisse inventam.' 'Herculem Graeci asserunt Iove et Alcmena[15] genitum, qui duos dracones a Iunone ad necem immissos puer gutture alliso peremerit. Aesculapium, Apollinis et Coronidos filium, adeo in medicina excelluisse ut ab incurabili morbo multos liberaverit. Ea re Iovem commotum eum interemisse, cuius morte irritatus Apollo Ciclopas, qui fulmen illud Iovi subministraverant, interfecerit. Unde iratus Iupiter Apollinem ad servitium Admeti regis impulerit.'

17 Alia quoque fuit Graecorum theologia, quam ab Athlantiis populis acceperint. 'Athlantii enim inquiunt Coelum apud se primum regnasse, qui filios quinque et quadraginta habuerit, quorum duodeviginti Ops castissima mulier ei genuerit, ob quod meritum Ops, quae est terra, in dearum numerum sit relata. Filias quoque Athlantem habuisse Basyliam et Cybelen, quam et Pandoram vocant. Basyliam post Coeli mortem Hyperioni fratri nuptam duos peperisse liberos, Solem et Lunam; Cybelen autem Hyperiona interemisse Solemque ad fluvium Eridanum praecipitasse; Lunamque cum haec sic facta percepisset de alto sese loco deiecisse. Mater vero furore concita crinibus solutis, tympanis et ululatibus bachans, circumvagabatur. Demum, postquam nullibi poterat inveniri, deificata fuit et arae templaque illi constituta sunt, cuius sacra cum cimbalis et tympanis fiunt. Sol vero atque Luna ad luminaria sunt translati.'

18 A Phrigum quoque theologia acceperunt Graeci. 'Phrigesque dicunt Maeona antiquissimum apud eos fuisse regem, a quo nata Cybele fistulam, quam syringam dixerunt, invenerit et Montana mater appellata est. Cybelen Athidi adultero iunctam, cum vero cognita res esset, interfecto Athide ac sociis eius a patre, commotam furore per universam regionem magnis ululatibus vagatam

He had satyrs as followers who brought him pleasure by their dances and goat songs. They say that he was the first inventor of theater and music."[43] "Hercules, the Greeks maintain, was born of Jupiter and Alcmena. When still a child he destroyed the two snakes sent by Juno to kill him by strangling them. Aesculapius, the son of Apollo and Coronis, they say achieved such heights in his medicine that he freed many from incurable illness. Disturbed by this Jupiter killed him, but Apollo, enraged because of his death, killed the Cyclopes who had supplied Jupiter with the thunderbolt. In his anger at this Jupiter compelled Apollo to serve king Admetus as a slave."[44]

The Greeks had another theology too borrowed from the peo- 17
ple of Atlas. "The people of Atlas say Coelus was their first king and he had forty-five sons. Eighteen of these Ops, a most virtuous woman, bore for him, as a reward for which Ops (who is also the earth) was deified. Atlas had daughters too, Basileia and Cybele, who was also called Pandora. After Coelus' death, Basileia married her brother Hyperion and bore two children, Sun and Moon. But Cybele did away with Hyperion and hurled Sun into the river Eridanus. When she realized this had happened, Moon threw herself down from a high place. Her mother was overtaken by madness and ranged around, with loosened hair, raving with drums and shriekings. Finally, after she could nowhere be found, she was deified and altars and temples were set up for her. Her rites were celebrated with cymbals and drums. Sun and Moon were turned into heavenly bodies."[45]

The Greeks borrowed from the Phrygians' theology too. "The 18
Phrygians say that Maeon was their most ancient king. His daughter Cybele invented the pipe called 'syrinx' and she was called Mountain Mother. Cybele committed adultery with Attis. When this affair was found out, Attis, together with his companions, was killed by her father. Driven mad by passion, she ranged over the whole region with loud wailings, consoling her grief with drums.

fuisse, tympanis dolorem suum consolantem, cumque Apollo Cybelem adamasset, Athidis corpus ab ea sepultum, quae divinos honores consecuta erat. Unde adolescentis mortem Phriges plangunt et aris structis Athida Cybelenque in deos colunt.' Prosequitur Phrigum theologia 'ex Athlante astrologo natas filias septem Athlantidas appellari, a quibus plures dii et heroes sint nati, a seniore quarum Maia, Iovi coniuncta, Mercurius fuerit procreatus; Saturnumque, filium Athlantis avaritia et impietate praeditum, sororem Cybelem duxisse uxorem, a qua Iovem suscepit, quamvis alium Iovem, Caeli fratrem, Cretae regem contendunt fuisse, qui decem filios procreaverit quos Curetas appellarunt. Saturnum vero in Sicilia Italiaque regnasse, a quo natus Iupiter oppositam patri vitam duxit. Alios etiam habuisse duos Saturnum ex Rhea filios, Iovem et Iunonem; ipsumque Iovem tres uxores: Iunonem, Cererem et Daphnem duxisse, a quarum prima Curetes genuerit, ab alia Persephonem, a tertia Minervam.' Multa praeter haec de diis, quos susceperit Graecia, dici possent, cum unicus poeta Hesiodus triginta deorum milia in terris fuisse commemoret, quod quidem illi faciliter concedere poterint qui statuas aeneas marmoreasque et ligneas sicut[16] et ipse pro diis habendas esse crediderint.

19 Satis multa dixisse videmur de diis quos ante urbem conditam diversae orbis provinciae coluerunt. Quos quidem deos Romani condita urbe non colere non potuerunt, praesertim cum Troianos eorum progenitores huiusmodi deorum superstitionibus plenos, sicut ostendemus, habuerint auctores, quamquam et ipsa re constat, et nonnullos ex Graecis sensisse videmus, Romanos in deorum susceptione multas Aegyptiorum Phoenicumque et Graecorum ineptias impietatesque omisisse. Sed praeter deos deasque alia nequaquam meliora a gentibus barbaris ad Romanos traducta[17]

When Apollo fell in love with Cybele, she buried Attis' body and she was honored as a goddess. This is why the Phrygians lament the death of the youth and have built altars and worship Attis and Cybele as gods."[46] The Phrygians' theology goes on to say that "the seven daughters born to Atlas, an astronomer, were called Atlantides, and from them a number of gods and heroes were born. The eldest of them, Maia, by union with Jupiter, gave birth to Mercury. Atlas' son Saturn, possessed of greediness[47] and impiety, married his sister Cybele and from her begat Jupiter, although they maintain that another Jupiter, Caelus' brother, was king of Crete. He begat ten sons who were called the Curetes. Saturn reigned in Sicily and Italy and his son Jupiter led a life opposed to his father. Saturn had two other children by Rhea, Jupiter and Juno. Jupiter himself had three wives, Juno, Ceres and Daphne, by the first of whom he begat the Curetes, by the second Persephone and by the third Minerva."[48] Much more could be said about the gods adopted by the Greeks, seeing that one poet alone, Hesiod, records that there were thirty thousand gods in the world. Indeed they could easily concede this to him given that they believed, just as he did himself, that statues of bronze, marble and wood were to be regarded as gods.[49]

I think I have said enough about the gods worshipped in differ- 19
ent parts of the globe before the foundation of the City of Rome. After Rome's foundation it was inevitable that the Romans would worship these gods, especially since the city's founders were their ancestors the Trojans and they, as I shall show, had an abundance of superstitious belief in gods of this kind.[50] It is both self-evident, however, and we see that some from among the Greeks realized, that the Romans in their adoption of gods avoided many of the follies and improprieties of the Egyptians, Phoenicians and Greeks. But apart from the gods and goddesses it is clear that other equally bad things were passed on to the Romans from the

fuisse videmus: fatorum et fortunae necessitatem, oraculorum responsa, auguria, somniorum vanas interpretationes, vaticinationes, nicromantiam et quaesita cum demonibus mortuisque colloquia. Cum tamen ex Graecis nonnulli fatorum et fortunae necessitatem tollere pro viribus sint adnixi, ostendentes, quod et verissimum est, ea stante omnem everti tollique philosophiam, iacere pietatem, iusticiamque interire, nullam fore virtutis laudem aut vitiorum vituperationem, nullumque expectandum esse laborum et bene gestorum fructum, nullam malefactorum punitionem extimescendam.

Beatus autem Aurelius Augustinus dum *Civitatem Dei* aedificat sic habet: 'Prorsus divina providentia regna constituuntur humana, quae si propterea fato quisquam tribuit, quia ipsam dei voluntatem fati nomine appellat,[18] sententiam teneat, linguam corrigat.' Ut ei videatur adhaesisse sententiae Seneca: 'Duc me, summe pater altique dominator poli, nulla parendi mora est, adsum impiger, fac nolle, comitabor gemens, malusque patiar facere quod licuit bono. Ducunt volentem fata, nolentem trahunt.' Et Cicero in libris *De fato* ex Homero: 'Tales sunt hominum mentes, qualis pater ipse Iupiter auctiferas lustravit numine terras.' Et tamen de unico ex eius fortunae cultoribus Tullo rege quid Plutarchus in *Problematibus* habeat ostendemus, qui scribit 'illum omnes actus suos fortunae ascripsisse, a qua sublatus fuerat ab ancilla matre ad regnum provectus. Hincque regem[19] Fortunae Primogeniae et Masculae templa erexisse, aliud Convertentis, aliud Bene Sperantis, aliud Fortunae videntis, quasi ab ea nos procul capiamur et negotiis ac rebus inhaereamus. Construxit etiam Fortunae parvae templum,

barbarian peoples: the binding force of fate and fortune, oracular responses, auguries, meaningless dream interpretations, prophecies, necromancy, and the seeking of conversation with demons and the dead. And yet some Greeks strove with all their might to remove the binding force of fate and fortune, demonstrating, and this is a great truth, that, if that holds, all philosophy is overturned and done away with, piety collapses and justice perishes, there would be no more praise for virtue or blame for vice, and we would have to expect no return for our labors and good deeds, and fear no punishment for wrongdoing.

St. Augustine, however, in the course of building his *City of God* 20
has the following: "Truly, human kingdoms are established by divine providence. If anyone attributes them to 'fate' for the reason that he calls the very will of God 'fate,' let him maintain his belief, but correct his language," so that he may seem to be in agreement with Seneca's opinion: "O supreme father and ruler of lofty heaven, guide me. Without delay I shall obey. Here I am, ready to act, suppose that I refuse, I shall follow with groans, and vilely I shall do under duress what I could have done as a good man. Fate leads the willing person but drags the unwilling." And Cicero, in *On Fate*, translating from Homer, "Such are the hearts of men as Jupiter, the father himself, brightened with his power the fruit-bearing lands."[51] Nevertheless I shall set out what Plutarch in his *Problems* says about King Tullius,[52] unparalleled among the worshippers of the goddess Fortune. "Tullius," he writes, "attributed all his actions to Fortune by whom he had been raised up, for he had a maidservant as a mother yet was promoted to the kingship. Hence as king he built temples of Fortune the Firstborn, and the Male, one of Fortune who Turns Around, one of the Giver of Good Hope, one of All-Seeing Fortune, signifying that we are caught by her from afar and are entangled in occupations and affairs. He also built the Temple of Little Fortune, as though he were teaching men to pay

quasi docens homines diligenter attendere, nec ea quae accidunt quamvis parva contemnere.'

21 Responsa vero simulacrorum, quod Aegyptiorum Phoenicumque inventum fuit, constat hominum malitia arteque malefica fuisse facta ad opes mendacio et multorum pernicie cumulandas. Carilao enim et Archilao, Lacedaemoniorum regibus, respondit Apollo melius fore si agri, quem bello quaesiverant, dimidiam Apollini partem darent. Itaque astuti et cauti homines animum ad id applicantes, ex abditis, penetralibus et profundissimis plerunque spelunchis responsa dantes, ea ab oraculis prodisse mentiebantur. Hi enim dispositos habuere per civitatem ministros investigantes cuius rei egentes essent vel advenae, vel cives, ut responsa excogitare possent. Habita autem indigentiae illorum notitia et necessariis ad id interrogantiunculis blande factis, si aliquid futurum coniecturis assequebantur, aperte respondebant. Sin vero dubia res coniecturis percipi nequisset, responsionis ambiguitate fallebant ut redargutionem effugere viderentur. Croesus, imperium Lydiae sperans augere, templum Apollini Delphico omnium orbis ditissimum erexit et deus ab eo consultus sua responsi ambiguitate destruxit. Sic enim vates oraculum dixisse mentitus est: 'intrepidus si Croesus Alim transmiserit amnem, imperium perdet magnum regnumque superbum.' Quandoque etiam cantando et verba quaedam inaudita responsionibus immiscendo multos decipiebant, nec parum fidei faciebat huiusmodi aditumm templorumque custodibus verborum elegantia et orationis gravitas, sive futuris a casu veris adhibita, sive in ambiguitatibus responsorum. Cum autem casu aliquid dictum eventu comprobaretur, id marmoreis incisum litte-

careful attention, and not to despise anything that happens, however small."[53]

21 As to oracular responses of statues — an invention of the Egyptians and Phoenicians — these, it is agreed, were a product of men's cunning and evil devices, for the purpose of accumulating wealth by deceit and by the destruction of many.[54] For instance, Apollo replied to the Spartan kings Charilaus and Archelaus that it would be better if they were to give to Apollo half the land they had gained by war.[55] Therefore clever and cunning men put their minds to it, and, giving responses from sanctuaries, innermost shrines and very often from the depths of caves, falsely claimed that these were put forth by the oracles. In fact they had agents stationed here and there throughout the city who investigated the wants of strangers or citizens so that they could devise their responses. With this information about what they required, for they had pleasantly made the requisite little inquiries, they would give a clear response, if they were able to guess correctly something that would happen. But if the matter was uncertain and could not be perceived by guesswork, they would give an ambiguous and cheating reply so that they would appear to avoid being proved wrong.[56] Croesus, who hoped to enlarge the Lydian empire, built the most sumptuous temple in the world for Delphic Apollo and the god, when consulted by him, destroyed him by the ambiguity of his response. The prophet falsely stated that the oracle said, "If Croesus fearlessly crosses the river Halys, he will destroy a great and proud empire."[57] Sometimes too they deceived many by chanting, and inserting certain strange words into their responses. To a large extent trust in the guardians of sanctuaries and temples of this kind was encouraged by the elegance of their words and the gravity of their speech, whether applied to events that accidentally turned out true or in their ambiguous responses. When something said by chance proved true in the event, it was inscribed in marble,

ris mandabatur ad fidem a ceteris comparandam; quae autem falsa fuissent, paene innumerabilia, nullus commemorabat. Ut non ignave iocatus fuisse videatur Dionysius ille Siculus, qui cum Apollinis Delphici templum donis aureis argenteisque refertum fuisset intuitus, quae illi affixerant qui per dei invocationem aliquo periculo liberati aut aliter beneficio affecti fuissent, dixit multo plura et prope infinita fore si quis promissa deo munera haberet quae, quia exauditi non fuerant, agitati confectique periculis et calamitatibus non dedissent.

22 Argumento quoque certissimo praedicta ab hominibus facta fuisse illud erit quod Hadriani imperatoris temporibus, quando maxime oracula desinere coeperunt, licet is Christianus non esset, subiecti quaestionibus praedicti oraculorum vates universam rem suis inventionibus ad turpes quaestus excogitatam edidere, modosque, de quibus supra diximus, patefecere qui tamquam seductores et malefici ultimo supplicio secundum leges affecti sunt. Unde postea proclivis fuit ad cultum Christianae religionis et fidei suscipiendum, quod in *Vita Alexandri Severi* Aelius innuit Spartianus his verbis: 'Iudaeis privilegia reservavit; Christianos passus est esse. Christo templum facere voluit, eumque inter deos recipere, quod Hadrianus cogitasse fertur, qui templa in omnibus civitatibus iussit fieri sine simulacris, quae hodie quoque quia non habuerunt numina Hadriani dicuntur. Etiam illa ad hoc parasse dicebat, sed prohibitus est ab iis qui consulentes sacra reppererunt omnes Christianos futuros si id fecisset.' Et Flavius Vopiscus[20] in Saturnini gestis rebus hanc inserit Hadriani epistulam ad supra-

to win credence from everyone else. The almost countless others which had turned out to be false no one recalled.[58] So that the joke of the famous Dionysius of Sicily seems to have had point. When he had observed that the Temple of Apollo at Delphi was crammed with gifts of gold and silver dedicated to the god by those who had been freed from some danger or had otherwise benefited by invoking him, he said there would be far more, an almost infinite number of them, if one were to have the gifts promised to the god which people, tormented and crushed by dangers and disasters, had not given because they had not been listened to.[59]

In addition a very reliable proof that the predictions were made up by people is the fact that, when oracles especially began to decline in the time of the emperor Hadrian, though he was not a Christian, the spokesmen of the oracles mentioned above were interrogated and admitted that the whole thing was an invention of their own for the purpose of dishonorable moneymaking. They divulged the practices I have already discussed and underwent capital punishment according to the laws for being confidence men and malefactors.[60] This is the reason that later on he was inclined to the adoption of the practice of the Christian religion and faith, as Aelius Spartianus implies in the *Life of Alexander Severus* saying, "[Alexander] preserved the Jews' privileges; he allowed Christians to exist. He wanted to build a temple to Christ and to include him among the gods. Hadrian is said to have had such plans because he gave instructions that in every city there should be a temple without images. Because they do not have specific deities, they are called today too Hadrian's temples. Alexander even said he was preparing them for this purpose, but he was prevented by those who examined the sacred victims and discovered that, if he did, all men would become Christians."[61] Flavius Vopiscus included in the history of Saturninus this letter of Hadrian referring to the 22

dicta facientem: 'Hadrianus Augustus Serviano consuli salutem. Ad Aegyptum quam mihi laudabas veni, totam levem, pendulam et ad omnia famae momenta volitantem. Illi qui Serapim colunt Christiani sunt et devoti sunt Serapi, qui se Christi episcopos dicunt. Nemo illic archisynagogus Iudaeorum, nemo Samarites, nemo mathematicus, non aruspex, non aliptes. Unus illis deus est, hunc Christiani, hunc Iudaei, hunc omnes venerantur gentes.' Divinationes vero, proximum supradictis malum, nonnullae gentes attentissime sunt secutae, sed minus id nocuit malum, quia multi ex eorum philosophis divinationem nullo modo utilem esse ea probaverunt ratione, quod sequi praevidebant omnia esse fatata, et quaenam utilitas fuisset, si futura omnino mala praevideas, quae nullo modo valeas evitare? Nulla enim omnino utilitas, sed maeror potius fuisset secutus qui hominum animos potius perturbasset. Et non tantum homines bonorum expectatione gaudent, quantum timore impendentium malorum torqueri consueverunt.

23 Non autem satis multum infortunii Romanis fuit deos deasque et fatorum, oraculorum auguriorumque, et ceterorum quae diximus malorum initia a gentibus barbaris accepisse, nisi ritus quoque sacrorum infandos ab iis pariter habuissent, quibus tamen populus Romanus pro sua prudentia minus flagitiose quam traditi erant est usus. Siquidem orgia Orpheus[21] adinvenit Thracibus, quae Dionysio a Bachis mulieribus celebrantur, et hae carnes crudas comedentes sacro furori initiabantur, et furentes ac Bachantes viros simul atque feminas in templis deorum noctu pernoctare cogebant. Cererem Romani ut castissimam coluerunt, adeo ut periculum castitatis facturae vittas eius matronae palam in templo

matters just mentioned: "Hadrian Augustus send his greetings to Servianus, consul. I have arrived in Egypt whose praises you were singing to me, [I have found it] wholly light-minded, inconstant and wavering according to every impulse of rumor. Those who worship Serapis are Christians and those who call themselves bishops of Christ are devotees of Serapis. There is no leader of a Jewish synagogue there, no Samaritan, [who is not] an astrologer, a soothsayer, a masseur. They have one god. He is worshipped by the Christians, by the Jews, by all nations."[62] Some nations to be sure have been scrupulous adherents of methods of telling the future by divination, an evil very like those already mentioned, but this evil did less harm because many of their philosophers proved that divination is of no possible use. They saw that it follows that everything happens by fate and what benefit would there have been if one could foresee every kind of future evil but not have any power to avoid it? Absolutely no benefit would have resulted but grief instead. This would have cast people's spirits into turmoil. People do not get as much joy from the anticipation of good, as they are usually wracked by fear of impending evils.[63]

The Romans would really not have come off so badly from hav- 23
ing adopted gods and goddesses from the barbarians and the mysteries of fates, oracles, auguries, and all the other evils I mentioned, if they had not in the same way received from them unspeakable sacrificial rites as well. These however the Roman people in its wisdom practiced with less infamy than they had been passed down, considering it is the case that Orpheus invented the Thracians' orgies which were celebrated in honor of Dionysus by female Bacchants and these were initiated into the sacred madness by eating raw flesh and, in their mad frenzy, they forced men and women together to stay overnight in the gods' temples.[64] The Romans worshipped Ceres as the chastest of goddesses, so much so that married women in public view in the temple touched her fillets to make trial of their chastity. For this reason the poet said,

tangerent. Unde poeta: 'Paucae adeo vittas Cereris contingere dignae.' Sed videamus quae fuerint merita propter quae deificata est: eam ferunt filiae luctu maestam cum a Bambone, nobili Coribanthum muliere, hospitio suscepta potionem multis confectam ex rebus, quam citrona appellant, sumere recusasset, indoluisse Bambonem, atque sublata veste genitalia membra Cereri ostendisse, quae hoc spectaculo delectata citrona susceperit atque biberit, unde dea meruerit appellari. 'Matris vero deorum sacra Phrigii quotannis crudelissimis certaminibus faciebant, sed Romani sacerdotes utriusque sexus, virum et feminam, ex Phrigia consecrantes urbem solemni pompa timpanorum sonitu perlustrabant.' Maiora sunt quae sequuntur et quorum pauca Romani vel modestissime duxerint imitanda.

24 'Rhodii hominem Saturno sacrificabant, quam crudelitatem cum postea duxerint mitigandam aliquem mortis supplicio damnatum ad Saturnalia usque servabant, quem ipso in festo gravatum vino imolabant. In Salamine insula Diomedi homo imolabatur, qui ab adolescentibus ter circum aram ductus, tandem a sacerdote hasta percussus et rogo impositus cremabatur. Dionysio Omadio[22] apud Chios homo crudeliter discerptus sacrificabatur. Lacedemoniique hominem Marti sacrificare soliti fuerunt. Et Phoenices in bellorum aut pestilentiae calamitatibus amicissimos homines Saturno solebant imolare. Et in Creta Curetes Saturno pueros sacrificabant. In Laodicia Syriae Palladi virgo imolabatur. Arabesque singulis annis puerum imolantes sub ara sepeliebant. Omnesque Graeci priusquam in suscepta prodirent bella hominem imolabant,' quod de Iphigenia bello Troiano factum praedicant. 'Phoenices in magnis calamitatibus atque periculis sui principis dilectissimum ex

"few indeed are worthy to touch Ceres' fillets."[65] But let us see what the merits were for which she was deified. They say that "she was mourning her daughter and was given hospitality by Baubo, a noble woman of the Corybantes. Because she refused to accept a drink called 'ciceon' made out of many ingredients, Baubo was saddened and lifting up her dress she showed Ceres her genitalia. Ceres, cheered by this sight, took up the 'ciceon' and drank it"[66] and this is how she earned the name of goddess. "The Phrygians used to sacrifice every year to the mother of the gods with very cruel contests, but the Romans, adopting priests of both sexes, a man and a woman, from Phrygia, used to traverse the city in a ritual procession to the sound of drums."[67] The things that follow are more momentous and the Romans considered few of them fit to be imitated even with the greatest discretion.

"The Rhodians used to sacrifice a man to Saturn. Later on they 24
considered this cruelty should be mitigated and they kept one of those who had been condemned to death until the festival of the Saturnalia, made him insensible with wine and sacrificed him during the festival. On the island of Salamis a man used to be sacrificed to Diomedes. He was led three times round the altar by the youths and in the end was struck by the priest with a spear, put on a pyre and burned. Among the Chians a man was sacrificed to Dionysus Omadios, cruelly torn limb from limb. The Spartans had the custom of sacrificing a man to Mars. The Phoenicians, too, in calamities of war or pestilence, used to sacrifice to Saturn their best-loved men. In Crete, too, the Curetes used to sacrifice boys to Saturn. At Laodicea in Syria a virgin used to be sacrificed to Pallas. The Arabs used every year to sacrifice a boy and bury him under the altar. All the Greeks used to offer human sacrifice before going out to war." This they say was done in the Trojan War in the case of Iphigenia. "It was the custom of the Phoenicians, in times of great calamity or danger for their ruler, to cut

filiis in redemptionis praemium iugulabant, unde Saturnus rex regionis, qui postea quam hominem exuit in Saturni stellam translatus est, cum unicum filium ex Anobret nympha haberet, Ieud dictum, quia maximo et periculoso bello civitas premebatur, regio indutum ornatu super constructam ad hoc praeparatamque aram imolavit. Aristomenes Messenius Iovi, quem appellant Ithometem, trecentos simul sacrificavit homines, in quibus Theopompus rex Lacedaemonius fuit.' Cum fame Athenienses propter Androgei caedem angerentur et ad auxilia deorum confugissent, Apollo iussit ut singulis annis septem mares totidemque feminas in Cretam sacrificandos mitterent, quod et diligentissime multis saeculis observatum fuisse traditur. 'Scythae quoscumque advenas ceperint—capiunt autem multos qui fluctibus et tempestate ad eos depelluntur—Dianae statim imolant.

'In Pellae civitate Thessaliae hominem Achivum Pelleo et Chironi singulis immolant annis. Dionysius Halicarnasseus[23] in primo de *Antiquitate Italica* refert Iunonem et Apollinem, quoniam decima hominum eis imolata non fuerat, magnas Italis calamitates induxisse, ut nullus in arboribus fructus ad maturitatem usque primam permanserit, nec spicae semine implebantur, nec herbae pecori sufficientes germinabant. Fontes deficiebant, mulieres abortu periclitabantur aut nati filii manci et distorti erant, ceteraque hominum multitudo crebrius quam solebant vexabantur. Cumque responso accepto nollent dii immolationem animalium hostiis faciendam, magna omnes ambiguitate tenebantur. Tuncque civitatum primates post reliqua multitudo ⟨ex⟩ Italia migrare coeperunt, et quasi amentes furentesque pellebant vicissim, ac pro certamine pellebantur, et multis Italiae civitatibus derelictis Graecia et

the throat of the most beloved of their children as the price of redemption. This is why Saturn, who was king of the country and subsequently was turned into the star Saturn after putting off his human form, dressed his only son Jeud (born by the nymph Anobret) in royal garb and sacrificed him on an altar specially prepared for the purpose, for his realm was hard pressed by a great and dangerous war. Aristomenes the Messenian sacrificed three hundred men simultaneously in honor of Jupiter of Ithome. Among them was the Spartan king Theopompus." When the Athenians were suffering from famine for the slaying of Androgeus and turned to the gods for help, Apollo bade them send every year seven men and as many women to Crete to be sacrificed. It is said they did this with the greatest care for many centuries. "All strangers the Scyths have taken captive (and they capture many, who are driven onto their shores by sea and storms) they sacrifice immediately to Diana.

"In the city of Pella in Thessaly they sacrifice an Achaean man 25
to Peleus and Chiron every year. Dionysius of Halicarnassus in *Antiquities of Italy* Book I relates that Juno and Apollo brought great calamities upon the Italians because they had not sacrificed a tithe of men to them. No fruit remained on the trees until it ripened, ears of wheat were not filled with grain, nor did sufficient grass grow for the herd. Springs were failing, women were put in peril by miscarriage, children were born either maimed or crippled, and the rest of the population were troubled more frequently than usual. When they got the response that the gods did not wish sacrifice to be made of animal victims, a great uncertainty took hold of every one. Then the chief men of their cities and subsequently the rest of the population began to leave Italy. And seeing that they were in a state of irrational frenzy they drove each other away and were driven away reciprocally as if by combat. Many cities in Italy were abandoned while Greece and the

barbaria Italis est repleta. Herculemque ferunt ara primum in Saturnino aedificata intemeratas hostias immolasse, et, ne quasi patrio ritu neglecto superstitione inani incolae turbarentur, simulacra vivi hominis in Tyberim fluvium deiiciebant hostiarum ornata modo, idque postea idibus Maiis a populo Romano factitatum est. Ea enim die pontifices virginesque Vestales, praetores aliique cives, quos sacris adesse fas est, animalibus de iure pontificio immolatis triginta hominum simulachra, quos appellant Argeos,[24] a ponte Subliceo in Tyberim dimittebant.'

26 Gentilium externorum religione, quantum ad Romanorum honestandam rem oportere visum est, ostensa, ad nostrum redibimus propositum. Inter multa vero quae Romana superstitio nobis dicenda exhibet, nihil non respuendum ac omnino abhominabile est praeter unum, quod viro Christiano in meliorem partem amplectendum convertendumque existimo, sacris scilicet ut appellarunt ac religioni Romanam gentem accuratissime intentam fuisse. Unde praeclarissima est illa Ciceronis *De haruspicum responsis* sententia: 'Quam volumus, patres conscripti, licet ipsi nos amemus, tamen nec numero Hispanos, nec robore Gallos, nec calliditate Poenos, nec artibus Graecos, nec denique hoc ipso huius gentis ac terrae domestico nativoque sensu Italos ipsos, ac Latinos, sed pietate et religione atque hac una sapientia, quod deorum immortalium numine omnia regi gubernarique prospeximus, omnes gentes nationesque superavimus.' Et Livius XLVII Gn. Cornelio praetori multa indicta quod cum M. Aemilio Lepido, pontifice maximo, iniuriose contenderet sacrorumque quam magistratuum ius potentius fuit. Sed quid[25] beatus Aurelius Augustinus scribit? Dum ille

barbarian lands were filled with Italians. Hercules, they say, first set up an altar on the Hill of Saturn[68] and offered undefiled victims and, in order that the local people would not be disturbed by baseless superstition, for having abandoned hereditary rite they used to cast into the Tiber river images of a living man, adorned in the manner of sacrificial victims. Subsequently this was habitually done by the Roman people on the Ides of May. On that day the pontiffs, and the Vestal Virgins, the praetors and the other citizens who are permitted to be present at sacrifices, sacrificed the animals according to pontifical law and threw from the Sublician bridge into the Tiber thirty images in human form, which they call 'Argives.'"[69]

Having set out the religion of the Gentiles of other countries as far as it seemed necessary in order to dignify the Romans' practices, I shall return to my main theme. The Romans' false religion furnishes much that I must tell of, but it is all to be repudiated and is completely abominable, save for one aspect and this, I think, a Christian ought to embrace and put in the best light. That is, the fact that the Roman people were scrupulously devoted to religious observances (*sacra*), as of course they called them, and to religion. This is the reason for that very splendid opinion of Cicero in *On the Responses of the Haruspices:* "However well we think of ourselves, senators, yet we have not surpassed Spain in numbers, nor Gaul in vigor, nor Carthage in cleverness, nor Greece in art, nor indeed Italy itself and Latium in this homegrown and native capacity for feeling that belongs to this land and its people, but in piety and religious devotion and this exceptional wisdom, the fact that we have discerned that the universe is guided and ruled by the sway of the immortal gods, we have surpassed all races and nations."[70] Livy in Book XLVII writes that a fine was imposed on the praetor Gnaeus Cornelius because he was wrongfully disputing with Marcus Aemilius Lepidus, the Pontifex Maximus, and religious rights prevailed over the magistrates'.[71] What is 26

a Romanis committerentur suorum sacrorum insaniae, 'dum tanta fierent mala, "calebant arae numinum Sabeo thure, sertisque recentibus halabant," clarebant sacerdotia, fana renitebant et uno eodemque tempore sacrificabatur, ludebatur, furebatur in templis.'

27 Igitur de Romanorum religione tractaturi partes primum proponemus, in quas eam dividi oportere iudicemus. Tribusque multarum et diversarum rerum aciebus armata religionis praedictae cognitio nobis tractanda occurrit. Nam prima in parte deos eorumque originem, sacra, caerimonias, ritus, adorationes, libationes et hostias, ipsarum postea rerum causa agentibus instituta erectaque templa, aedes, sacella, fana, aras, delubra simul ostendemus. Deinde secundo loco quaerendae utilitatis, opulentiae et amplitudinis artes sub religionis et deorum numinis integumento confictas, pontifices, flamines, sacerdotes, Salios, Vestales, sodales, fanaticos, Bacchides et maximam eiusmodi hominum turbam docebimus. Tertiam dehinc aciem ludi, spectacula, lectisternia, supplicationes et multa huiusmodi ad populorum delectationem luxumque et a seditionum tumultuationumque concitatione aversionem excogitata sub religionisque et deorum praetextu populo data complebunt. Deos etsi Romulus coluit, qui Lupercal in Palatino monte instituit, sacra diis aliis Albano ritu Graeco Herculi, ut ab Evandro instituta erant sicut Livius docet, fecit, tamen Numa Pompilius artifex religionis industrius fuisse videtur, quem Livius dicit 'ne luxuriarentur otio animi, omnium primum, rem ad multitudinem imperitam et illis saeculis rudem efficacissimam, deorum

it that St. Augustine writes? While the Romans engaged in those senseless rites of theirs, "while such great evils took place 'the altars of the divinities were warm with Sabaean incense and fragrant with fresh garlands,' the priesthoods were held in honor, the shrines gleamed" and at one and the same time "there were sacrifices, games and frenzied activities in the temples."[72]

And so to begin my treatment of Roman religion I shall first set out the parts into which I judge the topic should be divided. I find that the investigation I must hold into the aforesaid religion comprises three groups,[73] consisting of many different things. In the first part I shall set out together the gods and their origin, sacrifices, ceremonies, rites, prayers, drink-offerings and sacrificial victims and after that the temples, temple buildings, chapels, holy precincts, altars, and shrines established and built for the sake of these very practices. Then in second place I shall expound the arts of gaining advantage, wealth and consequence devised under the cover of religion and the powers of the gods—the pontiffs, flamens, priests, Salii, Vestals, members of associations, temple servants, followers of Bacchus, and the enormous throng of people of this kind. The third group will be filled up by games, shows, banquets for the gods, ritual thanksgivings and much of this kind devised for the people's delight and pleasure and to ward off the stirring up of sedition and riots, and provided for the people under the pretext of religion and the gods.[74] Even though Romulus paid due attention to the gods, set up the Lupercal[75] on the Palatine Hill and performed sacrifices for the other gods in the Alban fashion, for Hercules in the Greek, as they had been established by Evander, as Livy tells us,[76] yet Numa Pompilius seems to have been busier as a religious expert. Livy says that "so that their spirits should not go soft in peace, he thought that before all else fear of the gods should be inculcated into them, something that would have a most powerful effect on the inexperienced, and in those days, uncivilized crowd." He pretended that he had 27

metum incutiendum ratum esse,' simulasseque se cum Egeria colloqui et, monitum quae acceptissima diis essent sacra instituere, sacerdotes suos cuique deorum cultui praefecisse. Unde Cicero *Pro domo sua ad pontifices:* 'Equidem sic accepi, pontifices, in religionibus suscipiendis caput esse interpretari quae voluntas sit deorum immortalium.' Et in eadem oratione: 'Cum multa divinitus, pontifices, a maioribus nostris inventa atque instituta sunt, tum nihil praeclarius quam quod vos et religionibus deorum immortalium et summae rei publicae praeesse voluerunt, ut, amplissimi et praeclarissimi cives rem publicam[26] bene gerendo, pontifices religiones sapienter interpretando, rem publicam conservarent.'

28 Quanti etiam deos fecerint Romani Cicero in vetustissimis pontificii iuris legibus ostendit, quarum capita nonnullarum hic ponemus: 'Ad divos adeunto caste, pietatem adhibento, opes amovento. Qui secus faxit, deus ipse vindex erit. Separatim nemo habessit[27] deos neve novos, sed ne advenas nisi publice advectos privatim colunto, constituta a patribus delubra habento. Lucos in agris habento et Larum sedes. Divos et eos qui caelestes semper habiti colunto et illos quos in caelum merita vocaverunt, Herculem, Liberum, Aesculapium, Castorem, Pollucem, Quirinum, ast illa propter quae datur homini ascensus in caelum, Mentem, Virtutem, Pietatem, Fidem, earumque laudum delubra sunto, nec ulla vitiorum sacra solemnia obeunto.' 'Quod autem ex hominum genere consecratos, sicut Herculem et ceteros, coli lex iubet indicat omnium quidem animos immortales esse, sed fortium bonorumque

conversations with Egeria, and, advised by her about what would be most acceptable to the gods, established the religious observances and attached dedicated priests to each god's worship.[77] This is why Cicero says in *On His Own House*: "Indeed I have always understood, gentlemen of the Pontifical college, that the main thing in taking up religious obligations is to understand the will of the immortal gods,"[78] and in the same speech: "while many things, gentlemen, have been devised and established by our ancestors with godlike wisdom, there is none more striking than that they purposed that you be set in charge both of our religious obligations to the immortal gods and the supreme interests of the state, so that the citizens with the most substance and good fame might keep the state safe by administering it well, the pontiffs by understanding the demands of religion wisely."[79]

How much importance the Romans set on the gods Cicero allows us to see in his passage on the ancient laws of the Pontifical code, the main points of some of which I shall include here: "They shall approach the gods in purity. They shall practice due observance. They shall put aside wealth. Whoever does otherwise god himself will punish. No one is to have gods of his own, nor new ones, but they shall not worship foreign gods in private unless they have been introduced by the state. They shall have shrines established by their forefathers. In the countryside they shall have sacred groves and dwellings for the Lares and they shall worship as gods both those who have always been considered heavenly beings and those whose services have called them to heaven, Hercules, Liber, Aesculapius, Castor, Pollux and Quirinus, and those qualities on account of which human beings are permitted to rise to heaven, Intelligence, Virtue, Devotion to Duty, Good Faith; for these praiseworthy qualities there shall be shrines, but for none of the vices shall they observe the established rites."[80] "The fact that the law requires that those deified human beings (like Hercules and the rest) be worshipped shows that the souls of all are immortal 28

divinos. Bene vero quod Mens, Pietas, Virtus, Fides consecrantur manu, quarum omnium Romae dedicata publice templa sunt, ut illa qui habent — habent autem omnes boni — deos ipsos in animis suis collocatos putent.' Et idem Cicero *In Verrem* actione septima: 'Tuque Ceres et Libera, quarum sacra, sicut opiniones hominum ac religiones ferunt, longe maximis, atque occultissimis caerimoniis continentur, a quibus initia vitae atque victus, legum, morum, mansuetudinis, humanitatis exempla hominibus et civitatibus data ac dispersa esse dicuntur.' Praeterea ipse Cicero *Pro Murena:* 'Cum omnis deorum immortalium potestas aut translata sit ad nos, aut certe communicata nobiscum.'

29 Satis itaque hoc initio primae divisionis nostrae partis fundamenta iecimus, qui per Ciceronem et iuris pontificii documenta deorum venerationis et locorum in quibus adorarentur principium causamque ostendimus. Sed plura ad eam rem a M. Varrone afferemus: is, vir sanctorum nostrae religionis doctissimorum Hieronymi et Augustini iudicio doctissimus, est auctor deos ex Samothrace in Phrigiam advectos Aeneam ex Phrigia in Italiam detulisse, dictosque quod per eos spiremus et corpus, mentem ac rationem habeamus, quos fuisse vult Apollinem et Neptunum. Unde Virgilius: 'cum sociis natoque Penatibus et magnis diis' et 'iam pater Aeneas sacra, et sacra altera patrem afferet. Iliacos excipe Vesta deos.' Plutarchus in *Vita Numae Pompilii:* 'Ea quae de deorum simulacris Numa Pompilius statuit quam similia sunt prorsus Pythagorae documentis. Nam primum principium ille neque sensui

but those of the brave and the good are divine. It is well that Intelligence, Virtue, Devotion to Duty, Good Faith should be deified by *fiat*. All these qualities have temples publicly dedicated to them at Rome, so that those who have them (and all good men do have them) should believe that the gods themselves have been placed within their souls."[81] Cicero again in the seventh action of the *Verrine Orations*: "And you, O Ceres and Libera, whose sacred rites, according to human opinion and religious doctrine, consist of by far the most important and most secret ceremonies, by whom the origins of life and livelihood, of laws, the examples of customs, civilization and culture are said to have been given and distributed to mankind and cities."[82] Furthermore, Cicero himself says in *Defense of Murena*: "Since all the immortal gods' power has either been transferred to us or undoubtedly shared with us."[83]

I have, then, sufficiently underpinned the first part of my division by this introduction. By means of quotations from Cicero and the teachings of the Pontifical laws I have demonstrated the origin and cause of the worship of the gods and of the places in which prayers were addressed to them. But in regard to this matter I shall adduce more from Marcus Varro. He, a very learned man in the judgment of Jerome and Augustine,[84] the most learned saints of our religion, writes that Aeneas brought from Phrygia to Italy the gods that had been transported from Samothrace to Phrygia and that they were named [Penates] because through them we draw breath [deeply (*penitus*)] and possess body, mind and reason. His view is that they were Apollo and Neptune. For this reason Vergil says "with my companions and son, with the Penates and the Great Gods"[85] and "Now Father Aeneas shall bring here the sacred burden, and his father, just as sacred a burden. Vesta, welcome the gods of Ilium."[86] Plutarch in the *Life of Numa Pompilius*: "Numa Pompilius' ordinances about images of the gods are very similar to Pythagoras' teachings. Pythagoras thought that the first principle was not susceptible to sensation or emotion 29

neque perturbationi subiectum, sed mentem invisibilem et increatam esse censuit; hic autem Romanos prohibuit existimare imaginem dei aut hominis speciem, aut animalis habere formam, neque fuit apud eos picta, neque ficta dei prius species. Sed in prioribus CLXX annis templa quidem aedificabant sacraque tuguria erigebant, simulacrum vero nullum corporeum faciebant, perinde atque nefas esset deterioribus meliora assimilare, neque aliter atque intelligentia percipi deus posset. Sacra quoque ab Numa instituta, ritum, sanctimoniamque Pythagorae vehementer attingunt. Erant enim sine sanguine, eorumque plurima ex farina et libo rebusque vilissimis composita.'

30 Affirmat etiam Varro 'deos ab antiquis Romanis plus annos CLXX sine simulacris fuisse cultos.' Eorumque viginti selectos, ceteros appellavit plebeios; suntque selecti duodecim mares, octo feminae: Ianus, Iupiter, Saturnus, Genius, Mercurius, Apollo, Mars, Vulcanus, Neptunus, Sol, Orcus, Liber pater, Tellus, Ceres, Iuno, Luna, Diana, Minerva, Venus, Vesta. Et praeter hos utriusque sexus deos alia fuit deorum dearumque tanquam matrimonialis coniunctio, quam comprecationem appellaverunt, ut qui scilicet rem divinam uni fecisset, alteri quoque supplicasse videretur, et 'Latam Saturnus, Salatiam Neptunus, Oram Quirinus, Maiam Vulcanus, Miricem Quiricius, Nerienen Mars comprecationem suam habuit.' Attulit tamen aliam deorum divisionem Varro a Labeone sumptam, qui asseruit deorum partem esse bonam, partem malam, qui cultus diversitate internoscantur, cum mali caedibus hominum et tristibus supplicationibus, boni obsequiis laetis atque iocundis qualia sint lectisternia, atque ludi et convivia placarentur.

31 Et cum deos, ut diximus, selectos a Iano commendare incepisset,[28] quem 'tum bifrontem, tum quadrifrontem tanquam geminum faciebant,' de aliis minoribus tractavit, quorum seriem a

but was an invisible and uncreated intelligence. Numa forbade the Romans to suppose god's appearance was either in human shape or animal form. Nor in this earlier time did they have any painted or sculpted image of God. In the first 170 years they did build temples and put up sacred huts but they made no statues in bodily form, on the grounds that it was impious to liken the better to the worse and impossible to perceive god except by the intellect. The sacrifices established by Numa too come very close to Pythagorean religious observance and moral purity; for they were bloodless and most of them made with flour, cake and the cheapest things."[87]

Varro also affirms that "the Romans of old worshipped the gods 30
for more than 170 years without making statues of them."[88] He called twenty of them "select," the rest "plebeian." Twelve of the select are male, eight female: Janus, Jupiter, Saturn, Genius, Mercury, Apollo, Mars, Vulcan, Neptune, Sol, Orcus, Father Liber, Tellus, Ceres, Juno, Luna, Diana, Minerva, Venus, Vesta.[89] Apart from these gods of both sexes, there was another conjunction, of marriage, as it were, of gods and goddesses, which they called public supplication. The way it worked was that anyone who had made an offering to one would be taken to have prayed to the other too. Each had his own partner, "Saturn Lata, Neptune Salacia, Quirinus Hora, Volcanus Maia, Quiritius Mirices, Mars Nerienes."[90] Yet Varro adduced another division of gods that he borrowed from Labeo. The latter maintained that some of the gods were good, some evil, and these may be distinguished by their different forms of worship, since the evil are appeased by human sacrifice and mournful entreaties but the good by happy and joyful forms of worship such as banquets for the gods, games and feasts.[91]

Varro began his mention of the select gods, as I have said, with 31
Janus[92] of whom they made "sometimes a two-faced image, sometimes four-faces, as though he were double."[93] Then he treated the other lesser gods and traced their succession from the human

conceptione ad decrepiti hominis sepulturam perduxit in hunc maxime modum nostris hominibus perridiculum. 'Cum mas et femina coniunguntur, adhibetur deus Iugatinus; cum domum est ducenda quae nupsit officium id exhibet Domiducus. Ut autem in domo sit deus Domicius; ut maneat cum viro dea Manturna praestat.' Perductaque in mariti domum virgo super Priapum 'nimium masculum immanissimum et turpissimum fascinum, more honestissimo et religiosissimo matronarum sedere iubetur,' nec prius mariti cubiculum ingredi permittitur, quam aula et ceterae domus partes cubiculo continentes nucibus spargantur, quibus a multitudine conculcatis oppressae virginis eiulatus inter strepitum nequeat exaudiri. Dumque fuerint peragenda secreta, ut sine difficultate virginitas auferatur, dea Virginensis et deus pater Subigus et dea mater Prema,[29] deaeque Pertunda et Venus Priapo et ipsi deo praestant obsequium. Subsequiturque illico dea Mena, Iovis privigna, cruori me⟨n⟩struo praesidens, et Liber accurrit pater, quem sic vocatum esse volunt quod mares in coeundo per eius beneficium emissis seminibus liberentur. Nec tardius praestat officium dea Libera, et Venus dicta, illud idem mulieribus quod Liber viris praestans auxilium. Unde credidit, a Labeone doctus, Varro duobus his mari et feminae numinibus honores in templis marmore aut aere, Libero virilis corporis pudendam partem, femineam Liberae excisos adornatosque fuisse. Malum vero fuit obscurissimos a Romanis deos esse habitos Vituninum et Sentinum, quorum alter vitam in embrione, alter sensum puerperio largiebantur. Ut autem nulla pars vitae hominum praesidio numinum careret, dei per singulos aderant actus, 'tanquam opifices in vico argentario, ubi

being's conception to burial in old age,[94] in the following way that seems quite ridiculous to people of our era. "When male and female are joined, the god Jugatinus is summoned. When the bride must be taken home, Domiducus performs this duty. The god Domitius is responsible for her staying at home; the goddess Manturna for her remaining with her husband." When she has been escorted to her husband's home, the virgin is told to sit on the "excessively virile Priapus' huge and disgusting male phallus, in the very respectable and god-pleasing fashion of the married women."[95] She is not allowed to enter her husband's bedroom before nuts are scattered in the hall and the other parts of the house adjacent to the bedroom, and the crowd treads them under foot so that the cries of the virgin being taken cannot be heard for the din.[96] In the accomplishment of those private matters, so that she may lose her virginity without difficulty, the goddess Virginensis, the father-god Subigus, the mother-goddess Prema, the goddesses Pertunda and Venus do service for Priapus, who is a god himself.[97] Then there follows the goddess Mena, Jupiter's stepdaughter, who presides over menstrual blood[98] and Father Liber[99] runs up. They believe he has this name because males by his good graces are liberated in copulation from the semen they emit, nor is the goddess Libera, also called Venus, slower to fulfill her duty, providing the same help to women as Liber does to men.[100] For this reason it is Varro's belief, and he learned it from Labeo, that for these two divine powers, the male and the female, marks of honor were sculpted in marble or bronze and adorned in their temples, the male sexual organs for Liber and the female for Libera.[101] It was indeed wrong that the extremely obscure Vitumnus and Sentinus were considered gods by the Romans. The one bestowed life on the embryo, the other sensation on the infant at birth.[102] So that no aspect of human life should be without divine protection, there were gods present for all the individual episodes, "as if they were the artisans in the street of the silversmiths, where a

unum vasculum, ut perfectum exeat, per multos artifices transit.' 'Mulieri enim fetae in partu tres dei custodes adhibebantur, ne Silvanus deus illam vexaturus ingrederetur': Intercido, Pilumnus et Deverrinus, eorumque significandorum causa tres homines noctu domus limina circuibant. Primus, Intercidoni subministraturus, securi limen caedebat; pilo secundus pro Pillumno feriebat et scopis tertius deverrebat. Tandem Lucina quam parturiens invocaverat, Opis quoque dicta, opem afferebat. Et ne agrippae essent qui nascerentur, quos sic dictos fuisse constat quia perverso ordine pedibus primum ventre egrederentur, deae Perversa et Prosa advocabantur. Post quas Vagitinus deus os puerperii aperiens succedebat, et partum ad lucem Dispiter perducebat, praestoque aderat Levana, quae partum de terra levabat expositum. Sed et Rumina veniebat mammis praefecta mulierum, quas prisci 'rumas' appellavere, ut lac copiosissime praeberetur, quousque adveniente tempore Potina dea potionem, Edulica escam praebere possent. Nec parvum erat Cuminae deae opus, quae, etsi cunas ipsa non agitabat, ut leviter moverentur curabat.

32 Maiora deinceps dicenda sunt numinum collata hominibus beneficia. Mercurius inde, quasi medius inter homines currens, Hermes Graece ab hermonia id est sermone appellatus, loqui praestabat, quem effigiabant alas in capite et pedibus habentem, quod sermo hominum per aera volitet. Et Minerva, quam dixerunt temporibus Ogigi regis ad lacum Tritonis virginali primum apparuisse habitu, unde Tritonia sit dicta, artesque quarum fuit inventrix puerum edocebat. Pavoribus hominum ut arcerentur Paventia; spei eorum quae fortassis evenirent Venilia, voluptatibus

vessel passes through the hands of many craftsmen in order to come out finished."[103] "Three gods were employed to guard a pregnant woman in childbirth, lest the god Silvanus come in to disturb her," Intercido, Pilumnus and Deverrinus, and to represent them, three men go around the thresholds of the house by night. The first, in order to act as assistant to Intercido, would strike the threshold with an ax, the second with a pestle for Pilumnus and the third would sweep it with a broom.[104] Finally Lucina was summoned by women in labor. She brought aid (*opem*) under the name of Opis as well.[105] Lest those who were being born should be breach-born—they, it is well known, were so called because they came out of the womb the wrong way round with feet first—the goddesses Perversa and Prosa were summoned.[106] There followed after them the god Vaticanus, who opens the newborn baby's mouth, and Diespiter who brought him into the light of day, and Levana, who lifted the child from the earth where he had been laid, was ready at hand. Rumina came too, the goddess set over the woman's breasts, which the ancients called "rumae," so that milk might be supplied in abundance until as time went on the goddess Potina could supply drink (*potio*) and the goddess Educa food (*esca*). The goddess Cunina did not have a small task either. If she did not rock the cradles (*cunae*) herself, she saw to it that they were gently moved.[107]

Next I must speak of greater benefits of the gods conferred on 32
human beings. Mercury was responsible for speech, running in the midst as it were between human beings. In Greek he was called Hermes from "hermeneia," that is, speech. They used to depict him with wings on his head and feet because men's talk flies through the air. Minerva taught the boy the arts that she invented. They said that she appeared first, dressed like a maiden, in the time of King Ogygus at Lake Triton and so she was called Tritonia.[108] The goddess Paventia warded off men's fears, Venilia presided over their hopes that things might turn out well, Volupia

quibus fruerentur Volupia, actibus quibus se immiscerent Ageronia, stimulis quibus agerentur Stimula, strenue gestis quae contingerent Strenia, deae praeerant, fessis dea Fessona ut quiescerent, hostibusque pellendis dea Pellona praebebant auxilium, Numeria quoque dea quibusdam bene numerare, Cameria bene canere, Mars et Bellona ut bene belligerarent, Victoria ut vincerent, Honorinus deus ut honorarentur, Pecunia ut pecuniosi essent. Aesculanus et filius eius Argentinus dei, ut haberent aeneam argenteamque pecuniam praestabant. Et ut suum quoque deum improbi segnesque haberent, dea erat Murdea, quae praeter modum non moveret ac faceret hominem, ut inquit Pomponius, murcidum, ac nimis desidiosum et inactuosum.[30] Parvae etiam existimationis neque inter malos aut bonos deos posita fuit Fortuna Barbata, quae cultoribus suis malas speciosius vestiens, se spernentes male barbatos glabrosque reddebat; cum contra maiori deae Fortunae, quam omnipotentem appellaverunt, et deabus fatis multo maiorem quam oportuerit vim potentiamque, sicut supra ostendimus, tribuerint, Temin vero parum coluerint, quam Festus 'deam fuisse' dicit 'quae praeciperet hominibus id petere quod fas esset, eamque id esse existimabant quod fas est.' Et ne plures quam expediat perquiramus deos vitae hominum fortunisque adhibitos, Neniam gentiles voluerunt deam mortuos homines in funere comitari, unde et modulationes inter eiulandum plangendumque adhibitas 'nenias' vocavere.

33 Sed et suam sata segetesque et cetera hominibus usui futura deorum habuerunt turbam: Saturnumque deum in primis maximum, Iovis genitorem, praedicant 'nata ex sese devorare, quod semina unde nascuntur revertantur,' unde propter agriculturam falcem manu tenet effigiatus et, ne solus tanto munere fatigetur,

over pleasures they might enjoy, Agenoria over deeds in which they might get involved, Stimula over goads to action, Strenia over energetic achievements that might fall to their lot.[109] Fessona afforded help to the tired, that they might rest, the goddess Pellonia for repelling the enemy.[110] To certain people the goddess Numeria gave good counting, Camena good singing,[111] Mars and Bellona that they might fight well, Victoria that they might be victorious, the god Honos that they might be honored, Pecunia that they might be wealthy. The gods Aesculanus and his son Argentinus were at hand that they might have bronze and silver money[112] and there was the goddess Murcea so that the useless and lazy might have their own god too. She was to cause unusual inaction and to make him slothful [*murcidus*], as Pomponius says, and excessively lazy and inactive.[113] Bearded Fortune was of little account and not placed among the bad or good gods. She nicely covered the cheeks of her devotees, but made those who rejected her bare of cheek with a poor beard.[114] Though, on the other hand, as I showed above,[115] they attributed to the greater goddess Fortune (whom they named all-powerful) and the Fates a far greater strength and power than they ought, they worshipped Themis too little. Festus says she was "the goddess who taught men to strive after what was sanctioned and they thought she was that which is sanctioned."[116] Not to search out more of the gods given roles in men's lives and fortunes than is useful, the Gentiles said that the goddess Nenia escorted the dead at burial and this is why they called "neniae" the songs they performed amid the wailing and lamenting.[117]

Standing grain and crops too and everything else likely to be useful for mankind had their own throng of gods. In the first place they declare that the mighty god Saturn, Jupiter's father, "devours his offspring because seeds return to the place from which they come to birth." Hence, "for agriculture," he is represented holding a scythe[118] and so that he should not be tired out by having so large a task alone, they say the goddess Seia was put in charge of 33

deam Seiam ferunt satis frumentis quam diu sub terra sunt ; cum vero super terram herbescentes segetem faciunt deam Segetiam, frumentisque collectis atque reconditis ut tuto serventur deam Tutelinam esse praepositam; Proserpinam pariter frumentis germinantibus, deum Nodotum geniculis nodisque culmorum, involucris folliculorum deam Volutinam et, cum folliculi patescunt, ut spica exeat deam Patelinam, cumque segetes novis aequantur aristis deam Ostilinam, Floram frumentis florentibus, lactescentibusque deum Lacturcum, Maturam maturescentibus, et, cum runcantur, id est a terra auferuntur, deam Runcinam praefecerunt. Et, ne inculta agrorum viderentur a diis spreta, Diana silvarum, rurum dea Rusina, iugorum montium deus Iugatinus, collium dea Collacia, vallium dea Vallona curam habuit, nec deus Spinosus, ut spinas ex agris eradicaret Rubigoque non accederet, spernebatur. Quin potius deae Frutescae, ut fructus uberrimos daret, supplicabatur.

34 Quia vero Romanis a principio urbis conditae et multo tempore postea parcissimus fuit vini usus, parva ac omnino minima deorum turba vineis vinisque praefecta est quandoquidem solus Bachus tanti muneris curam habuit, qui multinomius Liber pater primo appellatus, cum bellasset in India et multas secum habuisset feminas, quae Bacchae dicebantur non tamen virtute nobiles, postea Bachus, quandoque Priapus, quandoque Bromius, quandoque Brotinus fuit dictus. Et quia custodiae huiusmodi solus erat

the sown grain (*sata*) as long as it is under the ground. When it springs up above ground and makes a crop (*seges*), they say it is the goddess Segetia. And when the grain was harvested and stored away, the goddess Tutilina was put in charge of keeping it safe (*tuto*). Likewise Proserpina was put in charge of germinating grain, the god Nodutus in charge of the joints and nodes of the stalks, the goddess Volutina of the sheaths (*involucris*) of the husks, and the goddess Patelana when the husks open (*patescunt*) to let out the ears of grain. When the crops stood level with ears newly formed they put the goddess Hostilina in charge, the goddess Flora when the crops are blooming (*florentibus*), the god Lacturcus when they are becoming milky (*lactescentibus*), the goddess Matuta when they are ripening (*maturescentibus*), and the goddess Runcina, when they are grubbed (*runcantur*), that is, removed from the soil.[119] So that the uncultivated fields would not seem rejected by the gods, Diana had charge of the woods,[120] the goddess Rusina of countryside (*rura*), the god Jugatinus of the mountain ridges (*iuga*), the goddess Collatina of the hills (*colles*), the goddess Vallonia of the valleys.[121] Nor did they neglect to request the god Spiniensis to root out thorns (*spinae*) from the fields, nor the goddess Rubigo (Rust) to come not near. Indeed prayers were made rather to the goddess Fructesea that she might provide a great abundance of good crops (*fructus*).[122]

Because right from the foundation of the City and for a long 34
time afterward the Romans used wine sparingly, a small and altogether minimal company of gods was put in charge of vineyards and wine, seeing that Bacchus alone was responsible for so great a task.[123] He had many names. He was first called Father Liber because he had waged war in India and had had with him many women, who were called Bacchants (for all that they were not renowned for courage).[124] Afterward he was called Bacchus, sometimes Priapus, sometimes Bromius, sometimes Brotinus.[125] And because he alone was responsible for a guardianship of this sort,

praefectus, omni spreta vinearum cura, unicae vindemiae, cum iam uvae maturascerent, intendebat, tantaque id actum est turpitudine ut modum pigeat pudeatque referre, quem omnino fuimus suppressuri, nisi quia nostris conducere Christianis arbitramur talia scire, quo nostrae religionis gravitatem et sanctam munditiem laetioribus animis amplectamur. Eruntque verba per beatum Aurelium Augustinum a Marco Varrone Labeoneque paululum immutata: 'Cum fierent Libero patri sacra in Italiae compitis, pudenda virilia cum honore plostellis[31] imposita primo rure transferuntur in compita, post in urbem. In oppido autem Lanuvio'—quod nunc civitas Indivina vocatum viro summo Prospero subest cardinali Columnensi—'uni Libero totus mensis tribuebatur, cuius diebus omnes verbis flagitiosissimis utebantur donec illud membrum per forum transvectum esset atque in loco suo quiesceret. Cui membro inhonesto matrem familias honestissimam imponere publico in loco coronam necesse erat, sic ab agris fascinatio repellebatur et matrona facere cogebatur in publico quod nec meretrici, si matronae spectarent, permitti debuit in theatro.' Ne domos etiam suas Romani spernere viderentur, tres illis deos dederunt ostiarios: 'Forculum foribus, Cardinem cardini, Limentinum limini.' Et ne maris cura esset abiecta, praeter Neptunum, Iovis fratrem, universo praefectum mari praeterque Amphitritem, quam deam Placidus grammaticus fuisse vult deam maris Neptuni matronam, Veniliam dixerunt deam unde maris quando venit ad litus, Salaciamque item deam eidem quando redit in salum esse praepositam.

he disdained all care of vineyards and turned his attention solely to the vintage at the time when the grapes were already ripening. This was performed with such a degree of obscenity that one is disgusted and ashamed to describe it. I was going to suppress it altogether, except that I think it benefits us Christians to have knowledge of such matters, so that with hearts all the gladder we may embrace the seriousness and holy cleanliness of our religion.[126] I shall quote with a few changes blessed Aurelius Augustine who draws on Marcus Varro and Labeo. "When in Italy at the crossroads rites were held for Father Liber, male genitalia were set up with honor on little carts, and first carried to the crossroads in the country, later into the city. In the town of Lanuvium" — this city is now called "Civitas Indivina," and is subject to an excellent man, Cardinal Prospero Colonna[127] — "a whole month was assigned to Liber alone. During the days of that month all used absolutely disgraceful language, until that phallus had been conveyed through the forum and come to rest in its proper place. A most honorable married woman had to place a crown publicly on this dishonorable member. So spells were averted from the fields and a married woman was compelled to do in public what ought not to have been allowed even to a prostitute in the theater, if there were married women among the spectators."[128] So that the Romans should not seem to neglect their houses too, they gave them three gods as doorkeepers: "Forculus for the doors (*fores*), Cardea for the hinges (*cardo*) and Limentinus for the threshold (*limen*)."[129] And so that management of the sea was not neglected, besides Neptune, Jupiter's brother, the superintendent of the sea over all, and besides Amphitryte, the goddess whom the grammarian Placidus thinks was goddess of the sea, Neptune's wife,[130] they said Venilia was the goddess put in charge of the sea's wave when it comes in (*venit*) to the shore, and likewise the goddess Salacia when it goes back out to the salt water (*in salum*).[131]

35 Romani tamen duce Romulo in asylo agentes eos primum colendos acceperunt ex supradictis diis, quos Troia avectos Albani primum, postea Laurentes per trecentos annos coluerant, qui videntur illi fuisse quos supra selectos diximus appellari. Et Tyberinum paulo post Romulus deinde Faunum et Picum, Pavorem et Febrem, ipsumque Romulum Titus Tatius rex et alias sensim turbas supradictas, demumque suos Caesares Romani in deorum numerum retulerunt. Quin etiam Albani patres primum, post Romanae urbis conditores fabulas pro miraculis acceperunt quae ante bellum Troianum Graecis Troianisque fuerant communes: Minotaurum bestiam fuisse inclusam labyrintho, quem cum intrassent homines inextricabili errore exire non poterant. Centauros equorum hominumque natura coniunctos. Cerberum tricipitem inferni canem. Phrixum et Hellem eius sororem ariete vectos mare tranasse. Gorgonem serpentibus crinitam se aspicientes in lapidem convertisse; Bellerofontem equo Pegaso pennis volante vectum fuisse. Amphionem citharae suavitate lapides attraxisse. Daedalum et Icarum filium coaptatis sibi pennis Creta in Italiam advolasse. Oedippum in Sphinga monstrum quadrupes indissolubilia hominibus cum vitae periculo proposuisse. Antaeum qui terrae contactu fortior resurgeret ab Hercule fuisse prostratum.

36 Sed iam satis multa de ineptis deorum fabularumque adinventionibus, ad sacra caerimoniasque veniamus plurima simul edocturi minutiora, quae in gentilium religione non minima habebantur. Ulpianus *De verborum significatione* dicit sacrum locum esse locum consecratum, sacrarium in quo sacra reponuntur. Et idem infra

When the Romans were living in the Asylum under the leadership of Romulus, however, from the gods listed above they first adopted as deserving worship those who had been brought from Troy and worshipped for three hundred years, first by the Albans, then by the Laurentines. These seem to have been the ones who I said above[132] were called "select" and a little later Tiberinus was included in the number of the gods by Romulus, then Faunus and Picus, Fright and Fever.[133] King Titus Tatius added Romulus himself, and gradually the Romans added the other companies I mentioned above, and finally their own Caesars. Furthermore the Alban fathers first and later the founders of the City of Rome took over the miraculous stories that the Greeks and Trojans shared before the Trojan War: that the Minotaur was a beast shut up in the labyrinth and that, when men had gone into it, they could not get out from the inextricable maze. Centaurs were a combination of horse and man. Cerberus was the three-headed dog of the underworld. Phrixus and his sister Helle crossed the sea riding on a ram. The Gorgon, who had serpents for hair, turned to stone those who looked at her. Bellerophon rode on the winged horse Pegasus. Amphion made stones move toward him by the sweetness of his lyre. Daedalus and his son Icarus fastened wings to themselves and flew from Crete to Italy. Oedipus risked his life putting riddles that men could not solve to the sphinx, a four-footed monster. Antaeus who rose up with increased strength after he had touched the earth was laid low by Hercules.[134] 35

But enough has now been said about the absurd fictions of the gods and myths. Let us come to religious observances and ceremonies, in connection with which I shall expound very many smaller items that in the Gentiles' religion were considered of no small importance. Ulpian says in *On the Meaning of Expressions* that a sacred place is a place that has been consecrated, a shrine (*sacrarium*) is where holy things (*sacra*) are stored and, further on in the same 36

sancta proprie dici quae nec sacra neque profana sunt, sed sanctione quadam sunt confirmata ut sanctae leges. Martianus vero sanctum esse vult quod ab iniuria hominum est defensum dicique a sagminibus, herbis quas legati populi Romani ferre solebant ne quis eos violaret. Cicero in *Legibus:* 'Sacrum sacrove commendatum qui clepserit raseritque parricida esto.' Idemque *De haruspicum responsis:* 'Nego unquam post sacra constituta, quorum eadem est antiquitas quae ipsius urbis.' Festus Pompeius: 'Curionia sacra quae in curiis fiebant.' Et infra: 'Fornacalia[32] sacra erant cum far in fornaculis torrebant, quod ad fornacem quae in pistrinis erat sacrificium fieri solebat.' Plutharcus in *Pauli Aemilii vita:* 'Sacra faciente Emilio fulmen aram percussit sacraque combussit.' Macrobius in *Saturnalibus:* 'Herculis sacris non licet mulieribus interesse, quia Herculi per Italiam transeunti mulier vinum petenti se aquam dixit non posse parebere.' Et Macrobius in *Saturnalibus* dixit: 'Sacra celebritas est cum sacrificia diis offeruntur, vel cum dies divinis epulationibus celebrantur, vel cum ludi in honorem aguntur deorum, vel cum feriae observantur.' Et infra idem: 'Sacrum est quicquid deorum habetur.' Virgilius: 'Sacra Dioneae matri divisque ferebam,' 'sacra Iovi Stigio quae nec incepta paravi.' 'Tibi enim, maxima Iuno, macto sacra ferens.' Et sanctum vult Trebatius idem quod religiosum, interdum neutrum id est incorruptum. Virgilius: 'Sancta ad vos anima atque istius inscia culpae descendam.' Hinc

source, what is sanctified (*sancta*) properly speaking is neither what is sacred or profane but what is confirmed by some sanction, such as the sanctified laws.[135] Marcianus' view is that the sanctified (*sanctus*) is what is protected from being injured by men. The word comes from *sagmina,* the herbs that ambassadors of the Roman people used to carry, so that no one would do them outrage.[136] Cicero in *On the Laws* says "whoever steals or makes away with a sacred object or anything entrusted to what is sacred shall be a parricide."[137] The same author in *On the Responses of the Haruspices:* "I say that never since sacred rites (*sacra*) were established and they are as ancient as the city itself."[138] Festus Pompeius: "The Curionia are sacred rites that were performed in the *curiae*"[139] and, further on, the Fornacalia (Feast of Ovens) "were rites at which emmer was toasted in little ovens, a sacrifice that used to happen at the oven (*fornax*) which was at the bakeries."[140] Plutarch in the *Life of Aemilius Paulus:* "While Aemilius was performing a sacrifice (*sacra*), lightning struck the altar, and burned the holy offerings (*sacra*)."[141] Macrobius in *Saturnalia:* "Women are not allowed to take part in Hercules' rites (*sacra*), because when he was traveling through Italy and asked a woman for wine, she said she could not provide him with water."[142] And Macrobius said in *Saturnalia,* "A sacred occasion is when sacrifices are offered to the gods or when festal days are celebrated with feasts for the gods or when games are put on in honor of the gods or when a holy day is observed."[143] And further on in the same source: "The 'sacred' (*sacrum*) is whatever is considered to pertain to the gods. Vergil: 'I was making sacred offerings (*sacra*) to my mother, the daughter of Dione, and the gods.' 'Things sacred (*sacra*) to Jupiter of the Underworld which I have duly begun and have ready.' 'To you, to you, mighty Juno, he sacrifices, bringing sacred offerings' (*sacra*)."[144] The same Trebatius is of the opinion that the term "sanctified" (*sanctum*) is the same as "protected by the gods" (*religiosum*), sometimes neither, that is, unsullied. Vergil: "I shall come down to you, an untainted

sanctae leges et sanctum virum integrum moribus 'nominaque sacrorum locorum sub congrua proprietate proferre pontificalis observatio est.' Aelius Spartianus Adrianum commendat imperatorem, quod sacra Romana diligentissime curavit, peregrina contempsit.

37 Post eamque sacrorum cognitionem de caerimoniis est dicendum, quas supra diximus Trebatium voluisse idem esse quod sacra, sed Livius libro quinto dicit Lucium Albinum de plebe unum virgines, sacerdotes, sacraque plaustro Caerae invexisse, unde caerimoniis enatum sit nomen. Et in septimo: 'Caeretibus qui[33] Tarquinensibus in populatione agri Romani consenserant ob memoriam servatorum sacrorum pax et indutiae in centum annos datae.' Festus Pompeius: 'Caerimoniarum causam alii ab oppido Caere dictam existimant, alii a caritate putant.' Adorationis et immolationis originem Plinius in *Naturali Historia* sic ponit: 'Numa instituit deos fruge colere et mola salsa supplicare, atque—ut auctor est Hemina—far torrere, quoniam tostum cibo salubrius. Is Fornacalia[34] instituit farris torrendi ferias et aeque religiosas terminis agrorum.' Nonius autem Marcellus: 'Ador frumenti genus quod epulis et immolationibus sacris putatur pium, unde adorare propitiare religiones.' Festus Pompeius: 'Ador farris genus, edor quod appellabatur, et fiebat tostum unde in sacrificio mola salsa efficitur, unde adorare.' Festus item: 'Immolare est mola id est farre molito et sale

(*sancta*) soul and free from knowledge of this fault."[145] For this reason the laws are "sanctified" (*sanctae*)[146] and a holy man (*sanctus*) is one of unblemished morality. "It is a pontifical practice to make known the names of the sacred places (*sacrorum*) with their matching owners."[147] Aelius Spartianus praises the emperor Hadrian because "he took very particular care of Roman sacred rites (*sacra*), and rejected foreign ones."[148]

After this examination of the sacred rites (*sacra*) I must discuss 37
religious observances (*caerimoniae*). As I said above, Trebatius held that these were the same as the sacred rites (*sacra*) but Livy says in Book V that Lucius Albinus, a plebeian, conveyed the Vestal Virgins, priests and sacred objects in a cart to Caere.[149] From this arose the name for ceremonies (*caerimoniae*). And in Book VII: "The people of Caere, who had come to an agreement with the people of Tarquinii over a raid on Roman territory, in memory of their preservation of the sacred objects were granted peace and a hundred years' truce."[150] Festus Pompeius: "Some think the origin of the word ceremonies was the town of Caere, others think it was from dearness (*caritas*)."[151] Pliny in *Natural History* presents the origin of worship (*adoratio*) and sacrifice (*immolatio*) as follows: "Numa began the practice of worshipping the gods with grain and making supplication with salted meal (*mola*) and, as Hemina says, of toasting emmer, because when toasted it is more wholesome as food. He established the Fornacalia, the festival for roasting emmer and the equally solemn holiday for the gods of the field boundaries."[152] But Nonius Marcellus says spelt (*ador*) is "a kind of grain that is considered holy for sacred banquets and sacrifices (*immolatio*), whence to pray to (*adorare*) is to appease the divine powers."[153] Festus Pompeius says spelt is "a kind of emmer wheat which is called *edor* and it was toasted. From it is produced the salted meal (*mola*) in sacrifice."[154] The word "to pray to" (*adorare*) comes from this.[155] Festus again: "To sacrifice (*immolare*) is to consecrate the victim with meal (*mola*), that is ground emmer, sprin-

hostiam perspersam sacrare.' Et idem infra: 'Mola vocatur far tostum sale aspersum, quod eo molito hostiae asperguntur.' Macrobius *Saturnalium*: 'Cum hostia caeditur fari non est fas, intercisa et porrecta licet. Rursus cum adoletur non licet.'

38 Plurima item nunc minutiora religionis gentilium vocabula unico doceamus contextu, videlicet sacrificium, consecratio, ornamentorum vasorumque vocabula. Dehinc superstitio, sacrilegium, dedicatio, piaculum, iusiurandum, eleemosina, abstinentia, virginitas, ieiunium, gestus inter faciendum rem divinam et demum hostiae quid sibi voluerint. Nonius Marcellus inter sacrificare et litare hoc dicit interesse: sacrificare est veniam dari petere, litare est 'propitiare.' Et Macrobius: 'Litare significat sacrificio facto placavisse deos.' Litare id est sacrificium rite facere. Cicero in *Legibus*: 'Nocturna mulierum sacrificia non sunto praeter illa quae pro populo rite fient.' Et Varro *De lingua Latina*: 'Romano ritu sacrificium mulieres cum facient capite sunto copertae.' Festus Pompeius: 'Arcanum sacrificii genus quod in arce fit ab auguribus, adeo remotum a notitia vulgari ut ne litteris quidem mandaretur, sed per memoriam successoribus relinquebatur.' Et infra: 'Iuvenalia[35] fingebantur Dianae sacra, quia ea aetas fortis est ad tolerandam viam. Diana enim putabatur dea viarum.' Item: 'Stata dicuntur sacrificia quae certis diebus fiebant.' Item 'sacrificium quod fiebat in monte Palatino palatuar dicebatur.' Livius in XXX: 'Philippi regis legati in senatum introducti sunt gratulantes de victoria; his petentibus

kled with salt,"[156] and further on, "toasted emmer, sprinkled with salt, is called meal (*mola*), because victims are sprinkled with ground emmer (*molire*)."[157] Macrobius in *Saturnalia:* "When the victim is being killed it is not lawful to utter the formula of judgment, but it is permitted when the victim has been cut up and laid out. Again when the victim is being burned, it is not allowed."[158]

Now let us explain together in one section the meaning of the 38
very many lesser terms belonging to the Gentiles' religion, viz. sacrifice, consecration, the words for the adornments and utensils, next superstition, sacrilege, dedication, expiation, the sworn oath, almsgiving, abstinence, virginity, fasting, the gestures during the performance of the rite of worship and finally the meaning of sacrificial victims. Nonius Marcellus defines the difference between sacrificing (*sacrificare*) and offering in propitiation (*litare*) this way: "To sacrifice is to ask for a favor to be granted, to offer in propitiation is to appease."[159] Macrobius says "to offer in propitiation means to have appeased the gods by making a sacrifice."[160] Thus to offer in propitiation is to perform a sacrifice in due form. Cicero in *On the Laws:* "There are to be no sacrifices carried out by women by night except those that are performed in due form on behalf of the people."[161] Varro, *On the Latin Language:* "When women make a sacrifice in the Roman manner they are to have their heads covered."[162] Pompeius Festus: A mystery (*arcanum*) is "a kind of sacrifice that is carried out on the citadel (*in arce*) by the augurs, kept so far away from common knowledge that it was not even put in writing, but handed down by memory to those who followed."[163] Further on: "Statues of Diana were made youthful because that age has the strength to endure travel. Diana was thought to be the goddess of the ways."[164] Again: "Sacrifices that happened on certain days are said to be 'fixed.'"[165] Again: "The sacrifice performed on the Palatine Hill was called 'Palatuar.'"[166] Livy in Book XXX: "King Philip's ambassadors, offering congratulations on the victory, were conducted into the senate. When they asked

ut sibi sacrificare in Capitolio donaque ex auro liceret ponere in aede Iovis Optimi Maximi, permissum ab senatu. Centum pondo coronam auream posuerunt.' Iam consecratio qua fieret ratione Cicero *Pro domo sua ad pontifices* sic docet: 'Video esse legem veterem tribuniciam, quae vetat iniussu plebis aedes, terram, aram consecrare.'

39 Ornamentorum religionis vasorumque modus fuit priscis castissimus, sed ornamenta unde habuerunt originem Livius in Numae gestis rebus sic edocet: 'Flaminem Iovi assiduum sacerdotem creavit insignique eum veste et curruli regia sella adornavit. Salios inde XII Marti Gradivo legit tunicaeque pictae insigne decrevit et super tunicam aeneum pectori tegmen' quali sacerdotes Christiani, sed aureo et argenteo et iaspidibus ornato, pectorali appellato utuntur. Et Festus: 'Albogalerus, a galea nominatus, est enim pileus capitis quo Diales flamines, id est Iovis sacerdotes, utebantur.' Et 'Flaminio vestimento flaminica[36] utebatur, Dialis uxor et Iovis sacerdos, cui telum fulminis eodem erat colore.' Item 'mortuae pecudis corio calceos fieri flaminibus nefas habebatur, quoniam sua morte extincta omnia funesta extimabantur.' Item 'tutulum[37] dicebant flaminicarum capitis ornamentum vitta purpurea innexa crinibus et in altitudine extructum.' Item 'flaminicas sacerdotissas, Diali addictas, scalas ultra tres gradus ascendere non licet, non comit caput, neque capillum depectit. Flamen solus habet galerum, quod maximus est.' Cicero in *Legibus*: 'In delubris omnibus

that they might be allowed to sacrifice on the Capitol and place gifts made of gold in the Temple of Jupiter Best and Greatest, permission was granted by the senate. They deposited a golden crown weighing one hundred pounds."[167] Now in what way consecration was performed Cicero tells us in *On His Own House* thus: "I observe there is an ancient tribunician law that forbids consecration of any building, land or altar without the express order of the plebeians."[168]

The people of the early days had religious adornments and 39
utensils of a very innocent kind. As to the origin of the adornments, Livy gives the following information in his history of Numa: "He appointed a flamen for Jupiter, as his standing priest, dignifying him with distinctive attire and the king's curule seat." "Next he chose twelve Salii for Mars Gravidus and decided on the distinction of an embroidered tunic with a bronze breastplate over the tunic."[169] The breastplate is like the one Christian priests make use of, called a pectoral, but theirs is of gold and silver and decorated with jaspers. Festus: "The white cap (*albogalerus*) got its name from the word for helmet (*galea*). It is the cap that the priests of Jupiter (*flamines Diales*) wear."[170] "The *flaminica,* the wife of the priest of Jupiter and the priestess of Jupiter, used the flamen's dress, the same color as the lightning bolt."[171] Again: "It was held contrary to religious law for flamens' shoes to be made from the skin of a dead cow, since everything that had died a natural death was considered ill-omened."[172] Again: "The head covering of the *flaminicae* was called a *tutulus,* with a crimson ribbon plaited into the hair, and it was built up to a height."[173] Again: "It was not permitted that the *flaminicae,* priestesses attached to the priest of Jupiter (*flamen Dialis*), go up more than three rungs of a ladder. She does not adorn her head nor comb her hair. The *flamen* [*Dialis*] alone has the white cap (*galerus*) because he is the most important."[174] Cicero in *On the Laws:* "In all the shrines a piece of textile

textile nec operosius quam mulieris opus menstruum. Color autem albus praecipue decorus deo est, cum in ceteris tum maxime in textili. Tincta vero absint, nisi a bellicis insignibus.' Plinius in *Naturali Historia:* 'Antiquior fuit plasticae quam fundendi aeris ars. Ex ea enim dii fiebant et domus civium ornabantur et dii fictiles erant. Hae enim tunc deorum effigies erant laudatissimae, nec paenitet nos illorum qui tales eos coluere. In sacris quidem tum non mirrinis, ut hodie cristallinisve, sed fictilibus libabant.' Seneca *epistola* XXXI ex Virgilio: 'Exurge modo et "te quoque dignum finge deo." Finges autem non auro nec argento: non potest in hac materia imago dei exprimi. Quin cogita illos cum propitii fuissent, fictiles fuisse.' Persius satyricus: 'Dicite, pontifices, in sancto quid facit aurum? Nempe quod Veneri donatae a virgine puppae.' Cicero in *Legibus:* 'Aurum et argentum in urbibus et privatim ⟨et⟩ in fanis invidiosa res est; tum ebur corpore extractum. Iam aes atque ferrum duelli instrumenta non fani.' Festus Pompeius de hac modestia religionis taliter scribit ut nostrae aetatis sacerdotibus ingentem inurat notam, qui nedum equo vehuntur, sed equitum turmas cum pari famulatu alunt. Inquit enim: 'Sacerdotis proprium est ut nec equo vehatur, nec plus quam tribus noctibus ab urbe absit, nec pileum deponat, ex quo flamen dictus est.' Et idem dicit 'pura sacerdotes vestimenta ad sacrificia habuisse, id est non obsita, non fulgurita, non funesta, non maculam habentia.'

Fuit etiam unum sacrificantibus vestimenti genus, quo sacerdotes cuiusque ritus et templi et dei pariter utebantur, quale est

[is permissible], and one not more elaborate than a woman could make in a month. Indeed, white is the color most fitting for a god in all other respects, but most of all in cloth. Dyed stuff should be kept away, except from military banners."[175] Pliny in *Natural History:* The art of modeling in clay was older than that of casting bronze. From clay gods were made and the citizens' houses were decorated, and the statues of the gods were made of clay. At that time these images of the gods were highly praised and we are not ashamed of those men for worshipping them in such a form. In fact in their sacrifices they did not then make offerings from fluorspar or crystal vessels, as today, but from ones of earthernware.[176] Seneca in *Letter* XXXI cites Vergil: "Rise up now and 'you too fashion yourself worthy of a god.' But you will not fashion from gold or silver. An image of a god cannot be modeled in this material. Rather ponder the fact that when they were favorable they were made of clay."[177] Persius the satirist: "Tell us, pontiffs, what does gold achieve in a temple? Surely the same as the dolls given by girls as gifts to Venus."[178] Cicero in *On the Laws:* "Gold and silver, both in private possession [and] in temples, provoke envy in cities, also ivory which is taken from a body. Again bronze and iron are the furnishings of war, not of a shrine."[179] Festus Pompeius writes about this restraint in worship in such a way as to brand the priests of our age with an enormous stigma. They, far from riding on one horse, keep squadrons of riders with household servants to match. Festus says: "It is the special duty of a priest not to ride a horse, and not to be away from the City for more than three nights, nor to take off the cap from which he derives the name of *flamen*."[180] The same author says that "priests had pure clothes for sacrificing, that is, ones that were not covered over, not struck by lightning, not polluted with death, and without stain."[181]

There was one kind of vestment for those performing sacrifice, 40
used alike by the priests of each rite, temple and god. It was like

camisium lineum album, quo Christiani utuntur sacerdotes et, cum esset latum adeoque oblongum ut discinctum per solum traheretur, postea cinctum pendentem supra cingulum faciebat undique sinum, qui ritus fuisse perhibetur Gabinus. Livius in quinto: 'G. Fabius ritu Gabino succinctus a Capitolio obsesso in Quirinalem collem sacra ferens ivit et rediit.' Et Virgilius: 'Ritu succincta Gabino.' Et Cicero *De haruspicum responsis:* 'Strophium quod Graece ophion dicitur pro insigni positum fuisse dicit, quod ponebatur in capitibus sacerdotum, et alii coronam fuisse dixerunt.' Quod ornamentum nostri Iohanni[38] Baptistae in imno attribuunt vespertino: 'Strophium bidentes.' Sed iam instrumenta et vasa religionis a Festo incipiamus ostendere: 'praefericulum[39] vas aeneum sine ansa patens ad summum velut pelvis, quo ad sacrificia utebantur.' Patenae 'vascula parva sacrificiis faciendis apta.' 'Infulae sunt filamenta[40] lanea, quibus sacerdotes et hostiae templaque velantur.' 'Inarculum virga erat ex malo punico inaurata, quam regina sacrificans in capite gestabat.' Acerra 'arcula thuraria in sacrificiis.' Achamum 'poculi fictilis genus, quo in sacrificiis utebantur.' Nonius Marcellus: 'Anclabris[41] mensa ministeriis aptata divinis; vasa quoque ea quibus sacerdotes utuntur anclabria appellabantur.' Festus: 'Secespita cultrum ferreum, oblongum, manubrio eburneo, rotundo, solido, vincto ad capulum argento et auro fixum, clavis aeneis aere Cyprio, quo flamines, flaminicae virgines pontificesque ad sacra utebantur. Dictum autem est secespita a secando.' Cicero *In Verrem,* actione tertia: 'Credo tum cum Sicilia florebat opibus et copiis magna artificia fuisse in ea insula. Nam domus erat ante istum praetorem nulla paulo locupletior, qua in domo haec non essent, etiamsi praeterea nihil esset argenti, patella grandis cum

the white linen tunic used by Christian priests. Since it was wide and so long that without a belt it trailed along the ground, later it was belted and, hanging over the belt, made a fold all round. This is said to have been the "Gabine fashion." Livy in Book V: "Gaius Fabius, belted in the Gabine fashion, went carrying the sacred objects from the Capitol, at that time under siege, to the Quirinal Hill, and returned."[182] Vergil: "[a crowd] belted in the Gabine fashion"[183] and Cicero says in *On the Responses of the Haruspices*, "The headband (*strophium*), called 'ophion' in Greek, was put on as a badge of office, because it was placed on the priests' heads, and others said it was a garland."[184] Christian writers say in the Vespers hymn that St. John the Baptist had this adornment: "Sheep [have produced] a headband."[185] Now, using Festus as our source, let us begin to describe the religious implements and utensils. "The *praefericulum* was a bronze vessel without a handle open at the top like a basin which they used for sacrifices."[186] *Patenae* were "little vessels suitable for use in sacrifices."[187] "*Infulae* are woolen fillets with which priests, victim and temples are draped."[188] "The *inarculum* was a gilded pomegranate twig which the queen wore on her head when sacrificing."[189] The *acerra* is a little incense box[190] used in sacrifice. The *achamum* is "a kind of earthenware cup which they used in sacrifice."[191] Nonius Marcellus: "The *anclabris* is a table used for service to the gods. The vessels which priests use were called *anclabria* too."[192] Festus: "The *secespita* is a long, sacrificial knife, of iron, with a round solid ivory handle, fastened to the hilt with a binding of silver and gold. The knife is studded with bronze rivets, of Cypriot bronze, and used by the flamens, *flaminicae*, Virgins and pontiffs for sacrifices. It is called *secespita* from cutting (*secando*)."[193] Cicero in the third action of the *Verrine Orations*: "I believe that there was immense production of works or art in the island at the time when Sicily was at the height of its wealth and resources. Before he was governor there was no house among the somewhat better off in which the following were not present,

sigillis simulacri deorum,[42] patera qua mulieres ad res divinas uterentur, turibulum, haec autem omnia antiquo opere et summo artificio facta.' Festus Pompeius: 'Simpulum[43] vas parvulum non dissimile cyatho, quo vinum in sacrificiis libabatur, unde mulieres rebus divinis deditae simpulatrices dictae.' 'Struppi vocantur in pulvinaribus fasciculi de verbenis facti, qui pro deorum capitibus ponebantur.' 'Suffibulum vestimentum album, praetextum, quadrangulum, oblongum, quod in capite Vestales virgines sacrificantes habebant, idque fibula comprehendebatur.'

41 Damnarunt et ipsi etiam Romani gentiles sacrilegia, per se ipsa a verbo nota, et superstitiones. Cuius verbi vim originem habuisse vult Aulus Gelius ab iis, qui filios superstites esse nimis importune ab diis efflagitarent, cum tamen omnis importuna ineptaque religio possit superstitio appellari. Livius in quarto: 'In ea rerum afflictione multiplex religio et pleraque externa invasit, novos ritus sacrificandi, vaticinando inferentibus in domos, quibus quaestui fierent capti religione animi, donec publicus iam pudor ad primores civitatis pervenit, cernentes in omnibus vicis sacellisque peregrina atque insolita piacula pacis deum exposcendae. Datum tamen negotium aedilibus, ut animadverterent ne qui nisi Romani dii neu quo alio more quam patrio colerentur.' Idem Livius XXIX: 'Pyrrhus Locros classe praetervectus thesauros Proserpinae intactos ad eam diem spoliavit. Classis postera die foedissima tempestate lacerata, omnesque naves, quae sacram pecuniam habuerant, in litora nostra eiectae[44] sunt. Pecuniam omnem conquisitam in

even if there was nothing else made of silver: a large offering dish with little figures and likenesses of the gods, a libation bowl that women use for service of the gods, an incense burner—all these made with antique workmanship and products of the highest skill."[194] Festus Pompeius: "*Simpulum:* a little vessel no different from the *cyathus* (ladle), with which wine was offered in sacrifices, whence women dedicated to divine affairs were called *simpulatrices.*"[195] "Little bundles of twigs laid on the couches to represent the heads of gods are called *struppi.*"[196] "The *suffibulum* was a quadrangular, oblong, white piece of cloth, with a red border, which the Vestal Virgins wore on their heads when sacrificing and it was fastened by a brooch."[197]

Even the Roman Gentiles themselves condemned sacrilege,[198] 41
known in its own right from the word, and superstitions.[199] The original meaning of the latter word came, according to Aulus Gellius, from those who made too insistent demands to the gods that their children outlive them,[200] though all demanding and inappropriate religious devotion may be called superstition. Livy in Book IV: "In that time of suffering there came in many kinds of religious dread, mostly from abroad. There were those who by divination brought new rites of sacrifice into the houses and souls entrapped by religious dread became a source of profit for them, until finally the public shame came to the notice of the leaders of the state, when they discovered in all the quarters and shrines foreign and unwonted sacrifices being made to propitiate the gods. The commission was given to the aediles that they should see to it that no gods except the Romans' be worshipped, nor in any other fashion than the ancestral."[201] Livy again in Book XXIX: Pyrrhus "sailing past Locri with his fleet, plundered the treasury of Proserpina which had been kept intact until that time. On the next day his fleet was shattered by a dreadful storm. All the ships which contained the sacred money were thrown up on our shores. He ordered all the money to be collected and restored to Proserpina's

thesauros Proserpinae referri iussit, nec tamen ei postea aliquid prospere evenit, pulsusque ita regno Lydiae atque inhonesta morte Argos ingressus occubuit.'[45] Dedicatio quid fuerit Cicero *Pro domo sua ad pontifices* sic ostendit: 'Postem teneri in dedicatione templi oportere videor audisse. Ibi enim postis est, ubi aditus est.' Livius VIIII: 'G. Flavius scriba, libertino patre genitus, aedilis, aedem Concordiae in area Vulcani summa nobilium invidia dedicavit. G.que Barbatus pontifex coactus consensu populi verba praeivit. Itaque ex auctoritate senatus lata lex, ne quis templum aramve iniussu senatus aut tribunorum plebis partis maioris dedicaret. G. Iunius Bubulcus dictator aedem Salutis, quam consul voverat, censor locaverat, dictator dedicavit.' Idem XXIII: 'Duumviri creati sunt Fabius Maximus, T. Attilius Crassus, aedibus dedicandis Menti Attilius, Fabius Veneri Ericinae, utraque in Capitolio est.' Et infra: 'Gnaeus Domitius, praetor urbanus, dedicavit aedem Fortunae Primogeniae in colle Quirinali, et in insula Iovis eadem dedicavit Gnaeus Servilius duumvir.' Valeriusque sic habet: 'Horatius Pulvillus, cum in Capitolio Iovi Optimo Maximo aedem dedicaret interque nuncupationem solemnium verborum postem tenens mortuum esse filium audisset, neque manum a poste removit.'

42 Iurisiurandi et sacramenti religio apud Romanos magni fuit momenti. Et quidem iurisiurandi religio duplex fuit: una cum quis requisitus aliquid diis in testes vocatis spopondisset aut affirmasset, ceu Marcus Attilius Regulus sese Carthaginem, nisi captivorum

treasuries. Even so thereafter nothing turned out well for him. Driven out of Italy he went to Argos and died an obscure and inglorious death."[202] Cicero demonstrates what dedication was in *On His Own House*: "I think I have heard that when a temple is dedicated the hand should be placed on the doorpost. For the entrance is where the doorpost is."[203] Livy Book IX: "Gnaeus Flavius, a scribe, son of a freedman, when he was aedile dedicated the Temple of Concord in the precinct of Vulcan and made himself very unpopular with the nobles. Gaius Barbatus the pontiff, compelled by the will of the people, dictated the formula first. So a law was passed by the senate's authority that no one should dedicate a temple or altar without the mandate of the senate or that of a majority of the tribunes of the people.[204] Gaius Junius Bubulcus when dictator dedicated the Temple of Safety which he had vowed as consul and contracted out when censor."[205] Again Livy Book XXIII: "Fabius Maximus and Titus Otacilius Crassus were elected as the Board of Two for the purpose of dedicating temples, Otacilius for that of Intelligence, Fabius for that of Venus of Eryx. Both are on the Capitol."[206] Further on: "Gnaeus Domitius as city praetor dedicated the temple of Fortune the Firstborn on the Quirinal Hill and Gaius Servilius when a member of the Board of Two dedicated the temple of Jupiter on the island."[207] Valerius Maximus says as follows: "When Horatius Pulvillus was dedicating the temple on the Capitol to Jupiter Best and Greatest and had his hand on the doorpost, while he was pronouncing the customary words, he heard that his son had died, but he did not take his hand from the doorpost."[208]

The religious sanction of the oath (*iusiurandum*) and of the pledge (*sacramentum*) was of great importance among the Romans. 42
In fact, the religious sanction of the oath was of two kinds. One was when someone of whom a demand had been made had called the gods to witness and promised or affirmed something, just as Marcus Attilius Regulus promised on oath that he would return

permutatio fieret, rediturum iureiurando spopondit. Formaque huius iurisiurandi erat talis: 'lapidem silicem tenebant iuraturi per Iovem haec verba dicentes: "Si sciens fallo, tum me Dispiter salva urbe arceque bonis eiciat ut ego hunc lapidem."' De quo Cicero *Legum* primo: 'Periurii poena divina exitium, humana dedecus.' Et infra: 'Poena violati iurisiurandi esto.' Altera iurisiurandi religio erat cum verbo inter loquendum per deorum numina sponte quis iurasset, quale erat cum Edepol, Mehercle et Medius Fidius dicebant, duorumque primo positorum loco facilis erat expositio: cum per Apollinis aedem primus, alter per Herculem se mentientem periurio obligasset. Tertii expositio altiorem habet indaginem: Sanctus Fidius et Semipater dii fuerunt Sabinorum, quos domo demigrantes in collem Quirinalem cum cetera supelletile detulerunt, idque numen verbis trinum, re unicum esse dixerunt, unde, licet tribus ipsis templum esset in Quirinali colle dicatum, unius tamen Sancti vocabulo appellabatur; obtinuitque eiusmodi nominis opinio sanctitatis magnam vim habere iusiurandum, quo in trino et unico numine medium esse quis Fidium affirmaret. Sacramentum autem esse dixerunt quo militiae ascribendi a sacerdotibus adigebantur, nec prius militare aut postquam eo absoluti essent in hostem pugnare poterant, unde est illud Catonis, qui filium militia per sacramenti relaxationem dimissum cum hoste manum conserere vetuit. Sacramenti etymologiam originemque sic refert Varro *De lingua Latina*: 'Sacramentum a sacro: qui petebat et qui inficiabatur uterque quingenta aeris ad pontificem deponebat.

to Carthage if the exchange of prisoners were not carried out.[209] The manner of this oath swearing was like this. "The ones who were going to swear an oath by Jupiter held a flint stone, speaking these words: 'If I knowingly deceive then may Diespiter keep the city and citadel safe and cast me out from my possessions, as I cast out this stone.'"[210] Cicero in *On the Laws* Book I says concerning this: "The divine punishment of perjury is death, the human punishment disgrace," and further on, "There shall be a punishment for violating an oath."[211] The second religious sanction of the oath was when someone in the course of speaking had sworn spontaneously by the divine powers with a word, as happened when they said "by Pollux," "by Hercules" and "by the God of Faith."[212] There was an easy explanation of the two first mentioned, since the first, if he were lying, had bound himself by a false oath by the temple of Apollo,[213] the second by Hercules. The explanation of the third involves a deeper investigation. Sanctus, Fidius and Semipater were gods of the Sabines. They brought them with the rest of their household goods when they moved from home to the Quirinal Hill. They said this deity was triple in word, single in reality. This was why, though the temple on the Quirinal was dedicated to the three, nevertheless it was called by the name of Sanctus alone.[214] A name of this kind made the opinion prevail that there was a great power of sanctity in an oath, by which one affirmed that Fidius was in the middle in a threefold and single deity. They called a pledge (*sacramentum*) that by which those who were being enrolled in military service were put on oath by the priests. They could not serve as a soldier beforehand, or, after they had been released from it, fight against the enemy. Hence that well-known saying of Cato's, who did not allow his son to engage with the enemy, after he had been dismissed from military service by the lifting of the pledge.[215] Varro in *On the Latin Language* gives the etymology and origin of the pledge (*sacramentum*) as follows: "The pledge (*sacramentum*) comes from the temple (*sacrum*). Both he

De aliis item rebus alio certo numero; qui iudicio vicerat suum sacramentum a sacro auferebat, victi ad aerarium redibat.' Posuimus mixta inter se superius quae de iureiurando et sacramento dicenda erant, ut ratio constet qua ducti opinamur sacramentum fuisse, in quibus rebus alia quam dei invocationis quae per iusiurandum fit obligatio rerum erat, sicut ex Varrone supra ostendimus.

43 Et hinc orta est sacramenti militaris adactio, in qua praeter invocatos iureiurando deos in fidei suae testes, alia item erat occulta obligatio stipendiorum et patriae rerumque amissionis, quam fidem fallens incurrebat; unde in *Vita beati Martini Turonensis* 'est sacramentis militaribus implicitus.' Qui autem iureiurando aliquid affirmabat solum deum, si fefellisset, habebat ultorem, et tamen Romani aliquando, ut sua dignitas servaretur, poenam ipsi et incommoda periurio adiunxerunt. Livius XXII: Post proelium Cannense 'cum egressi castris essent, unus ex iis, minime Romani ingenii homo, velut aliquid oblitus, iurisiurandi solvendi causa cum in castra redisset, ante noctem comites assequitur.' Qui postea reductus senatu iubente. Item Livius XXXI: 'G. Valerius Flaccus, quem praesentem[46] creaverant, quia flamen Dialis erat iurare in leges non poterat, magistratus autem plus quinque dies, nisi qui iurasset in leges, non licebat gerere.' Datus est qui iuraret pro fratre L. Valerius praetor plebesque scivit ut perinde esset, ac si ipse iurasset. Contra Numantinos rebelles missus, Q. Pompeius est superatus et pacem cum illis factam iureiurando sanxerat,

who was claiming reparation and he who was rejecting the claim deposited a sum of fifty asses with the pontiff. Likewise in cases concerning other matters, there was another fixed amount. The one who had won the case took back his deposit from the temple (*sacrum*). The loser's returned to the treasury."[216] Above I have combined together in my exposition what had to be said about the sworn oath and the pledge, so as to clarify the reason that that makes me think there was a pledge in matters in which there was, as I have shown above from Varro, an obligation different from that of an invocation of a god, which happens by a sworn oath.

From this arose the taking of the military pledge. In this be- 43
sides the swearing by the gods as witnesses of one's own fidelity, there was another concealed pledging of loss of pay and country and property, which he who broke his faith incurred. Whence in the *Life of St. Martin of Tours*: "he was bound by military pledges."[217] He who made an affirmation by an oath had only god as punisher, if he had not fulfilled his promise. Nevertheless, the Romans themselves sometimes made additional punishment and disadvantages follow upon perjury in order that their own dignity might be preserved. Livy Book XXII: After the battle of Cannae, "when all had departed from the camp, one of them, not at all a man of Roman character, went back to the camp as if he had forgotten something in order to release himself from his oath and then caught up with his companions before nightfall." Afterward he was taken back by order of the senate.[218] Again Livy Book XXXI: "Gaius Valerius Flaccus, whom they had appointed and was present, could not swear to observe the laws because he was flamen of Jupiter. But, unless he swore to obey the laws, he could not act as magistrate for more than five days." Lucius Valerius, who was praetor, was substituted to swear for his brother and the people voted that it would be just as if he himself had sworn.[219] Sent against the rebellious Numantines, Quintus Pompeius was defeated, had made peace with them and ratified it by an oath.

quam senatus cum non accepisset, ad iusiurandum exsolvendum idem remissus est. Missus item G. Mancinus iterum peiorem pacem fecit, quam S. P. Q. R. cum non approbaverit, Mancinus est Numantinis deditus, qui nudus ante portam ad iurisiurandi observationem expositus deridebatur, nec ab hostibus nec a suis recipiebatur. Suetonius *De Vespasiano*: 'Equiti Romano iurisiurandi gratiam fecit ut uxorem in stupro gravi compertam dimitteret, quoniam se numquam repudiaturum iuraverat.' Cicero *Pro Roscio comoedo*: 'At quid interest inter periurum et mendacem? Qui mentiri solet, peierare consuevit.'

44 Unico apud gentiles in loco 'eleemosina' verbum invenimus, quod apud Christianos frequentissimum habetur. Aelius enim Spartianus de Antonino Caracalla scribit: 'Non tenax in largitionem, non lentus in eleemosinam.' Et pariter unico in loco est 'exorzizatio.' Ulpianus *De extraordinariis cognitionibus*: 'Medicos fortasse et cetera si, ut vulgari verbo impostorum[47] utar, se exorcizavit.' Plinius abstinentiam commendans Romanorum inquit non degustasse eos vina aut novas fruges priusquam sacerdotes primitias libassent; quod quidem diximus quia et hoc eodem primitiarum vocabulo nostros sacerdotes uti videmus. Et omnibus sacris Cereris libationem vini esse prohibitam Macrobius scribit. Ieiunii et virginitatis ac castimoniae ob religionem priscis usus fuit. Livius in primo: 'Amulius Rheam Silviam neptem vestalem legit, ut spem partus adimeret.' Hieronymus ad Silvinam: 'Flamen unius uxoris ad sacerdotium admittitur. Flaminica quoque unius mariti uxor eligitur. Ad tauri Aegyptii sacra semel maritus assumitur, ut omittam virgines Vestae et Apollinis, Iunonisque Achivae et Dianae et

When the senate had rejected this peace treaty, he was sent back to discharge the oath. Again Gaius Mancinus was sent and made a worse peace treaty a second time. When the senate and Roman people did not approve it, Mancinus was surrendered to the Numantines. He was exposed naked before the gate in fulfillment of the oath and was mocked. Neither the enemy nor his own countrymen would take him in.[220] Suetonius, *Life of Vespasian:* "He excused a Roman knight of his oath, so that he might divorce his wife whom he had discovered in serious sexual misconduct, since he had sworn that he would never cast her off."[221] Cicero, *Defense of Roscius the Comedian:* "But what is the difference between a perjurer and a liar? The man who habitually lies has become accustomed to making false oaths."[222]

Only in one single place among the Gentiles have I found the word *eleemosina* (alms) which is used very often in Christian writers. Aelius Spartianus writes about Antoninus Caracalla: "He was not stingy in bestowing donations, not reluctant to give alms."[223] And in the same way *exorcizatio* (exorcism) occurs only once. Ulpian, *On Extraordinary Crimes:* "Doctors perhaps" etc. "if he exorcised himself, to use the vulgar word of impostors."[224] Pliny, praising the Romans' abstinence, says that they did not taste wine, or new crops, until the priests had offered the firstfruits.[225] (Indeed I have mentioned this because we observe that our priests too use this same word *primitiae* [firstfruits].)[226] And Macrobius writes that it was forbidden to make a drink-offering (*libatio*) of wine at all the sacrifices of Ceres.[227] The men of old observed fasting, virginity and chastity for religious reasons. Livy in Book I: "Amulius appointed his niece Rhea Silvia as a Vestal, to remove the prospect of her giving birth."[228] Jerome to Silvina: "A flamen is admitted to the priesthood if he has had only one wife. She too is selected as *flaminica* who has had only one husband. Only he who has been married once is allowed to take part in the sacrifices to the Egyptian bull, not to mention the Vestal Virgins and those of Apollo, 44

Minervae, quae perpetua sacerdotii virginitate marcescunt.' Livius XXXV: 'Prodigiorum causa libros Sibyllinos ex senatus consulto decemviri cum adissent, renuntiarunt ieiunium instituendum Cereri esse et id quinto quoque anno servandum.' Et Ovidius in *Fastis* dicit Numam Pompilium, quando orationem fecit pro frugibus, usu venereorum carniumque esu abstinuisse. Aelius Spartianus de divo Iuliano imperatore: 'Saepe autem nulla existente religione oleribus leguminibusque contentus sine carnibus cenavit.' Et Hieronymus, celeber Ecclesiae doctor, *contra Iovinianum* de ieiunio tractans: 'quasi non et superstitio gentilium castum matris deum observet et Isidis.'

45 Sed iam videamus hostias quarum duo genera esse inquit Trebatius: unum quo voluntas numinum per exta exquiritur, alterum in quo sola eius hostiae anima deo sacratur. Virgilius de primo: 'Mattat lectas de more bidentes,' 'pecorumque reclusis pectoribus inhians spirantia consulit exta.' De altero vero cum fecit Entellum victorem Erici mattare taurum: 'Hanc tibi Erix meliorem animam pro morte Daretis persolvo.' Hostias Placidus grammaticus inquit 'ab hostimento, id est aequamento,' et quandoque victimas dici 'quod ictae vi cadant, vel quia vinctae ad aram producuntur.' Cum Gelius dicat hostiam pro caesis hostibus a quolibet sacerdote, victimam eius qui vicerit manibus debere immolari. Et Festus Pompeius maximam hostiam esse dicit ovilli pecoris non ab amplitudine corporis, sed ab animo placidiore. Et infra: 'Solitaurilia[48]

and of Achaean Juno, of Diana and Minerva, who waste away in the perpetual virginity of their office."[229] Livy Book XXXV: "When because of portents the Board of Ten consulted the Sibylline books in accordance with a decree of the senate, they reported that a fast should be established in honor of Ceres and that this should be observed every fifth year."[230] Ovid says in *Fasti* that when Numa Pompilius prayed for crops, he abstained from sexual activity and from the eating of flesh.[231] Aelius Spartianus on the deified emperor Julian: "Often he dined happily on vegetables and beans without meat, though there was no religious obligation in force."[232] And Jerome, the celebrated Doctor of the Church, *Against Jovinian*, on the question of fasting: "As though the false religion (*superstitio*) of the Gentiles did not also observe the period of abstinence connected with the Mother of the Gods and Isis."[233]

Now let us consider sacrificial victims. Trebatius says they 45
are of two kinds: "One by which the will of the gods is sought through inspection of the entrails, the other in which the life alone of this victim is consecrated to the god. Vergil on the first: 'She slaughters the two-year-old sheep chosen according to custom' and 'poring over the opened breasts of the sheep, she consults the entrails still palpitating with life.' It is a case of the second kind when he has the victorious Entellus slaughter a bull in honor of Eryx. 'To you, Eryx, I render this better life in place of Dares' death.'"[234] Placidus the grammarian says the word for victims (*hostiae*) comes "from *hostimentum* (recompense), that is from a requital," and sometimes victims (*victimae*) are so-called "because they fall under a strong blow (*ictae vi*) or because they are brought to the altar bound (*vinctae*),"[235] though Gellius says that the *hostia* should be sacrificed by any priest in place of the slain enemies (*hostes*), while the victim (*victima*) must be sacrificed by the hands of the one who defeated the enemy (*vincere*).[236] Festus Pompeius says "'full-grown victim' is [said] of a sheep from the flock not because of its bodily size, but because of its more placid nature."[237]

hostiarum trium diversi generis immolationem significat: tauri, arietis, verris, quod omnes solidi integrique sunt corporis.' Plinius: 'Observatum a sacrificantibus si hostia, quae ad aras ducitur, fuisset vehementius reluctata ostendissetque se invitam altaribus admoveri, non esse admovendam, quia invito deo eam offerri putabant, quae autem stetisset oblata hanc volenti numini dari.' Virgilius: 'Et ductus cornu stabit sacer hircus ad aras.' Unde victimarii postea sunt introducti mansuefaciendis bestiis. Virgilius: 'Et statuam ante aras aurata fronte iuvencum.' Et Plinius item: 'Vituli ad aram humeris hominum allati non litant, nec claudicantes, nec tractae bestiae ad aras.' Et infra: 'Suis fetus sacrificio die quinto partus,[49] pecoris die octavo, bovis trigesimo. Caprae non immolantur Minervae, quia olivas rodunt. Deorum honori auratis cornibus hostiae maiores dumtaxat immolantur.' Quas perbelle, ut erant meritae, delusit G. Gallicula imperator, quem scribit Suetonius 'admota altaribus victima succinctum habitu pomparum[50] elato alte malleo cultrarium mattasse.' Cicero oratione *In legem agrariam Rulli* prima: 'Erant hostiae maiores in foro constitutae, quae ab iis praetoribus de tribunali sicut a nobis consulibus de consilii sententia probatae[51] ad praeconem et ad tibicinem immolabantur.' Nonius Marcellus: 'Furvum bovem, id est nigrum, immolabant Averno.' Quaedam item degustationes, quas liba appellabant, in hostiae locum offerebantur. Festus Pompeius: 'Muger[52] mucosus sal in pila

Further on: "*Solitaurilia* means a sacrifice of three victims of different species, a bull, a ram and a hog, because they are all whole and sound in body."[238] Pliny: "Those sacrificing observed the practice that if the victim had struggled violently when being led to the altar and had demonstrated that it was being brought to the altar unwillingly, it was not to be so brought, because they thought that it was being offered against god's will. The one that stood still when it had been presented they thought was being given to the god according to his will. Vergil: 'And led by the horn, the he-goat meant for the god will stand at the altar.'" For this reason later on assistants at sacrifices were introduced to keep the animals calm. "Vergil: 'And I will stand before the altars a steer with gilded horns.'"[239] And Pliny again: "Calves are not acceptable when brought to the altars on men's shoulders nor animals that are lame or that have been dragged to the altars,"[240] and further on: "the young of a sow is suitable for sacrifice on the fifth day after birth, of a ewe on the eighth, of a cow on the thirtieth." She-goats are not sacrificed to Minerva, because they nibble at olive trees. As a mark of honor to the gods, victims, provided they are fully grown, are sacrificed with gilded horns.[241] The emperor Gaius Caligula cheated them very nicely, as they deserved. Suetonius writes that "he was dressed in the manner of the priest's attendants and when the victim was brought up to the altar, he lifted the mallet on high and slaughtered the man who wielded the sacrificial knife."[242] Cicero in the first speech *On the Agrarian Law against Rullus*: "The fully-grown victims had been placed in the forum. After they had been approved by these praetors from their tribunal just as they are by us consuls at Rome according to the advice of the council, they were sacrificed with herald and flute player."[243] Nonius Marcellus: "They used to sacrifice a dark-colored, that is black, bull to Avernus."[244] Again certain tastings that they called *liba* (cakes) were offered in place of the victim. Festus Pompeius: "Muger

tunsum[53] et in ollam fictilem coniectum et in furno percoctum, quo dehinc in aquam misso Vestales virgines utebantur in sacrificio.' Et infra: 'Punicum genus libi translatum a Poenis; id etiam appellant probum quia erat ceteris suavissimum.' 'Pastillum in sacris genus fuit libi rotundi' et 'Suffimenta vocabant quae fiebant ex faba milioque molito mulso asperso. Ea diis eo tempore dabantur, quo uvae calente prelo premebantur.' 'Summanalia liba farinatia in modum rotae facta.' Festusque dicit panibus redimiri[54] caput equi immolati idibus Octobris in Campo Martio, quia sacrificium fiebat ob frugum eventum, et equus potius quam bos imolabatur, quod bos frugibus pariendis est aptus. Et Macrobius deam Carnam esse dicit cui mense Iunio sacrificatur petiturque ab ea ut intestina faciat salva; huic sacrificatur pulte fabacia et lardo, quia his rebus vires corporis roborentur. Et infra: 'In sacrificio quod protervia dicitur si quid superfuerat igne comburebatur.' Unde iocus ille Catonis in eum qui omnia bona simul cum domus incendio amiserat proterviam eum fecisse. Et flamen Vulcanalis Kalendis Maiis rem divinam facit Maiae, Vulcani uxori, et sus praegnans immolatur. Herculi et Cereri XII Kalendas Ianuarias faciunt sue praegnante et panibus et mulso.

46 Sed aliae fuerunt hostiae detestabiles. Festus enim scribit: 'Ver sacrum vovendi mos fuit Italis. Magnis enim periculis adducti vovebant quaecunque proximo vere nata essent apud se animalia immolaturos, sed, cum crudele videretur pueros et puellas immeritos interficere, perductos in aetatem adultam velabant atque ita

mucosus [Brine] is salt pounded in a mortar, collected in a clay pot and baked in the oven. It was then put in water and used by the Vestal Virgins in their sacrifice,"[245] and further on, "The *punicum* is a kind of cake, introduced by the Carthaginians. They also call it *probum* (good) because it was much sweeter than the rest."[246] "The *pastillum* is a sort of round cake used in sacrifice."[247] "They called *suffimenta* a preparation they used to make from beans, ground millet and a sprinkle of honeyed wine. These were offered to the gods at the time when the grapes were pressed by the warm winepress."[248] "*Summanalia* are cakes of flour, made in the shape of a wheel."[249] Festus says: "The head of the horse sacrificed on the Ides of October in the Field of Mars was crowned with bread because this sacrifice was made in thanks for a good harvest, and a horse rather than an ox was sacrificed because the ox is suited to producing crops."[250] Macrobius says there is a goddess Carna. Sacrifice is made to her in the month of June. She is asked to keep the intestines healthy. To her were made offerings were made of bean pottage and bacon, because these things build up the body's strength.[251] And further on: "In the sacrifice that is called 'Protervia' (For-the-road), if there was anything left over, it was burned. From this came that well-known witticism of Cato's at the expense of the man who had lost all his property at the same time as his house burned down, that he had performed a Protervia."[252] "The flamen of Vulcan offers sacrifice to Maia, Vulcan's wife, on the Kalends of May."[253] And "a pregnant sow was sacrificed."[254] They sacrifice to Hercules and Ceres on the twelfth day before the Kalends of January with a pregnant sow, bread and honeyed wine.[255]

But other victims were abominable. Festus writes: "The Italians 46
had the custom of promising a 'consecrated spring.' Induced by great dangers they vowed they would sacrifice all the living creatures born to them the next spring. But, since it seemed cruel to kill undeserving boys and girls, after they had raised them to adult age they would veil them and so drive them across their frontiers."[256]

extra fines suos exigebant.' Et Plutarchus in *Problematibus:* 'Mense Maio circa plenilunium de Ponte Sublicio simulacra in Tiberim iaciunt quae appellant Argivos, quod antiquis temporibus barbari ea incolentes loca Graecos quos ceperant eo pacto interfecerunt. Herculem postea admirati Graecum hominem ab huiusmodi caede abstinuerunt, docti ab eodem ut veterem superstitionem omittentes simulacra in fluvium iacerent.' Idem in *Pauli Aemilii vita* aliud refert sacrificium, multitudine hostiarium ceteris maximum: 'Ut religiosus sacrorum cultor, ubi lunam deductam perspexit, undecim tauros ei mattavit. Inde prima luce Herculi sacra faciens litavit adusque viginti hostias. Sacro igitur centum boum et ludis deo votis aciem per priores strui iussit.' De quo sacrificio hecatombon appellato Iulius Capitolinus in *Puppieni vita* sic habet: 'Tantum sane laetitiae in Balbino, qui plus timuerat, ut hecatombon faceret, quod tale sacrificium est: centum arae uno loco ex caespite construuntur et ad eas centum sues, centum oves mattantur. Iam si imperatorum sacrificium sit, centum leones, centum aquilae, et cetera huiusmodi animalia centena feriuntur, quod quidem Graeci fecisse dicuntur cum pestilentia laborarent et a multis imperatoribus frequentatum est.'

47 Ostendemus etiam aliquos ex multis variisque moribus, quos Romani in facienda re divina observaverunt. Macrobius ex Pauliniano asserit eum, qui sacra facturus sit, se in primis reum fateri. Nam reum dicit primam vocem esse sacrorum, sicut et apud nos confessio peccatorum ceteros divinae rei actus praecedere debet et subinde voluisse maiores damnari qui promissa vota non solvit. Plinius in *Historia Naturali* dicit in adorando dexteram ad osculum

Plutarch in *Problems:* In the month of May, around the time of the full moon, they throw figures from the Sublician Bridge into the Tiber. They call these "Argives" because in ancient times the barbarians who dwelled in these parts killed in this manner the Greeks they had captured. Later, out of admiration for Hercules, a Greek man, they abstained from killing of this kind. They were taught by him to give up their old superstition and throw figures into the river.[257] Again Plutarch in *Life of Aemilius Paulus* tells of another sacrifice, greatest of all because of the large number of victims: "As he was a scrupulous observer of sacrifices, when he saw that the moon had emerged from the shadow, he sacrificed eleven bulls to her. Then at first light he made sacrifice to Hercules, as many as twenty victims, and obtained favorable omens. Therefore, having vowed to the god a sacrifice of a hundred cattle and games, he ordered the battle line to be drawn up by the officers."[258] Concerning this sacrifice, called a "hecatomb," Julius Capitolinus in *Life of Pupienus* writes thus: "Balbinus (who had been very afraid) was so delighted that he performed a hecatomb, which is a sacrifice of this nature. A hundred altars made of turf are built in one place and at them a hundred swine and a hundred sheep are slaughtered. Now, if it is an imperial sacrifice, a hundred lions, a hundred eagles and a hundred each of other animals of this kind are slain. Indeed it is said that the Greeks did this when they were suffering from plague and it was frequently resorted to by many of the emperors."[259]

I shall now describe as well some of the many different customs 47
that the Romans observed in the performance of divine worship. Macrobius drawing on Paulinianus asserts that he who is about to perform a sacrifice first of all confesses that he is "guilty" (*reus*). For he says *reus* was the first word of sacred rites, just as in our case confession of sins must precede the other acts of worship, and next (he says) the forefathers laid it down that he who has not discharged the vows he promised is "condemned" to do so.[260] In *Natural History* Pliny says it was custom in worshipping to bring

referri consuevisse totumque corpus ea circumagi, sicut salutifero crucis signaculo adoraturi se communiunt Christiani. Macrobius in *Saturnalibus:* 'Vitulari in sacris est voce laetari.' Varro: 'Pontifex in sacris quibusdam vitulari solet.' Virgilius: 'Laetumque choro paeana canamus.' Et Hyllus *De diis* Vitulam dicit putari deam quae laetitiae praeest, unde vitulatio sacrum laetitiae post victoriam. Virgilius: 'Cum faciam vitulam pro frugibus, ipse venito.' Et item Macrobius: 'Terram dicunt Opem, cuius ope humanae vitae adiumenta quaeruntur. Huic deae sedentes vota concipiunt terramque de industria tangunt.' Festus Pompeius: 'Dici[55] mos erat Romae in omnibus sacrificiis precibusque "populo Romano Quiritibusque,"' quod est [a] Curensibus quae civitas Sabinensium potentissima fuit. 'Ignis Vestae si quando interstinctus esset, virgines verberibus afficiebantur a pontifice. Quibus mos erat tabulam felicis materiae tam diu terebrare quousque exceptum ignem cribro aeneo in aedem ferret. Et ignem ex domo flaminica efferri non licet nisi divinae rei causa.' 'Omen est votum mentis et vocis. Unde a sacrificantibus bona habentur omina, id est ut circumstantes et bona mente velint et mera oribus proferant,' quale est apud Christianos cum sacerdos ab altari ad populum conversus submissa voce pro se dicit orandum. Plinius dicit 'quandam genibus inesse religionem observantia gentium. Haec enim et supplices attingunt, ad haec manus tendunt, haec aras adorant.'

48 Sed iam nimis diu huiusmodi ineptiis immoramur. Templa itaque et cetera quae illi sacra dixerunt loca praesertim notiora,

the right hand to the lips and take it round the whole body,[261] just as Christians fortify themselves before worship with the redeeming sign of the cross. Macrobius in *Saturnalia*: "*vitulari* in sacred rites is to utter a cry of joy." Varro: the pontiff in certain sacred rites is accustomed to express joy (*vitulari*). Vergil: "let us sing in a chorus a happy paean of joy." And Hyllus in *On the Gods* says that Vitula is considered the goddess who is set over joy. For this reason a public rejoicing (*vitulatio*) is a rite of joy after a victory. Vergil: "when I sacrifice with a heifer (*vitula*) for the crops, come yourself."[262] And again Macrobius: "They call the earth 'Ops,' from whose resources (*ope*) support is sought for human life. They undertake vows to this goddess while sitting and deliberately touch the earth."[263] Festus Pompeius says: "It was customary at Rome in all sacrifices and prayers to say 'for the Roman people and Quirites,' that is, the people of Cures, which was a very powerful city of the Sabines."[264] "If Vesta's flame was ever extinguished, the Virgins were beaten with rods by the pontiff. Their custom was to drill a wooden board from a fertile tree until the fire might be taken up and carried into the temple in a bronze sieve," and "fire cannot be taken out of a house belonging to the flamen except for the purpose of divine worship."[265] "An omen is a mental and verbal prayer. For this reason good omens are to be observed by those sacrificing, that is, they ask that those present both wish for the good in their minds and make pure utterances,"[266] just as happens among Christians when the priest turning from the altar to the people says in a low voice that they should pray for him. Pliny says that, "in the usage of the nations, there is a certain religious power in the knees. For suppliants touch them, they stretch out their hands to them, they pray at them as if they were altars."[267]

But I have already lingered too long on nonsense of this kind. 48
Accordingly as I am going to describe the temples and all the other places they said were holy, especially the better known, this being

distributionis nostrae superius factae partem alteram, descripturi, eorum vocabula et ritus primo ostendamus. In ipsorum vero varietate vocabulorum templum, aedes, delubrum, fanum, tesca, ara sunt notiora. De templo sic habet Varro *De lingua Latina:* 'Omne templum debet esse continuo saeptum, nec plus quam unum introitum habere,' et praeter id 'templa esse dicunt singulis attributa diis, delubra vero multarum aedium sub uno tecto sacra sunt loca' unde 'curia hostilia templum est, sanctum non est.' 'Et in urbe Roma pleraeque sunt aedes sacrae, templa, eadem sancta.' Fani significatio magis ab opposito quam proprio et attributo vocabulo est nota. Profanum enim inquit Macrobius esse quod extra fanaticam causam sit quasi porro a fano id est religione remotum. Virgilius: 'Procul, o procul este profani.' Trebatiusque ait 'profanum' quod ex religioso vel sacro in usum hominum est conversum. Virgilius: 'Faune precor miserere—inquit—tuque optima ferrum Terra tene, colui vestros si semper honores quos contra Aeneadae bello fecere profanos.' Aliquotque loca, quod aedificia alicuius dei sunt, dicuntur tesqua quod ibi mysteria fiunt ut tueantur, tuesca dicta. Macrobius in *Saturnalibus:* '"Delubrum" Varro inquit locum esse in quo praeter aedem sit area assumpta deum causa, ut est in Circo Flaminio, vel in quo dei simulacrum sit affixum et dedicatum, sicut candelabrum ubi candela, ita delubrum ubi deus.' Virgilius: 'At gemini lapsu delubra ad summa dracones effugiunt, saevaeque petunt Tritonidis arcem. Sub pedibusque deae clipeique sub orbe teguntur.' Item: 'Nos delubra deum miseri quibus ultimus esset ille

the second section of the division I made above, let me first of all give an account of their names and rites. To be sure, among the various terms, the better known are temple (*templum*), temple building (*aedes*), shrine (*delubrum*), holy precinct (*fanum*), *tesca*,[268] altar. About the temple Varro in *On the Latin Language* says this: "Every temple should be enclosed without interruption, and not have more than one entrance,"[269] and besides this, "they say that temples are assigned to individual gods. Shrines (*delubra*) are holy places where many 'houses' (*aedes*) are under one roof."[270] For this reason "the Hostilian Meetinghouse is a space inaugurated for public business (*templum*) but is not sacred" and "in the City of Rome very many consecrated temple buildings are temples, the same being sacred."[271] The meaning of *fanum* is known more from its antonym than from the proper designation given to it. Macrobius says the "'profane' is that which is beyond the condition of belonging to a hallowed place, that is to say 'further apart from the hallowed place (*fanum*), that is, apart from religious scruple.' Vergil: 'Stand apart, apart, you unhallowed ones (*profani*).'" "And Trebatius says the term 'profane' is used of that which has been transferred from the religious or sacred sphere to the usage of men. Vergil: 'O Faunus, take pity I pray, he said, and you, Good Earth, hold fast to the steel, if I have always paid you honors which Aeneas' followers, on the contrary, have profaned by war.'"[272] Some places, because they are the buildings of some god, are called *tesca* "because they see (*tueri*) where mysteries take place, they were called *tuesca*."[273] Macrobius in *Saturnalia*: Varro says a "shrine" (*delubrum*) is a place in which, besides the temple building (*aedes*), an open space has been taken over for the sake of the gods, as it is in the Flaminian Circus, or in which an image of the god has been set up and dedicated; as a candelabrum is where a candle is put, so a *delubrum* where a god (*deus*).[274] Vergil: "But the twin snakes, gliding away, escape to the highest shrines and they make for the citadel of cruel Athena, and hide under the goddess's

dies.' Altare Festus Pompeius 'ab altitudine dici vult, quod antiqui diis superis in aedificiis a terra exaltatis sacra faciebant, diis terrestribus in terra, diis inferioribus in terra defossa.' Et infra: 'Terrentum locus est in Campo Martio dictus quod eo loco ara Ditis patris in terra occultaretur.' Primam aram Romae fuisse, quam Herculi Evander in foro Boario extruxit, Ovidius sic dicit: 'Cacus Aventinae timor atque infamia silvae,' noti sunt versus. Et infra: 'Instituitque tibi quae maxima dicitur aram.' Et Varro aras primitus fuisse appellatas existimavit, quod eas qui sacrificent teneant. Unde Macrobius dicit solam non posse orationem litare, nisi is qui deos precatur etiam manibus aram apprehendat. Virgilius: 'Talibus orantem dictis arasque tenentem audiit omnipotens.' Item: 'Tango aras medios ignes ac numina testor.' Fuerunt et arae apertis in locis. Plutarchus in *Problematibus*: 'Aedem Horae maiores perpetuo apertam esse voluerunt, quae et Hora est appellata quia circunspecta est, cum rebus humanis praesit provida dea, quam res humanas curantem et conservantem socordem et negligentem minime putant esse debere.' Aedemque Vulcani Romulus extra urbem posuit, quia cum incendiis urbs esset exposita Vulcanum quidem colendum, sed tamen urbe excludendum existimarunt. Laribus etiam locum sacrum attribuerunt, quod dixere lararium, eosque Aeneam Troia advexisse satis constat. Virgilius: 'Cum penatibus et magnis diis.' Cicero *Pro domo sua ad pontifices*: 'Quid est sanctius, quid

feet and her circular shield," and again: "We wretches, whose last day that day was, [wreathe] the shrines of the gods."[275] Festus Pompeius thinks that the word "altar" comes "from altitude, because the ancients performed sacrifices in honor of the celestial gods in buildings raised above the earth, and in honor of the terrestrial gods at ground level and in honor of the gods of the lower world in excavations below ground." And further on: "*Terentum* is a place in the Field of Mars, so-called because in that place the altar of Father Dis was hidden in the earth."[276] Ovid says that Rome's first altar[277] was that which Evander built in honor of Hercules in the Cattle Market: "Cacus, the terror and disgrace of the Aventine wood." The passage is well known. And further on: "He established for you the altar that is called the 'Great.'"[278] Varro thought that altars got their name originally because those who are sacrificing grasp them. For this reason Macrobius says one cannot perform a propitiation by words alone "unless he who is praying to the gods also takes hold of the altar with his hands." Vergil: "The All-Powerful god heard him as he prayed with such words with his hand grasping the altar." From the same author: "I grasp the altar, and call to witness the fires and the gods between us."[279] There were also altars in open places. Plutarch in *Problems:* The ancestors required that Hora's temple be continually open. She was named Hora too because she is heedful, since she, a provident goddess, is put over human affairs, and they do not think that she who cares for and watches over human affairs should be in the least careless or negligent.[280] Romulus put the temple of Vulcan outside the city. Because the city was vulnerable to fire, they thought Vulcan should be worshipped, but nevertheless kept outside the city.[281] They assigned a sacred place to the Lares too, which they called *lararium,*[282] and it is sufficiently well known that Aeneas brought them from Troy. Vergil: "with the Penates and Great Gods."[283] Cicero, *On His Own House:* "What is more

omni religione munitius quam domus uniuscuiusque civium? Hic arae sunt, hic foci, hic dii penates, hic sacra et religiones continentur.' Eos autem deos penates in larario domus custodes canem semper appositum habuisse et inde caninis fuisse pellibus contextos Plinius asserit Serviumque regem eos bovum oviumque effigie primum signasse.

49 Ut in praedicta locorum sacrorum institutione prudentius ceteris gentilibus egisse videantur Persae, quos Asconius Pedianus *secunda in Verrem actione* affirmat credidisse nulla diis templa esse condenda, cum uni deo Soli quem adorarent vix mundus ipse sufficiat. Econtra vero Romani ea in re eximiam curam vel potius superfluam susceperunt, quos non solum sideribus, sed quibuscunque etiam hominum passionibus templa et loca sacra erexisse videmus, quorum partem ordine ex Livio afferemus. Tarquinius Superbus Iovis Optimi Maximi templum ex praeda Suessae Pometiae aedificavit. Exinde aedes Mercurii dedicata. Post ob Veturiae matris et uxoris Coriolani factum Fortunae Muliebri templum est aedificatum. Camillusque dictator templum in Aventino Matutae matri dedicavit. Expiandae etiam vocis nocturnae quae nuntia cladis ante bellum Gallicum audita neglecta esset, iussum templum in nova via Alloquutiae. Et Terminus in Capitolio inventus moveri se non passus templum ibi habuit, aedesque Monetae Iunonis 'in area quae aedium Manlii fuerat aedificata.' Aedes paulo post Salutis a G. Iunio censore locata est. Carvilius[56] subinde consul aedem Fortis

inviolable, what more protected by every kind of sanctity then each individual citizen's house? Here are his altars, here his hearths, here his Penates, here his religious rites and observances have their center."[284] Pliny maintains that these Penates, the guardians of the house, always had a dog placed beside them in the Lararium and for this reason they were clothed with the skins of dogs.[285] And that "King Servius first marked them with the images of cattle and sheep."[286]

So that in the previously mentioned establishment of sacred 49
spaces the Persians may be seen to have acted more wisely than all the other Gentiles, for Asconius Pedianus in his commentary *On the Second Action of the Verrine Orations* affirms that they believed that "no temples should be built for the gods, since for the one god, the Sun, whom they worship, the world itself scarcely suffices."[287] The Romans on the other hand, took exceptional or, rather, excessive care in this matter. They, we observe, erected temples and sacred places not only for heavenly bodies, but also for every possible human passion. Some of these I shall adduce in due order from Livy. Tarquinius Superbus built the Temple of Jupiter Best and Greatest from the spoils of Suessa Pometia.[288] Next the Temple of Mercury was dedicated.[289] Later a temple was built in honor of Womanly Fortune to commemorate the deed of Coriolanus' mother Veturia and his wife.[290] When Camillus was dictator he dedicated a temple on the Aventine in honor of Mater Matuta.[291] "Also to propitiate the voice that spoke at night, which had been heard before the war with the Gauls and disregarded though it foretold disaster, a temple was ordered in the New Way for the god called 'he who speaks.'"[292] Terminus, since he was discovered on the Capitol and did not allow himself to be moved, had a temple there.[293] The Temple of Juno Moneta was built "on a site which had been that of Manlius' house."[294] A little later "the Temple of Safety was contracted for by Gaius Junius when he was

Fortunae de manubiis faciendam locavit. Et templum fuisse rostra Cicero oratione *In Vatinium testem* sic indicat: 'Produxeris iudicem in Rostris illo, inquam, inaugurato templo.'

50 Nunc ad ritus transeundum est. Festus Pompeius: 'Ritus, mos, consuetudo. Rite autem bene et recte.' Livius in primo: 'Pontificem deinde Numa M. Furium ex patribus legit, eique sancta omnia exscripta signataque attribuit, quibus hostiis, quibus diebus, ad quae templa sacra fierent, atque unde in eos sumptus pecuniae erogarentur. Cetera omnia publica privataque sacra pontificis scitis subiecit, ut esset quo consultum plebs veniret, nequid divini iuris negligendo patrios ritus peregrinosque asciscendo turbaretur.' Cicero in *Legibus:* 'Ritus familiae patriaeque servanto. Itaque ut cadat in cunctis anfractibus descriptum esto certasque fruges certasque bachas sacerdotes publice libanto, quae cuique divo gratae sint hostiae providento, quo quaeque privatim et publice modo rituque fiant discunto ignari a publicis sacerdotibus, ex patriis ritibus optima colunto.' Ritibusque ascribenda sunt ea quae a Livio tradita sunt: lacu Albano emittendam fuisse aquam, si Vehis potiri vellent, vates praedixisse et pariter a Delphis legatos attulisse, et Iunonem interrogatam nunquid vellet Romam ire, cum affirmasset, fuisse advectam templumque illi dicatum in Aventino. Et ancilia, caelo

censor."[295] Next when Carvilius was consul he "let out the contract for the Temple of Chance Fortune to be constructed from the general's spoils."[296] In his speech *Against Vatinius* Cicero demonstrates that the speaker's platform (*rostra*) was a space inaugurated for public business: "You have placed a judge on the *rostra*, that, I repeat, *templum* consecrated by the augurs."[297]

Now I must move on to the rites. Festus Pompeius. "A rite [is] 50
a usage or custom. But *rite* [means] well and properly."[298] Livy in Book I: "Next Numa chose Marcus Furius as pontiff from among the senators, and he made over to him all the holy rites, recorded and prescribed, showing with what victims, on what days, in what temples sacrifices should be performed and from what source the monies for these expenses should be paid out. All other public and private rites he made subject to the decrees of the pontiff so that there might be someone to whom the people might come for advice. This was to prevent divine law being thrown into confusion by the neglect of inherited rites or by the adoption of foreign ones."[299] Cicero in *On the Laws:* "They shall preserve the rites of the family and of the fatherland. Therefore let it be arranged to fall at all the sun's circuits. The pontiffs shall offer the prescribed crops and the prescribed fruits on behalf of the public."[300] "They shall make provision so that each victim be pleasing to each god. Those who do not know in what manner and with what rituals these private and public ceremonies are performed shall learn from the public priests."[301] "From among the ancestral rituals they shall observe the best."[302] The following matters recorded by Livy are to be included among the rites. He says the seers foretold that water had to be drained from the Alban lake if they wanted to get possession of Veii, and the envoys brought the same message from Delphi,[303] and Juno was asked if she wanted to go to Rome. When she said "yes," she was taken from there and a temple was dedicated in her honor on the Aventine.[304] And after the *ancilia* (sacred

demissa cum fuissent, iussu Nummae servata, illis Salios in solemnibus usos esse. De qua re sic habet Festus: 'Mamurri Veturi[57] nomen frequenter cantu Romani frequentabant hac de causa. Numae Pompilio e caelo cecidisse fertur ancile, id est scutum breve, quod ideo sic appellatur, quia ex utroque latere erat recisum, ut summum infimumque eius latus medio pateret; unaque edita vox omnium potentissimam fore civitatem quamdiu id in ea mansisset. Itaque facta eiusdem generis plura ideo miscerentur, ne internosci caeleste posset. Probatum opus est maxime Mamurri Veturi,[58] qui praemii[59] loco petiit, ut suum nomen intra carmina Salii canerent.' De quo ancili sic habet Cicero in *Philippicis*: 'Qui ita conservandus est ut id signum quod caelo delapsum Vestae custodiis continetur.'

51 His ad maiorem rerum[60] intelligentiam praemissis, loca simul cum ipsis ritibus ostendere pergamus, nec erit ab re multa repetere quae in *Romae* a nobis *instauratae* descriptione posuimus. Erit autem a Iove principium, quem omnia in omnibus esse voluerunt, ut dicat Virgilius: 'deum ire per omnes terras tractusque maris caelumque profundum.' Id tamen tantum numen a parricidio, adulterio stuprisque suam magnitudinem esse nactum confitentur, adeo ut in ludis scaenicis, deorum venerationi institutis, corruptorem pudicitiae Iovem turpissimi histriones canerent agerentque, ut populo placerent. Et adolescens ille Terentianus suum laudat adulterium Iovis dei exemplo, qui per auri impluvium Danaen, Acrisii filiam, corruperit. Sed eius ritus sacra et sacerdotes discutiamus. In aede ipsius Iovis Optimi Maximi, quae in Capitolio fuit, ubi

shields) had been sent down from heaven, they were kept safe by Numa's bidding.[305] The Salii used them in their ceremonies[306] and on this matter Festus writes as follows: "The Romans often repeated the name of Mamurius Veturius in their song, for this reason. It is said that a shield fell from heaven for Numa Pompilius. The *ancile* is a small shield that has this name because it had been cut away on both sides so that at the top and bottom it was broader than in the middle. At the same time a pronouncement was uttered that this would be the most powerful city of all, so long as the shield remained in it. So a number of the same kind were made and mixed up together so that the celestial one could not be recognized. The work of Mamurius Veturius was judged the best. Instead of a reward he requested that the Salii sing his name in their songs."[307] Cicero in *Philippics* says about this shield: "He who must be preserved in the same way as that statue which fell from heaven and is kept under the protection of Vesta."[308]

Now that I have set these things down in a preliminary way to 51
facilitate a greater understanding of the material, let us proceed to give an account of the places together with the rites themselves. Nor will it be beside the point to repeat much that I have already set down in my description in *Rome Restored*. Our beginning will be from Jupiter,[309] whom they affirmed was all in all,[310] so that Vergil says: "For god pervades all lands and the sea's expanses and the depths of heaven."[311] Nevertheless, they admit that this great god acquired his preeminence by means of parricide, adultery and rapes, so much so that in the theatrical shows established in reverence of the gods "the foulest actors used to sing and act the part of Jupiter, a corruptor of chastity,"[312] to please the people. And that young man in Terence commends his own adultery using the example of the god Jupiter, who seduced Danae, Acrisius' daughter, by a shower of gold.[313] Now let us discuss his rites, sacrifices and priests. In the Temple of Jupiter Best and Greatest himself on the Capitol, where punishment is now

nunc de facinorosis supplicium sumitur, et ad quam triumphi tantis ducebantur apparatibus, sacerdotes fuerunt perpetui epulones Iovis appellati, quos asserit Augustinus mensae ad auream eius statuam positae perpetuos fuisse convivas, ut mimorum ibi potius et parasitorum contubernia quam dei sacra celebrarentur. Fuitque moris eo in contubernio sermones et confabulationes quotquot inciderent, non minus cum Iovis statua quam ipsos inter se ipsos epulones deblacterare. Unde Seneca Cordubensis in superstitiosos invehens: 'In Capitolium—inquit—perveni. Puduit publicatae dementiae, quid non sibi vanus furor attribuit officii? Alius munera deo subicit, alius horas Iovi nunciat, alius lictor, alius unctor, qui vano motu brachiorum imitetur unguentem. Sunt qui ad vadimonia sua deum advocant. Sunt qui libellos offerant et illum causam suam doceant. Doctus archimimus senex iam decrepitus quotidie in Capitolio mimum agebat, quasi dii libenter expectarent, quem turba desierat; omne illic artificum genus operantium diis immortalibus desidet. Sedent quaedam in Capitolio, quae se a Iove amari putant.' Antedictique epulones et subditi eis aeditui cisternas et specus in Capitolio habuerunt subterraneas, quae appellatae sunt favissae, in quibus signa collapsa et aes aurumve sacrorum reponebant.

52 Libet vero quasdam ex legibus Iovis sacerdoti impositis a Plutarcho sumere: 'Sacerdotem Iovis cane et capra abstinere adeo voluerunt ut nec tangere nec nominare debeat, quia capra foetidum et libidinosum sit animal et comitiali addictum. Canis vero tumultuosum animal, quod omnibus sacris locis arcetur et in primis Iovis templo, ne sacerdoti ad ianuam sedenti et profugos in templum

exacted from criminals,[314] and to which the triumphal processions were led with such pomp and splendor, there were permanent priests called "feasters of Jupiter." Augustine maintains that these were standing guests at a table placed by his golden statue, the result being that there was a household of mimes and parasites there rather than celebration of the god's rites.[315] And in that companionship the custom was for the feasters themselves to make foolish conversation and talk, on as many topics as came up, no less with the statue of Jupiter than among themselves. This is why Seneca of Cordoba says in *On Superstition:* "I came to the Capitol, and I was ashamed of the folly revealed there. What duty has the groundless madness not arrogated to itself? One servant brings the god gifts, another tells Jupiter the time, one is a lictor, another a masseur, seeing that he imitates the act of rubbing in oil, moving his arms to no effect. Some summon the god to appear in court for them, others offer him lawyers' briefs and instruct him on their case. A well-trained leading mime actor, now a decrepit old man, used to act a mime every day on the Capitol, as if the gods would take pleasure in watching someone whom the crowd had abandoned. Every kind of artisan is idle there in the service of the immortal gods. Certain women who imagine that Jupiter loves them sit on the Capitol."[316] The feasters I have already mentioned and the sacristans under their authority had on the Capitol underground cisterns and caves, called *favissae*. They stored in them statues that had gone to wrack and ruin and bronze or gold belonging to the holy rites.[317]

I would like to take from Plutarch some of the laws imposed on 52
the priest of Jupiter. They required that the priest of Jupiter keep away from dogs and goats, so much so that he should neither touch them nor name them, because the goat is an animal that is stinking and lustful and subject to epilepsy. But the dog is one that gets involved in fights and is kept away from all sacred places, especially Jupiter's temple, lest it bark in an aggressive manner at the

reos excipienti sit latrando infestus. Sedentes enim ibi quicunque mane adibant, eo die ab omni verberatione et violatione tuti reddebantur et confugientes ad eum locum conservabantur, etiam si ligati erant solvebantur, loraque non per ianuam, sed per tectum abiciebantur.' Et infra: 'Sacerdotibus Iovis nec magistratum capere nec petere permittebatur, et tamen lictore utebantur ac sella curruli, quia regiae potestati par sacerdotii dignitas habebatur. Unde non vulgares, nec ignobiles homines ad sacerdotium promovebant.'

53 At de Matre Magna deum videamus quae, cum Berecynthia, Cibeles, Vesta et Ops et Proserpina sit dicta, cellam habuit prope templum Vestae apud Tyberim, et prope pontem nunc Sanctae Mariae prout in *Roma* ostendimus *instaurata*. Fuitque haec Magna deum Mater de qua Livius libro XXVIIII: 'Oratores Romani Pergamum ad regem venerunt. Is legatos comiter acceptos Pessimontem in Phrigiam deduxit, sacrumque iis lapidem, quem Matrem deum esse incolae dicebant, tradidit et deportare Romam iussit.' Quem Tybri advectum Scipio Nasica, optimus vir a senatu iudicatus, per Portam Capenam duxit in urbem, et cum Nasica templum ei vovisset, Metellus incepit, Augustus perfecit. Ovidius: 'Illa sedens plaustro porta est invecta Capena. Nasica cepit opus, templi non extitit auctor. Augustus nunc est, ante Metellus erat.' Eius deae, quam virginem et matrem fuisse mentiti sunt, simulacrum manu gestabat timpanum, turres habebat in capite. Unde Virgilius: 'Qualis Berecynthia mater invehitur curru Phrigias turrita per urbes.' Et contra eam posita erat sedes serviebantque illi

priest who sits at the door and welcomes criminals coming to the temple for refuge. For those who went up to them in the morning as they sat there were made safe for that day from beating and injury and those escaping to that place were protected and released, even if they had been tied up, and the straps were thrown away, not through the door, but the roof.[318] And further on: "Priests of Jupiter were not allowed to hold office nor to seek it, and yet they had the use of a lictor and a curule chair, because the priest's standing was considered on a par with the king's power. For this reason they did not promote common or ignoble men to the priesthood."[319]

But let us consider the Great Mother of the Gods, who, since 53
she was called Berecynthia, Cybele, Vesta, Ops and Proserpina,[320] had a chapel near the Temple of Vesta beside the Tiber and near the bridge now called St. Mary's, as I showed in *Rome Restored*.[321] She was the Great Mother of the Gods concerning whom Livy says in Book XXIX: "The Roman ambassadors arrived at Pergamum to see the king. He welcomed them in a friendly manner and escorted them to Pessinus in Phrygia. He handed over to them the sacred stone that the local inhabitants said was the Mother of the Gods and bade them transport it to Rome." It was carried up the Tiber, and Scipio Nasica, whom the senate judged the best man in Rome, brought it into the city through the Capene Gate. After Nasica had dedicated a temple in her honor, Metellus began it and Augustus completed it. Ovid: "Seated in a cart she was driven in through the Capene Gate. Nasica received her. The name of the founder of the temple is not extant. Now it is Augustus, earlier it was Metellus."[322] In representations, this goddess, whom they falsely said was both virgin and mother, carried a drum in her hand and had a turreted crown on her head. For this reason Vergil says "Just as the Berecynthia mother rides on a chariot through the Phrygian cities wearing a turreted crown,"[323] and a seat was placed facing her, and she was served by

sacerdotes Galli molles turpissime eunuchati, quos Plinius Samia testa virilitatem amputare affirmat, et Festus Pompeius dicit eos appellari a flumine Gallo quod accolunt. Et Livius in XXXVI: 'Livius, L. Scipionis legatus, classem in Europam ad Sexton oppugnandam traiecit. Iamque subeuntibus muros fanatici Galli primum cum solemni habitu ante portam occurrerunt, iussu sanctae matris deum venire memorant ad precandum Romanum ut parceret civibus urbique. Nemo eorum violatus est. Mox universus senatus cum magistratibus ad dedendam urbem progressus.' Et idem in XXVIII: 'Consul M. Fulvius Sangarium amnem transgressus ponte perfecto, praeter ripam euntibus Galli Matris Magnae a Pessimonte occurrere, cum insignibus suis vaticinantes fanatico carmine deam Romanis viam belli et victoriam dare imperiumque eius regionis.' Hi itaque Galli, sacerdotes eunuchi molles, apud deam se iactantes faciebant cimbalorum ferramentorumque iactorum ac manuum sonitum. Leoque adiungebatur solutus et mansuetus. Molles vero dicit beatus Augustinus 'contra omnem virorum mulierumque verecundiam consecratos, madidis unguento capillis, facie dealbata, fluentibus membris, incessu femineo, per plateas vicosque a populis unde turpiter viverent quaeritasse.' Nec immerito queritur et deflet ipse sanctus vir hoc crimen, hoc dedecus habere inter illa sacra professionem, quod in vitiosis hominum moribus vix habet inter tormenta confessionem. Castrati autem sunt ob memoriam Atys, quem formosissimum adolescentem, cum illa procax et impudica perdite et afflictim amasset, ob zelum muliebremque animi impotentiam eunucavit. Idemque Augustinus de seipso dicens sic Berecynthiae sacra commendat: 'Veniebamus

eunuch priests called Galli,[324] emasculated in a most shameful way. Pliny says they cut off their male organs with a shard of Samian ware,[325] and Festus Pompeius says they got their name from the river Gallus by which they dwelt.[326] And Livy in Book XXXVI: Livius, the legate of Lucius Scipio, "brought the fleet across to the European side to attack Sestus. When they were already beneath the walls, some inspired Galli, in their ritual attire, first ran up in front of the gate to prevent them. They said they came on the orders of the holy Mother of the Gods to beg the Roman leader to spare the citizens and the city. None of them was harmed. Presently the whole senate together with the magistrates came forth to surrender the city."[327] The same author says in Book XXVIII: The consul Marcus Fulvius "made a bridge and crossed the river Sangarius. As they went along the bank they were met by Galli devoted to the Great Mother of Pessinus, with their ritual adornments, prophesying in inspired song that the goddess was giving the Romans the path of war and victory and rule over this region."[328] So these Galli, effeminate eunuch priests, as they leaped about in the sight of the goddess sounded cymbals, clashed iron tools and clapped hands. An unleashed and tame lion accompanied her.[329] St. Augustine says the effeminates, "consecrated [to her] contrary to all male and female modesty, their hair damp with perfume, their faces whitened, with enervated limbs, a feminine gait, through the squares and streets sought from the people the means of their foul life."[330] Nor does this saint unjustifiably bewail and deplore the fact that "this offense, this infamy, which under torture is scarcely admitted to among men's corrupt customs, is openly declared in those sacred rites."[331] They were castrated in memory of Attis, a very handsome youth whom she made a eunuch out of jealousy and womanly lack of self-control since she, wanton and shameless, had madly and desperately loved him.[332] The same author, Augustine, talking about himself, writes in this way about the rites of Berecynthia: "I myself

nos etiam aliquando adolescentes ad spectacula ludibriaque sacrilegiorum, spectabamus arrepticios, audiebamus simphoniacos, ludis turpissimis, qui diis deabusque exhibebantur, oblectabamur Caelesti virgini Berecynthiae matri omnium, ante cuius lecticam die solemni lavationis eius talia per publicum cantabantur a nequissimis scaenicis, qualia non dico matrem deorum, immo vero qualia nec matrem ipsorum scaenicorum deceret audire.' Melius vero et prudentius quam viri in Iove suo mulieres in Matuta dea egerunt. Refert namque Plutarchus in *Problematibus* 'ancillis aedem Matutae ingredi fas non esse, unamque tantum mulieres introducere quam alapis caedunt, hancque unam ita pulsant, ut servas significent aditu prohiberi. Apudque eam deam suis filiis mulieres bona non optant, sed nepotibus tribuunt, quod Ino, quae et Matuta, miti quodam et humano ingenio fuisse et sororis filio mammam praebuisse; in filiis vero infelix fuisse videtur.'

54 Sed et vetustiora hoc principio tractemus. Evander Carmentem matrem, quae Latinas litteras prima dicitur invenisse, ex Arcadia in Italiam ducens attulit secum sacra quae dicta sunt Lupercalia. Unde Ovidius: 'Nam iuvenis nimium vera cum matre fugatus deserit Arcadiam Parrasiumque larem,' et alio loco: 'Quis vetat Arcadio dictos a monte lupercos. Faunus in Arcadia templa Lycaeus habet.' Livius in primo: 'Romulus in Palatino monte Lupercal fecit ludicrum, et a Palantia urbe Palatium appellat, unde nudi iuvenes Lycaeum Pana venerantes per luxum atque lasciviam currerent.' Et beatus Augustinus his verbis hoc exponit: 'Varro asseruit Circem

too when I was a young man sometimes used to go to the shows and games belonging to their impious ceremonies, I used to watch the ecstatic performers, listen to the musicians, take pleasure in the lewd entertainments that were put on in honor of the gods and goddesses, of the virgin Caelestis, Berecynthia mother of all, before whose couch, on the anniversary of her purification such things were sung in public by the basest performers as were not fit—I do not say for the mother of the gods, nay rather for the mothers of the performers themselves to hear."[333] In fact, the women behaved better and more wisely in relation to the goddess Matuta than the men in relation to their own Jupiter. For Plutarch in *Problems* tells that it is forbidden for slave women to enter Matuta's shrine, and the women bring in a single slave woman whom they hit and slap on the face, and they strike her like this to indicate that slave women are not allowed to enter. In this goddess' shrine women do not wish for blessings on their own children, but bestow them on their nephews, because Ino (who is also Matuta) seems to have been of a gentle and kindly nature, and to have given the breast to her sister's son, but to have been unfortunate in her own children.[334]

But let us also treat older matters beginning with this. When 54
Evander brought his mother Carmentis (she who is said to have first invented the Latin alphabet)[335] from Arcadia to Italy, he brought with him the rites called Lupercalia. So Ovid says: "The youth banished with his mother who spoke too truly, abandoned Arcadia and his Parrhasian home."[336] And elsewhere: "Who does not allow that the Luperci have been named after the Arcadian mountain? Lycaean Faunus has temples in Arcadia."[337] Livy in Book I: "Romulus celebrated the Lupercal festival on the Palatine and names the hill Palatium after the city Palantia. Whence it comes that naked youths ran about in honor of Lycaean Pan in debauchery and wantonness."[338] St. Augustine explains it in these words: Varro asserted that Circe transformed Ulysses' companions

socios Ulixis mutasse in bestias et Arcades, qui sorte ducti transnatabant quoddam stagnum, conversos fuisse in lupos. Unde Romanorum Lupercalia ex illorum semine sunt exorta.' Ovidius tamen aliam affert lupercorum originem, qui, diffuse narrata Romuli et Remi in Tyberim expositorum historia, Romanos dicit beneficii memores, quod lupa nutriendis infantibus praestitit, templum illi ad ficum Ruminalem extruxisse quod Lupercal sit appellatum. 'Venit ad expositos mirum lupa feta gemellos. Illa loco nomen fecit, locus ipse Lupercal. Magna dati nutrix praemia lactis habet.' Et nos eius templi locum fuisse ostendimus ubi ad superiorem Circi Maximi partem Caelius mons desinit in Sancti Gregorii aedibus in viam Appiam vergentibus. Sed ad rem: eius templi sacerdotes Luperci, sicut vult Varro, appellati divinam rem suam nudi agebant, nec in templo solum, sed per vicos urbis ac compita discurrentes, quin etiam, praeter sacerdotes, quicumque, mares et feminae, sacrificio volebant communicare, nudi per templum urbemque catervatim Lycaeum nescio quod carmen canentes procedebant. Et Festus Pompeius: 'Creppos dicit lupercos esse dictos a crepitu pellicularum, quem faciunt verberantes. Mos enim erat Romae in Lupercalibus nudos discurrere et pellibus obvias quasque feminas ferire.' Unde notum est Marcum Antonium, cuius immiti ingenio insaniam addiderat Gaii Caesaris victoria, ut Pani Lycaeo Lupercalia celebraret nudum, nudatis omnia membra matronis et virginibus sociatum, curru per urbem fuisse vectum, quem puellae pariter nudae traherent, quo die Cesari coronam regni imponere est adnixus.

into beasts and that the Arcadians, who, chosen by lot, swam across a certain pool, were turned into wolves. For this reason he says that the Roman Lupercalia were sprung from their seed.[339] Ovid, however, puts forward another origin for the Luperci.[340] After narrating at length the story of the exposure of Romulus and Remus on the Tiber bank, he says that the Romans, mindful of the benefit that the she-wolf bestowed by feeding the infants, built a temple in her honor near the Ruminal fig tree[341] and that this was called the Lupercal. "A she-wolf that had given birth miraculously came to the abandoned twins." "The she-wolf gave the place its name, the place itself was the Lupercal. The nurse has a great reward for the milk she gave."[342] I have shown that the location of this temple was where the Caelian Hill comes to an end near the upper part of the Great Circus, at the church of St. Gregory that faces onto the Appian Way.[343] But back to our subject. The priests of this temple, called "Luperci" according to Varro,[344] performed their divine rite naked, not only in the temple but also when they ran about through the streets and crossroads of the city. In fact, apart from the priests, anyone, male or female, who wanted to take part in the sacrifice processed naked in bands through the temple and the city singing some Lycaean song or other.[345] Festus Pompeius says the "'Luperci' were called *creppi* from the snapping noise (*crepitu*) they make with their hides as they do their beating. For it was the custom at Rome for the Luperci to race around naked during the Lupercalia and to whip with strips of hide every woman they met."[346] For this reason it is well-known that Mark Antony, to whose innate cruelty Gaius Caesar's victory had added madness, on the day when he attempted to place the royal crown on Caesar's head, rode naked through the city in a chariot to celebrate the Lupercalia in honor of Lycaean Pan escorted by married women and maidens who were completely naked. The chariot was drawn by girls who were equally naked.[347]

55 Hercules quoque, cum Evandrum Cachi timore liberasset, ob memoriam vaccarum quas eo mactato receperat, bovem aeneum in foro obtinuit, quod inde Boarium appellarunt. Fuitque ad id forum ab ipso deo templum aedificatum Ara Maxima appellatum, eo in loco vel prope contiguo ubi ecclesiam Sancti Georgii ad Velabrum esse videmus. Livius in secundo: 'Ara Maxima Herculi ab Evandro dicata. Hic sacra Romulus prima ex omnibus peregrina cepit.' Herculi vero rem divinam facientes scribit Plutarchus alium neminem ex diis nominare, quia semideus sit habitus vel quod soli, dum ageret in humanis, ara ab Evandro dicata est. Canem amoveri volunt, quia Cerberus Herculi fuit infestus, vel quia, Licinio puero a cane occiso, ab Ipothomatibus, proelio decernere coactus multos ea pugna ex amicis, fratrem quoque perdidit. Et Ovidius de Hercule: 'Immolat et illic taurum, tibi Iupiter, unum. Victor et Evandrum ruricolasque vocat. Constituitque sibi quae Maxima dicitur Aram. Hic ubi pars urbis de bove nomen habet.' Augustinus autem de hoc templo habet infra scripta eius dei, quem solum virtus in aethera sustulerit indigna, quae tamen vel ideo toleranda erunt quia deam nobis nunc primum notam efficiunt Larentinam, perpetui meretricii infamia nobilissimam. Herculius[61] aedituus otiosus atque feriatus lusit thesseris secum utraque manu alternante, in una constituens Herculem, in altera se ipsum, sub ea condictione ut si ipse vicisset, de stipendio templi cenam sibi pararet amicamque conduceret. Si autem victoria Herculis fieret, hoc idem de pecunia sua voluptati Herculis exhiberet. Deinde cum a se ipso tanquam ab Hercule victus esset, debitam cenam et nobilissimam meretricem Larentinam deo Herculi dedit. At illa, cum dormisset

Hercules, too, when he had freed Evander from fear of Cacus, 55
received a cow of bronze in a forum to commemorate the cows which he had recovered by slaying Cacus. And from this it was called the Cattle Market.[348] At this forum there was a temple built by the god himself, called the Great Altar, in that spot or quite near it where we see the church of St. George at the Velabrum is located.[349] Livy in Book II: The Great Altar was dedicated by Evander in honor of Hercules. Here took place the first from among the foreign rites that Romulus adopted.[350] Plutarch writes that when they are sacrificing to Hercules they do not mention any other of the gods by name for the reason that he is considered a demigod, or because the altar was dedicated by Evander to him alone, while he was living among mortals. They require dogs to be kept away, because Cerberus was hostile to Hercules, or because when the boy Licinius had been killed by a dog, Hercules was forced by the Ipothomates[351] to decide the issue in a battle and lost many of his friends in that fight, and his brother too.[352] Ovid says about Hercules: "There the victor sacrificed a bull to you, Jupiter. He invited Evander and the country people [to the feast] and set up for himself the altar which is called the Great here where a part of the city takes its name from an ox."[353] Augustine writes about this temple the account I quote below, unworthy of this god who alone was raised to heaven by his virtue. Nevertheless we must bear with it for the reason that now for the first time it gives us information about the goddess Larentina, notorious as a habitual prostitute. A sacristan of Hercules, when at leisure and on holiday, was playing dice with himself, first with one hand, then the other, making the one stand for Hercules, the other for himself, on condition that, if he himself won, from the temple's revenue he would treat himself to a dinner and hire a girl. But if Hercules had the victory he would offer the very same from his own savings for Hercules' pleasure. Then when he was beaten by himself, as it were by Hercules, he gave the god the dinner he

in templo, vidit in somnis Herculem sibi esse commixtum sibique dixisse quod inde discedens cui primum iuveni obvia fieret apud illum esset inventura mercedem, quam sibi illa credere deberet ab Hercule persolutam. Ac sic accidit: eunti cum primus iuvenis ditissimus Carutius occurrisset, eamque dilectam secum diutius habuisset, illa herede defunctus est. Quae amplissimam adepta pecuniam, ne divinae mercedi videretur ingrata, quod acceptissimum putavit numinibus, populum Romanum etiam ipsa scripsit heredem atque illa non comparente inventum est testamentum. Quibus meritis illam ferunt honores meruisse divinos. Sed Festus dicit Larentia esse festa Accae Larentiae, quam Aulus Gelius scribit Romuli nutricem fuisse, quae, ex duodecim filiis unum morte cum amisisset, Romulus in eius locum sese Accae Larentiae filium dedit seque et ceteros eius filios fratres Arvales appellavit, et exinde mansit collegium fratrum Arvalium numero duodecim, cuius sacerdotii insigne est spicea corona et alba infula. Et Varro scribit 'fratres Arvales dictos quod sacra publica faciunt ut fruges ferant arva.' Et Valerius tradit Accam Larentiam fuisse sepultam in Velabro, celeberrimo urbis loco.

56 Venerem minus miraremur obscenos habuisse in sacrificiis ritus nisi diceret Augustinus Romanos non erubuisse aliquando Vestam Venerem appellare, forsan ea ratione quod tres fuerunt Veneres: una virginum, quae etiam Vesta, cui puppas donasse virgines Persius poeta innuit; aliam coniugatarum, in cuius sacris Adon amatus eius apri dente extinctus deplorabatur; alia meretricum, cui Phoenices donum dabant de prostitutione filiarum, ante quam eas iungerent maritis. Habuit vero templum Veneris Erycinae dictum

owed him and the famous prostitute Larentina. When she had fallen asleep in the temple, she dreamed that Hercules had intercourse with her and said to her that when she left the place she would find her pay with the first young man she met and she should believe that Hercules had discharged it. And so it happened. As she left, the first to meet her was the very rich youth Carutius. He loved her and after keeping her with him for a long time, he died leaving her as heir. Having received a substantial fortune and in order not to seem ungrateful for the god's pay, she too made the Roman people her heir, supposing that this would be most pleasing to the gods. When she passed away, the will was found and they say for such services she earned divine honors.[354] But Festus says "the Larentia [i.e., Larentalia] are the festival of Acca Larentia,"[355] whom Aulus Gellius writes was Romulus' nurse. When she had lost one of her twelve sons, "Romulus gave himself as a son to Acca Larentia in his place and named himself and her other sons 'Arval Brethren.' From that time on the college of the Arval Brethren remained twelve in number. The emblem of this priesthood is a garland of ears of wheat and a white fillet."[356] Varro writes "they were called Arval Brethren because they perform public sacrifices so that the plow lands (*arva*) may bear crops."[357] And Valerius tells the story that Acca Larentia was buried in the Velabrum, one of the city's most public places.[358]

We would be less surprised that Venus had obscene rites in her 56
sacrifices did not Augustine tell us that the Romans were not ashamed to call Venus Vesta on occasion, perhaps for the reason that there were three Venuses: one a goddess of virgins, who is also Vesta, to whom the poet Persius implies that maidens gave dolls. Another of wives, at whose rites the death of her lover Adonis by a boar's tusk is lamented. Another of prostitutes; to her the Phoenicians used to make a gift raised from prostituting their daughters before they married them to their husbands.[359] She had the temple called of Venus of Eryx outside the Colline

extra portam Collinam nunc Salariam, ubi ingentia in vinetis fundamenta cernuntur. De quo Ovidius: 'Templa frequentari Collinae proxima portae nunc decet.' Et Veneris illius primae virginis Augustinus tale refert vidisse sacrificium: 'Ante illud delubrum, ubi simulacrum illud locatum conspiciebamus, universi undique confluentes, et ubi quisque poterat stantes, ludos qui agerentur intentissimi spectabamus, intuentes alternato conspectu hinc meretricum pompam, illinc virginem deam; illam suppliciter adorari, ante illam turpia celebrari. Num ibi pudibundos mimmos, num verecundiorem scaenicam vidimus? Cuncta obscenitatis implebantur officia, sciebatur virginali numini quid placeret, et exhibebatur quod de templo domum matrona doctior reportaret. Nonnullae prudentiores avertebant faciem ab impuris moribus scaenicorum, et artem flagitii furtiva intentione discebant.' At post impudicae et turpis deae obscenitates, deae unius rituum prudentiam ostendamus. Romae coli dicit Plinius in aede Voluppiae deam Angeroniam ore obsignato. Et Macrobius addit: 'Id a principio sic institutum fuisse, quod qui angores suos dissimulando supprimant perveniant deae beneficio ad maximam voluptatem.'

57 Ad turpes ritus redeamus. Templum fuit ante urbem conditam Iunonis Lucinae a luco dictum, in quo erat qui ab Esquiliis ad ripas Tyberis pertinebat, eoque luco Tarquinii reges in novalia purgato agrum ibi seminarium habuere, cuius segetem messi maturam populus Romanus pulso Tarquinio Superbo et regno illi abrogato in Tyberim furcis abiecit. Unde insula urbi inclusa fieri coepit, isque

Gate, now Salarian, where huge foundations are visible in the vineyards. Ovid says the following about it: "Now it is fitting that the temple nearest to the Colline Gate be filled with crowds."[360] And of that first Venus, the virgin, Augustine reports that he saw a sacrifice of the following kind: "Before that shrine, where that image was placed for us to gaze upon, we all flocked together from all sides. Standing each where he could, we would watch with the greatest attention the shows which were being performed, looking from side to side at the parade of prostitutes here and the virgin goddess there. That goddess was being humbly worshipped, in her presence her lewd rites were being celebrated. Did we see there mime actors with a sense of shame, did we see a more respectable actress? All the obligations of obscenity were fulfilled. They knew what would please the virgin goddess, and they put on a show that would send a married woman home from the temple better informed. Some, who were more discreet, kept their faces turned away from the performers' indecent behavior and learned the art of shame by paying stealthy attention."[361] But after an immodest and lewd goddess' obscenities, let us describe the good sense of one goddess' rites. Pliny says the goddess of Suffering and Silence is worshipped at Rome in the Temple of Pleasure with her mouth sealed. Macrobius adds that this was so established from the beginning because those who suppress their sufferings by concealing them attain the greatest pleasure through the favor of the goddess.[362]

Let us return to lewd rites. Before the City's foundation, there 57
was a temple of Juno Lucina named after the grove (*lucus*) where it was located, which extended from the Esquiline to the banks of the Tiber.[363] When they had cleared and plowed this grove for the first time, the Tarquin kings had there a field for sowing. After the expulsion of Tarquinius Superbus and the termination of his reign, the Roman people harvested the crop of this field when it was ripe and tossed it into the Tiber with pitchforks. This was the

campus Marti consecratus postea dictus est Campus Martius, ut non sit dubitandum id Iunonis Lucinae templum fuisse, ubi nunc est ecclesia Sancti Laurentii in Lucina. Refert vero Ovidius ei templo sacerdotem ex Lupercalibus praefuisse, ad quem cum irent mulieres concipere nequeuntes, is ante se denudatas prostratasque flagello verberans hircinis confecto pellibus, ut conciperent efficiebat. 'Monte sub Esquilio multis incaeduus annis Iunonis magnae nomine[62] lucus erat' et infra: 'Gratia Lucinae: dedit haec tibi nomina lucus. Augur erat, nomen longis intercidit annis. Ille caprum mattat, iussae sua terga puellae pellibus exsectis[63] percutienda dabant.' Eiusque moris meminit Iuvenalis: 'Condita pyxide Lydae atque nec prodest agili palmas praebere luperco.' Eademque Iuno, Iovis soror et coniunx, maiorem primariamque habuit aedem, Iovi Tarpeio proximam. Ovidius: 'Si thorus in pretio est, dicor matrona Potentis. Iunctaque Tarpeio sunt mea templa Iovi,' in qua idem fiebat qui et Iovi cultus, cum dicat Seneca contra superstitiones scribens praeter alios actus insanos fuisse per singulos dies quasdam mulieres, quae Iunonis et pariter Minervae suam ibi cellam habentis simulacris propius accendentes, et digitos ornantium modo moventes capillos earum disponere simulabant, cum aliae essent, quae tunc speculum tenentes, dearum oculis illud supponerent inspiciendum. Et Varro *De lingua Latina* dicit Iunonem, quod una cum Iove iuvat, terram esse Iunonemque Lucinam invocari, quod partus a principio ab ea in lucem editur. Cicero autem *Pro Murena* Iunoni sacra fecisse consules sic ostendit: 'Nolite a sacris Iunonis Sospitae, cui omnes consules facere necesse est, domesticum et suum consulem avellere.'

origin of the island enclosed by the city. The field dedicated to Mars was later called the Field of Mars,[364] so that it is not to be doubted that the temple of Juno Lucina was where the church of St. Laurence in Lucina now stands.[365] Indeed, Ovid tells that the priest set over the temple was one of the Luperci. Wives who could not conceive went to him and he, beating them with a whip made from goatskins as they lay naked and prostrate before him, would cause them to conceive.[366] "At the foot of the Esquiline Hill a sacred grove, uncut for many years, was called great Juno's." Ovid further on: "Thanks to Lucina! the sacred grove (*lucus*) gave you this name."[367] "There was an augur (his name has disappeared with length of years). He slaughters a he-goat. At his bidding the girls present their backs to be beaten with strips of hide."[368] Juvenal mentions this practice: "Lyde in her box of potions [does not help], nor is it of help to offer his palms to the running Lupercus."[369] The same Juno, Jupiter's sister and wife, had a bigger, main temple next to that of Tarpeian Jupiter. Ovid: "If value is put on the marriage couch, I am called wife of the Powerful. My temple is linked to that of Tarpeian Jove."[370] In her case there was carried out the same type of worship as Jupiter received, since Seneca in his work *On Superstition* says that, among other foolish activities, there were certain women who every day would go up close to the statues of Juno and Minerva (she had her shrine there) and pretend to arrange their hair, moving their fingers in the fashion of hairdressers, since there were others who then held up a mirror in front of the goddesses' eyes for them to look into.[371] Varro in *On the Latin Language* says Juno is the earth because she together with Jupiter helps (*iuvat*) and Juno is invoked as Lucina because the newborn initially is brought into the light (*lux*) by her.[372] Cicero, however, in *Defense of Murena* demonstrates as follows that the consuls sacrificed to Juno: "Do not deprive the rites of Juno the Preserver, to whom all consuls must sacrifice, of the consul who is especially her own."[373]

58 Operosum fuerit singulos deorum ritus, sicut in aliquibus supra fecimus, disctincte describere, praesertim cum tales fuerint quos non nisi erubescentes possumus scribere. Sicut M. Ciceronem vel hac una re divino virum ingenio erubuisse et suis qui extant libris se vivo per urbem Romam disseminatis indignitatem rei damnasse videmus. Nam in libro quem *De natura deorum* accuratissime scripsit haec per Q. Lucilium Balbum dialogo respondentem dicit: 'Videsne igitur ut a physicis rebus bene ac utiliter inventis ratio sit tracta ad commenticios deos, quae res genuit falsas opiniones erroresque turbulentos et superstitiones paene aniles; et formae enim deorum et aetates, vestitus ornatusque notescunt, genera, praeterea cognationes, coniugia, omniaque traducta ad consuetudinem imbecillitatis humanae. Nam et perturbatis animis inducuntur, accepimusque deorum cupiditates, aegritudines, iracundias.' Quare ad ritus alios veniemus qui totam civitatem multis diebus feriatam tenebant. Sacra fuerunt Cereris quando Proserpina eius filia ab Orco fuit rapta et paulo post inventa, quarum dearum nominis interpretationem hanc Varro *De lingua Latina* ponit: Ceres quod gerit fruges; Proserpina Luna quod ut serpens modo sit a dextris, modo a sinistris. Earumque dearum sacra licet ab Atheniensibus Eleusina a loco dicta maiore celebrarentur apparatu, Romani tamen in lunae defectu et Romae et ubicunque agerent maximo aeneorum tinnitu ea celebravere; ad cuius moris strepitum perpulchre Iuvenalis allusit cum mulierem notare volens garrulam atque contentiosam dixit: 'Una laboranti poterit succurrere Lunae.' Servatum autem extra urbem a Romanis eum morem Plutarchus in

It would be laborious to give a precise description of the rites of the gods one by one as I have done above in some cases, especially since they were such that I cannot write of them without blushing. Just as we see that Marcus Cicero, a man of divine character, especially because of just this one matter, was embarrassed by and condemned its shamefulness in books which survive and were disseminated throughout the City of Rome during his lifetime. In the book *On the Nature of the Gods* which he wrote with much care he says this through the mouth of Quintus Lucilius Balbus, a respondent in the dialogue: "Don't you see that from good and useful discoveries about nature reason has been led to adopt false gods. This state of affairs has generated false opinions, disturbing errors, and superstitions almost worthy of old women. The appearances and the ages of the gods, their dress and arms are known; furthermore, their genealogies, relationships, marriages, in short, everything has been adapted to the habits of human weakness. For they are also represented with emotional disturbances and we have heard tell of the gods' lusts, sorrows and angers."[374] So we shall come to other rites that used to keep the whole city on holiday for many days. The festival of Ceres commemorated the time when her daughter Proserpina was carried off by Orcus and found soon after. Varro in *On the Latin Language* sets down this interpretation of the goddesses' names. Ceres because she brings (*gerit*) crops.[375] The moon is called Proserpina because like a snake (*serpens*) she is now on the right hand, now on the left.[376] Though these goddesses' rites (called Eleusinian from the place where they took place) were celebrated by the Athenians with greater splendor, the Romans nevertheless during an eclipse of the moon celebrated them at Rome, or wherever they were living, by great clashing of bronze. Juvenal nicely alluded to the noise of this practice when, wishing to criticize a talkative and argumentative woman, he said, "she on her own could rescue the struggling moon."[377] Plutarch demonstrates in the *Life of Aemilius Paulus* that the 58

Vita Pauli Aemilii sic ostendit: 'Luna obscurari coepit ac, deficiente lumine multisque coloribus mutatis, tandem nusquam apparuit; Romanis, ut moris est, tinnitu aeris lumen eius revocantibus et ignes multis facibus ad caelum tollentibus nihil simile a Macedonibus factum.' 'Termino sacra fiebant quod in eius tutela fines agrorum esse putabant. Denique Numa Pompilius statuit eum qui terminum exarasset et ipsum et boves sacros esse. Terminusque quo loco colebatur super eum foramen patebat in tecto, quod nefas esse ducebant terminum intra tectum consistere.'

59 At vero aedes ipsi gentiles templaque sicut et nostri rite consecrantes augusta appellavere. Unde vult Ovidius Augustum fuisse dictum quasi rite a populo sacerdotibusque dicatum, eademque ab origine auguria sunt dicta quasi ea Iupiter manu sua dare et augere sit visus. Is vero augurandi mos latam in urbe Romana habuit provinciam, ut augures tanto praeficiendi sacerdotio ex maioribus praestantioribusque urbis deligi consueverint. Unde gloriatur in *Bruto* M. Cicero se a Q. Hortensio, viro clarissimo, in collegium augurum fuisse cooptatum, et Q. Mucium Scaevolam augurem videmus inter primarios omnium aetatum viros connumerari, quem in templo Vestae, quo nihil in urbe Roma habitum est sanctius, aram ipsam amplexantem Syllae carnifices interfecerunt, cuius sanguine ignis ille virginum cura perpetuus paene fuit extinctus. Eratque, sicut Paulus Aemilius dicere fuit solitus, summa eius sacerdotii potestas, quod nec senatus cogi, nec conveniendi locum habere poterat, nisi quando et ubi augures praescripsissent. Locum

Romans maintained this practice outside the city: "The moon began to grow dark, losing its light and undergoing many changes of color, and finally disappeared. The Romans, as is their practice, called her light back by clashing bronze and raising the fires of many torches to the sky, but the Macedonians did nothing of this kind."[378] "Sacrifices were made to Terminus because they thought the boundaries of the fields were under his protection. Finally Numa Pompilius decreed that if anyone dislodged a boundary stone while plowing both he himself and his oxen would be forfeited to the god. The place where Terminus was worshipped had a hole kept open in the roof above the god because it was considered sacrilege to set up Terminus within a roofed structure."[379]

Indeed the Gentiles themselves, duly consecrating, as we do, 59
the gods' dwellings and temples, called them "august." For this reason Ovid maintains Augustus was so-called as if duly dedicated by the people and priests and from the same root comes the word auguries, as though Jupiter has been seen to give and augment (*augere*) them[380] with his own hand. Indeed this practice of taking the auguries held wide sway in the City of Rome, so that the augurs used to be selected for so important a priestly duty from the city's more important and eminent men. For this reason Marcus Cicero in *Brutus* takes pride in the fact that he was co-opted into the college of augurs by the illustrious Quintus Hortensius.[381] And we see that Quintus Mucius Scaevola, the augur, is numbered among the leading men of all ages, he whom Sulla's butchers killed as he clung to the altar in the Temple of Vesta—no place in the City of Rome was considered holier than this. His blood almost extinguished that flame kept eternal by the Virgins' care.[382] The power of this priesthood was supreme, as Aemilius Paulus used to say, because the senate could not be convened nor could it have a place to meet except when and where the augurs had prescribed.[383] I have shown that the place for taking the auguries was

vero inaugurandi ostendimus fuisse in curia veteri, ubi nunc Sancti Petri ad vincula est ecclesia, quam titulo cardinalatus nunc obtinet vir summus Nicolaus de Cusa, Germania oriundus, philosophia theologiaque egregie et mathematicis eloquentiaque eximie ornatus, licet aliquando alibi inaugurarentur. Nam Festus Pompeius 'tesca' vel 'tesqua' dicit esse loca augurio designata, et 'posimirium'[64] esse pontificale pomerium ubi pontifices auspicabantur.

60 Artem vero inaugurandi ab ipsis servatam facile ostendere possemus, nisi fomentum addere vereremur quorundam ex nostris insaniae, qui nimium auguriis credere videntur, ut mustelae occursum, bestiolae omnium mundissimae et homini amicissimae, ut corvi crocitatum, noctuae ac bubonis cantum territi expavescant. Melius Cicero, qui Nonio optimam spem habere licere dicenti quod septem aquilae in castris Pompeii essent captae, inquit: 'Recte moneres si adversus picas nobis pugnandum foret.' Et non insulse consul ille qui pullarios nuntiantes pullos non addicentes sacris pasci nolle iussit illos ut biberent proici in profluentem. Et Labieno, in castris Pompeii divinationibus auguriisque innixo, dicenti Pompeium superaturum deridens respondit Cicero eos hac spe ductos castra nuper amisisse. Sed omnium maxime graviter et vere sensit doctissimus Varro, qui deos dixit otiosos et feriatos fore si sua consilia corniculae crederent aut corvo hominibus indicanda. Et tamen ut levitatem eorum arguamus, qui se avium volatui aut occentui committunt, augurandi particulam ex Varrone docebimus. Augures cum se in supremam curiae veteris partem recepissent, vestem induti sacerdotalem, lituum, quae virga erat manu tenentes elevata, spatium in caeli ambitu quem prospicerent designabant. 'Idque templum appellavere, quod tribus modis dicitur:

in the Old Meetinghouse where the church of St. Peter in Chains now stands[384] (its titular cardinal is now Nicholas of Cusa,[385] a very distinguished man, German in origin, exceptionally graced with theology, philosophy, mathematics and eloquence), though sometimes the auguries were taken elsewhere, for Festus Pompeius says *tesca* or *tesqua* are places marked out for the taking of auguries[386] and *posimirium* is the pontifical *pomerium* where the pontiffs took the auspices.[387]

60 I could easily describe the art of taking the auguries kept up by them, did I not shrink from adding fuel to the madness of some among us who seem to give too much credence to auguries so that they are in fear and dread of chancing upon a weasel, the cleanest of all little animals and the most friendly to mankind, or of the croaking of a raven and the song of a night owl. Better is Cicero. When Nonnius said they could have the highest hope because seven eagles had been captured in Pompey's camp, he said, "Your advice would be good, if we were going to have to fight against magpies."[388] And that consul was no fool who, when the chicken-keepers told him that the chickens were not giving good omens and refusing to eat, ordered them to be thrown into running water so that they might drink.[389] When in Pompey's camp Labienus, relying on divination and auguries, said that Pompey would be victorious, Cicero replied derisively that led on by this hope they had just lost the camp.[390] The most learned Varro has the most weighty and true opinion of all. He said that the gods would have nothing to do and be on holiday if they entrusted a crow or a raven to communicate their decisions to men.[391] Nevertheless to prove the frivolity of those who put themselves under the protection of the flight or song of birds, I shall expound a short section from Varro on the taking of auguries. When the augurs had withdrawn into the uppermost part of the Old Meetinghouse, dressed in priests' garb, holding with raised hand the augur's staff (*lituus*), which was a rod, they would mark out the circumference of an

a natura, ab auspicando, a similitudine, in caelo qua attuimur[65] templum; id quatuor modis: sinistra ab oriente, dextra ab occasu, antica ad meridiem, postica ad septentrionem. In terris dictum templum locus augurii intra fines qua oculi conspiciunt, idest intuemur[66] a quo templum.' Et de littuo sic habet Livius in primo: Numa Pompilius augurio creatus rex. 'Inde ab augure, cui deinde honoris gratia publicum id sacerdotium perpetuum fuit, deductus in arcem in lapide ad meridiem versus consedit. Augur ad laevam eius capite velato sedem[67] cepit, dextra manu baculum sine nodo aduncum tenens, quem littuum appellarunt, regiones ab oriente ad occasum determinavit, dextras ad meridiem partes, laevas ad septentrionem.' Oculis enim intentissimis[68] aves augurium facientes—nam aliquae nullius erant augurii—sinistrorsumne an dextrorsum, et canentesne an tacite advolarent, diligenter observabant, bonum inde aut malum futurae quam animo meditarentur rei ex eorum disciplina vel potius insipientia elicientes. Nec movere debebit quenquam quod multi scripserunt occentum soricis Fabio Maximo dictaturam abstulisse, cum id potius augurum invidia sit factum dictaturam alteri cupientium demandari, aut quod Livius in primo refert, si Attius Navius quia cotem novacula discidit, auguriis sacerdotioque tantus honos accessit, ut nihil belli domique postea inauspicato fieret, consilia populi, exercitus vocati, summa rerum, ubi aves non addixissent, dirimebantur. Profecto enim id fuit quod Augustinus in *Civitate Dei* dixit scripsisse Porphirium a daemonibus fuisse divinationes augurum, aruspicum, vatum atque somniorum et miracula magorum.

area in the sky to watch. "This they called a *templum;* the word is used in three ways: from nature, from taking the auspices, from a likeness. Where we look at it in the sky [it was called] a *templum.* It has four parts: left on the east, right on the west, front toward the south, back toward the north. On the earth what is called a *templum* is a place for augury within borders where the eyes view, that is, look (*tueri*), from which comes the word *templum.*"[392] Livy in Book I says the following about the staff. Numa Pompilius was appointed king by means of augury. "Accordingly an augur, who was subsequently honored with this public priesthood in perpetuity, escorted him to the citadel where he took his seat on a stone facing the south. The augur with his head veiled sat on his left, holding in his right hand the crooked staff free from knots, which they called a *lituus,* and he fixed the boundary lines from east to west, the right quarters to the south, the left to the north."[393] With eyes concentrated they would carefully observe the birds that give an augury (for some are of no augural significance) whether they flew to the left or the right, and whether they sang or were silent, thence eliciting in accordance with their doctrine, or rather their folly, good or bad for the future event they were pondering. Nor should it influence anyone that many wrote that a shrew mouse's cry robbed Fabius Maximus of the dictatorship,[394] since it happened rather by the augurs' ill will that the dictatorship was entrusted to the other of the two candidates. Or Livy's account in Book I: If, because Attius Navius cut a whetstone with a razor, "such great honor accrued to the auguries and the priesthood, that after that nothing might be done in war or domestic affairs without the sanctions of the auspices, public meetings, callings up of armies and the weightiest affairs were put off when the birds had not given their assent."[395] To be sure this was the reason why Augustine said in *City of God* that Porphyry wrote that the predictions of augurs, soothsayers, prophets and dreams and the miracles of sorcerers were owing to demons.[396]

61 Multa igitur de augurum disciplina et auguriis iterato dicturi ab eo incipiemus, quod nostris hominibus, ne hanc extimescant vanitatem, plurimum prodesse debebit. Plinium scilicet scribere in augurum disciplina fuisse nulla auspicia pertinere ad eos qui ingredientes observare ea neglexerint. Et ne in primario eiusmodi rerum verbo erretur Nonius Marcellus docet 'auspicium esse avium inspectionem, augurium rerum omnium coniecturam.' Livius in decimo: rogatio promulgata ut, cum quatuor augures, quatuor pontifices tunc essent, placeret augeri sacerdotum numerum, et quatuor pontifices, quinque sacerdotes de plebe omnes legerentur. Inter augures enim constat imparem numerum debere esse, vocatae tribus ingenti consensu accepta est rogatio. Ita octo pontificum, novem augurum numerus factus. Et XXVII Livius: 'In locum M. Marcelli L. Aquilius Paetus augur creatus inauguratusque.' Cicero in *Legibus* sacerdotum genera duo esse dicit: 'unum quod praesit caerimoniis et sacris, alterum quod interpretetur fatidicorum et vatum effata incognita, quorum causa S. P. Q. R. asciverit. Interpretes autem Iovis Optimi Maximi publici augures signis et auspiciis postea vidento, disciplinam tenento, sacerdotesque vineta, virgeta et salicta publica auguranto, quique agent rem duelli, quique populare auspicium praemonento, ollique obtemperanto, divorumque iras providento, hisque parento, caelique fulgura regionibus ratis denotanto, urbemque et templa et agros liberata et

Therefore, as I am going to say much about the augurs' doctrine and the auguries, I shall begin by repeating the point that it should be greatly to the good of our contemporaries not to fear this deception. To be sure, Pliny writes that it was the case in the augurs' doctrine that no auspices affected those people who, when they were embarking on something, had not troubled to observe them,[397] and, so that no mistake is made as to the chief term in matters of this kind, Nonius Marcellus informs us that "*auspicium* was the observation of birds, *augurium* the interpretation of all things."[398] Livy in Book X: A law was proposed that, since there were then four augurs and four pontiffs and it was decided to increase the number of priests, they should choose four pontiffs and five augurs, all from the plebeians. For it is agreed among the augurs that their number should be uneven. The tribes were summoned and the law was passed with massive agreement. Thus the number of the pontiffs became eight and of the augurs nine.[399] Livy in Book XXVII: "In place of Marcus Marcellus, Lucius Aquilius Paetus was elected and installed as augur."[400] Cicero in *On the Laws* says there are two kinds of priests, "one to be in charge of ceremonies and sacrifices, the other to interpret the unfamiliar utterances of soothsayers and prophets, for the sake of which the Senate and People of Rome has approved. The interpreters of Jupiter Best and Greatest, the public augurs, should afterward see with signs and auspices, and maintain their doctrine. And the priests perform the augural ceremony in regard to the vineyards and osier thickets and public willow plantations. And they should give prior advice of an omen to those who manage warfare and those who manage the people's business, and they shall obey and they shall foresee the gods' angry signs and give heed to them and take note of lightning flashes from heaven by means of ratified regions, and keep the city and *templa* and fields liberated and demarcated. And whatever the augurs shall declare to be unalterably 61

effata[69] habento. Quaeque augures iniusta, nefasta, vitiosa, dira defixerint, irrita infectaque sunto, quique non paruerit capitale esto.' 'Quid vero maius si de iure quaerimus quam posse a summis imperiis, a summis potestatibus comitia tollere, consilia vel instituta dimittere, vel habita repudiare? Quid gravius quam rem susceptam dirimi si unus augur aliter dixerit? Quid magnificentius quam posse discernere ut magistratu se abdicent consules? Quid religiosius quam cum populo, cum plebe agendi ius dare, aut non dare? Quid legem si non iure rogata sit tollere?' 'Iam vero permultorum exemplorum et nostra est plena res publica et omnia regna omnes populi, cunctaeque gentes, quam augurum praedictis multa incredibiliter vera cecidisse viderunt.' 'Omnes magistratus auspicium iudiciumque habento, ex iis quae senatus esto, eius decreta rata sunto.' 'Omnibus magistratibus auspicia dantur et iudicia, ut esset populi potestas ad quem provocatur, auspicia, ut multos inutiles conatus impedirent mora. Saepe enim populi impetum iniustum auspiciis dii immortales represserunt. Auspicia servanto, auguri parento.

62 'Est autem boni auguris meminisse maximis rei publice temporibus praesto esse debere, Iovique Optimo Maximo se consiliarium atque administrum datum.' Et M. Varro: 'Augur consuli adest tum cum exercitus imperatur ac praeit quid eum dicere oporteat.' Cicero *Philippicorum* secundo: 'Quo enim tempore me

unjust, unlawful, contrary to the auspices, ill-omened, these things must be void and invalid. He who does not obey them is to be punished by death."[401] "Indeed, if we are discussing their legal rights what is greater than to be able to remove the assemblies from the magistrates with the highest authority, from the highest powers, to adjourn councils even when they have begun, or to repudiate them once held? What more important than for business that has been undertaken to be broken off, if a single augur has said otherwise? What more splendid than to be able to determine that consuls resign from their magistracy? What more full of religious awe than to give or withhold the right of convoking the plebeian or popular assemblies? What than abrogating a law, if it has not been passed with favorable auspices?"[402] "Indeed not only is our commonwealth full of numerous examples but all kingdoms, all peoples and all races have seen how many things turn out true in an unbelievable fashion in accordance with the augurs' predictions."[403] "All magistrates are to have the right of taking the auspices and to have jurisdiction, and the senate shall consist of these. Its decrees shall have legal validity."[404] "Rights of taking the auspices and the power of jurisdiction are given to all magistrates: jurisdiction so that there is a power of the people to whom appeal may be made, and rights of taking the auspices so that they may block many useless attempts by delay. The immortal gods have often checked an unjust impulse of the people by means of the auspices."[405] "They shall observe the auspices, they shall obey the augur.

"It is the duty of a good augur to remember that he should be 62
of service in the greatest crises of the commonwealth, that he has been appointed as an adviser and assistant to Jupiter Best and Greatest."[406] Marcus Varro: "the augur is present with the consul at the time when the army is summoned and says in advance what he is to say."[407] Cicero in the second *Philippic*: "At the time

augurem a toto collegio expetitum Gn. Pompeius et Q. Hortensius ⟨nominaverunt⟩, neque enim licebat a pluribus nominari.' Festus Pompeius scribit quinque genera signorum observasse augures ex caelo, ex avibus, ex bipedibus, ex quadrupedibus, ex diris.[70] Alites volatu auspicium facientes istae putabantur: buteo,[71] sanqualis,[72] inmusulus,[73] aquila, vulturius,[74] inebrae[75] aves quae in auguriis aliquid fieri prohibebant. Oscinum augurium a cantu avium, oscines aves auspicium ore facientes; supervaganea dicebatur ab auguribus avis quae ex summo cacumine vocem emisisset, dicta ita quod omnia supra vagatur aut canit. Puls potissimum dabatur pullis in auspiciis, quia ex ea necesse erat aliquid decidere quod tripudium faceret, id est terripuvium:[76] puvire[77] enim ferire est. Bonum enim augurium esse putabant, si pulli per quos auspicabantur comedissent, praesertim si eis edentibus aliquid ab ore decidisset, sin autem omnino non edissent, arbitrabantur periculum imminere. Plutarchus in *Problematibus:* 'Metellus pontifex maximus, prudens et civilis, post sextilem mensem Augustum vetuit auspicari, quod adultis et perfectis avibus auspicando antequam aestas advenerit sit prudentiae. Autumno autem aves partim inutiles sunt, partim morbidae, partim pulli imperfecti, et aliquae propter anni tempus alio devolant.' Et idem: 'Qui prius auspices nunc augures in captandis auguriis luminaria semper accensa etiam interdiu habere voluerunt, ut scilicet an ventus esset intelligerent, quo prohibente aves dubiae et perplexae volant, nec aliquid certi cursus ostendere possunt, sed cum flamma cernitur recta et constans de avium quieto volatu iudicant.' Et infra: 'In auguriis

that Gnaeus Pompeius and Quintus Hortensius nominated me as augur at the request of the whole college (for nomination by more was not permitted)."[408] Festus Pompeius writes that "augurs observed five kinds of signs: from the sky, from birds, from bipeds, from quadrupeds, from ill-boding events."[409] "Birds that give a sign by their flight were thought to be the following: buzzard, *sanqualis, inmusulus,* eagle, vulture."[410] "From among birds those were called 'restraining that stopped something being done when the auguries were taken.'"[411] "*Oscinum* is an augury from the song of a bird." "*Oscines* are birds that give a sign from their song."[412] "A bird which uttered a call from the topmost point was called *supervaganea* by the augurs, and it is so-called because it roams or sings above everything (*supra vagatur*)."[413] "In the taking of the auspices pulse porridge especially was given to chickens because a bit of it would have to fall to make the *tripudium,* that is *terripuvium,* for *puvire* is 'to strike.' They considered it a good omen if the chickens they were using to take the auspices ate greedily, especially if a part fell from their beak while they were eating. But if they did not eat at all they thought danger was threatening."[414] Plutarch in *Problems:* When Metellus, a wise and good statesman, was Chief Pontiff, he did not allow the auspices to be taken after the month of *Sextilis* (August) because it is wise to take the auspices from full-grown and perfect birds before summer has come. In autumn birds are partly useless, partly sick, partly ungrown chicks, and some migrate because of the time of year.[415] The same author: They required that those who were once called *auspices,* now *augures,* always keep lamps alight even during the day when the auguries were being taken, so that they might realize if there was a wind. The birds' flight is unsure and confused if a wind impedes them and their flight paths cannot display anything definite. But when the flame is seen upright and constant they can make determinations from the birds' undisturbed flying.[416] And further on: In taking of the auguries they made much use of the vulture, because

vulture plurimum utuntur, quia Romulo in condenda urbe XII apparuerunt vel quia, ut ait Herodotus, vultur nemini nocet animali, quae nisi cadavera comedit, nec aves mortuas attingit, et quod vultures omnes feminae Zephiro, ut arbores, impregnantur unde purior ceteris avibus.' Item augures, si ulcus haberent, augurandi causa sedere prohibebantur, quia integros et sanos corpore et mente eos esse oportet qui sacra peragunt. Ceteris sacerdotibus, simul ac ad iudicium ducti ac damnati sunt, alium substituunt, augurem vero donec vita suppetat, licet maximorum criminum convictum, sacerdotio non multant, quia non honoris nec magistratus, sed scientiae atque artis cuiusdam potius nomen est augur, quae non potest auferri, sicut nec medico medicina ars, nec musico cantandi peritia. Alium vero non istituunt, quod sacerdotum numerum ab initio constitutum merito tuentur.

63 'Caduca auspicia dicunt cum aliquid in templo excidit. Clivia auspicia dicebant quae aliquid fieri prohibebant; omnia enim difficilia clivia, unde et clivi loca ardua. Pedestria auspicia arbitrantur, quae dabantur a vulpe, lupo, serpente, equo ceterisque animalibus quadrupedibus. Piacularia auspicia arbitrabantur quae sacrificantibus tristia portendebant cum aut hostia ab ara aufugisset, aut percussa mugitum dedisset, aut in aliam partem corporis, quam oporteret, cecidisset. Pestifera auspicia cum cor in extis, aut caput in iocinere non fuisset. Praepetes aves dicuntur quae se ante auspicantem ferunt. Nam praepetere dicebant anteire.' Et Plinius aves edocet auspiciis adhibendas. Cornices sunt inauspicatae garrulitatis; corvi in auspiciis soli videntur intellectum habere significationum suarum, pessima eorum significatio cum glutiunt vocem

twelve appeared to Romulus at the founding of Rome or because, as Herodotus says, the vulture harms no living thing—it eats only dead bodies and does not touch dead birds—and because vultures, being all female, are impregnated by the west wind like the trees. For this reason it is purer than all the other birds.[417] Again, if augurs have a sore they are forbidden to sit to take the auguries because those who deal with divine matters must be whole and healthy in body and mind.[418] For all other priests the minute they are taken to court or condemned they provide a substitute, but they do not deprive an augur of his priesthood during his lifetime, even if he has been convicted of the most heinous charges. This is because "augur" is a name not of an office or a magistracy but rather of a particular knowledge or skill, which cannot be taken away, just as a doctor cannot be deprived of his medical skill or a musician of the knowledge of how to sing. They do not appoint another because they rightly keep to the number of priests determined at the beginning.[419]

"Auspices are called 'fallen' (*caduca*) when something has been 63
dropped in the *templum*.[420] They called auspices 'preventive' (*clivia*) which stopped something being done. For all difficult things are preventive. For this reason steep slopes are called *clivi*."[421] "They considered auspices 'pedestrian' that were given by a fox, a wolf, a snake, a horse and the other four-footed animals. They considered auspices as 'requiring expiation' which predicted unhappy outcomes for those offering the sacrifice, such as when the victim escaped from the altar or bellowed when struck or fell on the wrong side of the body. They said auspices were 'baleful' when there was no heart in the entrails or head in the liver. Birds are called 'flying before' (*praepetes*) that present themselves in front of the man taking the auspices, for they said 'to go in front' was *praepetere*."[422] Pliny too gives information about the birds to be used for taking auspices. Crows' "chattering is unlucky." "In auspices ravens alone seem to have an understanding of their own prognostications." "It

velut strangulati. Bubo funebris et maxime abhorrens publicis praecipue auspiciis deserta incolit. Itaque in urbibus aut omnino in luce visus dirum ostentum est. Privatorum domibus insidere scio non fuisse feralem. Capitolii cellam intravit propter quod urbs lustrata. Anser pervigil Capitolium servavit a Gallis. Gallinae nigrae digitis imparibus ad rem divinam idoneae. Est inter aves ardeolarum genus, quos leucos vocant, altero oculo carere tradunt, optimi augurii cum ad Austrum volant. Solvi enim pericula metusque Nigidius ait. Galli gallinacei 'horum sunt tripudia solistima.[78] Hi magistratus nostros quotidie regunt, domosque ipsi suas claudunt ac reserant. Hi fasces Romanos impellunt aut retinent, iubent acies ac prohibent, victoriarum toto orbe partarum auspices. Hi maxime terrarum imperio imperitant.' Similem vero huic verborum levitatem prior Plinio Livius in quinto dixit: 'Auspiciis hanc urbem conditam esse, auspiciis bello ac pace, domi, militiae, omnia geri quis est qui ignoret? Quid enim est si pulli non pascentur? Si ex caveis tardius exierint? Si ocecinerit[79] avis? Parva sunt haec, sed parva ista non contemnendo maiores nostri maximam rem hanc fecerunt.' Et libro nono: 'L. Papirius dictator a pullario monitus ad auspicium repetendum Romam profectus.' Item decimo: 'Papirius Cursor consul pullarium in auspicium immittit, et, cum pulli non pascerentur, pullarius auspicia mentiri ausus, tripudium solistinum consuli nuntiavit. Locatus in prima acie qui mentitus fuerat interfectus est. Consul "dii in proelio sunt—inquit—habet poenam noxium caput ante consulem." Hoc dicente consule, cor-

is a very bad omen when they swallow their cry as if they have been strangled." "The eagle-owl is funereal and the most averse, especially in public auspices; it lives in uninhabited places. Therefore when it is seen in cities or in any case by daylight it is a disastrous portent. I know of its sitting on the houses of private people without fatal consequences. It went into the inner sanctum of the Capitol and on this account the city was purified."[423] The vigilant goose saved the Capitol from the Gauls.[424] Black hens with unevenly numbered claws are suitable for sacrifice.[425] Among birds is a species of "heron, called 'white.' They are said to have one eye missing and be an excellent omen when they fly southwards. For danger and fear are removed, Nigidius" says.[426] Domestic fowl. "Their omens are *tripudia solistima*. They control our magistrates from day to day and open or shut their houses. They set in motion or restrain the Roman fasces, command or prevent battle formation, being the auspices of victories won over the whole world. They hold the greatest dominion over the dominion of the world."[427] Before Pliny, Livy in Book V said some equally frivolous words: "Who is there who does not know that this city was founded under the auspices, that everything in war and peace, at home and in the field is carried out under the auspices?" "What does it matter if the chickens do not feed? If they are too slow to come out of their cages, if a bird has given a call? These are trivialities, but by not despising these trivialities our ancestors made this commonwealth very great."[428] In Book IX: "Lucius Papirius when dictator was warned by the chicken-keeper and set out for Rome to take the auspices again."[429] Again in Book X: Papirius Cursor when consul "sent the chicken-keeper for an omen" and "since the chickens were not feeding the chicken-keeper dared to falsify the omens and he reported to the consul a perfect omen from feeding." He who had falsified the omen was placed in the front line and was killed. "'The gods are present in the battle,' the consul said, 'The guilty party has been punished before the con-

vus clara voce occinuit.' Unde et ipse Cicero oratione *In Catilinam* tertia hanc fatuitatum disciplinam laudibus effert: 'Auruspices ex Etruria iidem iusserunt simulacrum Iovis facere maximum et in excelsum contra atque fuerat ad orientem collocare, ac se sperare dixerunt, si illud signum, quod videtis, Solis ortum et forum curiamque conspiceret, fore ut ea consilia quae clam essent patefierent.' Et *De haruspicum responsis* idem Cicero: 'Quanta maiorum nostrorum fuerit sapientia perspicere possunt qui statas solemnesque caerimonias pontificum rerum bene gerendarum auctoritate, augurum, fatorum, veteri praedicatione Apollinis, vatum libris et portentorum explanationis Etruscorum disciplina contineri putarunt.'

64 Unde Ciceronis sententiam secuti sunt posteri, quod Flavius Vopiscus in Aureliani principis rebus gestis sic ostendit: 'Die tertia iduum Ianuarii Fulvius Sabinus praetor urbanus dixit: "Referimus ad vos, patres conscripti, pontificum suggestionem et Aureliani principis litteras, quibus iubet ut inspiciantur fatales libri, quibus spes belli terminandi sacrato deorum animo continetur. Scitis enim ipsi, quotienscunque gravior extitit aliquis motus, eos semper inspectos, neque prius mala publice esse finita quam ex iis sacrificiorum processit auctoritas." Tunc surrexit primae sententiae Ulpius Sillanus atque ita locutus est: "Sero nimis de re publica pontifices retulerunt, qui puri, qui mundi, qui sancti, qui vestitu animisque sanctis sunt, Commodi templum ascendite. Subsellia laureata consternite. Veteranis manibus libros evolvite. Varia rei publicae quae sunt aeterna perquirite. Patrimis matrimisque pueris carmen indicite. Nos sumptum sacris, nos apparatum sacrificiis,

sul.' As he said this, a raven gave a loud call."[430] For this reason even Cicero himself in the third speech *Against Catiline* lauds this doctrine based on stupidities. "The same soothsayers from Etruria told them to make a very large statue of Jupiter and put it in a high place facing east, contrary to how it had been before, and they said that they hoped that if that statue, which you now behold, looked upon the sunrise and the Forum and the Senate house, those designs that were secret would be brought to light."[431] Cicero too in *On the Responses of the Haruspices*: "They can discern how great was our ancestors' wisdom, for they thought the fixed and regular ceremonies were preserved by the authority of good management of the pontiffs, in the augurs' predictions, in Apollo's ancient prophecy, in the soothsayers' books and the Etruscans' doctrine of explaining portents."[432]

For this reason later authors adhered to Cicero's opinion, as 64
Flavius Vopiscus shows in the *History* of the emperor Aurelian, as follows: "On the third day before the Ides of January, Fulvius Sabinus, the city praetor, said, 'We put before you, conscript fathers, the pontiffs' recommendation and a letter from the emperor Aurelian in which he orders that the Books of Fate be consulted. In them is contained by the gods' holy will our hope of bringing the war to an end. For you yourselves know that, whenever some serious disturbance has arisen, they were always consulted and that the ills were not publicly brought to an end until the command to make sacrifice issued from them.' Then Ulpius Silanus, who had the right to give his view first, got up and spoke as follows: 'Much too late have the pontiffs made a proposition about the commonwealth: you who are pure, clean, holy, hallowed in dress and spirit, go to the Temple of Commodus. Spread the benches decked with laurel. Unroll the books with experienced hands. Search out the various matters of the state which are eternal. Prescribe a song for the children with living fathers and mothers. We shall decree expenses for the divine rites, equipment for the sacrifices,

nos aris tumultuarias indicemus hostias." Haec interrogati plerique senatores sententias dixerunt. Itum est deinde ad templum, inspecti libri, proditi versus, lustrata urbs, cantata carmina, amburbium celebratum, amburbana promissa, atque ita solemnitas quo iubebatur modo expleta est.' Litterae autem, quas supra Fulvius Aurelianum scripsisse dicit, fuerunt hae: 'Aurelianus Augustus senatui amplissimo salutem. Miror vos, patres conscripti, tamdiu de aperiendis libris Sibyllinis dubitasse, proinde quasi in Christianorum ecclesia non in templo deorum omnium tractetis. Agite igitur et castimonia pontificum caerimoniisque solemnibus iuvate principem necessitate publica laborantem. Inspiciantur libri, quae facienda sunt celebrentur.' Profuit tamen multis in rebus Romanum hunc principem religionis cultum servantem deos timuisse. Nam, cum vetus Apollonius Thianeus philosophus ipsi Aureliano desolationem Thianae meditanti sic dixisset: 'Aureliane, si vis vincere, nihil est quod de civium meorum nece cogites. Aureliane, si vis imperare, a cruore innocentium abstine. Aureliane, clementer te ages, si vis vincere,' urbem ille liquit intactam.

65 Sed iam aliquos particulares videamus effectus quos ab auguriis provenisse dixerunt. Plinius: 'Siculo bello ambulante in litore Augusto, piscis e mari ad pedes eius exiliit. Quo argumento vates respondere Neptumnum patrem adoptantem eum sibi Sextum Pompeium repudiasse.' Et infra: 'Picus Martius in capite praetoris urbani Lucii Tuberonis[80] in foro iura pro tribunali reddentis sedit ita placide, ut manu praehenderetur. Respondere vates exi-

hastily procured victims for the altars.'"[433] "A number of senators were asked and spoke their opinions." "Then they went to the temple, the books were inspected, the verses made known, the city purified, the songs sung, the expiatory procession (*amburbium*) performed, the Amburbana [Ambarvalia] promised and the ceremony was completed in the way it was ordered."[434] The letter that Fulvius says above that Aurelian wrote was as follows: "Aurelianus Augustus sends greetings to the most splendid senate. 'Senators, I am surprised that you have hesitated for so long about opening the Sibylline books, as though you were deliberating in a Christian church and not in the temple of all the gods. Come, then, and by the pontiffs' purity and by the solemn ceremonies give aid to your emperor since he is hard pressed by a public crisis. Let the books be consulted; let what needs be done be performed.'"[435] In many matters this Roman emperor, nevertheless, benefited from maintaining religious observance and fearing the gods. When Aurelian was contemplating the destruction of Tyana Apollonius of Tyana, a philosopher of the old school, said: "'Aurelian, if you wish to conquer, there is no reason why you should plan to slaughter my fellow citizens. Aurelian, if you wish to rule, abstain from the blood of innocents. Aurelian, you will conduct yourself with mercy, if you wish to conquer,'" he left the city intact.[436]

Now let us consider some specific successes which they attrib- 65
ute to the auguries. Pliny: "During the Sicilian war, when Augustus was walking beside the shore, a fish leaped out of the sea at his feet. On the basis of this the soothsayers gave the response that Father Neptune, adopting him as his own, had cast off Sextus Pompeius."[437] Further on: A woodpecker, Mars' Bird, "sat so quietly on the head of the city praetor, Lucius Tubero, when he was handing down judgment in the forum from the tribunal, that it could be grasped by a hand. The soothsayers predicted that if it

tium imperio portendi si occideretur, at si dimitteretur, praetori.' Dimissa est. Et praetor brevi mortuus prodigium implevit. Gallinam cum lauri ramusculo cecidisse in sinum Liviae Drusillae, quae fuit imperatrix, et hucusque servatum ut ex ea lauro imperatores fuerint laureati.

66 Fuerunt quoque minores auguribus subditi sacerdotes 'estispices,' quos ab inspiciendis extis dixerunt. Omentis enim extisque et fibris animalium sua inspectis disciplina futura hominibus praedicebant, eosque sic descripsisse Virgilium supra ostendimus: 'Pecorumque reclusis pectoribus inhians spirantia consulit exta.' Cuius insaniae ab historicis poetisque infinita sumi possent exempla, ex quibus nonnulla ponemus. 'Syllae cuius tempora' sicut inquit Augustinus 'talia fuerunt ut superiora, quorum vindex esse videbatur, illius comparatione quaererentur. Cum primum ad urbem contra Marium castra movit, adeo laeta exta immolanti fuisse scribit Livius ut custodiri se Postumius aruspex voluerit capitis supplicium subiturus, nisi ea quae in animo Sylla haberet diis iuvantibus implevisset.' Et Suetonius de Caesare dicit, cum somniasset se matri struprum intulisse, coniectores eum ad amplissimam spem incitavisse. Sed et Cornelius Tacitus de Vespasiano scribit: 'Iudaeam inter Syriamque Carmelus est. Ita montem vocant. Sacrificanti in eo Vespasiano, cum spes occultas animo versaret, Basilides sacerdos inspectis extis "quicquid est"—inquit—"Vespasiane, quod paras, sive domum extruere, sive prolatare agros, sive ampliare servitia, datur tibi magna sedes ingentis termini."'

were killed, it presaged the empire's doom, but if it were let go, that of the praetor." It was let go and the praetor's death soon after fulfilled the omen.[438] A hen carrying a bay twig fell into Livia Drusilla's lap. She was empress and to the present day the custom has persisted that emperors should be crowned with bay from that tree.[439]

There were also the inspectors of entrails (*extispices*), lesser 66
priests under the authority of the augurs. Their name came from the inspecting of entrails (*extis*),[440] for when, using their doctrine, they had inspected the bowels, innards and entrails of animals, they predicted things that would happen to people in the future. I have shown above that Vergil described them as follows: "poring over the opened breasts of the sheep, she consults the entrails still palpitating with life."[441] I could have taken an infinite number of examples of this folly from the historians and poets. I shall set down some of them. "Sulla's times were such," as Augustine says, "that the preceding period, of which he seemed to be the avenger, was thought preferable in comparison with his. Livy writes that when Sulla first moved camp toward the city to attack Marius, he performed a sacrifice and the entrails were so auspicious that Postumius the diviner said he was willing to be imprisoned under sentence of death if Sulla did not accomplish his intentions with the gods' help."[442] Suetonius said that when Caesar had dreamed that he raped his mother, the interpreters spurred him on to the highest of hopes.[443] Cornelius Tacitus writes about Vespasian: "Between Judea and Syria is Carmel, for so they call the mountain." "When Vespasian was sacrificing on it and pondering secret hopes in his heart, Basilides the priest consulted the entrails and said 'Vespasian, whatever it is that you are planning, whether to build a house, enlarge your estate, or increase the number of your slaves, a great dwelling place of limitless boundary is given to you.'"[444] This was fulfilled when he was elevated to the imperial

Quod ad imperium evectus implevit. Sed unica M. Varronis quam praemisimus respondeat sententia: non solum otiosos, sed sordidissimos fuisse deos, si in iecorum, [iocinerum] et viscerum sterquilinio sua occuluerunt consilia, hominibus ab insanis sacerdotibus manifestanda. Ut optabilius fuerit valuisse apud maiores Ciceronis *Pro A. Cluentio* sententiam: 'pietate et religione et iustis precibus deorum mentes non contaminata superstitione, neque ad scelus perficiendum caesis hostiis posse placari.' Ubi enim fuisse deos alibi quam in stercore existimabimus, quando ea acciderunt, quae Plinius enumerat, iis qui quaesiverunt ostensa? 'Marco enim Marcello, cum periit ab Hannibale, caput iecoris defuit, defuit et G. Mario cum immolaret Uticae. Item G. principi Kalendas Ianuariis, cum iniret consulatum, quo anno interfectus est, Claudioque, successori eius, quo mense interemptus est veneno. Pyrrho regi quo die periit praecisa hostiarum capita ⟨repsisse⟩.'

67 Sed et praebendis quoque laetis et prosperis dii in stercore iacuerunt. Divo namque Augusto, Spoleti sacrificanti primo potestatis suae die, victimarum iocinera replicata intrinsecus ab una fibra reperta sunt, responsumque duplicaturum intra annum imperium. Gemina item divo Augusto apparuere iocinera, quo die apud Actium vicit. Sed et magici fuerunt et mathematici, quos accuratissime Cicero et Plinius impugnant, quibus et Livius consentire videtur cum regem Tullum, quia Iovem mala religione solicitabat, fulmine cum tota domo flagrasse dicit. Et Augustinus in *Civitate Dei* dicit adversus magicas artes Romanorum esse leges praesertim

throne. Let Marcus Varro's unparalleled saying (that I have put by way of preface) serve as a reply. He said the gods would not only have been idle but also very squalid if they concealed their advice in a dung heap of livers and entrails, to be revealed to men by mad priests.[445] How much more desirable would it have been for Cicero's opinion in *Defense of Cluentius* to have prevailed among the ancients. He said that "the gods' favor can be won by duty toward man and toward the gods and righteous prayers, not by impure superstition nor by victims slaughtered in order to accomplish a crime."[446] Where else than in dung shall we judge the gods to have been, when these things listed by Pliny were what resulted for those who sought portents? "In the case of Marcus Marcellus, when he died at Hannibal's hands, the head of the liver was missing. It was also missing for Gaius Marius when he was sacrificing at Utica.[447] Likewise for the emperor Gaius on the Kalends of January when he was entering into the consulship in the year in which he was killed. And for his successor Claudius, in the month in which he was done away with by poison."[448] "In King Pyrrhus' case on the day he died the heads of the victims crawled around after they had been cut off."[449]

But in order to disclose happy and advantageous events too the 67
gods located themselves in dung. For when the deified Augustus was sacrificing at Spoleto on the first day he was in power, the victim's livers were found folded back to the inside from one lobe. The prediction was that within the year his *imperium* would be doubled.[450] Likewise double livers appeared for Augustus on the day he was victorious at Actium.[451] But there were also sorcerers and astrologers, whom Cicero and Pliny[452] attack with great attention to detail. Livy appears to agree with them when he says King Tullus was consumed by lightning along with his whole house because he was trying to influence Jupiter by bad religious rites.[453] Augustine too in *City of God* says that the Romans

duodecim tabularum. Et Asclepiadem in primis dicit Plinius adimere magicae vanitates ut abrogaret herbis fidem, eumque probare bonis argumentis dicit si magia fuisset vera potuisse Romanos contra Cymbros et Teutones,[81] contra Afros, contra Gallos, et ceteros providisse, si herbarum arte magica fames tolleretur et portae urbium reserarentur. Et Aelius Spartianus de Didio Iuliano imperatore scribit fuisse sibi eam amentiam ut per magos pleraque faceret, quibus putaret odium populi deliniri. Quasdam enim non convenientes Romanis sacris hostias imolaverunt, carmina profana cantaverunt, et ea quae dicunt ad speculum fieri, in quo puer praeligatis oculis incantato vertice aliqua respicere dicitur. Mathematicos vero Suetonius asserit a Tiberio imperatore expulsos fuisse, sed deprecantibus et se artem desituros promittentibus veniam dedisse. Cornelius autem Tacitus mathematicos dicit genus hominum potentibus infidum, sperantibus fallax, quod in civitate Romana et vetitum semper et retentum fuit, quos postea Vitellium imperatorem asserit expulisse.

68 Sed et alios habuerunt prisci sacrificulorum, praestigiorum et precationum et variarum observationum mores, a quibus partim in urbe Roma vetitis, partim a superstitiosis in usu habitis, plurimae oriebantur insaniae. Livius XXII: 'Interim ex fatalibus libris sacrificia aliquot extraordinaria facta, inter quae Gallus et Gallina, Graecus et Graeca in foro Boario sub terram demissi sunt vivi.' Et item infra Livius XXV: 'Tanta religio et ea maxima ex parte externa civitatem incessit ut homines aut dii alii viderentur effecti,

had laws against the arts of magic, especially the laws of the Twelve Tables.[454] Pliny says that Asclepiades above all deprives the Magi's deceits of force in order to destroy confidence in herbal remedies. Asclepiades argued with good evidence that if there were any truth in magic, if hunger might be removed magically by plants and city gates unbarred, the Romans could have taken precautions against the Cimbrians and Teutones, the Africans, the Gauls and all the rest.[455] Aelius Spartianus writes that the emperor Didius Julianus "was so mad as to use sorcerers to carry out a number of things by which he thought he could mitigate his unpopularity with the people. For they sacrificed certain victims that did not conform to Roman rites, they sang profane chants and [he did] those things which they say are done at a mirror in which a boy, with his eyes blindfolded and charms said over his head, is said to look at some things."[456] Suetonius affirms that the astrologers were expelled by the emperor Tiberius but that he pardoned them when they begged and promised to give up the practice.[457] Cornelius Tacitus says astrologers are a type of man, treacherous to the powerful, misleading of those with expectations, which was always both barred from and allowed to remain in the City of Rome.[458] He affirms that later the emperor Vitellius expelled them.[459]

The Romans of old had other customs of minor priests, of 68
conjuring tricks, of prayers and observances of different kinds, some of which were forbidden in the City of Rome, while others were kept in use by the superstitious. From them very many mad deeds sprang. Livy Book XXII: "Meanwhile by the direction of the Books of Fate some unusual sacrifices were performed, among which a Gallic man and woman and a Greek man and woman were buried alive in the Cattle Market,"[460] and again, further on, Livy Book XXV: "So great a passion for religious devotion, for the most part of foreign origin, invaded the community that it seemed that the human beings or the gods had been trans-

nec iam in secreto modo, sed in publico etiam, ac foro Capitolioque mulierum turba erat nec sacrificantium, nec precantium deos more patrio. Sacrificuli ac vates ceperant hominum mentes, quorum numerum auxit rustica plebs, ex incultis diutino bello infestisque agris egestate et metu in urbem compulsa. Et quaestus ex alieno errore facilis quem velut ex concessae artis usu exercebant. Marcus Aemilius praetor edixit, ut quicunque libros vaticinios praedicationisve aut artis sacrificandi haberet, eos libros omnes litterasque ad se ferret.' Maioremque in praedictis auctoritatem habuit precatio, cui faciendae ⟨de⟩ scripto,[82] sicut scribit Plinius, praeibat aliquis et alius adhibebatur custos, ne erraretur in verbis. Alius item praeponebatur qui linguis faveri a circunstantibus iuberet, quemadmodum apud nos servatur cum sacram in ecclesia lecturus lectionem alta dicit voce: 'Iube Domine benedicere,' cui boni ominis[83] fit responsio, ut digna in eius corde et labiis sacrorum dogmatum sit enuntiatio. Dicebant enim gentiles: 'Favete linguis omnes et tu tibicen cane,' ne aliud in terra exaudiatur. Vestalem itaque praecationem fuisse asserit Plinius, qua aquam illa cribro attulit, et parietes ab incendiis precationibus fuisse circumscriptos et Vestales creditum mancipia fugitiva nondum urbem egressa retinuisse in loco precationibus; unde et traditum morem dicit primum anni diem laetis precationibus invicem faustum ominari.

69 Observationes, cum fuerint propemodum infinitae, nonnullas ponemus. Sanguinem gladiatorum ex vulnere morientium bibebant, ut procul a comitiali essent; quod tamen scribit Plinius cum

formed. No longer just in secret but also in public, in the Forum and on the Capitol, there was a throng of women whose sacrifices and prayers to the gods were not in the ancestral manner. Minor priests and soothsayers had taken over peoples' minds. The population was increased by the common people from the countryside, driven into the city by want and fear, from fields that were uncultivated during the long war and had become dangerous. There were also easy profits to be made from others' delusion and they exploited their trade as if they were practicing a legitimate skill." Marcus Aemilius the praetor issued an edict that anyone who had books of prophecies, or of soothsaying or of sacrificial procedure, should bring all such books and documents to him.[461] In such matters, prayer had greater power when someone dictated the formula from a written version, as Pliny writes, and another attendant was used so that no mistake be made in the words. Again, another was given the function of bidding those attending to keep holy silence.[462] The same custom is maintained when he who is about to read the holy lesson in church says out aloud, "O lord, give thy blessing." The auspicious reply is made to him that worthy proclamation of holy teaching be in his heart and on his lips. The Gentiles used to say, "All observe holy silence" and, "You, piper, play" so that nothing extraneous might be heard on earth.[463] Pliny affirms that there was a Vestal prayer, which enabled her to fetch water in a sieve and that prayers protecting from fires were written on walls.[464] It was also believed that the Vestals by prayers stopped runaway slaves from escaping if they had not yet left the City.[465] For this reason he says it was a traditional custom that the first day of the New Year was given propitious omens by cheerful good wishes to one another.[466]

As for the observances, since they were almost infinite in number, I shall set down a few. They drank blood from the wounds of dying gladiators to keep epilepsy at bay. Nevertheless Pliny writes that this aroused horror when it was seen or done in the arena.[467] 69

spectaretur aut fieret in arena horrorem attulisse. Et observatio illa erat qua Augustum scribit Suetonius adeo tonitrua et fulgura expavisse, ut semper et ubique pellem vituli marini circumferret pro remedio, et qua Caesar, post unum ancipitem vehiculi casum, semper domum egrediens carmine ter repetito securitatem itinerum aucupabatur,[84] sicut nos, domus limitem transgressuri, signaculo crucis praemisso divinam ab adversis tuitionem imprecamur. Publicaque illa fuit observatio cum in oppugnationibus ante omnia evocabantur a Romanis sacerdotibus dii, sub quorum tutela urbs aut oppidum id erat, promittebantque illi vel illis diis eundem aut ampliorem locum Romae alibique. Ideoque Romae deus tutelaris ignorabatur ne posset ab hoste aliquo evocari. Publica etiam observatio illa erat de qua Cicero *In Vatinium* Iove fulgurante cum populo agi nefas esse, et laurum in sinu Iovis poni quotiens laetitiam novam victoria attulerit, in profanisque usibus pollui laurum et oleam fas non esse, et ne propitiandis quidem numinibus accendi ex his altare aramve debere. Et Plutarchus in *Problematibus* scribit cum in ceteris Dianae templis cervorum cornua affigere mos esset, in ea tantummodo quae erat in Aventino bovum affixa fuisse, quod Antronius Horatius in Sabinis bovem insigni specie et magnitudine natam a divino quodam monitus siquis imolasset totius Italiae imperio eius civitatem potituram. Cornelius sacerdos eo ad Tybrim lavandi specie iusso immolaverit et Romae imperium Italiae peperit.[85]

Et praestigia damnans Suetonius de Vespasiano dicit nuntiata fuisse 'ex urbe praestigia Neronem diebus ultimis monitum per quietem ut tensam Iovis Optimi ex sacrario in domum ⟨Vespasiani⟩

And there was that observance whereby Suetonius writes that Augustus was so afraid of thunder and lightning bolts that he always carried around with him everywhere a sealskin to counteract them.[468] Caesar, after one dangerous accident in his carriage, always repeated an incantation three times to ensure a safe journey when he left home,[469] just as we, when we are about to cross the threshold of our house, pray for divine protection against misfortune by first making a little sign of the cross. There was a public observance when they put a city under siege. The Roman priests first of all "called forth" the gods under whose protection this city or town was and promised this or those gods the same or a grander place at Rome or elsewhere. This is why the name of Rome's guardian god was unknown, so that he could not be "called forth" by some enemy.[470] There was also a public observance mentioned by Cicero in *Against Vatinius* that it was forbidden to transact business with the people when Jupiter was sending lightning.[471] Bay was placed in Jupiter's lap whenever a fresh victory brought happiness.[472] It was not permitted for bay or olive to be polluted in profane uses and even to propitiate the gods they ought not to be used in lighting a fire in any receptacle for offerings or on any altar.[473] Plutarch writes in *Problems* that though it was the custom to nail up stags' horns in all the temples of Diana, horns of cattle were nailed up only in the temple on the Aventine. This was because, when a heifer of outstanding beauty and size had been born in the Sabine territory, Antronius Horatius was advised by a soothsayer that, if anyone sacrificed it, his city would acquire rule over all Italy. Ordering him to the Tiber on the pretext that he should wash, Cornelius the priest sacrificed the heifer and brought about Rome's rule over Italy.[474]

Condemning conjuring tricks, Suetonius says about Vespasian 70
that "deceptions were reported from Rome that Nero in the last days of his life was advised in a dream to take the sacred chariot of Jupiter the Best from its shrine to the house of Vespasian and

et in circum deduceret,' quorum etiam praestigiorum Iudaeos scribit poenas dedisse 'cum in oriente percrebruisset vetus et constans opinio esse in fatis ut eo tempore Iudaeae praefecti rerum potirentur.' Iudaeique id ad se trahentes rebellarunt et urbe amissa ad exterminium sunt adducti. Quorum tamen praestigiorum aliquid certioris eventus habuisse est visus Iosephus nobilis Iudaeus, qui, cum Vespasiani iussu coniiceretur in vincula, constantissime asseveravit fore ut ab eodem absolveretur, verum iam imperatore; quod et postea factum fuit. Quod autem supra Cicero in *Legum* libris 'divorum iras providento hisque parento' dixit ad prodigia spectat; de quibus eodem libro 'prodigia et portenta ad Etruscos et aruspices, si senatus iussit, deferunto, Etruriaeque principes disciplinam dicito, quibus divis decreverint procuranto, iisdemque fulgura et ostenta pianto.' Prodigia autem Nonius Marcellus dicta vult quod porro sint adigenda. Et infra: 'Prodigia semper esse pessima, quod deorum sint irae vel minae.' Livius VIII: 'M. Rutilio tertium T. Manlio Torquato tertium consulibus prodigium lapidibus pluit.' Et libro XXII: 'Quod autem in Piceno lapidibus pluisset novendiale sacrum edictum est, urbs lustrata, hostiae maiores quibus edictum est diis, donum ex auro pondo XL ad Lanuvinum Iovem portatum, et signum aeneum auratum Iunoni in Aventino, lectisternium Caere et Romae, a iuventute supplicatum Fortunae in Algido, et inde Romae omnibus diis et Genio maiores hostiae. Attilius Soranus praetor vota suscipere iussus si in decem annos

from there to the Circus."[475] He writes that the Jews were punished for these deceptions too, when "an old and persistent opinion had spread abroad in the east that the rulers of Judaea were destined to take over the world." The Jews, taking this as referring to themselves, rebelled, lost their city and were brought to destruction.[476] Nevertheless, from among these deceptions, Josephus, a noble Jew, seemed to have had one that turned out more reliably. When Vespasian ordered him to be imprisoned, he most steadfastly maintained that he would be released by the same man, but when he was emperor.[477] This did happen later on. As to what was quoted above from Cicero's *On the Laws*, that "they shall foresee the gods' angry signs and give heed to them," this refers to prodigies, concerning which he says in the same book: "Prodigies and portents are to be referred to the Etruscans and the soothsayers, if the senate has commanded, and the leading men are to pronounce the doctrine from Etruria. Let them make atonement to those gods they have decreed and for the same gods let them expiate lightning bolts and portents."[478] Nonius Marcellus thinks that "prodigies (*prodigia*) were so called because they had to be driven away (*porro*)" and, further on, "that prodigies are always utterly harmful" in as much as "they are the gods' angers or threats."[479] Livy Book VIII: When Marcus Rutilius and Titus Manlius Torquatus were in their third consulships, a prodigy, a rain of stones, occurred.[480] And in Book XXII: "Because there had been a rain of stones in Picenum, an edict declared a nine days' sacrifice, the purification of the city, the offering of fully-grown victims to those gods decreed by the edict, a gift of gold weighing forty pounds carried to Jupiter at Lanuvium, a gilded bronze statue to Juno on the Aventine and ceremonial banquets for the gods at Caere and Rome. A supplication was made by the youth to Fortune on Mt. Algidus and then at Rome fully-grown victims to all the gods and to Genius. Attilius Serranus the praetor was ordered to discharge

rei publicae eodem stetisset statu.' Et infra Livius XXIII: 'Prodigia eo anno multa nuntiata sunt. Quoque magis credebant simplices ac religiosi homines, eo plura nuntiabatur.' Et XXIIII verum ex ingenio fateri coactus sic habet: 'Prodigia procurarunt quae nuntiata erant et alia ludibria oculorum auriumque credita pro veris.' Ostentaque proximo loco Romanis fuerunt, quae Ulpianus *De verborum significatione* dicit Labeonem diffinisse cum contra naturam alicuius rei genitum factumve est aliquid. Duoque eorum genera esse: cum quid contra naturam nascitur, tribus manibus aut pedibus homo, alterum cum quid prodigiosum videtur, quae Graeci fantasmata dicunt. Plinius: 'Subsedit in Cumano arbor gravi ostento, paulo ante Pompeii Magni bella civilia, paucis ramis eius eminentibus.' Ostentumque est cum arbores in capitibus statuarum vel in atriis enascuntur vel in arboribus ipsis alienae. In Capitolio bis bello Persei enata palma victoriam triumphosque portendit, quae tempestatibus prostrata, eodem loco ficus enata est in Messalae et G. Cassii censorum lustro, a quo tempore pudicitiam prostratam Piso gravis auctor est.

71 Monstra subsequuntur quae Nonius dicit deorum monita esse. Et Festus 'monstrum dictum velut monestrum, quod moneat aliquid futurum; prodigium velut praedicium, quod praedicat; portentum quod portendat, ostentum quod ostendat.' Tenitas esse inquit Festus 'deas sortium dictas, quod tenendi habeant potestatem.' Videmusque bina fuisse sortium genera. Unum quas 'sortes Virgilianas' appellavere, cum aperto Virgilii codice destinati in ordine et numero versus qui forte occurrissent in augurium

the vows if at the end of ten years the commonwealth remained in the same state."[481] Livy further on, in Book XXIII: "In that year many prodigies were reported—and the more the simple and pious folk believed them, the more were reported."[482] And in Book XXIV, compelled to admit the truth by his own intelligence, he writes: "they expiated the prodigies that had been reported and other visual and aural delusions of eyes and ears taken as true."[483] For the Romans portents came next. Ulpian, in *On the Meaning of Expressions*, says Labeo defined them as when something was born or done contrary to the nature of the particular thing. "There are two kinds of these, when anything is born contrary to nature, a man with three hands or feet, the second when something unnatural is seen—the Greeks call these 'apparitions' (*fantasmata*)."[484] Pliny: "In the territory of Cumae not long before the civil war of Pompey the Great a tree sank leaving a few of its branches protruding. A serious portent was involved."[485] It is considered a portent when trees spring up on the heads of statues or in courtyards or on unrelated trees. Twice during the war against Perseus a palm sprang up on the Capitol presaging victory and triumphs. This was thrown down in a storm and a fig sprang up in the same place in the censorial term of Marcus Messalla and Gaius Cassius. Piso gives weighty authority that from this time chastity was overthrown.[486]

Next come warnings (*monstra*). Nonius says they are the gods' 71
admonitions (*monita*)[487] and Festus says "a *monstrum* is so called as if a 'monestrum,' because it warns (*monere*) of a future event, *prodigium* as if a prediction (*praedicium*), because it predicts (*praedicere*) and a *portentum* because it portends (*portendere*), an *ostentum* because it shows (*ostendere*)."[488] Festus says *Tenitae* are goddesses of lots, "so-called because they had the power of holding (*tenere*)."[489] We see that there are two kinds of lots. The one, which they called "sortes Vergilianae," was when a book of Vergil was opened and the verses that had turned up by chance were chosen in order and

accipiebantur. De quo Aelius Spartianus in *Adriani vita:* 'Quo quidem tempore cum solicitus de imperatoris erga se iudicio Virgilianas consuleret sortes, in hos incidit versus: "Quis procul ille tamen ramis insignis olivae sacra ferens, nosco crines incanaque menta regis Romani, primam qui legibus urbem fundabit, Curibus parvis et paupere terra."' Alterum fuit sortium genus vetustissimum a sacerdotibus confictum responsisque oraculorum adsimile, quod inscripta foliis arborum tabellisque diversorum eventuum elogia ad deorum pulvinaria erant a sacerdotibus ita disposita, ut, cum illi aut orati voluissent aut sponte constituissent, certo decussa artificio in id spei aut timoris populos et principes viros inducerent, quod sibi conducibile aut delectabile existimarent. Hinc illud est apud Livium libro XXII: prodigii a sacerdotibus procurandi loco habitum 'sortes attenuatas, id est sponte sua in altare tamquam e caelo delapsas, unamque excidisse ita scriptam "Mavors telum[86] suum concutit."' Cernere autem ex Livio quales adhibitae fuerunt procurationes, ex quibus omni sacerdotio maxima accessit delectatio et utilitas, iocundissimum est. 'Decembri enim mense' quaerendis voluptatibus summae idoneo huius procurandae sortis gratia 'ad aedem Saturni Romae immolatum est, lectisterniumque imperatum, et eum lectum senatores straverunt, et convivium fuit publicum, ac per urbem Saturnalia die ac nocte clamata, populusque eum diem festum perpetuo habere ac servare iussus.' Vota quoque prisci impetrandis a deo concupitis emisere, quae ut implerent constantissime sunt adnixi. Livius in Tulli regis rebus gestis: 'In re trepida duodecim vovit Salios fanaque Pallori et Pavori.' Et libro

number and taken as an augury. Aelius Spartianus says about this in the *Life of Hadrian:* "at the time when he was worried about what the emperor thought of him, he consulted the 'sortes Vergilianae' and hit upon these lines: 'Who is that far off, marked out by olive branches and carrying holy emblems? I recognize the gray hair and beard of a Roman king, he who first will base the city on laws, from the small town of Cures and its poor land.'"[490] The other kind of lot was the very old one manufactured by the priests, and similar to the responses of oracles. According to this leaves of trees and tablets were inscribed with responses concerning various events. These were arranged on the couches of the gods by the priests in such a way that a certain contrivance made them fall down when the priests had either acceded to prayers or come to an independent decision. They encouraged peoples and leading men to that pitch of hope or fear that they thought of advantage or pleasure to themselves. From this comes that passage in Livy Book XXII: It was considered as equivalent to a prodigy that should be expiated by the priests "that the lots had shrunk in size, that is, fallen onto the altar of their own accord as if from heaven and one fell out with the following inscription 'Mars shakes his spear.'"[491] It is very agreeable to see from Livy the nature of the expiations used, which were the greatest source of pleasure and advantage for all the priesthoods. "In the month of December" (which is eminently suitable for the seeking of pleasure), for the sake of expiating this oracle "there was a sacrifice at the Temple of Saturn in Rome, orders were issued for a banquet of the gods and the senators prepared this couch and there was a public feast. Throughout the city the cry 'Saturnalia' rang out for a day and a night and the people were ordered to make that day a holiday and observe it forever."[492] The ancients also uttered vows in order to obtain their desires from God and they strove very faithfully to discharge them. Livy in his history of King Tullus: "in a critical situation he vowed to establish twelve Salii and shrines to Paleness and

V: 'Dictator M. Furius Camillus Veios capturus decimam Iovi Pithio vovit et Iunoni hospitium promisit.' Et Hannibalem Livius bellum meditantem Romanum facit secundis se votis obligasse. Qua de re plura dicere omittemus, quia apud priscos pariter et apud nostros et pari forma est acta.

72 Multa superius a nobis sunt ostensa per quae prisci futura scire, providere et avertere conabantur. Unum hoc loco libet ostendere, per quod certiora et oculis subiecta sacrorum auxilio occultari posse credebant. Ad vallem Egeriae, quam fuisse tenemus ad sextum decimum ab urbe lapidem, ubi Cinthianum est summi viri Prosperi cardinalis Columnae oppidum, lacus illi subiectus sicut semper alias nunc Nemorensis est dictus, quo in loco templum erat Fortunae virilis. Eius sacerdotem virgines, quamprimum viri potentes esse inciperent, a parentibus ductae adibant. Isque eas omnino nudatas undique inspiciens, vitia corporis apparentia indicabat. Et admonitae virgines cum Fortunae thura imolassent, vitium illud maritum qui contingebat perpetuo celari impetrasse tenebant.

Fright"[493] and in Book V: The dictator Marcus Furius Camillus, who would capture Veii, vowed a tithe to Jupiter Pythius and promised Juno a home.[494] Livy makes Hannibal have pledged himself with vows a second time when he was planning the war against Rome.[495] I shall omit more that could be said on this matter because the ancients acted in it in a similar way and fashion to ourselves.

I have shown above a number of ways by which the ancients 72
attempted to learn, foresee and avert future events. Here I would like to make known one way by which they believed indubitable and visible things could be concealed by the help of divine worship. In the vale of Egeria, which I believe to have been sixteen miles from Rome where there is now the town of Cynthianum, which belongs to an eminent man, Cardinal Prospero Colonna, there is a lake lying below it called now, as it always has been, Nemorensis.[496] Here there was a temple of Male Fortune. To its priest parents brought young girls as soon as they began to be ready for a husband. He looked at them carefully from all sides, completely naked as they were, and pointed out their visible physical defects. When the girls thus advised had made an offering of incense to Fortune, they believed that they had ensured that that defect would forever be concealed from their eventual husband.[497]

LIBER SECUNDUS[1]

1 Confictas iam et sub religionis velamine a priscis gentilibus ad luxum, fastum opesque quaerendas vario excogitatas modo artes, pontificum scilicet flaminumque et sacerdotum institutiones primum, post cetera quae religionis fuere secundo hoc volumine ostendemus. Pontifices Varro *De lingua Latina* scribit dictos esse a ponte Sublicio quem saepe fecerunt. Additque Festus maximum esse dictum pontificem 'quod maximarum rerum, quae ad sacra et religionem pertinent, iudex sit vindexque contumaciae privatorum magistratuum ⟨que⟩.' Pontifices vero alii duorum fuerunt generum, ex patriciis maiores et minores ex plebe. Quantae autem dignitatis fuerit pontifex maximus Livius libro XLVII ostendit quod 'Gn. Cornelio praetori multa indicta est, quia cum M. Aemilio Lepido pontifice maximo iniuriose contenderat. Sacrorum enim quam magistratuum ius potentius fuit.'

2 Eademque pontificis maximi dignitas ab eius modo creandi[2] apparet. Livius enim XXV scribit: 'Comitia pontifici maximo creando[3] sunt habita, res ingenti certamine acta. Creatus est Licinius Crassus qui aedilitatem currulem petiturus erat. Ante hunc intra CXX annos nemo praeter P. Cornelium pontifex maximus creatus fuerat qui sella curruli non sedisset.' Cicero autem oratione *In legem agrariam Rulli* secunda dicit comitiis pontificum non nisi decem et septem tribus fuisse vocatas. Et Suetonius Tranquillus de C. Caesare: 'Pontificatum maximum petiit non sine profusissima largitione, in qua reputans magnitudinem aeris alieni, cum mane

BOOK II

In this second volume I shall now describe the devices that the Gentiles of old, under the pretext of religion, fabricated and contrived in various ways to acquire luxury, splendor and wealth: first to be sure the institutions of pontiffs, flamens and priests, and next everything else belonging to the sphere of worship. The pontiffs, Varro writes in *On the Latin Language*, got their name from the Sublician Bridge (*pons*), the construction of which they often supervised.[1] Festus adds that the Chief Pontiff was so called "because he is the judge of the chief matters relating to sacred rites and religion, and punisher of citizens' and magistrates' contumacy."[2] The other pontiffs were of two kinds: the major came from the patricians, the minor from the plebeians.[3] Livy in Book XLVII demonstrates the superior authority of the Chief Pontiff, because "a fine was imposed on the praetor Gnaeus Cornelius because he had illegally disputed with Marcus Aemilius Lepidus, the Chief Pontiff: religious rights prevailed over those of the magistrates."[4] 1

Similarly the Chief Pontiff's standing can be seen from the mode of his appointment. Livy writes in Book XXV: "Elections were held to appoint the Chief Pontiff. The matter was resolved amid enormous competition. Licinius Crassus, who was about to stand for the curule aedileship, was appointed. Before him, over a period of 120 years, no one besides Publius Cornelius [Calussa] had been elected Chief Pontiff without previously having held a curule position."[5] Cicero, however, says in Book II of *On the Agrarian Law against Rullus* that only seventeen tribes were summoned for the pontifical elections.[6] Suetonius Tranquillus says about Gaius Caesar: "He was a candidate for the office of Chief Pontiff and gave very lavish bribes. Having in mind the size of the debt 2

ad comitia descenderet, praedixisse matri osculanti fertur domum se nisi pontificem non reversurum. Atque ita potentissimos duos competitores multumque aetate et dignitate antecedentes superavit, ut plura ipse in eorum tribubus suffragia quam uterque in omnibus tulerit.' Unicum tamen video Romanorum imperatorem non ad luxum et fastum, sed ad clementiae et pietatis instrumentum quaesivisse pontificatum. Suetonius enim scribit Titum Vespasianum, qui iure optimo appellatus est 'deliciae humani generis,' 'pontificatum maximum ideo se professum accipere ut puras servaret manus fidemque praestitisse, quod numquam posthac auctor fuerit cuiusquam necis, nec conscius, quamvis interdum ulciscendi causa non deesset.' Qua in re intellegi potest primas fuisse pontificis maximi partes manus ab effusione humani sanguinis continere, quo posthabito respectu alii omnes Romani imperatores voluerunt pontificatu maximo exornari.

3 Flamines Varro dicit 'dictos quod caput vinctum habent filo et cognomen accipiunt ab eo deo cui sacra faciunt. Sed partim sunt aperta ut Martialis et Vulcanalis, obscuriora partim ut Dialis a Iove, Furialis a Furida,[4] cuius in fastis feriae[5] erant Furinales.' Et Livius dicit 'Numa Pompilius[6] flaminem Iovi assiduum sacerdotem creavit insignique eum veste et curruli regia sella adornavit. Huic duos flamines adiecit: Marti unum, alterum Quirino.' Quod autem flamines etiam a pontifice maximo crearentur Livius XXVI[7] ostendit: 'G. Flaminius flamen captus a P. Licinio pontifice maximo. Ut animum eius cura et sacrorum et caerimoniarum cepit, ita repente exuit antiquos mores ut nemo in tota iuventute patrum primoribus probatior haberetur.' Creatos etiam fuisse flamines a

involved he is said to have warned his mother when she kissed him as he went down to the polls in the morning that he would come home as Chief Pontiff or not at all. His victory over two extremely powerful rivals, far surpassing him in age and rank, was so decisive that he received more votes in their tribes than the two of them received in all the tribes."[7] There is only one Roman emperor whom I know of as having sought the office of Chief Pontiff not for luxury and splendor, but as a means of exercising mercy and piety. Suetonius writes that Titus Vespasianus, who, with perfect justice, was called "the delight of the human race," "declared that he accepted the office of Chief Pontiff for the purpose of keeping his hands clean, and he kept his word, in that after this he was never responsible for, or an accomplice in, the death of any man, although sometimes he did not lack reasons for taking revenge."[8] Thus it can be understood that the first duty of the Chief Pontiff was to keep his hands from the shedding of human blood. Once this consideration lost importance, all the other Roman emperors wanted to have the honor of being Chief Pontiff.

Varro says: "The flamens (*flamines*) were so called because they have their heads bound with a thread (*filum*) and they are given an additional name from the god whose rites they perform. Some of these names are self-evident, such as 'of Mars' and 'of Vulcan.' Others are less obvious, such as Dialis from Jupiter, Furi[n]alis from Furida (who has a Furinal Festival in the calendar)."[9] Livy says Numa Pompilius "appointed a flamen for Jupiter to be his standing priest, dignifying him with distinctive attire and the king's curule seat. He added two more flamens, one for Mars, the other for Quirinus."[10] Livy demonstrates in Book XXVI that the flamens were also appointed by the Chief Pontiff: "Gaius Flaccus was chosen flamen by Publius Licinius, the Chief Pontiff. When responsibility for the sacred rites and ceremonies captured his attention, he so suddenly discarded his old ways that no one among all the young men was considered of better character by the leading 3

dictatore urbium et oppidorum ostendit Cicero in *Miloniana* oratione: 'Milo Lanuvium, ex quo erat municipio et ubi tum dictator, profectus est ad flaminem prodendum.' Item infra: 'Interim cum sciret Clodius iter solemne, legitimum, necessarium Miloni esse Lanuvium ad flaminem prodendum quod erat dictator Lanuvii Milo.'

4 'Maximae dignationis flaminem fuisse Dialem inter XV flamines' dicit Festus 'et, cum ceteri discrimina maiestatis suae haberent, pro minimo habitum Pomonalem, quod Pomona dea levissimo fructui agrorum pomis praesideret.' Et flamini Diali anulum quidem gerere non licebat solidum aut aliquem in se habere nodum. Et flamini iurare Diali fas non erat,[8] quod parva in re ei fidem non habere absurdum esset cui divina summa credita essent. Flamenque Dialis cum flaminicam haberet uxorem, ea mortua sacerdotio se abdicabat quia, cum uno et eodem tempore uxor cum eo sacraretur, multa essent in sacris quae illa mortua agi nequirent et statim alteram superducere cum difficile, tum iniquum atque impium videbatur. Palatualem flaminem ad sacrificandum ei deae constitutum fuisse in cuius tutela Palatium esse putabatur Festus asserit, cum Plutarchus in *Problematibus* affirmet Iovis sacerdoti, quem flaminem Dialem vocavere, farinam frumentumve tangere non licuisse, quia frumentum res corrupta ac paene putrida: farina ex frumento contrita et nondum in panem redacta res sit imperfecta. Hederam flamen Dialis si attigisset piaculum ei erat, nec iter facere poterat ubi umbracula ab ea arbore desuper imminerent,

senators."[11] That flamens were also appointed by the chief magistrates of cities and towns Cicero demonstrates in his speech *Defense of Milo*: "Milo set out for Lanuvium, the town he came from and where at the time he was chief magistrate, in order to appoint a flamen."[12] Again further on: "Meanwhile since Clodius knew that Milo had to make a ritual, legal and necessary journey to Lanuvium in order to declare the election of a flamen, because Milo was chief magistrate at Lanuvium."[13]

Festus says "the flamen of Jupiter had the highest status of the 4
fifteen flamens and, since all the others were differentiated in rank, the flamen of Pomona was considered least in status, because the goddess Pomona looked after fruit (*poma*), the least important agricultural product."[14] The flamen of Jupiter was not allowed to wear a solid ring[15] or have any knot on his person.[16] He was not permitted to swear an oath because it would be ridiculous not to believe in a trivial affair someone entrusted with the most important divine matters.[17] The flamen of Jupiter had a wife, the *flaminica*. If she died he resigned his priesthood, the reason being that since his wife was consecrated together with him at one and the same time, many of the rites could not be performed if she were dead. To marry another wife straight away seemed difficult as well as not right and disrespectful.[18] Festus declares that "the flamen of Palatua was instituted to sacrifice to the goddess who was thought to watch over the Palatine."[19] Plutarch affirms in *Problems* that the priest of Jupiter, whom they called the flamen of Jupiter, was not allowed to touch either flour or yeast, it is because yeast is a corrupt and almost rotten thing. Flour is an incomplete thing, because it has been ground from wheat and not yet turned into bread.[20] If the flamen of Jupiter touched ivy, he had to perform an expiation. Nor could he travel where shady bowers from that tree leaned over from above, the reason being that it is an unfruitful tree and completely

quia arbor sterilis et omnino hominibus inutilis, quae propter fragilitatem semper alteri inhaeret solaque viriditate et umbra delectat, unde non temere in domibus nasci prohibetur. De pontificum flaminumque verbo et officio satis multa sunt dicta.

5 'Sacerdotes' Varro inquit 'universos a sacris dictos esse.' Fuerunt enim pontifices, flamines et ceteri omnes rebus praefecti sacris appellati pariter sacerdotes, per ea autem quae Cicero oratione *In legem agrariam Rulli* secunda habet videmus, etsi pontifices populi suffragiis, flamines vero a populo, vel a principe, vel a dictatore, vel pontificibus creabantur, neutros tamen potuisse sacerdotium ita populi suffragiis habere, quin ipsos oportuerit a collegio pontificum cooptari. Comitiis pontificum non nisi XVII tribus vocabantur 'atque hoc idem de sacerdotiis Gn. Domitius tribunus plebis, vir clarissimus, tulit quod populus per religionem sacerdotia mandare non poterat, ut minor pars populi vocaretur; ab ea parte qui esset factus, is a collegio cooptabatur.' Unde tractus mos apud nos videtur eos, qui a principibus sive populo et aliquo collegio ad dignitates eliguntur, oportere nihilominus a Romano pontifice et eius collegio cardinalium confirmari.

6 Collegium vero quid fuerit appellatum in oratione *De haruspicum responsis* idem Cicero sic ostendit: 'at vero domum meam P. Lentulus consul pontifex maximus, L. Lentulus flamen Martialis, L. Claudius rex sacrorum, Sex. Caesar flamen Quirinalis, L. Cornelius, Q. Albinovanus, Q. Terentius, pontifices minores, omnes liberaverunt.' Sicque ex quinque sacerdotiis maioribus collegium constabat. Ad quam ut videtur imitationem collegium Romanae

useless to mankind, always clinging to another because of its weakness and giving pleasure solely by its greenness and shade. Hence it is not allowed for good reason to grow in their homes.[21] Enough has been said about the terms for the pontiffs and the flamens and about their duties.

"Priests (*sacerdotes*) in general," Varro says, "were so called from 5
sacred rites (*sacra*)."[22] The pontiffs, flamens and all the rest who were put in charge of sacred matters were called priests in the same way. We see from what Cicero writes in Book II of *On the Agrarian Law against Rullus* that, even if the pontiffs were appointed by popular election, and the flamens on the other hand by the people or by the emperor or magistrate or by the pontiffs, neither were able to achieve the priesthood by popular election without having themselves to be co-opted by the college of the pontiffs. Only seventeen tribes were summoned for the pontifical elections[23] "and Gnaeus Domitius, tribune of the plebs and a very distinguished man, passed the same law with respect to the [other] priesthoods. Because the people, prevented by a religious impediment, could not confer priesthoods, a smaller section of the popular assembly was to be convoked. Whoever was chosen by this section was co-opted by the college."[24] This seems to be the origin of our custom, that those who are chosen for high office by the leading men or by the people and some college must nonetheless be confirmed by the Roman Pontiff and his college of cardinals.

In *On the Responses of the Haruspices* Cicero explains what the col- 6
lege was: "In fact, Publius Lentulus, the consul and Chief Pontiff, Lucius Lentulus, the flamen of Mars, Lucius Claudius, the king for sacrifices (*rex sacrorum*), Sextus Caesar, the flamen of Quirinus, Lucius Cornelius, Quintus Albinovanus, Quintus Terentius, the minor pontiffs, all released my house."[25] Thus the college consisted of the five major priesthoods.[26] In imitation of this, as it seems, the college of cardinals of the Roman church is composed of

ecclesiae cardinalium ex tribus maioribus sacerdotiis est confectum: episcopis videlicet septem urbi Romae propinquioribus, presbyterisque parrochias urbis principales et diaconibus parrochias item alias minores administrare solitis.

7 Sed unum praeterire hoc loco nolumus, a quo omnis gentilium Romanorum religio causam videtur originemque habuisse. Sacerdotes ipsos utriusque sexus a maximo ad minimum sacerdotia habuisse quorum[9] proventus erant tanti et tales ex quibus[10] nedum rem sustentabant familiarem, sed fomenta inde ad fastum eis luxumque proveniebant, cum tamen sacerdotes ipsi uxorem[11] filiosque et familias ex sacerdotio aeque ac patrimonio alentes, publicis omnibus praeter admodum pauca muneribus fungerentur et militiae ac mercaturae aut opificio prout cuique contingerat libebatque vacarent. Eaque sacerdotia fuerunt qualia nos Christiani propriore vocabulo beneficia appellamus.

8 Sacerdotiorum autem sicut et beneficiorum duo fuisse genera videmus: unum quod sacris esset addictum locis, quae rei publicae aut principum aut pontificum collegii collationis essent. Alterum quod[12] aedis aut sacelli iuris esse[n]t a patrefamilias ea ratione erecti dedicatique, ut et sacrorum cura et fructuum ipsius sacerdotii perceptio ad solam gentem familiamque suam perpetuis successionibus devolveretur, quae sacerdotia a priscis gentilicia, beneficia a nostris iuris patronatus appellata sunt. Livius nono: 'Gens Potitia cuius ad aram Herculis familiare sacerdotium erat,' et Cicero *Legum* primo: 'De sacris haec sit una sententia, ut conserventur semper et deinceps familiis prodantur, et perpetua sint sacra ut ne

members of the three major priesthoods, that is, the seven bishops in the immediate vicinity of the City of Rome, priests who usually minister to the city's main parishes and deacons who likewise usually minister to other lesser parishes.

But there is one fact I do not wish to pass over here, for 7
it seems to have been the cause and origin of the whole religion of the Gentiles of Rome. The priests of both sexes, from the greatest to the least, derived great revenues from their priesthoods from which they not only maintained their households but derived encouragement for splendor and luxury. The priests, while themselves supporting their wife, children and households from the priesthood as well as from their estates, nevertheless performed all public offices except for a very few and were free to engage in military service and trade or work according to the circumstances or desires of the individual. These priesthoods were of the kind that we Christians call "benefices," to use a more suitable term.

We see that there were two kinds of priesthoods just as there 8
are of benefices: one was attached to sacred places which belonged to a common fund of the state or of the emperors or of the pontifical college. The second kind were under the jurisdiction of a temple or chapel erected and dedicated by the head of a household with the intention that both the responsibility for the rites and the collection of the profits of the priesthood itself might devolve in unbroken succession to his own family and household alone. The ancients called such priesthoods "of the *gentes,*" but our contemporaries "benefices subject to patronage." Livy in Book IX: "The clan of the Potitii who held the hereditary priesthood at the altar of Hercules."[27] Cicero too in Book I of *On the Laws:* "Let there be this one principle about the rites: that they shall be maintained forever and be handed down within families in succession. Let the sacrifices be in perpetuity." "So that memory of the rites not be lost

patrisfamilias morte sacrorum memoria occideret, ut esset ea adiuncta ad quos eiusdem morte pecunia venerit.' Et Cicero *De haruspicum responsis:* 'Multi sunt etiam in hoc ordine qui sacrificia gentilicia illo ipso in sacello stato loco anniversaria[13] factitarunt.' Et Cornelius Tacitus de Othone: 'At recens ab exilio reversos adolescentes avitis et paternis sacerdotiis in solacium reposuit.' Idemque Tacitus de Vitellio: 'Extructis in Campo Martio aris inferias Neroni incessit; caese publice victimae coronataeque, facem Augustales[14] subdere quod sacerdotium ut Romulus Tacio regi, ita Caesar Tiberius Iuliae genti sacravit.'

9 Primi generis sacerdotiorum publice institutorum quincuplex fuit proventus: sacra enim construentes fundantesque loca, varias fundorum possessiones stipendiaque adiungebant a quibus sacerdotum alimonia proveniret. Unde Livius Numam Pompilium facit, cum flamines et Vestales instituisset de quibus supra est dictum, stipendia eis de publico statuisse, quod quidem alios omnes sacrorum fundatores locorum imitatos fuisse nullus addubitabit. Alioquin magni et amplissimi cives Romani nunquam aut sacerdotia cumulare studuissent aut pro ipsis sacerdotiis tantopere contendissent.[15] Et Livius XXX, cum Fabium Maximum filium in locum patris mortui pontificem creatum dixisset, duo ipsum[16] sacerdotia habuisse addit. De Caesare autem Suetonium dicere videmus: anno XVII aetatis flamen Dialis designatus a L. Sulla sacerdotio multatus. Sulla enim, qui[17] animos Caesaris et eloquentiam suspitioni maximae duceret haberique oportere palam praedicaret,

when the father of the family dies, let them be enjoined on those to whom the property comes by the same man's death."[28] Cicero, *On the Responses of the Haruspices:* "There are many too belonging to this order who have frequently made the annual sacrifices of their clan in that very shrine, the place appointed for this."[29] Cornelius Tacitus on Otho: "but lately as a consolation he restored the young men who had returned from exile to their grandfathers' and fathers' priesthoods."[30] And the same author Tacitus on Vitellius: "An altar was built in the Field of Mars and he performed rites in honor of Nero. Victims were slaughtered on behalf of the state and decked with garlands; the 'Augustales' applied the torch. They were a priesthood which Tiberius Caesar dedicated to the Julian clan, just as Romulus dedicated an order of priests to King Tatius."[31]

For the priesthoods of the first kind—those established on behalf of the state—there were five sources of revenue; for when 9
they were arranging and establishing sacred places, they would add various ownerships of estates and stipends from which the priests' sustenance would come. For this reason Livy says that, when Numa Pompilius had instituted the flamens and Vestals (I spoke about them above),[32] he decreed stipends for them from the public treasury.[33] No one will doubt that all the other founders of sacred places copied this. Otherwise the great and noble citizens of Rome would never have taken pains to accumulate priesthoods or competed so fiercely for them. After he said in Book XXX that Fabius Maximus the son was elected pontiff in place of his dead father, Livy adds that he had two priesthoods.[34] We see that Suetonius says of Caesar: When he was sixteen years old, and had been nominated priest of Jupiter, he was deprived of his priesthood by Lucius Sulla. For Sulla, who held Caesar's courage and eloquence in the greatest suspicion, and openly proclaimed that he must be "kept," proceeded to weaken him by depriving him of the priest-

nervos illi adimere in sacerdotii multa perrexit,[18] a quibus fomenta potentiae et amplitudinis accepisset.

Stipes secunda proventus sacerdotiorum pars dicta erat quod nostri oblationes eleemosynasque appellant. De hisque Cicero *Legum* primo: 'Praeter Idaeae Matris familias eosque iustis[19] diebus ne quis stipem cogito.' Quod autem Cicero familias dicit aliud a praedictis tribus generibus, pontificum, flaminum et sacerdotum singulorum dei alicuius cultui dedicatorum genus indicat, quod procedente tempore multiplicatum est. Multi enim utriusque sexus in eandem familiam ad alicuius dei cultum convenientes ex unis[20] eisdemque sacerdotiis ac stipum et legatorum redditibus convivebant variisque vocabulis et cognominibus censebantur. Cicero *Pro A. Cluentio Habito*: 'Martiales quidam Larini appellabantur ministri publici Martis atque ei deo veteribus institutis religionibusque Larinatum consecrati,[21] quorum cum satis magnus numerus esset cumque item in Sicilia multi Venerei sint.' Aelius Spartianus scribit Hadriano imperatori in deorum numerum[22] relato flamines et sodales senatum[23] constituisse. Et Suetonius de Galba: 'Ob res in Africa gestas et in Germania ornamenta triumphalia accepit et sacerdotium triplex inter XV viros sodales inter Augustales cooptatus.' Aelius Spartianus: 'Clipeum Hadriano magnificentissimum posuit et sacerdotes instituit. Puellas alimentarias in honorem Faustinae Faustinianas constituit.' 'Meruit flamines, circenses, templum et sodales Antonianos.' Faustinae uxori in radicibus Tauri montis novas puellas Faustinianas instituit. Dati

hood which had provided him with the support for his power and wealth.[35]

The second source of revenue for priesthoods was called reli- 10
gious donations (*stipes*), which men of our times call offerings (*oblationes*) and alms (*eleemosynae*). Cicero says of them in Book I of *On the Laws*: "No one is to collect donations, except the households of the Idaean Mother, and they on the days when it was permitted."[36] As to what Cicero calls "households," this reveals a kind in addition to the three kinds I have already spoken of, the pontiffs, the flamens and the individual priests dedicated to the worship of any one god—a kind that multiplied as time went on. Many people of both sexes, gathering together in the same household for the worship of some god, lived together from one and the same priesthood and from the income of donations and bequests, and they were called by a range of terms and titles. Cicero in *Defense of Cluentius*: "At Larinum there were certain people called 'Martiales,' public servants of Mars, and they were dedicated to this god by the ancient institutions and religious ordinances of the Larinates. Since there was quite a large number of them, and since likewise in Sicily there were very many temple servants of Venus. . . ."[37] Aelius Spartianus writes that the senate established flamens and brethren (*sodales*) for the emperor Hadrian after his deification.[38] Suetonius *on Galba*: "For his deeds in Africa and Germany he was awarded triumphal ornaments and three priesthoods, being co-opted to the Board of Fifteen, the Brethren [of Titus] and the Augustales."[39] Aelius Spartianus: "He [Antoninus Pius] set up a most magnificent shield in honor of Hadrian and he established a college of priests." "In honor of Faustina he founded the order of charity girls called 'the Faustinian girls.'" "He was granted flamens and circus games, a temple and the Antoninian Brethren."[40] He [Marcus Aurelius] established a new order of girls called "the Faustinian girls" in honor of his wife Faustina at the foot of Mt. Taurus. When he himself died, he was given brethren,

sodales et satellites et flamines ipsi mortuo. Sodales autem fuerunt quales nostri appellant societates saecularium, satellites quales multos per orbem[24] habemus: Sanctae Mariae Theotonicorum in Germania et sancti Iacobi de spata in Hispania. Flamines noti sunt. Et infra Cicero: 'Stipem sustulimus nisi eam quam apud paucos dies propriam Idaeae Matris excipimus. Implet enim animos superstitione et exhaurit domos.' Unde constat priusquam ea lex ferretur consuevisse omnes, qui sacerdotia haberent, illa quaestu per stipem petitam facto pinguiora reddidisse.

11 Tertia sacerdotiorum opulentia a solutionibus proveniebat quas inferiora impetraturi superioribus impendebant, quale apud nos est cum Pontifici Romano fructus primos antistites et his minores ac subditi sacerdotes pro habitorum modo beneficiorum pecuniam dissolvunt. Suetonius enim de Claudio imperatore dicit 'eum sextercium octogies pro introitu novi sacerdotii impendere coactum.'[25] Quarta iam pars ad sacerdotiorum exuberantiam proventuum donationes et legata fuere. Nam viventes ut deos haberent propitios multa sacerdotibus largiebantur. Felicitati autem, ut appellabant, animarum consulturi etsi multa alia testamento legabant, epulum raro aut fere[26] nunquam praetermittebant quod qua fieret ratione in multis, quae per Italiam extant, marmoreis sepulcris apparet. Ravennae nam apud sacram Petri apostoli aedem, quae seraphici Francisci vocabulo et fratrum eius ordinis habitatione notior est, marmoreo in sepulchro, a Classensi oppido tribus distante passuum milibus pridem avecto, haec legati in epulum est inscriptio: 'Dis manibus Flaviae Quinti filiae Salutari[27] coniugi carissimae.

guards (*satellites*) and flamens.[41] "Brethren" were comparable to what men of our time call societies of lay people. "Guards" were like the many we have throughout the world, for example, the Knights of St. Mary of the Germans in Germany[42] and of St. James of the Sword[43] in Spain. Flamens are well known. Cicero further on: "We have prohibited the collection of donations with the exception of that which belongs specifically to the Idaean Mother and takes place on a few days. For it fills men's minds with credulity and drains their homes of wealth."[44] For this reason it is evident that before that law was proposed all who had priesthoods used to make them more profitable by the income they gained by seeking donations.

The priesthoods' third source of wealth were the payments 11
which those wanting to obtain positions lower in rank paid to their superiors, as happens today, when bishops pay the first-fruits to the Roman Pontiff,[45] and lesser priests who are the bishops' subordinates pay them money for benefices they have received. Suetonius on the emperor Claudius says that "he was compelled to pay eighty thousand sesterces as the entry fee into a new priesthood."[46] Now, gifts and legacies were the fourth source of revenue to make the priesthoods overflow with wealth. For the living made many lavish gifts to the priests so that the gods might look on them favorably, but to provide for the felicity, as they called it, of their souls, they made many other bequests in their wills,[47] yet rarely or almost never failed to mention a feast. The way in which that was done is seen on many marble tombs that are extant throughout Italy. At Ravenna in the holy church of St. Peter the Apostle, which is better known under the name of the angelic St. Francis and by the house of the Franciscans, on a marble tomb transported long ago from the city of Classis three miles away there is the following inscription of a bequest for a feast: "Sacred to the shade of Flavia Salutaris, daughter of Quintus, dearest wife. Lucius Publicius Italicus, a decurion, while

Lucius Publicius Italicus decurio ornamentum sibi vivens posuit. Hic collegio fabrum militiae Ravennatis sextercia triginta vivens dedit, ex quo redditu[28] quotannis decurionibus collegii fabrum militiae Ravennatis in aede Neptuni quam[29] ipse extruxit die Neptunialiorum praesentibus sportulae nummi bini dividerentur et decurionibus XXVIII centeni quinquaginta quotannis darentur, ut ex ea summa, sicuti soliti sunt, arcam Publiciorum Flaviani et Italici filiorum et arcam in qua est posita Flavia Salutaris, uxor eius, rosis exornent de nummis XXV sacrificentque ex XXII et de reliquis ibi epulentur. Ob quam liberalitatem collegium fabrum militiae Ravennatis inter benemeritos quotannis rosas supra se et Flaviam Salutarem uxorem eius mittendas ex XXXV sacrificiumque faciendum de XXII per magistros decrevit. P. Haelius Cissus sibi et Ligariae Artimialdi vivens posuit. In agro pedes XV infra pedes XXV. Hic locus heredem non sequitur.' Aliaque sepulcra Maceratae et alibi in Piceno extare videmus, quibus similia epulorum legata elegantibus litteris inscripta sunt. Unde, quod a pluribus[30] factum esse constat, omnes tenemus testamento legasse epulum quotannis ad sepulcrum rosis et variis respersum odoribus pro hereditatum facultatibus exhibendum, cui quidem epulo[31] non magis cognatos affinesque quam magistratuum quos gesserant opificiorumque, quae exercuerant[32] collegia, aut legionis in qua militassent ordinum ductores et commilitones interesse iubebant.[33] Idque, etsi sacerdotibus pro divina re facienda convocatis et commodo et delectationi multis cedebant modis, maiorem brevi post afferebat utilitatem. Cum enim contingeret aut herede absque legi-

still living set up this monument for himself. In his lifetime he gave thirty thousand sesterces to the college of workmen of the service at Ravenna, from which revenue every year gifts of two nummi each were to be distributed to the decurions of the college of workmen of the service at Ravenna who were present on the day of the festival of Neptune in the temple of Neptune which he built and 2,850 each were to be given every year to the decurions, so that from that sum they may, as they were accustomed to, adorn with roses the coffin of the Publicii, sons of Flavianus and Italicus, and the coffin in which has been placed Flavia Salutaris his wife, from up to twenty-five nummi, and make sacrifice from up to twenty-two and feast there from the rest. On account of this generosity the college of workmen of the service at Ravenna decreed them among the benefactors and that every year roses be strewn over him and his wife Flavia Salutaris from thirty-five nummi and a sacrifice be made from up to twenty-two nummi by the presidents."[48] "Publius Aelius Cissus while still alive erected this for himself and Ligaria Artimialdis. Fifteen feet in the field twenty-five feet below. This place does not follow the heir."[49] We see that other tombs still exist at Macerata[50] and elsewhere in Picenum with elegant inscriptions referring to similar bequests of feasts. For the reason that this was evidently done by many, I hold that all made a legacy in their will of a feast to be carried out every year according to the heirs' resources at the tomb which was strewn with roses and an assortment of perfumes. They invited to participate in that feast not so much relatives by birth and marriage as the associations of the magistracies they had performed and of the work in which they had been engaged, or the officers and fellow soldiers of the legion in which they had served. Even though, when priests were convened to perform a sacrifice, they yielded in many ways both to advantage and pleasure, yet shortly afterward this feast provided more profit. Since it might come about that the feast disappeared or

timis successoribus defuncto aut vetustate ipsa epulum absoleri in oblivionemque deduci, hereditatis portio pecuniam legato subministrare[34] solita per septemvirum diligentiam redigebatur in pontificum collegii potestatem. Ex hisque sacerdotia, quae a nostris appellari diximus beneficia, collegio pontificum distribuente fomenta novasque institutiones habuerunt.

12 Septemviri enim epulonum apud priscos haud secus quam nostrae religionis episcopi legatorum ad pias causas executionis curam habebant, cum tamen omnia templa, praesertim maiora, suos particulares habuerint[35] epulones sicut de Iovis templo supra ostendimus, in quo Aurelium Augustinum diximus affirmare epulones perpetuos fuisse, qui ad auream mensam Iovis statuae appositam perpetui erant convivae ut mimorum ibi potius et parasitorum contubernia quam dei sacra celebrarentur. Festus autem scribit 'epolones' dixisse maiores eos qui postea epulones appellati sunt, datumque fuisse nomen iis quod epulas Iovi ceterisque diis instituendi potestatem haberent. Fueruntque epulones a quibus scribit in VIIII Livius tibicines fuisse a commessatione solita prohibitos, unde Tibur concesserunt et nemo erat qui sacris praecineret, sed Tiburtini sopitos remiserunt curru et ius vescendi illis restitutum est. Eundem vero morem[36] epulandi in sacris locis ad legatorum executionem fuisse etiam a Christianis per multa tempora servatum Augustinus in *Dei civitate* his verbis ostendit: 'Quaecumque igitur adhibentur religiosorum obsonia in martyrum locis ornamenta sunt memoriarum[37] non sacra vel sacrificia mortuorum

fell into oblivion either because the heir died without legitimate successors or because of the very length of time it had existed, the part of the legacy which usually supplied the money for the bequest by the care of the Board of Seven was brought under the control of the college of pontiffs. As the college of pontiffs made the distribution, the priesthoods that I said we call benefices acquired support and new foundations from these funds.

Among the ancients the Board of Seven of Banquets,[51] no differently from the Christian bishops, had the responsibility of managing legacies for good causes, although all temples, especially the more important ones, had their own special banquet priests (*epulones*), as I showed above in the case of the Temple of Jupiter.[52] I said that Aurelius Augustine stated that in that temple there were permanent banquet priests who were standing guests at a golden table placed by his statue, the result being that there was a household of mimes and parasites there rather than celebration of the god's rites.[53] Festus writes that the ones who were later called "epulones" were called "epolones" by the ancestors. The name was given them because they had the right of setting up banquets (*epulae*) for Jupiter and the other gods.[54] The banquet priests were the ones by whom, Livy writes in Book IX, the flute players were banned from the customary banquet, which was the reason why they departed for Tivoli and there was no one to play at the sacrifices. But the people of Tivoli sent them back sound asleep in a cart, and their right to take part in the meal was restored.[55] Augustine demonstrates in *City of God* that the same custom of feasting in holy places to discharge the terms of a bequest was preserved for a long time even by Christians: "Therefore whatever victuals the pious consume in the places of the martyrs, these are to honor their memory and are not sacred or sacrificial rites given to the dead as though they were gods. Those who bring their own 12

tanquam deorum. Quicumque epulas suas eo deferunt, quod quidem a Christianis melioribus non fit et in plerisque terrarum nullatenus est consuetudo, cum apposuerunt orant.' Septemviri autem epulonum quantae fuerint auctoritatis ex verbis Auli Gellii licet cognoscere, qui eos facit maioribus sacerdotibus pares, flaminibus, auguribus, quindecim viris sacrorum his verbis. Virgines Vestales XX fuerunt quas pontifex maximus ex omni civitate capiebat, quae non essent filiae flaminis, auguris, quindecim viri sacrorum aut[38] septemviri epulonum. Fuisse autem ditissimos septemviros epulonum, quod plerumque videmus illis accidere qui multas etiam alienas tractant pecunias, unum extat argumentum quod eius collegii unus sepulcrum habuit Romae extans, quod insigne videmus paene integrum et falso ab imperitisque Remi appellatum, portae urbis olim Trigeminae, post Ostiensi et nunc sancti Pauli proximum. Id enim monumentum in piramidem supra urbis moenia, quibus est inclusum, surgens litteras inscriptum est semicubitales septemvirum epulonum eius auctorem nostro etiam saeculo conservantes.

13 Quinta sacerdotiorum opulentiae pars fuerunt damnatorum et vi aut iure patria pulsorum bona, quae ipsis in patriam aliquando reversis aut populus aut magistratus nunquam posse restitui cupiebant. Idque facile intelliget qui vitam et orationem Ciceronis perleget, in qua domum suam a pontificibus compellente Clodio, tribuno plebis, in templum Libertatis consecratam ab eisdem obtinuit liberari. Partibus quinque emolumenti et redituum proventuumque sacerdotiorum sive beneficiorum generaliter explicatis, unicam legatorum replicare et diffusius tractare libet, ex qua apparebit

feasts there (and this in fact is not done by Christians who know better and in most countries it is by no means the practice), pray when they have set them down."[56] That the Board of Seven of Banquets had considerable standing can be learned from Aulus Gellius' words. According to him they are the equals of the major priests, the flamens, the augurs and the Board of Fifteen in charge of the celebration of rites. He says there were twenty Vestal Virgins, chosen by the Chief Pontiff from the whole civic community, provided that they were not daughters of a flamen, augur, one of the Board of Fifteen in charge of the celebration of rites or one of the Board of Seven of Banquets.[57] The Board of Seven of Banquets were very rich, as we very often see is the case with those who handle large sums of money for others. One proof of this exists today, the tomb that belonged to one of that college and that still exists at Rome. This conspicuous tomb, which is almost intact and wrongly called "the tomb of Remus" by the ignorant, is to be seen right next to the city gate which was once called the Triple Gate, later the Ostian Gate and now St. Paul's Gate. This pyramidal-shaped monument rises up above the city walls, by which it is enclosed, and has an inscription in letters half-a-cubit high which preserve even to our own age the information that he for whom it was built was a banquet priest.[58]

The fifth source of wealth for the priesthoods consisted in 13
the property of those condemned and expelled from their homeland by force or the law, and which, by the wish of either the people or the magistrates, could never be restored to them should they at any time return home. This will easily be understood by anyone who peruses Cicero's life and the speech in which he managed to get his house released by the pontiffs after it had been consecrated as a temple of Liberty at the urging of Clodius, tribune of the plebs.[59] Now that I have explained in general terms the five sources of remuneration, revenues and profits for priesthoods (or benefices), I shall go back and treat the single case

priscos gentiles felicitatem beatitudinemque, ut appellabant, animarum in campis Elysiis ducendam per temporalium bonorum in legata post mortem dandorum distributionem diligentius quam nostros vitam per dei contemplationem aeternam quaesivisse. Sed prius quod de campis Elysiis diximus aliquali ex parte ostendamus. Tibullus in *Elegis*: 'Ipsa Venus campos ducet in Elysios, hic choreae cantusque vigent, passimque vagantes dulce sonant tenui gutture carmen aves. Fert casiam[39] non culta seges, totosque per agros floret odoratis terra benigna rosis. At iuvenum series teneris inmixta puellis ludit et assidue proelia miscet amor. Illic est, cuicunque rapax mors venit amanti, et gerit insigni mirtea serta coma.' Econtra autem quia inferna etiam sicut nos poenarum loca crediderunt, Tibullus de eis sic habet: 'At scelerata iacet sedes in nocte profunda abdita, quam circum flumina nigra sonant, Tesiphoneque impexa[40] feros pro crinibus angues saevit et huc illuc impia tuba fugit.[41] Tum niger in porta serpentum Cerberus ore stridet et aeratas excubat ante fores.' Virgilius autem de Elysiis campis: 'Devenere locos laetos et amoena virecta fortunatorum nemorum sedesque beatas. Largior hic campos aether et lumine vestit purpureo solemque suum sua sidera norunt, pars in gramineis exercent membra palaestris, contendunt ludo et fulva luctantur arena, pars pedibus plaudunt choreas et carmina dicunt,[42] nec non Treicius longa cum veste sacerdos obloquitur numeris septem discrimina vocum, iamque eadem digitis, iam pectine pulsat eburno.' Et infra: 'Nulli certa domus, lucis habitamus opacis riparumque

of legacies more fully. This will show that the Gentiles of old sought to obtain their souls' felicity and blessedness (as they called it) to be spent in the Elysian Fields, by a distribution of temporal goods to be bestowed in bequests after death, more assiduously than our contemporaries seek eternal life through the contemplation of God. But first let me partly explain what I meant by the Elysian Fields. Tibullus in his *Elegies:* "Venus herself will bring me into the Elysian Fields. Here dancing and song flourish and flitting everywhere birds make their sweet song resound from their slender throats. Without tending, the land bears garland flowers and throughout the fields the generous earth blooms with sweet-smelling roses. A line of youths and maidens sport mingled together and love stirs up constant battles. In this place is any lover visited by greedy death and he wears a myrtle wreath in token on his hair."[60] On the other hand, because like us they believed that the underworld was a place of punishment, Tibullus says this about it: "The abode of criminals lies hidden in bottomless darkness. Black rivers boom around it. Disheveled Tisiphone, with wild snakes for hair, rages and the crowd of the wicked flees hither and thither. Then black, snake-mouthed Cerberus hisses in the gateway and keeps watch before the bronze doors."[61] Vergil on the Elysian Fields: "They arrived at the happy places and the pleasant greensward of the groves of the fortunate and the abodes of the blessed. Here more generously the air clothes the plains with brilliant light and they know their own sun and their stars. Some exercise on grassy athletics grounds. They compete in wrestling and struggle on the golden sand. Others stamp the beat of the dance and sing. The Thracian priest as well in his long robe sounds the seven separate notes in accompaniment to the rhythm, striking them now with his fingers, now with a plectrum."[62] And further on: "No one has a fixed home. We live in shady groves and we stay on cushioning banks and in meadows kept fresh by

thoros et prata recentia rivis incolimus.' De inferis vero eadem et multo maiora quam Tibullus habet Virgilius.

14 Sed iam ad legata revertamur. Valentiniano secundo, imperatore Romano eius[43] nominis secundo, apud Mediolanum agente, tumultus in urbe Roma ingens fuit inter Christianos gentilesque ex huiusmodi causa concitus. Erant[44] per id temporis Christiani in urbe adeo aucti ut gentilium sectam opibus et numero aequarent enitebaturque[45] una quaeque pars et quotidie variis quaerebat modis et artibus[46] alteram superare. Accidit autem Christianos aram quae in curia veteri, ubi nunc sancti Petri ad vincula celebris est ecclesia, gentilium superstitionis erat suo cultui dedicare, quod cum audivere pagani, ad arma tumultumque est concursum, nostris quod intentaverant conservare, illis impugnare ac in suam redigere idolatriam adnitentibus. Sed, quod erat propinqui et imperium obtinentis tunc etiam integrum imperatoris metus ingens, obtinuerunt utriusque partis graves viri rem ad principis iudicium deferendam. Missusque est Mediolanum a gentilibus vir nobilitate, eloquentia ac dignitate insignis Simachus patritius ex cuius oratione quam habuit extante ista sumimus. Isque, inter cetera quae diffuse dixit alio tempore et loco diligentius narranda, a Valentiniano postulavit Vestalibus reddi legatorum ius percipiendorum, quod paulo prius quam ea dedicaretur, de qua diximus, a Christianis ara eisdem Vestalibus iussu imperatoris sublatum erat. Simachusque inter orandum pluries dictum saepe[47] repetivit tanti iam pridem fuisse urbi Romae legata Vestales potuisse capere ac distribuere ut neminem illae in populo in urbe ipsa sinerent mendicare. Constansque et perseverans in fide catholica Valentinianus, quam beatus Ambrosius ecclesiae doctor in illo roborabat, ita in sententia

streams."[63] About the underworld Vergil has the same as Tibullus and much more besides.

But let us now return to legacies. When Valentinian II, the 14
second Roman emperor of this name, had his court at Milan, there was a huge commotion between the Christians and Gentiles in the City of Rome, provoked by the following cause. At that time the Christians in the city had so increased that they equaled the Gentiles' sect in wealth and numbers. Each party was striving and seeking every day to outdo the other by various ways and means. It happened that the Christians dedicated to their own form of worship an altar belonging to the Gentiles' false religion, which was in the Old Meetinghouse where the famous church of St. Peter in Chains now is.[64] When the pagans[65] heard of this, all rushed to riot and take up arms, those on our side striving to keep what they had laid under threat, the pagans striving to fight back and to restore it to their own idolatry. But because there was a great fear of the emperor, who was near at hand and still held undiminished power, the influential men on both sides managed to have the affair referred to the emperor's judgment. The patrician Symmachus was sent to Milan by the Gentiles. He was a man of outstanding rank, eloquence and influence. The speech which he delivered is still extant and I have excerpted these passages from it. Among all the rest that he expressed at length and that must be recounted more carefully at another time and place, he demanded of Valentinian that there be restored to the Vestals the right of accepting legacies which had been taken away from them by the emperor's command a little before that altar I mentioned was dedicated by the Christians.[66] In the course of his speech Symmachus repeatedly said that it had long been of very great importance to the City of Rome that the Vestals could receive and distribute legacies for as a result they allowed no one among the people in the city itself to go begging. Constant and steadfast in the Catholic faith which blessed Ambrose Doctor of

perstitit ut nec aram nec legata Vestalium Simachus pro gentilium secta obtinere potuerit.

Sed iam satis pontifices, flamines, sacerdotes eorumque ad lasciviam, ad opes, ad amplitudinem fomentum sacerdotia quid apud priscos gentiles fuerint docuimus. Cetera nunc ostendere pergamus quae eorundem superstitio habuit. Agonalia Iani sacra ad nonam diem Ianuarii festa erant, quorum nominis origo quincuplex reddebatur[48] quod minister sacrorum hostiam feriturus, ne iniussus ageret, cultrum tenens elevatum continuo sacerdotes agendi tempus rogabat una, et quod pecudes non venirent sed agerentur alia, tertia quod pro Agnalibus ab agnis, qui[49] imolabantur, corrupte agonalia appellarentur, et quarta quod pecudes visa in aquis cultri, quo feriendae erant, umbra animis angerentur. Quintam meliorem Ovidius in *Fastis* existimavit, agonalia scilicet verbo Graeco a ludis similibus appellari, observatumque esse eo in sacrorum ritu hostiam non victimam immolari, cum hostia sicut docuimus pro caesis hostibus a quolibet sacerdote, victima eius qui hostes vicerit manibus debeat imolari. Fiebantque huiusmodi sacra ad templum Iani quod paene integrum ad sanctum Georgium in Velabro patentibus quadrifariam portis *Romam instaurantes* extare docuimus. Februa a Romanis triplici ratione piacula sunt appellata, aut vetere vocabulo a lana quam regem sacrificulum aut flaminem Dialem immolaturi peterent sacerdotes, aut pari vetustate vocabuli a farre frugibus mixto, aut a ramis de pura arbore caesis, quibus sacerdotes consueverint coronari. Ovidius in *Fastis:* 'Februa

the Church kept strong in him, Valentinian stood so firm in his determination that Symmachus could not win either the altar or the legacies of the Vestals for the Gentiles' sect.[67]

But I have now given sufficient information about the role in 15
pagan antiquity of the pontiffs, flamens and priests and their priesthoods, an encouragement for licentiousness, wealth and splendor. Now let us proceed to set out all the rest that their false religion involved. The Agonalia was a festival sacred to Janus held on January 9. Five different explanations of the name's origin were related. One was that, when the attendant at the sacrifice was about to strike the victim, lest he proceed (*agere*) without being bidden, as he held the knife aloft he would forthwith ask the priests if it was time to act (*agere*). Another was that the beasts did not come, but were driven (*agi*). The third was that the name Agonalia was a corruption of Agnalia, derived from the lambs (*agni*) that were sacrificed. The fourth was that the sheep felt distress (*angi*) when they saw in the water the reflection of the knife by which they were going to be struck. Ovid in *Fasti* thought the fifth explanation the best, that is, that the festival was called Agonalia by a Greek word for similar games (*agones*),[68] and that in this sacrificial ritual they observe the rule that a *hostia* not a *victima* was slain, since, as I have shown,[69] the *hostia* should be sacrificed by any priest in place of the slain enemies (*hostes*), while the victim (*victima*) must be sacrificed by the hands of the one who defeated the enemy (*vincere*). Sacrifices of this kind were performed at the temple of Janus which I have shown in *Rome Restored* is extant today almost intact near St. George in the Velabrum and has four open archways.[70] Purifications were called "februa" by the Romans for three reasons: either from an old word for the wool that the priests, when they were going to sacrifice, asked for from the king for sacrifices (*rex sacrificulus*) or the priest of Jupiter, or from an equally ancient word for spelt mixed with grain, or from boughs, cut from an undefiled tree, with which the priests were customarily crowned.

Romani dixere piacula patres. Pontifices ab rege petunt et flamine lanas quae veterum lingua februa nomen habent. Quaeque capit lictor domibus purgamina certis, torrida cum mica[50] farra vocantur idem; nomen idem ramo, qui caesus ab arbore pura casta sacerdotum tempora fronde tegit.' Macrobius in *Saturnalibus:* poenas a nocente Saturnalibus exposcere piaculare est, et infra, regi sacrificulo flaminique 'non licet videre feriis opus fieri et ideo per praeconem nunciabatur ne quid ageretur' quamquam Festus petios dicit appellatos, qui taliter flamines praecedebant 'et praecepti negligens multabatur.'[51] Praeter poenam opus qui fecisset porcum pro piaculo dabat. Plutarchus in *Problematibus:* eos quos in agro externo obiisse falso nuntiatum esset cum postea reversi fuissent, non ianua in domum recipiebant, sed tegulis dimittebant quod piacula omnia sub divo fieri consueverunt.[52] Plinius in *Naturali Historia:* 'Mirtea verbena Romani Sabinique, cum propter raptas[53] virgines dimicare voluissent, depositis armis purgati sunt, quo in loco Veneris Cluicinae[54] signa sunt: purgare enim cluere prisci dixere.'

16 Et vulgata priscis temporibus opinio obtinuit februa esse omnia quibus malefactorum conscientia purgaretur delerenturque[55] peccata aut manes animabus defunctorum placidi redderentur, unde inter februa fuit habita aquae aspersio qua, sicut et nos, gentiles utebantur, quamquam mos ipse prius a Graecis quam a Romanis originem habuit, unde Peleus traditur absolvisse Patroclum et ab Acasto absolutum fuisse Peleum a caede Phoci fratris sui, cum

Ovid in *Fasti:* "Our Roman fathers called purifications 'februa.' The pontiffs ask the king and flamen for pieces of wool called 'februa' in the tongue of the men of old. The means of purification—the toasted spelt and salt—that the lictor takes from certain houses are called by the same name. The same name is given to the bough which, cut from an undefiled tree, with its leaves decks the holy brows of priests."[71] Macrobius in *Saturnalia:* punishing a guilty man during the Saturnalia is an act requiring expiation,[72] and further on, the king for sacrifices (*rex sacrificulus*) and the flamen are "not allowed to see work being carried out during festivals and for this reason an announcement was made by a herald that nothing be done" (although Festus says those who thus went before the flamens were called "petii")[73] "and anyone disregarding the warning was fined." Anyone who performed work, besides being punished, would offer a pig in expiation.[74] Plutarch in *Problems:* when those who had been falsely reported to have died on a foreign field had come back, they did not admit them into the house by the door but let them down through the tiles, for the reason that all expiatory rites were usually performed under the open sky.[75] Pliny in *Natural History:* "After the Romans and the Sabines had resolved to fight because of the abduction of the young girls, they put down their arms and were purified by myrtle branches in the place where the images of Venus of the Sewer (*Cluacina*) are, because the ancients used *cluere* (to purify) for *purgare* (to clean)."[76]

And in early times the opinion commonly prevailed that purifications (*februa*) were everything by which the consciousness of wrongdoing was cleansed and sins were wiped away or their spirits made peaceful for the souls of the dead. For this reason among purifications was counted sprinkling with water, which the Gentiles used just as we do, although the actual custom originated among the Greeks before the Romans. For this reason Peleus is reported to have absolved Patroclus and Peleus himself was absolved by Acastus of the murder of his own brother, Phocus, 16

interim Aegeus Medeam aquae aspersione lustraverit, quam opinionem Ovidius damnat his versibus: 'Ah[56] faciles nimium, qui tristia crimina caedis fluminea tolli posse putatis aqua.' Virgilius tamen facit Aeneam cum iusta Miseno solvisset 'sparsisse eum rore levi[57] dixisseque novissima verba.' Cicero *Legum* primo: 'Caste iubet lex ad deos ire, animo videlicet in quo sunt omnia; nec tollit castimoniam corporis, sed cum observetur ut casto corpore multo etiam animis id observandum magis. Nam illud vel aspersione aquae vel dierum numero tollitur, animae labes ne diuturnitate vanescere ne ⟨a⟩ manibus ullis elui[58] potuit.' Et Macrobius in *Saturnalibus*: 'Constat diis superis sacra facturum corporis ablutione purgari, cum vero inferis litandum est satis actum videtur si aspersio sola attingat.' Aeneas Virgilianus: 'Donec—inquit—me flumine vivo abluero' et infra: 'Annam,[59] cara mihi nutrix, huc siste sororem. Dic corpus properet fluviali spargere lympha.' Et alibi: 'Sparserat et latices simulatos fontis Averni.' Nec non cum Misenum sepulturae mandari refert: 'Idem ter socios pura circumdedit unda spargens rore levi.' Et cum Aeneam facit apud inferos ianuam Proserpinae consecrantem: 'Occupat Aeneas aditum corpusque recenti spargit aqua.' Fuit etiam prope portam Capenam, nunc Appiam aqua Mercurii appellata, ad quam, cum convenisset populus Romanus, unusquisque lauri ramo alterius caput ea aspergebat aqua Mercurium invocans, ut aspersi peccata praesertim periuria mendaciaque dilueret.

17 Maiora autem certioraque Februa fuerunt per XII dies continuos Februarii celebrata. Unde mensem illum nomen inde

whereas Aegeus purified Medea by a sprinkling of water, a belief Ovid condemns with these verses: "Ah, too ready to believe, you who think that the grievous charge of murder can be removed by river water."[77] Yet Vergil says that Aeneas, when he had performed Misenus' funeral rites, "sprinkled him with light dew and spoke a final farewell."[78] Cicero in Book I of *On the Laws:* "The law bids us approach the gods in purity, that is, purity of the heart, for that contains everything, nor does it exempt physical purity, but, since the law that the body be pure is respected, so much the more should it be respected that the heart too be pure. The body's impurity is removed by a sprinkling of water or by a number of days passing, but the soul's stain cannot fade with time nor can it be washed away from any departed spirit."[79] Macrobius in *Saturnalia:* "It is agreed that someone intending to sacrifice to the gods above is cleansed by washing the body, but when a propitiatory offering is made to the gods of the underworld, a sprinkling alone is thought to be enough." Vergil's Aeneas says: "'until I have cleansed myself with running water,' and further on, 'dear nurse, bring Anna, my sister, here. Tell her to hasten to sprinkle her body with river water,' and elsewhere, 'she had sprinkled water feigned to come from the spring of Avernus.'" "So also, when he tells of Misenus' burial 'he, too, three times encircled his companions with pure water, sprinkling them with light dew' and when he describes Aeneas dedicating the bough to Proserpina in the underworld 'Aeneas gains the entrance way and sprinkles himself with fresh water.'"[80] Moreover near the Capene Gate (now the Appian Gate)[81] there was what was called the "Water of Mercury." The Roman people came together there and sprinkled that water on each others' heads with a bough of bay while invoking Mercury, so that they might wash the sprinkled man's sins away, especially perjuries and lies.[82]

More important and more established purifications were celebrated for twelve days in a row in February.[83] For this reason many 17

nactum fuisse multi existimaverunt, hisque diebus, cum pro impetranda[60] mortuorum animabus quiete omnis populus piaculis sacrificiisque circa sepulchra accensis facibus caereisque esset intentus, interdictum erat virginum viduarumque matrimoniis et vestem induti atram omnes consuetum domi dimittebant ornatum. Sed paulo postquam horrida cessaverant Februa dies succedebant laetissimi, Caristia[61] appellati, quibus diebus agnati affinesque alternato convenientes officio primum defunctos enumerabant, quos ab anteactis Caristiis[62] amisissent. Exinde superstitibus pariter enumeratis finem eiulatibus defunctorumque complorationi imponendum constituebant et genio in conviviis commessationibus ceteroque applausu pro viribus supraque indulgebant. Romuli caedis casus feriatam una die tenebat urbem per Kalendas quae inde Caprotinae sunt[63] appellatae, quod ea die ad paludem capreae, in *Roma instaurata* descriptam, fuerit a patribus discerptus. Sed et Terminalia dies suos habuerunt festos, inde dicta quod deus Terminus sexto ab urbe Roma miliario via Laurentina, ferme ubi sancti Sebastiani passionis est locus, magno populi concursu celebrantur. Estque is Terminus quem, cum dedicaretur Capitolium, ferunt ceteris diis Iovi cedentibus remansisse. Idque M. Varro scribit optimum fuisse visum Romanis augurium, quasi vero intelligi potuerit Romani imperii terminos quocumque producerentur inde removeri repellique nequire.

18 Diximus *Romam instaurantes* Equiriam[64] fuisse viam, qua rhedis a monumento Augusti, nunc Augusta appellato, ad Circum Flaminium, nunc Agonem, currebatur, quae quidem via ecclesiae continens esset sanctae Mariae nunc in Equiria[65] appellatae. Sed quantum attinet ad praesens opus Equiria[66] diebus quoque duobus

thought this was the origin of the month's name.[84] During these days, since the whole populace was concentrated on atonements and sacrifices to obtain rest for the souls of the dead, lighting torches and tapers around the tombs, there was a prohibition on marriage with virgins and widows[85] and all dressed in black garments and put away at home the adornment they usually wore. But a little after the somber purifications came to an end, there followed the very joyful days called "Caristia," days during which relatives by blood or marriage, coming together in turns, first counted up those who they had lost since the last Caristia and then, after counting up the living in the same way,[86] resolved that they must put an end to wailing and lamenting for the dead and indulged their pleasure in feasts and banquets and every other enjoyment[87] with all their might or more so. The anniversary of Romulus' slaying kept the city on holiday for one day during the Kalends that are thence called *Caprotinae*. This was because on that day he was torn to pieces by the senators at the "Goat's Marsh" (*Palus Capreae*), which is described in *Rome Restored*.[88] The festival of Terminalia too has its own holidays. It was so named because a great crowd flocked together to celebrate the god Terminus at the sixth milestone from Rome on the Laurentine Way[89] almost at the place where St. Sebastian was martyred.[90] He is the Terminus whom they say, at the time when the Capitol was dedicated, remained behind, though all the other gods gave place to Jupiter.[91] Marcus Varro writes that this seemed an excellent omen to the Romans, as though in fact it could be understood that however far the boundaries of the Roman empire were extended they could not be moved or driven back from that point.[92]

In *Rome Restored* I said that Equirria was a road down which 18
they raced in chariots from the Mausoleum of Augustus (now called "Augusta")[93] to the Flaminian Circus (now called "Agone").[94] Indeed this road skirted the church now called St. Mary in Equiria.[95] But as far as the present work is concerned, Equirria

ultimis Februarii nomen fuit, in quibus Marti deo is agitandi rhedas et equos ritus[67] in sacrificium tribuebatur. Pulchrum vero fuerit loca per quae is rhedarum equorumque a Marte,[68] sicut illi praedicabant, impulsorum cursus fiebat mente ingenioque inspicere. Campi Martii proprium, in quo deligendis magistratibus comitia haberentur, locum fuisse ostendimus, cui columna coclis Antoniana fuit apposita eique[69] continebat campo Augusti forum, templo Martis contiguum, quod ipse princeps quo tempore arma in Brutum Cassiumque cepit votum, postea quam Augusti nomen accepit opere sumptuosissimo exaedificavit. Cuius quidem templi columnationes adeo fuere sublimes, ut dicat Ovidius: 'Digna giganteis sunt haec delubra triumphis.' Unde videmus eas quae extant columnas stabulo summi viri Dominici Capranicensis, Cardinalis Firmani, supereminentes multis frustis esse compactas, quod nullas ditissimus potentissimusque princeps habere potuerit integras tam sublimes. Ut autem demus inditia eius templi reliquiarum cum dictis columnis extantia, sunt plateae presbyterorum appellatae continentes quibus[70] ecclesia imminet sancti Stephani parva, sed marmoribus picturisque ornata et a columna Antoniana, qua in occidentem solem vergit, paucis parvisque civium aedibus separata hisque in civium domibus et presbyterorum platea[71] praeter columnatum aliae tanti templi reliquiae[72] nunc visuntur.

19 Sed ad rem. Scribit Plinius fuisse in foribus templi illius Martis Apollinem eburneum ingentis magnitudinis, et Ovidius, quem Augusto adulari oportuit, dicit in summo eius fastigio diversa fuisse signa ex aere eximii operis. Hinc Aeneam, qui Anchisa genitorem Troiae excidio humeris asportaret, et alios gentis Iuliae ac Caesarum progenitores, inde ipsum Caesarem Augustum de patris sui interfectoribus superatis occisisque triumphantem, ut iam

was also the name of the last two days of February, on which this ritual of driving chariots and horses was given to Mars as an offering.[96] It would be a fine thing to see with the mind's eye the places through which this race of chariots and horses driven, as they stated, by Mars,[97] took place. There was, as I have shown, a specific place in the Field of Mars in which the elections to appoint magistrates were held,[98] where the spiral column of Antoninus Pius was set up.[99] And there bounded this Field the Forum of Augustus adjacent to the Temple of Mars.[100] The emperor himself vowed to build it at the time when he took up arms against Brutus and Cassius, and he completed the building most splendidly after he took the name Augustus.[101] The columns of the temple were so tall that Ovid says "this shrine was fit for Giants' triumphs."[102] Whence we see that these columns (which stand towering over the stables of the eminent Domenico Capranica, Cardinal of Fermo)[103] were put together from many pieces because no emperor however rich and powerful could have had such lofty ones from a single block. But to give extant evidence of the remains of this temple with the said columns, they are next to the square called "of the Priests."[104] Near them is the church of St. Stephen. It is small but ornamented with marbles and paintings and it is separated from the Antonine column on its west side by a few small private houses. In these private houses and in the Square of the Priests besides the colonnade other remains of this very large temple are now seen.

But to return to our subject. Pliny writes that there was an 19
ivory Apollo of great size on the doors of that Temple of Mars,[105] and Ovid, who had to flatter Augustus, says that on its rooftop there were various bronze statues of outstanding workmanship: on the one side, Aeneas who was carrying his father Anchises on his shoulders away from the destruction of Troy, and other ancestors of the Julian family and the Caesars; on the other, Caesar Augustus himself triumphing over his father's killers whom he had

mente et animo perspicere liceat per ornatissimum undique Campum Martium et post per forum Augusti omnium urbis praeter magnum Romanum speciosius, deinde ad fores templi Martis, ut diximus, ornatissimas viam fuisse equos agentibus et spectantibus pulcherrimam. Nec vero soli deo Marti optime de Romano populo merenti, sed infami quoque mulieri Florae habiti sunt honores; eam, nobilissimum sui temporis scortum, et amasse Pompeium et ab ea fuisse dilectum Plutarchus est auctor. Quae sicut et Larentina, cum pecuniae ingentis meretricio quaesitae populum Romanum instituisset heredem, in dearum numero est relata illique ludorum honores dati, Floralia appellati, ad clivum[73] Capitolinum mense Maio celebrabantur, quos quidem ludos meretrices egisse nudatas cum alibi, tum maxime constat apud Senecam ubi epistola LXXXXVII[I] scribit: 'Catone sedente populum Romanum negasse permissum sibi postulare[74] Florales ludos nudatarum meretricum.' Ut iam aequiore sit tolerandum animo nostri temporis prostitutas eo propemodum loco tabernas habere et casas ubi Florae meretricis dedecus quotannis ludorum gloria honestabatur. Quia vero domum Flora apud Pompeii theatrum habuerat non indecenter aut accidit aut de industria factum videtur, ut qui amore iuncti[75] fuerant honorum quoque monumenta habuerint coniuncta, campusque ex deiectis domibus meretricis in eius memoriam decusque Florae appellatus, nunc etiam id retinet nomen estque omnium praesentis Romanae urbis camporum arearumque publicarum commerciis et populi frequentia celebratissimus, praesertim postea quam in Pompeii theatro pridem sicut *Romam instaurantes* diximus collapso speciosissimas ornatissimasque aedes quidam, Flora et eius sodalicio dignus, sed nec nostris nec cuiuspiam

defeated and slain.[106] Now one may see in the mind's eye that the road through the Field of Mars adorned on all sides and after that through the Forum of Augustus, the most splendid of all in the city apart from the great Roman Forum, and then to the doors of the Temple of Mars, which were highly decorated, as I have said, was a very beautiful one, both for those driving the horses and for those looking on. Nor were honors paid only to the god Mars, who deserved very well of the Roman people, but also to Flora, a woman of ill fame. Plutarch tells us that she was the most celebrated prostitute of her time and that Pompey loved her and he was held dear by her.[107] Like Larentina she too was deified, since she had made the Roman people heir to the huge fortune she amassed by her trade.[108] She was honored with games called the Floralia and these were celebrated in May on the rise of the Capitol.[109] It is confirmed in other sources, but most importantly in Seneca, that prostitutes performed these games naked. He writes in *Letter* XCVII that as long as "Cato was in the audience the Roman people, it is said, did not allow themselves to ask for entertainment by naked prostitutes at the Floralia."[110] So that now it must be borne with more equanimity that prostitutes of our own time have booths and huts in almost the same place where every year the prostitute Flora's shame was honored with the glory of games. As Flora lived near Pompey's theater, it either happened fittingly or seems to have been brought about on purpose that those who had been bound in love should have linked memorials of their honors too. After the demolition of her house, the Field was called Flora's in her memory and honor, a name it still keeps today.[111] Of all the squares and public spaces of the present-day City of Rome, it is the most celebrated for trade and crowds of people, especially now that a certain man, worthy of Flora and her companions, but not fit to be commemorated in my or anyone else's writings (he disdained renown along

litteris per famam quam semper simul cum virtutibus sprevit conservandus magno sed in solo alieno extruxit impendio bene merenti Ursinae genti commodum allaturo.

20 Lustria fuerunt dies festi Martis dei ritibus consecrati, in quibus ad VII Kalendas Maii tubae, aquilae aliaque Romana signa militaria lustrabantur, ut originem inde potuerit habuisse mos per aetatem quoque nostram servatus, cum per diem natalem martyris Georgii vexilla et omnem pompam castrensem ex urbibus deferentes in nemora nostri milites etiam ipsi lustrare videntur. Saturnaliaque et ipsa fuerunt dies festi Saturno dicati, quorum feriationem omnium longissimam et luxuriem maximam[76] Senecae verbis libet ex *Epistulis* describere: 'December est mensis cum maxime civitas sudat, ius luxuriae publicae datum est, ingenti apparatu sonant omnia tanquam quicquam inter Saturnalia intersit et dies rerum agendarum. Adeo nihil interest ut mihi videatur non errasse qui dixit olim mensem fuisse Decembrem, nunc annum.' Nec tamen parum similia esse videntur quae eodem mense per Christi Dei nostri natalia[77] committuntur a nostris. Et Bachanalia, Libero patri Bacho dicata, temporis longitudine per autumnum Saturnalibus paria maiore luxu celebrata sunt. Nudi enim viri[78] cum nudatis omnia membra mulieribus, matronis viduis et virginibus ad sacra conveniebant, quae non nisi nocturna erant, caput omnes pariter femoraliaque pampinis et uvarum racemis cincti alios item uvarum racemos manu tenebant, et, tumultuario invicem commixti coetu in sublime saltantes variaque gesticulatione brachia cervicem caputque moventes, carmen Bacho inconditum decantabant, nec prius erat saltationis modus quam defatigati et toto corpore vacillantes, partim resupinarentur proximioribus inhaerentes, partim in pavimentum fanatici amentesque procumberent,

with the virtues) has built on the site of Pompey's theater, ruined long ago as I said in *Rome Restored,*[112] a very splendid and ornate palace at great expense, but on another's ground, to bring advantage to the well-deserving family of the Orsini.[113]

The Lustria was a festival dedicated to the rites of the god Mars 20
in which on April 23 trumpets, eagles and other Roman military standards were purified.[114] This might be the origin of the custom preserved up to our own time too, when on the birthday of St. George the Martyr our soldiers take flags and all their military array out from the cities into the woods and they too seem to carry out a lustration.[115] The Saturnalia was a festival dedicated to Saturn.[116] I want to describe its holiday, the longest of all, and its very great indulgence in words from Seneca's *Letters:* "It is December, the month above all when the city is in a sweat. License is given to public festivity. Everything resounds with large-scale preparations as though there were some difference between the Saturnalia and days of business. In fact the difference is so nonexistent that I think the man was not wrong who said that December once was a month, but now it is a year."[117] But still the festivities in which we engage during the same month for the birth of Christ our God seem very similar. The Bacchanalia,[118] dedicated to Liber, Father Bacchus, was like the Saturnalia in length, extending through the autumn, but was celebrated with greater debauchery. Naked men, together with women bared in every limb, wives, widows and young girls, flocked to the rites which took place only at night. All alike tied round their heads and loin cloths vine leaves and bunches of grapes and they held other bunches of grapes in their hands and, in turns mingling with the riotous throng, leaping on high, moving arms, neck and head in various gestures, chanted an improvised song to Bacchus. There was no end to the dancing until, exhausted and their whole body unsteady, some fell on their backs clinging to those closest to them, others on their fronts on the floor in a mindless ecstasy. So that

ut recte senserit M. Varro talia nisi ab amentibus fieri non potuisse.

21 Quid vero incestuum constuprationumque in huiusmodi nocturnis conventibus sit commissum Livius XL libro his verbis scribit: 'Hispala originem Bachorum expromit; primo sacrarium id feminarum fuisse. Esoponem sacerdotem omnia tamquam deum monitu immutasse, nocturnum sacrum ex diurno quinos singulis mensibus dies initiorum fuisse, ex quo inde promiscua sacra sint et permixti viri feminis et noctis licentia accesserit, nihil ibi facinoris, nihil flagitii praetermissum. Plura virorum inter sese quam feminarum stupra. Si qui minus patientes dedecoris sint et pigriores ad facinus pro victimis immolari, nihil nefas ducere. Viros, velut mente capta, cum iactatione fanatica corporis vaticinari; matronas Bacharum habitu crinibus pansis cum ardentibus facibus decurrere ad Tybrim, demissasque in aquam[79] faces, quia vivum sulphur cum calce insit, integra flamma efferri.' Prosequiturque Livius paulo infra: 'Institutum fuisse ne quis maior viginti annis initiaretur, captari[80] aetates et erroris et stupri patientes. Consules in rostra ascenderunt et contione advocata cum solemne carmen praecationis, quod fari prius quam populum alloquantur magistratus consueverunt, peregissent ita coepit: "Bachanalia tota iam pridem Italia et nunc per urbem etiam multis locis esse non fama modo accepisse vos, sed crepitibus etiam ululatibusque nocturnis qui personent tota urbe certum habeo. Primum igitur mulierum magna pars est et is fons mali huiusce[81] fuit. Deinde simillimi feminis mares, stuprati et constupratores, fanatici, vigiles vino strepitibusque nocturnis attoniti. Maiores nostri ne nos quidem, nisi

Marcus Varro opined correctly that such things could be done only by people not in their right senses.[119]

Livy in Book XL describes in the following words what unchaste deeds and debaucheries were perpetrated in nocturnal gatherings of this kind: "Hispala revealed the origin of the Bacchic rites. At first this sanctuary was reserved for women. The priestess Paculla brought about a complete change, as if by the bidding of the gods. The rite became nocturnal instead of diurnal. There were five days of initiation each month. From the time when the rites became open to all, and the association of men with women and the license afforded by night were added, no crime, no deed of shame there was left undone. The debaucheries of men with each other were more numerous than those of the women. If they were less tolerant of misbehavior and less ready to engage in misdeeds, they were sacrificed as victims. They regard nothing as forbidden. Men prophesy as if possessed, tossing their bodies around in ecstatic agitation. Married women in Bacchic garb with loosened hair would run down toward the Tiber with blazing torches, and when the torches were plunged into the water they were lifted out with the flame still burning because they were made of live sulfur mixed with the lime."[120] Livy continues a little further on: "the practice had been established that no one over twenty should be initiated; they took age groups tolerant of wrongdoing and debauchery."[121] "The consuls mounted the speaker's platform and called a meeting of the people. When they had completed the regular prayer formula which the magistrates usually spoke before they address the people, the consul began thus: 'I am sure that you have grasped, not only by report, but also by the nocturnal uproar and cries that echo throughout the city, that the Bacchanalia have long been all over Italy and are now also in many places throughout the city. First, then, the majority are women and this has been the source of this evil. Next, men very like the women, debauchees and debauchers, people possessed, sleepless, befuddled by wine 21

cum aut vexillo in arce posito comitiorum causa aut exercitus eductus esset aut plebi concilium tribuni edixissent, aut aliqui ex magistratibus ad concionem vocassent, forte temere coire voluerunt.[82] Et ubicunque multitudo esset, ibi et legitimum rectorem multitudinis censebant debere esse."' 'Senatus[83] consulto cautum ne qua Bachanalia in urbe, neque in Italia essent.' Nec parvum ad ea tollenda momentum habuisse videtur Lentuli Cornelii Surae factum, quem constat ad urbis incendium caedemque civium primam Saturnalium noctem cum coniuratis destinavisse.

22 Ludos etiam scaenicos et theatrales flagitiosissimos ad deorum cultum institutos et ea ratione ipsum item theatrum a principio aedificatum fuisse scripsit Aurelius Augustinus, dicens 'ludos scaenicos spectacula turpitudinum et licentiam vanitatis, non hominum vitiis, sed deorum iussis Romae institutos, cum propter sedandam pestem corporum dii eos sibi iusserint exhiberi,' quos postea asserit obscenis vocibus et motibus histrionum fuisse actos, praesertim cum Fugalia celebrarentur, vere taliter appellata quod pudor inde et honestas dedita opera fugarentur, ut[84] merito ipse Augustinus exclamet:[85] 'Quanto iustius et honestius in Platonis templo libri eius legerentur quam in templis daemonum ⟨Galli⟩ abscinderentur, molles consecrarentur secarenturque insani et quicquid aliud vel turpe vel turpiter, crudele vel crudeliter in theatris et deorum sacris celebrari solet!' Qualiter autem omnes ludi fierent scaenici difficile fuerit docere, quod singulis paene vicibus ex histrionum ingenio ac industria variarentur.[86] Et satis constat omnes fabulas, a Plauto Terentioque et aliis comicis confictas, in

and nocturnal uproar. Our ancestors did not wish even us to come together by chance [and] for no purpose except when either the flag had been raised on the citadel for an election, or the army had been led out or the tribunes had decreed an assembly of the plebeians or some from among the magistrates had summoned a public meeting. And wherever there was a crowd, there too they thought there should be a lawful controller of the crowd.'"[122] "By a decree of the senate measures were taken that there should be no Bacchanalia in the City or in Italy."[123] What was done by Lentulus Sura appears to have had no small influence in getting rid of them. It is well known that he with fellow conspirators fixed on the first night of the Saturnalia for firing the city and slaughtering the citizens.[124]

Aurelius Augustine wrote that the most disgraceful stage and 22
theatrical shows were established for worship of the gods and that it was for this reason that the theater itself had been built in the first place, saying "that the theatrical festivals, the exhibitions of lewd deeds and the free rein given to frivolity were established at Rome, not by human immorality, but by divine command," "since the gods bade shows be put on for them to quell a plague."[125] Later on he states that these shows were acted by actors using obscene words and gestures, especially when the Fugalia (Feast of the Flight) was celebrated, rightly named thus, because modesty and decency were deliberately put to flight from them (*fugare*).[126] So that Augustine himself rightly exclaims, "How much better and more decent would it be to read Plato's books in a temple dedicated to him than for the Galli to be castrated, eunuchs consecrated and madmen mutilated in demons' temples and whatever other foul or cruel deed they used foully or cruelly to perform in theaters and in rites of the gods!"[127] It would be difficult to explain how all the stage shows were performed because on almost every particular occasion they varied according to the actors' talent and design and it is well enough known that all the plays devised by Plautus and Terence and the other comic poets were acted on the

scaena et theatro ab histrionibus eorumque ministris personatis deorum cultui spectante populo fuisse actas, unde scribit in *Vita Ciceronis* Plutarchus Aesopum, cum in theatro repraesentasset Athreum consultantem de iudicio Thiestis ex ingenti dolore mentis impotem, quendam ex ministris, quod ipse non observato tempore celerius adventasset, sceptro percussisse ac interfecisse. Cetera quae his scaenae actionibus competant in *Roma* docuimus *instaurata*.

23 Faciet autem ludorum mentio propter scaenicos suborta ut cetera de ipsis dicturi ferias prius in quibus fiebant doceamus, quamquam non solum ludos, sed et funebria et spectacula et pompas eodem paene contextu dicere oportebit, quae omnia suos dies feriatos habere, ut rite fierent, oportebat. 'Feriarum' Festus Pompeius inquit 'alias sine festo fuisse, ut Nundinas, alias cum festo, ut Saturnalia, quibus adiungebantur epulationes ex proventu fetus pecorum frugumque'; quamquam et idem Festus alio loco vim verbi exprimens dicit 'ferias a feriendis victimis esse dictas.' Nundinas aliqui Romulum, aliqui Tatium instituisse dicunt, quas 'Hortensius lege sanxit nefastas esse, ut rustici qui nundinandi[87] causa in urbem veniebant, lites componerent legesque acciperent. Nefasto enim die praetorem loqui non licebat.' Feriarum publicarum quatuor esse genera voluit Varro, aut enim stativae sunt, aut conceptivae aut imperativae, aut de quibus diximus nundinae. Stativae omnes populi communes certis et consuetis diebus ac mensibus et in fastis[88] observationibus annotatae, in quibus sunt Agonalia et Lupercalia superius a nobis descripta. Conceptivae quae quotannis

stage in the theater by actors and their servants wearing masks as a form of divine worship with the people as spectators. So Plutarch writes in his *Life of Cicero* that when Aesop was playing Atreus in the theater, at the point where he is deliberating about punishing Thyestes, out of his mind because of his great suffering, he struck one of the attendants with his scepter and killed him, because, not having kept his eye on the time, he came on too soon.[128] Everything else that pertains to these stage performances I have expounded in *Rome Restored*.[129]

Since mention of the games has come up in connection with theatrical shows, this will prompt me to explain first the festivals in which they took place, though I intend to say other things about them. It will be necessary, however, to speak in almost the same context not only of the games, but also of funeral rites, and shows and processions, all of which had to have their own festival days so that they might be duly performed. "Some religious festivals," Festus Pompeius says, "had no holiday, like market days (*Nundinae*), others had one, like the Saturnalia. Included in the Saturnalia were banquets supplied by the products of herds and of crops."[130] Yet the same Festus in another place where he is explaining the meaning of the word, says that "religious festivals (*feriae*) were so called from the slaughtering (*ferire*) of the victims."[131] Some say Romulus established market days, others Tatius.[132] "Hortensius by a law made them free of legal business (*nefastae*), so that country people who came in to the city to go to market might settle their disputes" and accept rulings. "For on a day free of legal business (*nefastus*) the praetor was not allowed to utter the formula of judgment."[133] It was Varro's view that "there were four kinds of public festivals. They are either fixed, or moveable, or commanded or the market days," which I have spoken of. "The fixed were shared by the whole people on determined and customary days and months, and marked in the calendar for observance. Among them are the Agonalia and the Lupercalia," which I have 23

a magistratibus vel a sacerdotibus accipiuntur in dies certos[89] vel incertos, ut sunt Latinae, Sementinae, Paganalia, Compitalia. Imperativae sunt quas consules vel praetores pro arbitrio indicunt. Erant praeterea feriae propriae familiarum, ut Claudiae, Aemiliae, Iuliae, Corneliae et aliarum. Erant singulorum, ut natalium, funerum et expiationum atque frugum susceptiones, quae feriarum pars latius patebat quod tribus temporibus feriae et dies festi erant. 'Rubigalia primo a Numa instituta[90] anno regni sui XI° ad VII Kalendas Maii, quia tunc segetes rubigo occupat.' 'Floralia quarto Kalendas Maias anno urbis quingentesimo sextodecimo ex oraculis Sibyllae, ut omnia bene deflorescerent.' 'Vinalia priora in Kalendas Martii degustandis vinis,' Vinalia altera ad XIII Kalendas Septembris, quod festum tempestatibus leniendis institutum est. Sementinae fuerunt feriae a sementibus faciendis; Paganicae agriculturae causa. Et demum feriae stultorum appellatae sunt Quirinalia quod eo die sacrificabatur ab iis,[91] qui solemni die aut non potuerant rem divinam facere aut ignoraverant. Quibus omnibus in diebus feriatis nihil omnino, quod non eius diei religio exposceret, fieri licebat, quamquam Scaevola, sicut et Hebraeorum consuetudo habet, licere voluit feriis ea fieri, quae neglecta nocerent, ut puta qui bovem fossa extraxisset, tignum domus ruinosum tibiis sustentasset.

24 Post ferias vero et nundinas, quoad expediens fore visum est descriptas, funebria nobis ideo sunt dicenda, ut in eis, qui exhibebantur, ostensis ludis alios cum spectaculis pompisque describendos ordine afferamus. Funebria mortuis primum a Numa

described above.[134] "The moveable are those which every year are set down by the magistrates or by the priests on determined or undetermined days, like the Latin festival, the Sementivae, the Paganalia, the Compitalia. The commanded are those that the consuls or praetors set according to their own judgment. Moreover there were religious festivals belonging to specific clans such as the Claudian, Aemilian, Julian, Cornelian and others. There were those of individuals, such as the markings of birthdays, funerals, expiations and crops."[135] This last category of festival was more capacious, because there were festivals and holidays on three occasions. First of all, "the Robigalia established by Numa in the eleventh year of his reign on April 25, because that is when rust attacks the crops,"[136] "the Floralia on April 27 established in the 516th year of the City in conformity with the Sibylline oracles, so that all would flower well."[137] "The first Vinalia on March 1 for tasting the wine,"[138] the second Vinalia on August 19, a festival instituted to ward off storms.[139] The Sementivae festival was from the sowing of seeds, the Paganicae for the sake of agriculture,[140] and, finally, the Quirinalia was called the Festival of Fools, because on that day sacrifice was performed by those who either could not perform their divine worship on the regular day, or were in ignorance of it.[141] On all of these holidays nothing at all was permitted to be done that was not required by the religious provisions of that day. Scaevola however (and this is Jewish practice too) had the view that it was permissible for those things to be done on festivals that would cause harm if they were neglected, as, for instance, one who had pulled an ox out of a ditch, or one who had propped up with supports a collapsing house beam.[142]

Now that the holidays and market days have been described as 24
far as seemed useful, I must talk of the funeral rites, so that after I have set out the games exhibited during them, I may bring forward in due order the others that must be described along with the shows and processions. Livy demonstrates that funeral rites for

Pompilio instituta fuisse Livius sic ostendit: 'Nec caelestes modo caerimonias, sed iusta quoque funebria placandosque manes ut idem pontifex doceret.' Ipsa vero funebria quam parce haberi deceret Cicero *Legum* primo sic dicit: 'Deorum Manium iura sancta sunto, hos[92] leto dato divos habento, sumptum in illis[93] luctumque minuunto.' Et infra: 'Minuendi sunt sumptus lamentationesque funeris.' Quibus autem modis et causis minuerentur lamentationes ipse Nonius Marcellus sic ostendit: 'Minuebatur populo luctus aedis dedicatione, cum a censoribus lustrum condebatur, cum votum publice susceptum solvebatur. Privatis autem cum liberi nascerentur, cum honos in familiam veniret, cum pater aut liberi aut vir aut frater ab hoste captus domum rediret, cum puella desponsaretur, cum propiore quis cognatione quam is qui lugebatur nasceretur, cum in festo ceteris consensissent.' Sequitur Cicero in *Legibus:* 'Mulieres genas ne radunto neve lessum funeris ergo habento.' Erat enim lessus lugubris eiulatio. Sequiturque Cicero: 'Haec laudabilia et locupletibus fuisse cum plebe communia, quod quidem maxime rectum est[94] tolli fortunae discrimen in morte. Coronam tamen virtute partam et ei qui peperisset et eius parenti sine fraude esse lex repositam iubet.' Hinc refert Livius Valerio Publicolae, post tres consulatus defuncto, ob paupertatem funus publice duci oportuisse. Pariter Menenio Agrippae, conciliatori plebis cum patribus, et Q. Fabio Maximo in funus aera fuisse collata.[95] Quadragesimoque octavo Livius pariter: 'M. Porcium Catonem filii in

the dead were first established by Numa Pompilius: "that the same pontiff should give instructions for not only ceremonies for the heavenly gods, but also due rites of burial and propitiation of spirits of the dead."[143] Cicero in Book I of *On the Laws* tells us how frugally the funeral rites themselves should be performed: "Let there be sanctified rites of the deified departed. Give them to death, consider them gods, curtail expenditure on them and mourning."[144] And further on: "the expenses of the funeral and the wailings at it should be curtailed."[145] Nonius Marcellus explains how and why the wailings were curtailed: "For the whole people mourning was brought to an end by the dedication of a temple, when the *lustrum* was completed by the censors, when a vow undertaken on behalf of the state was discharged. For private people on the other hand mourning was brought to an end when children were born, when honor came into the family, when a father or children or husband or brother taken captive by the enemy returned home, when a girl was betrothed, when a closer relative was born than the one who was being mourned, when they had come to harmony with the others at a festival."[146] Cicero continues in *On the Laws:* "women shall not tear their cheeks, nor have a keening (*lessus*) on account of a funeral." A *lessus* was a sorrowful cry.[147] Cicero continues, saying that: "these provisions were praiseworthy and shared by the wealthy and the common people alike because it is especially right that distinction of fortune be removed in death." "Nevertheless the law requires that the garland won by courage be assigned to him who had won it and to his father with immunity."[148] Hence Livy reports that when Valerius Publicola passed away after being consul three times, because of his poverty they had to give him a funeral at public expense.[149] Likewise for Menenius Agrippa who reconciled the plebeians with the senators.[150] Coins were collected for the funeral of Quintus Fabius Maximus.[151] In Book XLVIII Livy says likewise that "Marcus Porcius Cato spent very little, according to his ability

praetura mortui funus tenuissimo ut potuit (erat enim pauper) sumptu fecisse.' Et 'M. Aemilium Lepidum, qui princeps senatus sextis iam censoribus lectus erat, antequam expiraret, praecepisse[96] filiis lecto se strato [sine] linteis, sine purpura efferrent,[97] in reliquum funus ne plus quam aeris denos consumerent.'

25 Sed post hanc priscorum moderationem tam multa funeribus sepulcrisque ornamenta, tam ingentes sumptus posteri adhibuere ut ceteram omnem privatae impensae insaniam superaverint, de quibus omnibus ordine est dicendum. Prius tamen mores parandi cadaveris, post funeris sepulcrique impensam ostendemus. Qui coniunctores erant, uxor, filii aut fratres paterve aut genitrix, defuncto oculos claudebant et post parum, patefacto undique cubiculo introductis ex familia viciniaque[98] qui inspicere voluissent, terni quaternique mortuum altissimis vocibus nomine ter inclamitabant. Quo tacente qui advenerant conclamatum esse in publicum efferebant. Quod autem nonnulli aliquando, pro mortuis post conclamationem habiti in rogumque elati, ad flammae contactum palpitantes liberari nequissent, aqua omnes ferventi lavare mos fuit, qua tamquam expergefacti se vivere ostenderent. Exinde everricator, quem Festus inquit, iure accepta hereditate, iusta[99] facere defuncto debuisse, certo scoparum genere adhibito domum purgabat; cupressi ramo domus ostio in funeris indicium superposito, quod eam arborem Diti[100] sacram constat succisam nequaquam a radicibus pullulare. Si autem defunctus vir fuerat alicuius vel minimae dignitatis, praeco cives ad funus convocabat. Erantque verba

(because he was poor), on the funeral of the son who died when he was praetor" and "Marcus Aemilius Lepidus, who had been chosen leader of the senate by six pairs of censors, before his death gave his sons instructions that they should carry him out to burial on a bier spread with linen without purple and that on the rest of the funeral they should spend less than a million sesterces."[152]

But after this restraint of the men of old, later generations used 25
so many embellishments in funerals and graves and outlaid such huge expenses that they exceeded all the other extravagances of private spending. I must speak about all of that in due order. First, though, I shall outline the practices followed in laying out the corpse, and, after that, the expenses of the funeral and grave. The closer relatives, wife, sons, or brothers or father, or mother, would close the eyes of the deceased. After a while the bedroom was opened up completely, and those of the household and neighborhood who wanted to look on were admitted. Three or four at a time would call upon the dead man by name three times at the top of their voices. If he remained silent, those who had come in would make a public announcement that he had been called upon. Because from time to time some, who were regarded as dead after being called upon, and were placed on the pyre, had not been able to be set free when they struggled on contact with the flame, it was the practice to wash everyone with boiling water so that they might be woken up by it, as it were, and demonstrate that they were alive.[153] Next is the sweeper (*everriator*). He as Festus says, being the lawful heir, is he who has to perform the funeral rites for the deceased, by purifying the house with a certain kind of broom.[154] A cypress branch was placed above the house door as a sign of a death, because this tree, sacred to Dis, is known to be incapable of sprouting from its roots once it has been felled.[155] If the deceased had been a man of some standing, even the least, a herald would summon the citizens to the funeral.[156] The form

ut inquit Varro: [olli] ollus fato functus est. Polinctores exinde cadaverum curatores et vespeliones urendi humandive periti suum et ipsi praestabant officium. Nam, quod Plutarchus in *Problematibus* habet, in aede Libitinae, quae et Venus, omnia ad funus pertinentia publice parata erant. Qua ex re homines frugalitatis admonitos intelligere voluerunt Venerem, sicut advenientibus viam, ita decedentibus sepulturae instrumenta praebere. Vespeliones autem sic appellavere maiores quod pauperes maximus in civitate numerus, cum mane solemni et sumptuoso funere efferri nequirent,[101] vespere ab illis obscuriore per umbram modo deportarentur, appellabaturque id populare feretrum sandapila,[102] quod Suetonius in *Domitiani gestis rebus* sic edocet: 'Cadaver eius populari sandapila[103] per vespeliones asportatum.'

26 Sed, dum mortui in domo fieret comploratio, lugentes pelles insidebant mulieresque, quem nunc Romae servant morem, genas olim unguibus lacerasse hinc constat quod lege id prohibitum fuisse scribit Cicero. Funebres interea tibiae carmen ferale decantabant aderantque mulieres, pretio conductae praeficae[104] appellatae, et flendo[105] fortia defuncti facta miris in caelum et confictis et falsis saepius quam veris laudationibus extollentes, quarum et aliarum id genus muliercularum ineptae eiulationes et voces nenia appellatae[106] sunt, quae sic diffinit Festus: 'Nenia carmen, quod in funere laudandi gratia canitur ad tibiam. Sunt, qui eo verbo finem significari putant, quia volunt nenia ideo dici quod voci similior querimonia flentium sit. Quidam autem nenia dictum nomen ab

of words was, as Varro says: So-and-so has met his end.[157] Next the *pollinctores*, who prepared the corpse,[158] and the *vespillones*, expert in burning and burying, would also perform their office. For as Plutarch says in *Problems:* In the temple of Libitina (she is also Venus) everything needful for a funeral was available at public expense. By this means they wanted people to be put in mind of frugality and understand that just as Venus provides the way for new arrivals, so she provides the means of burial for those departing.[159] *Vespillones* (corpse-bearers) were so called by the ancestors because the poor, the majority of people in the city, could not be borne out to burial in the morning with a customary and costly funeral, and so were carried out by them in the evening (*vespere*) in a less visible manner under the cover of darkness.[160] The bier used by the people was called "sandapila," about which Suetonius in *Life of Domitian* gives the following information: "His corpse was carried out by corpse-bearers (*vespillones*) on the bier (*sandapila*) used by the people."[161]

While the deceased was being lamented in the house, the 26
mourners would sit on skins[162] and, from the fact that Cicero writes that it had been forbidden by law, we know that the women once rent their cheeks with their nails,[163] a custom which they still keep up in Rome today. Meanwhile the funeral pipes sounded the dirge and women called "praeficae" were hired to weep and extoll to the skies the deceased's brave deeds[164] with extraordinary praises, more often fabricated and false than true. The foolish wailings and utterances of these and other females of this kind were called a dirge (*nenia*). Festus defines it as follows: "A dirge is a song sung to the accompaniment of the flute at a funeral to praise the deceased. There are some who think this word means 'end' because they want it to have this name because the lamentation of those weeping is very like this word. Some say however that the *nenia* got its name from the designation for the last intestine,

extremi intestini vocabulo, quod Graece "extremum" significat.' Praetexta vero pulla uti, quod genus vestimenti est oblongum, talare et atrum, illi a quo funus fieret et nulli licuisse alio Festus est auctor. Mulieres vero defuncti propinquas in luctu albis vestibus indutas, sicut et ipsum mortui corpus fuisse, Plutarchus in *Problematibus* asserit redditque[107] causam primo cadaveris quod iam quasi emeritum et gravi certamine liberatum ad sepulchrum deduci splendidum oportuerit, et propinquos decuisse dicit defuncti corpus indumenti colore et specie imitari. Infectae enim coloribus vestes superfluitatem prae se visae sunt ferre ac sumptum, nec satis decuisse atro aut purpureo coloribus dolosis, sed potius alio amiciri coniunctos exemplo defuncti, qui purus et omni commixtione vacuus tinctorio corporis veneno liberatus esset.

27 Sepeliendi corpora duplicem fuisse morem videmus. Cicero enim *Legum* primo antiquissimum dicit fuisse genus sepulturae illud quo apud Xenophontem Cyrus utitur, quo[108] corpus terrae redditur et ita locato et sito quasi operimentum matris obducitur, gentemque Corneliam usque ad memoriam suam hac sepultura fuisse humatam. Et Livius in primo dicit Aeneae ultimum operum mortalium fuisse apud Numicum amnem, ubi situs sit, Iovemque Indigetem appellari. Et libro CXVIIII Livius dicit victum ab Hirtio et Caesare Antonium in Gallias confugisse ac Hirtium, qui post victoriam ex vulnere ceciderit,[109] et L. Pansam ex vulnere defunctum in Campo Martio sepultos esse. In *Legibus* item Cicero: 'Gaii Marii reliquias apud Anienem dissipari iussisse Sullam victorem, acerbiore odio incitatum quam si tam sapiens fuisset quam vehemens, quod, suo corpori cum timeret accidere, primus e patriciis

because in Greek it means 'last.'"[165] Festus says that no one else but the person conducting the funeral is allowed to wear a dark-colored *praetexta*.[166] This is a kind of elongated garment that is ankle length and black. Plutarch in *Problems* maintains that the women relatives of the deceased dressed in white while they were in mourning and the body of the deceased too was clothed in white. First of all he explains why this is so in the case of the corpse: because it has now, as it were, served out its time and been freed from the grievous struggle, it ought be taken to the grave looking bright. He says too that it was fitting that the relatives imitate the corpse of the deceased in the color and appearance of their dress. Dyed garments seemed to make a display of excess and expense. It was not fitting that the relatives be dressed in black or crimson, cheating colors, but in another color, following the example of the deceased, for he, pure and free from all admixture, had been released from the body's dye, a poison.[167]

We see that there were two ways of burying bodies. Cicero in 27
Book I of *On the Laws* says that the most ancient kind of interment was the one Cyrus used in Xenophon, by which the body is returned to the earth and so placed and laid as though it were covered by the coverlet of its mother. The Cornelian clan were interred by this mode of burial right up to his day.[168] Livy says in Book I that the last of Aeneas' mortal deeds was near the river Numicus, where he lies interred, and that he is called Jupiter Indiges.[169] In Book CXIX Livy says that Antony fled to Gaul when he was defeated by Hirtius and Caesar, and Hirtius, who fell of a wound after the victory, and Lucius Pansa, who died of a wound, were buried in the Field of Mars.[170] Cicero in *On the Laws* again says that "Sulla as victor ordered Gaius Marius' remains to be scattered in the Anio. If he had been as wise as he was violent, he would not have been motivated by so bitter a hatred. Since he feared that this would happen to his own corpse, he was the first of the patrician Cornelii who expressed the wish to be cremated."

Corneliis igni[110] voluit cremari.' Et tamen sequitur Cicero declarare Ennium de Africano: '"Hic est ille situs" vere, sitosque dici illos qui conditi sint eumque morem ius pontificale confirmare.' Et Plinius: 'Quin[111] defunctos sese multi fictilibus soliis condi maluere.' Nonius Marcellus: 'Membrum abscidi mortuo dicebatur cum digitus eius decidebatur, ad quod servatum iusta[112] fierent reliquo corpore combusto.' Et item[113] Plinius: 'Hominem fulgure exanimatum cremari fas non est, condi terra religio tradit.' Et infra: 'Cremare corpus non fuit veteris instituti, terra condebantur, ante Sullam dictatorem nemo crematus est. Is, quia Marii cadaver ludibrio fuit extractum, cremari voluit.' Quod autem Plinius dicit Sullam primum fuisse crematum de patriciis verum fuit, sed prius consuevisse mortuorum corpora cremari infra ex Virgilii versibus XI libri ostendemus et Terentius in *Andria* ostendit. Additque Plinius linum inventum est quod igni non absumitur. In rogum funebris eius lini tunica corpori obducta favillam ab reliquo separat cinere. Nasciturque in desertis adustisque sole Indiae, ubi non cadunt imbres, assuescitque vivere ardendo; rarum invenitur, difficile textu propter brevitatem, aequat pretia ingentium margaritarum. Et Suetonius in *Galliculae vita* cor inquit veneno tactum igne non comburi.

28 Usum autem comburendi corpora non diu durasse Macrobius innuit, qui scribit urendi corpora mortuorum usum suo saeculo non fuisse, quem Hadriani principis temporibus satis constat floruisse, additque quo tempore igni corpora dare fuit honor 'si quando venisset ut plura simul cremarentur, solitos fuisse funerum

Nevertheless, continues Cicero, Ennius says about Africanus, "'Here he lies.' Truly, those who have been buried are said to lie and the pontifical law confirms this practice."[171] Pliny: "Moreover many preferred to be buried in clay sarcophagi when they were dead."[172] Nonius Marcellus: "A limb was said to be cut off from the dead man when his finger was cut off and this was kept and given rites of burial after the rest of the body was burned."[173] And again Pliny: "It is not right to cremate a man killed by a lightning bolt; the teaching of religious law is that he is buried in the earth."[174] And further on: "Cremation of the body was not an old practice. They were buried in the earth. Before Sulla the dictator no one was cremated. He ordered that he be cremated because Marius' corpse was exhumed to be treated with disrespect."[175] Pliny's statement that Sulla was the first to have been cremated was true as far as the patricians were concerned, but I shall demonstrate below on the basis of lines from Vergil Book XI and (Terence's *Andria* shows) that there had been an earlier custom of cremating corpses.[176] Pliny adds that a kind of linen was invented which was incombustible. On the funeral pyre a tunic of this linen covering the body keeps the ashes of the dead man apart from all the other ash. It grows in deserts and in parts of India scorched by the sun where there is no rainfall and it becomes used to staying alive while burning. It is rarely found and difficult to weave because of its short length. It costs as much as pearls of huge size.[177] Suetonius in *Life of Caligula* says the heart affected by poison does not burn in the fire.[178]

Macrobius implies that the practice of cremation did not last long. 28
He writes that the practice of cremating the bodies of the dead was not employed in his own era,[179] though it is agreed that it flourished in the era of Hadrian. He adds that at the time when cremation was an honor, "if it ever happened that a number were to be burned at the same time, the officials who looked after funerals used to add one female for every ten male bodies."[180] In this

ministros denis virorum corporibus addere singula muliebria,' itaque citius et facilius arsisse. Non licuisse autem mortuos in urbibus sepeliri Cicero sic ostendit in legibus civilibus caveri '"hominem mortuum in urbe non sepeli, neve urito." Credo propter ignis periculum.' In urbe tamen sepulti sunt clari viri, quibus ante hanc legem habitus est honor ut Publicolae aut G. Fabricio; Aeliusque Spartianus Antoninum Pium inquit intra urbes sepeliri mortuos vetuisse, idque obstinatius servasse Athenienses scribit Servius Sulpicius[114] ad Ciceronem de morte M. Marcelli his verbis: 'Ab Atheniensibus locum sepulturae intra urbem impetrare non potui, quod religione se impediri dicerent, neque tamen id ante concesserant.' Et Plutarchus in *Problematibus* dicit, eius qui triumphasset, demum combustus esset, licebat ossa capere et in urbem deferre ac locare mortui honoris causa, quorum posteris in forum delatis facem subiciebant, ut statim sublati honore sine invidia uterentur.

29 Sed iam satis ea sunt dicta quae circa corpus fiebant, cetera sunt dicenda quae honori corporis vel potius suorum in eo adhibebantur. Primaeque erunt laudationes funerariae, de quibus Cicero in *Legibus*: 'Honoratorum virorum laudes in contione memoranto easque ad cantus ad tibicinem[115] prosequantur.' Livius XXVII: Marcellus filius patrem M. Marcellum consulem interfectum laudavit. Et Suetonius Tranquillus C. Caesarem scribit annos natum duodecim aviam et postea Tiberium annos agentem novem patrem defunctum pro rostris laudasse, Pliniusque orator, ad Romanum de Virginio Rufo defuncto scribens, 'triginta annis gloriae suae ipsum[116] supervixisse et posteritati suae interfuisse' scribit, 'qui laudatus fuerit a consule Cornelio Tacito, ut supremus felicitati suae

way they burned more quickly and easily. Cicero demonstrates that there was a provision in the civil law that forbade the dead to be buried in cities: "'Do not bury or burn a dead man inside the city.' I believe because of the danger of fire."[181] Yet outstanding men were buried in the city, the honor being paid them before this law was passed, as, for example, Publicola or Gaius Fabricius.[182] Aelius Spartianus says that Antoninus Pius prohibited burying the dead within cities.[183] The Athenians clung rather tenaciously to this, as Servius Sulpicius says writing to Cicero concerning the death of Marcus Marcellus, in these words: "I could not obtain from the Athenians a burial plot within the city because they said they were prevented by religious scruple, nor on the other hand had they granted this before."[184] Plutarch in *Problems* says that it was permitted to gather the bones of one who had had a triumph, provided he had been cremated, and bring them into the city and deposit them there as a sign of honor to the dead. The bodies of their descendants were brought into the Forum and the torch applied, so that as they were immediately removed they would enjoy the honor without ill will.[185]

But enough now has been said about what happened to the 29
corpse. I must discuss all the other practices employed in the funeral to honor the deceased's corpse, or rather his relatives. First will be funerary eulogies, concerning which Cicero says in *On the Laws:* "Pronounce a eulogy of honored men in a public meeting and accompany them with songs and flute playing."[186] Livy Book XXVII: Marcellus, the son, pronounced the eulogy for Marcus Marcellus, his father, who was killed when consul.[187] Suetonius writes that when Gaius Caesar was twelve years old he spoke a eulogy for his grandmother standing on the speaker's platform,[188] as later on did Tiberius for his dead father, when he was nine.[189] Pliny the orator in a letter to Romanus about Virginius Rufus' death writes that "he outlived his glory by thirty years and enjoyed his fame to come among posterity. His eulogy was spoken by the consul Cornelius

cumulus accesserit laudator eloquentissimus.' Quod autem supra in *Legibus* scribit Cicero ad tibicinem et cantum mortuorum laudes prosequendas esse servat in plerisque locis urbi Romae propinquis nostrae aetatis consuetudo.

30 Secundus mortuo honor non verbis ut superior, sed re et multa grandique impensa adhibitus fuit. Gladiatorium munus, quod quale fuerit, postremus fere scriptorum ex priscis, quorum scripta ad nos pervenerunt,[117] Aelius Spartianus in *Maximi sive Pupieni et Albini gestis rebus* ad alium tamen propositum sic habet: 'Unde tractum sit ut proficiscentes ad bellum imperatores gladiatorium munus et venatus darent brevi dicendum est. Multi dicunt apud veteres hanc devotionem factam contra hostes, ut tum sanguine litato specie pugnatorum vim quandam Fortunae satiarent; ituros quoque ad bellum Romanos debuisse pugnas videre et vulnera et ferrum et ruentes inter se cohortes, ne in bello intuentes hostes timerent aut vulnera aut sanguinem horrerent.' Sed quod Spartianus dicit veteres consuevisse Livius XXVIII sic ostendit: 'Scipio Carthaginem ad vota solvenda diis munusque gladiatorium,[118] quod mortis causa patris patruique paraverat, edendum rediit. Gladiatorum spectaculum fuit non ex eo genere hominum, ex quo lanistas comparare mos est, servorum qui sanguinem venalem habent, voluntaria omnis et gratuita opera pugnantium fuit. Nam alii iussi ab regulis suis ad specimen insitae genti virtutis ostendendum, alii ipsi professi se pugnaturos in gratiam ducis. Alios aemulatio et certamen ut provocarent provocative haud abnuerent traxit, quidam qui disceptando controversias finire nequiverant aut

Tacitus, so that, as the ultimate crown of his good fortune, was added his having the most eloquent of eulogizers."[190] As to what Cicero writes above in *On the Laws,* that praise of the dead must be accompanied by song and flute playing,[191] this custom survives to our own day in many places in the vicinity of the City of Rome.

The second honor paid to the dead was carried out not by 30
words (like the one above), but by deeds and at very great expense. About the nature of the gladiatorial show Aelius Spartianus, almost the last of the ancient writers whose works have come down to us, in the *Life of Maximus or of Pupienus and Balbinus* has the following information, though this was not his main purpose: "A brief account must be given of the origin of the custom by which commanders setting out for war put on a gladiatorial show and wild-beast hunts. Many say that in the old days this was a solemn ritual (*devotio*) directed against the enemy so that by offering blood in a semblance of combat at that time they might satiate a certain power of Fortune. They also say that the Romans, when about to go to war, were obliged to look on fights and wounds and steel and cohorts clashing lest on seeing them in war they might fear the enemy or take fright at wounds or blood."[192] But Livy in Book XXVIII illustrates that which Spartianus says was the custom of the men of old: "Scipio returned to Carthage to discharge his vows to the gods and to put on a gladiatorial show that he had planned in memory of his father and uncle. The gladiators for the show did not consist of men of the kind from which it is the custom to match *lanistae,*[193] slaves who offer their life blood for sale. The service of those who fought was all voluntary and free. Some were impelled by their own chieftains to display an example of the natural courage of their race; others gave the reason that they would fight out of respect for their general. Rivalry and emulation led others to challenge or not to refuse a challenge. Some who could not or would not settle a dispute by discussion made mutual agreements that the winner would take all and came to a decision

noluerant,[119] pacti inter se ut victorem res sequeretur, ferro decreverunt, neque obscuri generis homines, sed clari illustresque.'

31 Patet itaque ex superioribus Livii verbis gladiatores ex lanistis et servis redimi[120] consuevisse et magno quidem pretio, cum infra ostensuri simus huiusmodi perditissimorum hominum,[121] vitam in certissimum discrimen exponentium pretio dum nudi acutis mucronibus decertant, raro quempiam ultra sextam victoriae palmam reportasse, quam quidem palmam Festus lemuscatam[122] appellari solitam dicit, nisi forte credemus miseratum[123] eosdem populum Romanum cum bini et nudi quandoque quaterni aut multa simul paria unico concursu digladiarentur a caede et vulneribus revocasse, cum scribat Cicero in *Legibus:* 'Etenim si in gladiatoriis[124] pugnis et infimi generis omnium conditione atque fortuna timidos et supplices et ut vivere liceat obsecrantes etiam odisse solemus, fortes et animosos et se acriter ipsi morti offerentes servare cupimus, eorumque nos magis miseret, qui nostram misericordiam non requirunt quam qui illam efflagitant.' Et infra patebit multa eorum paria ad dictam excarnificationem saepenumero fuisse exhibita.

32 Sed ad rem: scribit XVI Livius Decium Iunium Brutum fuisse primum, qui munus gladiatorium in honorem defuncti patris dedit. Unde mirari soleo qua ductus ignoratione Valerius Maximus scripserit gladiatorium munus primum in foro Boario Appium Claudium Fulviumque consules dedisse. Et Plinius: Gaio principi XX paria gladiatorum[125] fuere in ludo; in his duo, qui contra comminationem aliquam non conniverent, ob id invicti. Et infra: G. Terentius Luctatius primus XXX paria gladiatorum in foro per

by the sword, and they were not men of unknown family, but outstanding and illustrious."[194]

Therefore it is apparent from Livy's words cited above that gladiators used to be bought from among *lanistae* and slaves, and indeed at a great price. In contrast, below I am going to show that rarely any of the desperate men of this kind who for a fee expose their lives to the most certain danger while, unprotected, they fight with sharp blades, won the palm of victory more than six times (Festus says that this palm was customarily called "lemniscata"),[195] unless we happen to believe that the Roman people took pity on them when they were fighting for life or death in pairs and without armor, sometimes in fours, and many pairs all at the same time in a single encounter, and called them back from slaughter and wounds. For Cicero writes in *On the Laws*: "Indeed if in gladiatorial fights and in the case of men of the lowest class in position and fortune we tend even to dislike those who are afraid, and are suppliants, and who beg to be allowed to live, yet we desire to save those who are brave and full of spirit and voluntarily offer themselves keenly to death. We pity those more who do not ask for our pity than those who beseech it."[196] Further on it will be shown that many pairs of gladiators were often put on show in the aforesaid butchery. 31

But back to our subject. Livy in Book XVI writes that Decimus Junius Brutus was the first to put on a gladiatorial show in honor of his deceased father.[197] For this reason I always wonder what ignorance it was that made Valerius Maximus write that the consuls Appius Claudius and Fulvius put on the first gladiatorial show in the Cattle Market.[198] And Pliny: In the principate of Caligula there were twenty pairs of gladiators in the gladiatorial school, among them two who never flinched in the face of any threat, and for this reason remained undefeated.[199] And further on: Gaius Terentius Luctatius was the first to show thirty pairs of gladiators 32

triduum dedit. Macrobiusque in *Saturnalibus* scribit lapidandum Vatinium testem gladiatorium munus dedisse eodem quo lapidabatur tempore, ut populo moriens et diis simul Erebi placeret. Suetoniusque scribit: Augustum Caesarem 'gladiatores sine intermissione edi' vetuisse et Tiberium 'munus gladiatorium in memoriam patris et avi Drusi diversis temporibus ac locis primum in foro, secundum in amphitheatro, rudiariis quoque quibusdam revocatis auctoramentum centenum millium dedit.' Rudem vero virgam fuisse constat, qua praetor gladiatores sexagenarios ab eo munere eximebant, quos, cum probi fuissent qui multas reportassent lemuscatas, Tiberius ad maiorem ludorum suorum magnificentiam revocatos centenis nummum milibus donavit. Gallicula vero 'munera gladiatoria partim in amphitheatro Tauri, partim in saeptis aliquot dedit, quibus inseruit catervas Afrorum Campanorumque pugilum ex utraque regione lectissimorum.'

33 Cumque populus ad ea spectacula[126] frequentissimus convenisset Saeptaque, qui locus semper tecto caruit, et pariter theatrum per aestatem ferventissimam lineis et quandoque bissinis intecta essent velis, Gallicula ipse, perniciosus sordidissimusque princeps, reductis eiusmodi velis aestuantem in spectaculo populum vi contineri iussit. Claudius vero, princeps et ipse ineptus, post munera gladiatoria multipliciter data, cum aliud requirenti populo daturus avaritia distineretur, quaestoribus vim attulit ut[127] pecuniam sternendis viis paratam in id munus impenderent. Scribitque Suetonius Claudium 'quocumque gladiatorio munere vel suo, vel alieno gladiatores, etiam forte prolapsos, iugulari iussisse.

in the Forum for three consecutive days.[200] Macrobius writes in *Saturnalia* that the witness Vatinius, sentenced to be stoned, put on a gladiatorial show at the same time as he was stoned,[201] so that as he died he might find favor both with the people and with the gods of the underworld. Suetonius writes that Augustus Caesar forbade "gladiators to be exhibited without any intermission"[202] and that Tiberius "put on gladiatorial shows in memory of his father and grandfather Drusus at different times and in different places, the first in the Forum and the second in the amphitheater and gave a payment of one hundred thousand sesterces to certain retired gladiators (*rudiarii*) whom he induced to reappear."[203] It is agreed that this staff (*rudis*) was the rod with which the praetor released from their duty gladiators who had turned sixty.[204] The good ones were those who had been awarded many *lemniscatae*, and Tiberius induced them to reappear with a payment of one hundred thousand sesterces to make his games more magnificent. "From time to time" Caligula "put on gladiatorial shows, some in the Amphitheater of Taurus, some in the Voting Pens. He included among them gangs of African and Campanian boxers, choosing the best from each region."[205]

The people flocked to these shows in great numbers. The Vot- 33
ing Pens (a place which was always unroofed) and in the same way the theater throughout the burning heat of summer had been covered by awnings made of linen and sometimes of sea silk.[206] Caligula, a ruinous and very despicable emperor, ordered the awnings of this type to be removed and the people, who were sweltering, to be kept at the show by force.[207] Claudius, also a foolish emperor, had put on gladiatorial shows of many kinds.[208] When the people requested another and he was going to give it but was held back by avarice, he put pressure on the quaestors to outlay on that show the money that was intended for paving the roads.[209] Suetonius writes that Claudius "ordered that in all gladiatorial

Cumque par quoddam mutuis ictibus concidisset, cultellos sibi parvulos ex utroque ferro in usum suum fieri sine mora iussisse.'[128] Aelius Spartianus scribit Hadrianum per sex continuos dies gladiatorium munus exhibuisse. Et Antoninum Pium ex publico sumptum gladiatoriis muneribus instituisse, pariterque Iulius Capitolinus M. Antoninum philosophum 'gladiatoria spectacula omnifariam temperasse,' quod quidem optimi principis temperamentum adeo valuisse videmus, ut post Maximum sive Pupienum et Albinum, de quibus supra diximus, nemo id funestissimum munus horridumque ediderit. Unde quod scribit Cassiodorus facile credimus Theodericum regem Gothorum, secta Arrianum et tamen Christianum, id ipsum munus Romanis optantibus ita denegasse, ut nunquam postea editum fuerit vel petitum.

34 Tria nunc simul dicenda nobis occurrunt funebrium apparatibus solita adhiberi. Nam ludi funebres simul cum gladiatorio munere fuerunt quandoque editi, quae funera scribit Festus simplediaria maiores appellavisse. Hisque ludis et visceratio quandoque et epulum addita fuere, quos quidem ludos illis similes fuisse tenemus, de quibus paulo inferius cum spectaculis dicturi sumus. Scribit XXIII Livius 'M. Aemilii Lepidi, qui bis consul augurque fuerat, filii tres Lucius, Marcus, Quintus ludos funebres per triduum et gladiatorum[129] paria duo et viginti per triduum in foro dederunt.' Et XXXI Livius: 'Ludi funebres eo anno per quatriduum in foro mortis[130] causa Valerii Laevinii et Publii a Publio et Marco filiis eius facti et munus gladiatorium datum ab his; paria XXV pugnarunt.' Et XL ac XLI Livius: 'Publii Licinii funeris

shows, whether his own or another's, gladiators who fell, even accidentally, should be killed. When a certain pair had killed each other, he immediately ordered little knives to be made from each of their swords for his own use."[210] Aelius Spartianus writes that Hadrian put on a gladiatorial show that lasted for six days in succession,[211] and that Antoninus Pius established a maximum expense from public funds for gladiatorial shows.[212] Equally, Julius Capitolinus writes that the philosopher Marcus Aurelius "in every way restrained gladiatorial shows."[213] We see that this restraint of an excellent emperor was so influential that after Maximus (or Pupienus) and Balbinus, mentioned above,[214] no one put on this fatal and ghastly show.[215] For this reason I am ready to believe Cassiodorus when he writes that Theoderic, king of the Goths, an Arian and yet a Christian, refused the Romans hoping for such a show in such a way that never afterward was one put on or requested.[216]

Now we are confronted with and must discuss together three things that that usually contributed to the pomp and splendor of funerals. Funeral games were sometimes put on in conjunction with a gladiatorial show. Festus writes that the ancestors called these funerals "simpludiarea."[217] Sometimes both a dole of meat (*visceratio*) and a banquet were added to these games. I consider that these games were like those that I am going to describe a little further on in conjunction with the shows.[218] Livy writes in Book XXIII that "Lucius, Marcus and Quintus, the three sons of Marcus Aemilius Lepidus (who had been consul twice and augur), put on in his honor funeral games lasting three consecutive days, and showed twenty-two pairs of gladiators in the Forum for three consecutive days."[219] And Livy in Book XXXI: "In that year funeral games lasting four consecutive days were put on in the Forum in memory of Valerius Laevinus' and Publius' death by Publius and Marcus his sons and they put on a gladiatorial show at which twenty five pairs fought."[220] Livy in Books XL and XLI: "On the 34

causa visceratione data gladiatores CXX pugnaverunt et ludi funebres per triduum facti. Post ludos epulum, quo cum toto foro strata triclinia essent, tempestas cum magnis procellis coorta coegit plerosque tabernacula statuere in foro. Eadem paulo post quam disserenasset sublata.' Quid autem inter viscerationem datam et epulum interfuerit, etsi infra in morum partibus diffuse certiusque dicturi sumus, tamen paucis hic docebimus. Cum Publii Licinii praestantis ditissimique civis curatores funeris, praeter ludos et gladiatores oculis tantummodo populi Romani satisfacturos, cibum quoque intenderent praebere, honoratioribus epulo opipare et laute dato gratificaturi, plebem prius et multitudinem inverecundam, quae ad stipem facile conflueret, visceratione paverunt. Quae visceratio, etsi ab initio verbi originem habuit, quando animalibus caesis rem divinam facturi viscera iis, qui sacrificio intererant, dispertiebantur, tamen postea in consuetudinem[131] tractum est viscerationem quoque appellari cum carnes, sive crudae sive coctae, quandoque panis vinumque cum illis domum perferentibus[132] singulis praebebantur.

35 Epulum fuit estque quod et convivium appellatur, ciborum etiam variorum lautus decensque apparatus. Sed triclinium hic, veteri Latinoque more, aliter quam multis retro saeculis, sicut et nostro per abusionem factum videmus, a Livio positum est. Non enim pars aliqua domus, sicut nunc utimur, triclinium fuit, sed coacta in locum unum parandae paucorum cenae supellex necessaria. Et quidem triclinii verbum habuisse originem constat a tribus lectis, qui contigui sternerentur, super quibus convenientes ad convivium, sicut Turchi et Graeci nunc faciunt, accubarent. Hinc

occasion of Publius Licinius' funeral a dole of meat was made and 120 gladiators fought. Funeral games lasting three successive days were put on, and a banquet after the games. During this when dining couches (*triclinia*) had been prepared and laid all over the Forum, a storm came up with strong gusts of wind and forced a great number of people to erect tents there. These were taken down soon after the weather had cleared up."[221] We are going to discuss in greater detail the difference between the donated dole of meat (*visceratio*) and the public banquet (*epulum*) below in the section on customs.[222] Nevertheless I shall explain it briefly here. In addition to games and gladiators which would satisfy only the eyes of the Roman people, those organizing the funeral of Publius Licinius, an outstanding and very wealthy citizen, intended to offer food as well. They planned to gratify the upper classes with a sumptuous and elegant banquet (*epulum*). They first fed the people and the shameless multitude ready to flock to a charitable handout with a dole of meat (*visceratio*). Even though initially the origin of the term *visceratio* was from when those who intended to offer worship by slaughtering animals shared the flesh (*viscera*) among those present at the sacrifice, yet later on it became the custom that it was called "visceratio" too when meat, raw or cooked, and sometimes bread and wine with it, were provided to individuals to take home.[223]

A banquet (*epulum*) was and is the same as what is also called a 35
dinner party (*convivium*), a lavish and handsome provision of foods of various kinds. But here Livy put "triclinium" according to the old Latin custom, not in the way we see the term has been abused in many past centuries, as in ours too. For a *triclinium* was not a part of a house, as is our present usage, but the furnishings, collected into one place, necessary to prepare dinner for a few people.[224] Indeed, it is agreed that the word *triclinium* originated from the three couches laid out touching each other, on which those coming to the dinner party reclined, as Turks and Greeks do

Horatius: 'Saepe tribus lectis videas cenare quaternos, e quibus unus avet praeter eum qui praebet aquam.' Et Iuvenalis: 'Ergo duos post si libuit menses neglectum adhibere clientem, tertia ne vacuo cessaret culcitra lecto, "una simus" ait.' Et Virgilius: 'Inde toro pater Aeneas sic orsus ab alto.' Sed postea sicut in multis factum esse videmus, triclinium mutatae[133] rei formae verbum remansit. Et apparatus ad mensam factus triclinium est dictus, quod auleis tapetisque quosdam, alios velis purpureis aut bissinis, argenteis nonnullos eburneisve cratibus[134] et laminis obduxisse, infra in partibus morum allatis singulorum, qui usi sunt nominibus ostensuri sumus, qua in clausura poculorum, patinarum, craterarum, vinariorum aquariorumque vasorum ex argento, aurove et cristallinorum myrrinorumque abbacus omnis continebatur. Ubi igitur toto foro strata erant triclinia, quae multa tanto in spatio esse oportuit, tempestas cum procellis coorta coegit plerosque tabernacula statuere.

36 Sepulcra deinceps dicenda sunt, de quibus Cicero *Legum* primo: 'Iam tanta religio est sepulcrorum, ut extra sacra et gentem inferri fas neget lex esse idque apud maiores nostros Tarquinius in gente Popilia iudicavit.' Et infra: 'Decretum a pontificum collegio non esse ius in loco publico fieri sepulcrum.' Item in *Legibus*: 'Duae praeterea leges sunt de sepulcris, quarum altera privatorum aedificiis, altera ipsis sepulcris cavet. Nam quod[135] "rogum bustumve novum" vetat "proprius sexaginta pedes adduci aedes alienas invito domino," incendium veretur acerbum. Quod autem vestibulum sepulchri, "bustumve usu capi" vetat, tuetur ius sepulcrorum. Haec

today. For this reason Horace says: "Often you may see dining on three couches four guests, one of whom loves [to insult indiscriminately everyone] except the provider of the water."[225] And Juvenal: "'Therefore if after two months have gone by he is pleased to invite the neglected client so that the third cushion not be unused on an empty couch, he says 'Let's get together.'"[226] And Vergil: "Then from his lofty couch Father Aeneas began thus."[227] But, as we see has happened in many cases, later on the form of the thing changed, but the word *triclinium* was kept for it. The furnishings made for the table were called "triclinium." That certain people covered it with hangings and tapestries, others with awnings of crimson or sea silk, some with silver or ivory lattice and leaf, I am going to show further on in the section on morals, adducing the names of the individuals who used such things.[228] In this enclosure, a whole sideboard of cups, dishes, mixing bowls, wine flasks, water jugs and vessels made of silver or gold or crystal and fluorspar was contained. When therefore the dining couches were laid out all over the Forum (there must have been many in such a large space), a storm arose with strong gusts of wind and forced a great number of people to erect tents.[229]

Next I must talk about graves, concerning which Cicero says in 36
On the Laws Book I: "Now there is so much religious concern for graves that, according to the law, it is sacrilege to inter anyone in them who is outside the clan and its rites. In the time of our ancestors this was the judgment made by Torquatus in the case of the Popilian clan,"[230] and further on: "It was decreed by the college of pontiffs that it is unlawful to put a grave in a public space."[231] Again in *On the Laws*: "Furthermore there are two laws concerning graves, one of which makes provision to protect the buildings of private individuals, the other the graves themselves. As to the forbidding of 'a new funeral pyre or tomb to be brought nearer than sixty feet to another's house against the wishes of its owner,' that is out of fear of a calamitous fire. But the forbidding of a grave's

in XII tabulis secundum naturam, quae norma legis est. Reliqua sunt in more.' Et infra: 'Poena est "si quis bustum" etiam id credo appellari tumbam "aut monumentum" inquit Solon[136] "aut columnam violaverit, iecerit, fregerit." In primis sepulcrorum magnificentiam esse minuendam, "quam legem eisdem paene verbis nostri decemviri in decimam tabulam coniecerunt."' 'Vetat etiam lex ex[137] agro culto, eove qui coli possit, ullam partem sumi sepulchro,' 'extruique vetat altius quam quod quinque diebus absolveretur, nec lapide extrui plusve poni quam quod capiat laudem mortui incisam quatuor heroicis versibus, quos longos appellat Ennius.' Cicero etiam *Philippicorum* octavo: 'Maiores quidem nostri statuas multis decreverunt, sepulcra paucis, sed statuae intereunt tempestate, vi, vetustate. Sepulcrorum autem sanctitas in ipso solo est, quod nulla vi moveri neque deleri potest, atque, ut cetera extinguntur, sic sepulchra fiunt sanctiora vetustate.'

37 Nonius Marcellus: monumentum ad memoriam posteritatis. Et infra: 'monumentum est, quod[138] mortui causa aedificatum est et quicquid ob memoriam alicuius factum est, ut fana, porticus, scripta et carmina. Sed monumentum quamvis causa mortui sit factum, non tamen significat ibi sepultum.' Marcianus in *Digestis*: 'Monumentum sepulcri id esse divus Hadrianus rescripsit[139] quod munimenti[140] causa, id est muniendi eius loci causa factum.' Florentinus *De religione et sumptibus*[141] *funeris*: 'Monumentum generaliter[142] res in posterum memoriae causa prodita, in qua, si corpus vel reliquiae inferantur, fiet sepulcrum. Si vero nihil eorum inferatur, erit monumentum memoriae causa factum, quod Graeci cenotaphium appellant.' Cicero Attico: 'Fanum fieri volo, neque mihi

forecourt 'or the tomb to be acquired by another by virtue of use' protects the rights of graves. These, in the Twelve Tables, are according to nature, which is the pattern of the law, others are a matter of custom."[232] And further on: "'There is a penalty, Solon says, 'if anyone violates, casts down, smashes a tomb' (I believe this is also called a 'tumba') 'or monument or column.'" Above all he said that magnificence of graves was to be curtailed, "a law that our Board of Ten included in the Tenth Table in almost the same words." "The law also forbids that any parcel of land which has been or could be cultivated be used for a grave" "and forbids the grave to be built up higher than could be completed in five days or more to be erected in stone or built than could take a commemoration of the dead inscribed upon it in four hexameters, lines which Ennius calls 'long.'"[233] Likewise Cicero says in the eighth *Philippic*: "Our ancestors decreed statues for many, graves for a few. But statues perish by weather, assault, old age. The sanctity of graves, however, is in the soil itself, which cannot be moved or destroyed by any physical force. As everything else is destroyed by age, so graves become more sacred."[234]

Nonius Marcellus: A monument is built as a memorial for posterity.[235] Further on: "A monument is what is built for the sake of the deceased, and whatever is made in memory of someone, as for instance a shrine, a colonnade, writings and poems. Although a monument is made for the sake of the deceased, it does not mean he is buried there."[236] Marcianus in the *Digest*: "The deified Hadrian said in a rescript that the grave monument is for the sake of commemoration, that is, made for the sake of protecting (*munire*) this place."[237] Florentinus, *Religious Things and Funeral Expenses*: "A monument in general is something handed down to posterity as a memorial. If a body or remains are interred in it, it becomes a grave. If none of these is interred, it will be a monument made as a memorial, which the Greeks call a cenotaph."[238] Cicero to Atticus: "I want it to be a shrine and I cannot be talked 37

hoc erui potest sepulcri similitudinem effugere.' Plinius Cornelio Tacito de villa Virginii Ruffi et eius sepulcro: 'Libuit etiam monumentum eius videre et vidisse paenituit. Est enim adhuc imperfectum, nec difficultas operis in causa modici ac potius exigui. At ille mandaverat caveratque ut divinum illud etiam immortale factum versibus inscriberetur: "Hic situs est Ruffus, pulso qui Vindice quondam, imperium asseruit non sibi, sed patriae."' Et Montano Plinius: 'Est via Tiburtina intra primum lapidem monumentum Pallantis, ita inscriptum: "Huic Senatus ob fidem pietatemque erga patronos ornamenta praetoria decrevit et sextertium centies quinquagesies, cuius honore contentus fuit."' Servius Sulpicius Ciceroni de obitu M. Marcelli: 'Nos in nobilissimo orbis terrarum gymnasio Achademiae locum delegimus, ibique eum combussimus, posteaque curavimus, ut eidem Athenienses in eodem loco monumentum marmoreum faciendum curarent.'

38 Sepulcra autem et funeralibus expletis et quandoque postea floribus odoramentisque fuisse sparsa multis legimus in locis. Plinius in *Historia Naturali*: Scipioni florum honos a populo Romano, funus ei e publico stipe collata et sparsi flores quacunque delatus. Cicero oratione *Pro L. Plancio*[143] indignabundus: 'Sepulcrum L. Catilinae,[144] floribus ornatum, hominum audacissimorum ac domesticorum hostium conventu epulisque celebratum est.' Hinc Virgilius Octavio Augusto et eius sorori in Marcello adulatus: 'Heu, miserande puer, si qua fata aspera rumpas tu Marcellus eris. Manibus[145] date lilia plenis, purpureos spargam flores animamque nepotis, his saltem accumulem donis et fungar inani munere.' Idemque mos, cum in plerisque regionibus Italiae, tum maxime in

out of it. [My concern is] to avoid the likeness to a grave."[239] Pliny to Cornelius Tacitus about Virginius Rufus' villa and his grave: "I wanted to see his monument and I was sorry to have seen it, for it is still unfinished. The reason is not difficulty in the building, which is modest, or rather, tiny. But he had given instructions and stipulated that that divine, even immortal, deed, be inscribed on it in these verses: 'Here lies Rufus, who by the routing of Vindex once set free the imperial power, not for himself but for his country.'"[240] And Pliny to Montanus: "On the Tiburtine Way, before the first milestone, there is a monument to Pallas with the following inscription: 'To him the senate decreed praetorian insignia and fifteen million sesterces in return for his loyalty and duty toward his patrons. He was content with the honor alone.'"[241] Servius Sulpicius to Cicero on the death of Marcus Marcellus: "I chose a place in the Academy, the most famous lecture hall in the world. There we burned him. Later I arranged that the same Athenians should be responsible for setting up a marble monument on the same spot."[242]

We read in many places that both when the funeral was over 38
and sometimes on later occasions the grave was strewn with flowers and perfumes. Pliny in *Natural History:* A tribute of flowers was paid to a Scipio by the Roman people. His funeral was from contributions collected from the people and flowers were strewn wherever he was carried.[243] Cicero, full of outrage, in his speech *Defense of Lucius Plancius:* "Lucius Catilina's grave was decorated with flowers, and reckless and violent men, enemies of their country, marked it by coming together and feasting."[244] Hence Vergil, who is flattering Augustus and his sister Octavia, on Marcellus: "Alas, poor boy, if you break the harsh decrees of Fate, you will be Marcellus. Give me lilies in handfuls. Let me strew crimson flowers, and these gifts at least let me heap up for my offspring's shade and perform an unprofitable service."[245] The same custom is preserved everywhere in our time both in many regions of Italy and

subiectis Apennino collibus Romandiolae alicubi aetate nostra servatur. Adhibita etiam sunt post funeralia in templis et publicis in locis ornamenta. Plinius: 'Caesar, postea dictator, in aedilitate munere patris funebri omni apparatu arenae argenteo usus est. Ferasque etiam argenteis vasis incessere[146] tunc primo visum.' Et Macrobius templorum ornamenta clipei, coronae et huiusmodi donaria, quod nostra quoque aetas in nobilibus et honoratis viris servat. Iulius autem Capitolinus de M. Antonino philosopho: Iussit ut filii septennis mortui, qui erat Caesar, imago aurea [a] circensibus per pompam ferretur et ut Saliarii carmini insererent.

39 Quid gentiles nostri circa mortuorum corpora egerint satis hactenus et abunde videmur dixisse. Pauca nunc dicenda sunt nobis de his[147] quae bonorum sive malorum animis tam defunctorum quam vivorum contingere existimabant. Cicero *Legum* primo, cum multa de poenis disseruisset transgressoribus legum inferendis, haec habet: 'Sed nimis saepe aliquos videmus poenas evadere. Non enim recte existimamus quae poena divina sit et opinionibus vulgi rapimur in errorem, nec vera cernimus. Morte aut dolore corporis aut luctu animi aut offensione iudicii, hominum miserias ponderamus, quae fateor humana esse et multis bona viris accidisse. Sceleris est poena tristis et praeter eos eventus, qui sequuntur, per se ipsam[148] maxima est; tantum dixerim duplicem poenam esse divinam, quod constat ex vexandis vivorum animis, et ex fama mortuorum, ut eorum exitium et vivorum iudicio et gaudio comprobetur.' Idemque Cicero oratione *In Pisonem:* Deinceps post mortem de tranquillitate bonorum, poenis impiorum habetis explicatum. 'Nolite enim putare, patres conscripti, ut in scaena videtis,

especially in the hills of Romagna lying beneath the Apennines. After the funeral, adornments were employed as well in temples and public places. Pliny: "Caesar, who later became dictator, in his aedileship, at the gladiatorial games for his father's death, had all the equipment used in the arena made of silver. Then for the first time they decided to attack wild beasts with silver weapons."[246] Macrobius says the adornments of temples are shields, garlands and offerings of this kind,[247] a practice our age too maintains in the case of noble and honored men. Julius Capitolinus, writing about Marcus Antoninus the philosopher: He commanded that a golden image of his dead seven-year-old son, who was Caesar, be carried in the procession at the circus games and that they include mention of him in the song of the Salii.[248]

So far I seem to have said more than enough about the prac- 39
tices of our Gentiles in relation to the bodies of the dead. Now a little must be said about what they thought happened to the souls of the good or the wicked, both in death and in life. Cicero in Book I of *On the Laws,* after much discussion of the punishments that must be imposed on those who break the laws, says the following: "But only too often we see that some escape punishment. We do not have a correct view of the nature of divine punishment, and we are swept up into error by the mob's opinions, and we do not discern the truth. We weigh people's misfortunes by death or physical pain or mental suffering or losing a case at court, which I admit are part of human life and have happened to many good men. The penalty of crime is grim, and apart from the results which follow upon it, in itself is very great. I would say only that divine punishment is twofold: it consists in torment of the minds of the living and in their having such a reputation when they are dead, that the living not only regard their end as fitting but rejoice at it."[249] The same Cicero in his speech *Against Piso:* Next you have an explanation of the serenity of the good and the punishments of the wicked after death.[250] "Don't suppose, conscript fathers, that,

homines consceleratos impulsu deorum terreri Furiarum taedis ardentibus: sua quemque fraus, suum facinus, suum scelus, sua audacia de sanitate et mente deturbat. Hae sunt impiorum Furiae, hae flammae, hae faces.' Et *Philippicorum* XIII: 'Illi igitur impii, quos cecidistis, etiam ad inferos poenas parricidii luent. Vos vero, qui extremum spiritum in victoria effudistis, piorum estis sedem et locum consecuti. Brevis autem a natura vita nobis data est, at memoria bene redditae vitae sempiterna.' Cicero item[149] in oratione *Pro Roscio Amerino:* 'Nolite enim putare, quemadmodum in fabulis saepenumero videtis, eos qui aliquid impie scelerateque commiserint agitari et perterreri[150] Furiarum taedis ardentibus. Sua quemque fraus et suus terror maxime vexat, suum quemque scelus agitat amentiaque afficit, suae malae cogitationes amentiaeque animi terrent, hae sunt impiis assiduae domesticaeque Furiae.' Et *In Vatinium testem* Cicero: 'Cum inaudita et nefaria scelera susceperis, cum inferorum animas elicere, cum puerorum extis deos manes ad te citare soleres.' Noniusque Marcellus: 'Lemures' dicit 'sunt larvae nocturnae, terrificationes imaginum et bestiarum.' Festus autem, quem Christianum fuisse videmus, sic scribit: 'Mundum gentiles ter in anno patere putabant, diebus his: postridie Vulcanalia et ante diem tertium Nonas Octobris, et ante diem[151] sextam Idus Novembris. Inferiorem enim eius partem consecratam diis Manibus arbitrantes clausam omni tempore, praeter hos dies, qui supra scripti sunt, credebant, quos dies etiam religiosos iudicaverunt ea de causa, quod his diebus ea, quae occulta et abdita religionis deorum Manium essent, in lucem adducerentur et patefierent, nihil eo tempore in re publica geri voluerunt. Itaque per hos dies non cum

as you see it on the stage, wicked people are put into a state of terror by the Furies' blazing torches at the instigation of the gods. Each man is driven out of a healthy state of mind by his own fault, his own villainy, his own crime, his own audacity. These are the Furies of the wicked, these the flames, these the torches."[251] And in *Philippics* XIII: "Those wicked men, whom you killed, will be punished as parricides even in the underworld, whereas you who have breathed your last in victory have attained the seat and dwelling place of the good. The life given to us by nature is brief. But the memory of a life nobly laid down is eternal."[252] Cicero again in the speech *Defense of Roscius of Ameria*: "Don't suppose that, as you often see in plays, those who have committed some impious or wicked deed are hounded and terrified by the Furies' blazing torches. Each man is particularly tormented by his own evil deed and his own terror. His own crime drives him mad, and his frenzy stirs him up. His own evil thoughts and mad passions terrify him. These are the constant and personal Furies of the wicked."[253] And in *Cross-examination of Vatinius* Cicero: "Although you have committed unheard of and wicked crimes, although you were accustomed to summon the souls of the dead, although you conjured spirits of the dead to you by the entrails of children."[254] Nonius Marcellus says: "Lemurs are ghosts in the night, shades and beasts that terrify."[255] But Festus (we see he was a Christian) writes as follows: "The Gentiles thought the *mundus* (lower world) was open three times a year on these days; the day after the Festival of Vulcan (August 24), October 5 and November 8. Because they thought its lower part was dedicated to the spirits of the dead, they believed that it was closed all the time except for those days which are recorded above. They judged those days taboo as well, since on them when those concealed and hidden things having to do with reverence of the spirits of the dead were brought out into the light and revealed, they required that no public business be carried out at that time. Thus on those days battle was not

hoste manus conserebatur, non exercitus scribebatur, non comitia habebantur, non aliud quicquam in re publica, nisi quod ultima necessitas exegisset, administrabatur.'

40 Suetonius de G. Gallicula: 'Satis constat, priusquam mortuus transferretur,[152] hortorum custodes umbris inquietatos, in ea quoque domo, in qua occubuerat, nullam noctem sine aliquo horrore transactam, donec ipsa domus incendio consumpta sit.' Et de Nerone: 'Saepe confessus est agitari se materna specie umbrisque Furiarum accedentibus. Quin et facto per magos sacro evocare manes et exorare tentavit. Peregrinatione quidem Graeciae Eleusinis sacris, quorum initiatione impii et scelerati voce praeconis summoventur, interesse non ausus est.' Ut supradictis omnibus addere non vereamur quod beatus Aurelius Augustinus in *Civitate Dei* sic scribit: 'Et quoniam creberrima fama est, multique se expertos vel ab eis, qui experti sunt, de quorum fide dubitandum non esset, audisse confirmant, Silvanos et Faunos, quos vulgo incubos vocant, improbos semper extitisse mulieribus et earum appetisse et peregisse concubitus, et quosdam daemones, quos Dusios Galli[153] appellant, adsidue hanc immunditiam et tentare et efficere, plures talesque asseverant, ut hoc negare impudentiae videatur non audeo diffinire.'

41 Sed ad gentiles redeundum est. Cum supradicta suorum animis viventium ac mortuorum animabus accidere crederent, eis post sepulturae et funebrium obita munera parentabant,[154] non dissimiliter nostris quando ad septimum diem aut anniversarium divina in animarum suffragia celebrant officia. Cicero in *Philippicis:* 'ut parentalia cum supplicationibus miscerentur.' Et infra: 'ut cuius

engaged with the enemy, the army was not enrolled, voting assemblies were not held, no public business was carried out except what was absolutely necessary."[256]

Suetonius on Gaius Caligula: "It is well known that before the 40
body of the dead man was moved to another place, the caretakers of the garden were disturbed by ghosts. In the house too in which he had met his end no night passed without something horrific until the house itself was destroyed by fire."[257] And on Nero: "He often confessed that he was pursued by his mother's ghost and by shades of Furies coming upon him. Indeed he even tried to summon the ghost and appease it by having a rite performed by the Magi. In his tour of Greece he did not dare to participate in the Eleusinian mysteries, from the initiation into which the herald makes an announcement warning the wicked and criminal to depart."[258] Not to be afraid of adding to all that has already been said that which St. Augustine writes in *City of God*, as follows: "Since there have been frequent reports and many confirm that they have experienced or that they have heard from those who have experienced (whose reliability could not be doubted) that vexatious Silvani and Fauni (commonly called nightmares) have always appeared to women and wanted to and did sleep with them, and more people and of great standing have asserted that certain demons, whom the Gauls call 'Dusii,' constantly attempted and carried out this foulness, so that it seems reckless to deny it. I do not venture to state definitely."[259]

But I must return to the Gentiles. Since they believed that the 41
things I have mentioned above happened to the minds of their relatives when they were alive and their souls when they had died, they made offerings to the dead (*parentare*) after the offices of burial and funeral had been executed, not very differently from our contemporaries when they celebrate divine services in intercession for their souls on the seventh day, or on the anniversary of death. Cicero in *Philippics*: "that the offerings to the dead (*Parentalia*) be

sepulcrum nusquam extet, ubi parentetur, ei publice supplicetur.' Plutarchus in *Problematibus:* cum ceteri Romani Februario mortuis inferias mittere et parentare consuevissent, Decimus et Brutus, ut Cicero scribit, id Decembri faciebant, quia Saturno is mensis consecratus est, quem in[155] inferorum deorum numero habent. Et cum Saturnalibus et voluptati ac genio[156] omnes nimium indulgeant, hi nonnullas etiam diis inferis et mortuis voluptates impartiebantur. Et infra Plutarchus: faba parentando absumitur, quia in ea animas mortuorum Pythagorici esse dixerunt; flaminicamque ob id ea non vesci Varro tradit, quando in flore litterae lugubres reperiantur. Satis iam supraque ostendimus quid virorum cuiuscumque status funebribus sepulturisque et animarum statui curandum esse gentiles opinati sunt, maiora nunc Caesaribus suis imperatoribus a populo Romano excogitata et tributa ostendamus. Quid enim maius, ne dixerim dementius, quam homines id quaerere, ut hominem et plerumque sordidissimum sese deum facere existiment et intentent. Notum esse non dubitamus adeoque vulgatum, ut a nobis particulariter scribi non oporteat, principum Romanorum plurimos in numerorum deorum fuisse relatos, sed quo id fieret modo, quis adhiberetur in re ordo, apud Latinos nondum invenimus.

42 Nuper vero Marcus Barbus, patritiae gentis Venetus ecclesiae Tarvisinae[157] antistes venerandus, a nostro Omnibono Brendulensi[158] Vicentino, Graecis Latinisque litteris apprime erudito, munus nobis attulit, quale bonarum artium studiis innutritos et qui detulit et qui misit in nascentem *Romam triumphantem* conferre

combined with public thanksgivings (*supplicationes*)," and, further on, "that he who has no grave anywhere where offerings to the dead may be made, may have public thanksgivings made to him."[260] Plutarch in *Problems:* Though all the other Romans had customarily made offerings to the dead and to relatives in February, Decimus and Brutus, as Cicero writes, used to do it in December, because this month is sacred to Saturn, whom they regard as one of the gods of the underworld. And since at the Saturnalia all give themselves up very much to pleasure and good living, they bestowed some pleasures on the gods of the underworld and the dead too,[261] and Plutarch further on: Beans are employed when making offerings to the dead because the Pythagoreans said the souls of the dead were in them.[262] Varro said that the flamen's wife did not eat beans because letters of ill omen are found on their flowers.[263] I have now described more than enough of the Gentiles' views of what had to be undertaken for funerals, burials and the state of the soul of people of all classes. Now let us show the greater honors the Roman people devised for and bestowed upon the Caesars, their emperors. For what is greater, not to say crazier, than for men to have the idea that they are making a man, and for the most part a very despicable one, into a god? I have no doubt that the fact that most of the Roman emperors were deified is well known and such common knowledge that I do not need to write about it particularly, but I have not yet found in the Latin authors how this was done or what procedure was used in the matter.

Recently however, Marco Barbo, a Venetian of patrician family, 42
venerable bishop of Treviso,[264] brought me a gift from my friend Ognibene from Brendola near Vicenza,[265] a man exceptionally well studied in Greek and Latin literature, a gift such as was fitting both for him who carried it and him who sent it, men nurtured in studies of the liberal arts, to bestow on *Rome in Triumph* as it

decuit. Ea est traducta ex Herodiano scriptore Graeco Severi imperatoris deificatio, quam ipsius Omniboni verbis paene totam inserimus: 'Mos est Romanis consecrare imperatores, qui superstitibus filiis vel successoribus moriuntur, et eiusmodi honorem deificationem appellant. Luctus quidam per omnem urbem ostenditur, festa celebritate permixtus. Corpus enim defuncti pro ritu hominum sumptuoso funere sepeliunt, sed ceream imaginem defuncto simillimam fingunt, quam sub vestibulo praetorii proponunt in eburneo lecto, magno atque sublimi vestibus aureis instrato, et imago illa sub aegrotantis specie pallida percumbit et ab utraque lecti parte ad multum diei sedent, laeva quidem senatus omnis vestibus atris indutus, dextra vero mulieres, quae virorum vel parentum dignitate honorem et gloriam sortitae sunt. Earum autem quaelibet conspicitur neque aurum gestans, neque monilibus ornata, sed vestibus albis exilibus induta, maerentium speciem praebens. Atqui septem dies haec quae dicta sunt continuo geruntur, et introeuntes medici passim ad lectum accedunt et aegrotum diu contemplati gravius utique habere pronunciant. Postquam vero diem obiisse visus est, lectum humeris tollentes, equestris ac senatorii ordinis nobilissimi delecti iuvenes per Sacram Viam deferunt, et ad[159] vetus forum magnum proponunt, ubi magistratus Romani imperium deponunt. Utrimque vero gradus quidam in schalarum modum constructi sunt, et in altera parte puerorum chorus ex nobilissimis atque patriciis consistit, in altera mulierum ex iis,[160] quae digniores esse videntur, et utrique hymnos in defunctum canunt et laudes verendo et lamentabili carmine conditas. Post haec lectum suscipientes, per urbem deferunt in Campum Martium, ubi forma quaedam[161] quadrangula aequis lateribus, qua latissime campus patet, aedificata est in tabernaculi modum, quod materia fixum est alia quidem nulla, praeter quam lignorum ingentium. Id

comes into being. This is the account of the deification of the emperor Severus, translated from the Greek author Herodian. I include almost the whole of it in the words of Ognibene himself. "It is the Roman custom to place among the gods emperors who die with sons or successors to survive them. They call this kind of honor 'deification.' Throughout the whole city a certain public mourning is displayed mingled with festive celebration. They bury the deceased's body in a splendid funeral in the customary manner but they fashion a wax image exactly resembling the deceased. They put this on display in the entrance hall of the palace on a large and lofty ivory couch, draped with golden covers, and that image lies on the couch, pale, in the guise of one who is ill, and they sit on either side of the couch for most of the day, on the left all the senate dressed in black, on the right those women, who because of the position of their husbands or fathers, have acquired honor and glory. None of these women is seen wearing gold jewelry or decked with necklaces, but dressed in simple white garments, showing that they are in mourning. What I have just described lasts for seven days without a break. Everyday[266] doctors enter and approach the couch. After looking at the sick man for a long time, they announce that he is definitely worse. After it appears that he has died, chosen young men, the noblest of the equestrian and senatorial orders, lift up the bier on their shoulders, bear it along the Sacred Way and display it in the old Roman Forum at the spot where the Roman magistrates lay down their power. On both sides tiers of steps have been built. On one side sits a chorus of children from noble and patrician families, and on the other side, one of women, chosen from those who seem to be of greater standing. Both sing hymns in honor of the deceased and eulogies composed in reverential and sorrowful verse. After this they take up the bier and bear it through the city to the Field of Mars to where a certain square frame in the shape of a hut has been built entirely out of huge wooden beams where the field

quidem interius totum[162] est aridis fomitibus plenum, exterius aureis vestibus et eburneis signis tabulisque pictis ornatum. Infra vero alterum brevius positum est, forma et ornatu simile. Tertium autem et quartum perficitur[163] et sub ultimo, quod est minimum, aquila iacet. Aedificii formam turribus quispiam comparet, quae in portubus eminentes noctu per ignem naves in tutas stationes dirigunt, pharos eos vulgo[164] appellant. Ad secundum igitur tabernaculum deferunt lectum ibique et aromata et omne suave olentium genus, sive fructus sint, sive herbae succique, imponunt ac coacervatum fundunt. Nam neque gens est ulla, neque civitas, neque cum dignitate quisquam vel honore, qui non suprema haec munera in honorem pietatis ambitiose mittat. Ubi vero aromatum acervus ingens[165] aggestus fuerit et locus omnis expletus, equitatio fit circa aedificium illud et omnis equester ordo circumvehitur, moderatione quadam et cursus replicatione, versus interea pirrichios decantando. Currus etiam circunvehuntur personatis quibusdam purpura amictis onerati, quibus similitudo quaedam superinducta[166] est Romanorum ducum aut imperatorum ex iis,[167] quorum fama nominisque celebritas integrior extat. His itaque confectis, qui ad imperium successurus est facem tabernaculo admovet[168] et reliqui deinceps ignem undique circumponunt omniaque illico, utpote arido fomite et aromatum congerie plena, igni valido corripiuntur. Ex tabernaculo autem ultimo atque brevissimo velut a pinnaculo quodam aquila simul cum subiecto igne dimittitur aetherem petitura, quae a Romanis de terris in caelos imperatoris animam vehere creditur cum aliis diis perpetuo mansuram. Hoc honore filii patrem consecrantes ad praetorium deducuntur.'

43 Hanc vero funebrium magnificentiam aliqua ex parte Virgilius imitatos fuisse Troianos facit *Aeneide* XI, cum mandarentur sepulturae corpora in proelio defunctorum: 'Aurora interea miseris

opens out most broadly. Within, it is completely full of dry firewood, on the outside it is adorned with cloth of gold, ivory figures and paintings. On top[267] is placed a second structure, not as high, similar in shape and decoration, a third and fourth are completed and below the last, which is the smallest, an eagle is placed.[268] One might compare the building's shape to the high towers which stand in ports and at night guide ships into safe moorings by means of a fire. They are commonly called 'phari.' They carry the bier up to the second story. There they put spices and all kinds of sweet-smelling things, whether fruit, herbs or juices, and pour them out in heaps. For there is no nation or city, no man of standing or honor who does not vie to send these tributes as a dutiful gift.[269] When the huge pile of spices has been heaped up and the whole place filled, they put on a cavalry display around that building, and the entire equestrian order rides round it, in a certain regular and repetitious pattern, while chanting Pyrrhic verses. Chariots too are driven around it carrying some masked men dressed in crimson. They wear masks resembling Roman generals and emperors selected from those whose fame and renown is unblemished. On the completion of these rites the successor to the empire applies a torch to the hut and the others then set it on fire on all sides. All is immediately consumed by the fierce fire, full as it is of dry firewood and the heaps of spices. From the last and smallest story, as if from a gable, the eagle is set free at the same time as the fire is lit beneath, so that it makes for the upper air. The Romans believe that the eagle conveys the emperor's soul from earth to heaven, and that it will remain there forever with the other gods. After deifying their father by this rite the sons are escorted to the palace."[270]

Vergil in *Aeneid* XI represents the Trojans as imitating to a 43
certain extent magnificent funeral rites of this nature, when they committed to burial the bodies of those who had died in battle:

mortalibus almam extulerat lucem referens opera atque labores. Iam pater Aeneas, iam curvo in litore Tarchon constituere piras, huc corpora quisque suorum more tulere patrum, subiectisque ignibus atris, conditur in tenebras alta caligine caelum. Ter circum accensos cincti fulgentibus armis decurrere rogos, ter maestum funeris ignem lustravere in equis ululatusque ore dederunt. Spargitur et tellus lacrimis, sparguntur et arma; it caelo clamorque virum clangorque tubarum. Hic alii spolia occisis direpta Latinis coniciunt igni, galeasque ensesque decoros frenaque ferventesque rotas; pars munera nota ipsos clipeos et non felicia tela. Multa boum circa mattantur corpora morti. Saetigerosque sues captas ex omnibus agris in flammam iugulant pecudes. Tum litore toto ardentes spectant socios semiustaque servant busta, neque avelli possunt, nox humida donec invertit caelum stellis ardentibus aptum.'

44 Superiorem quoque referendi[169] in numerum deorum morem aliqua ex parte imitari videmus funeris Romanorum pontificum curatores. Aedificata enim forma tabernaculi in turris phareae formam ('castrum doloris' nostri appellant), sericinis undique pendentibus ornatur,[170] et sedet[171] ad sinistram longus atra veste indutorum ordo, lectusque sub tabernaculo amplissimus aureis contegitur, super quem videri volunt mortuum iacere pontificem. Non autem medici sicut in superiori per septem dies ad simulacrum hic conveniunt, sed stantes hinc inde ad lectum servi, et ipsi atrati ventilabrum perinde muscis abigendis frequenter agitant, ac si in lecto iaceret[172] vel aegrotans vel defunctus pontifex, quem multis ante diebus condiderant sepulturae. Sumpsisse etiam videmos nostros et multorum supra saeculorum nobiles et honoratos morem

"Dawn meanwhile had lifted up her kindly light for wretched mortals, bringing back work and troubles. Now Father Aeneas, now Tarchon, had set up pyres on the curving shore. Hither they each brought the bodies of their men in the manner of their forefathers, and when the murky fires have been lit beneath, the lofty sky is folded in darkness by the gloom. Three times girt in shining armor they paraded around the blazing piles, three times on horseback they circled around the sad funeral fire and uttered howls. Earth and armor are wet with tears. Shouting of men and blaring of trumpets rises to the sky. And now some hurl into the flames spoils stripped from the slain Latins, helmets and ornamented swords, bridles and swift wheels, others offerings that were familiar to the dead, their own shields and luckless spears. Around, many head of oxen are sacrificed to death, and into the flame they slaughter and cast bristly boars and cattle seized from all the countryside. Then everywhere on the shore, they gaze at their comrades as they blaze and watch the half-burned pyres, nor can they tear themselves away until dank night revolves the sky studded with blazing stars."[271]

We observe that those who organize the Roman popes' funerals 44
imitate to a certain extent the practice of deification described above.[272] A frame of a hut is built in the shape of the lighthouse tower (we call it a castle of grief) and decorated on all sides with hanging silks. A long row of people dressed in black sits on its left. Beneath the tabernacle there is a very splendid bed covered with cloth of gold. They wish to make it appear that the dead pope is lying on top of this. Doctors do not, as in the rite described above, gather here for seven days beside the replica, but standing beside the couch on either side, servants, they too dressed in black, frequently wave a fan to drive the flies away just as if the pope, whom many days before they had placed in the grave, were lying on the couch either sick or dead. We see too that our nobles and distinguished men and those of many past centuries have adopted their

ornandi defunctorum suorum, praesertim arma tractare aut magistratus[173] administrare solitorum funebria, equitibus nonnullis atra ipsis et simul equis veste intectis circa ducendum funus obequitare iussis, qui et ipsi cum Virgilianis: 'Lustravere in equis ululatusque ore dederunt.'

45 Reliquum est nobis in religionis partibus ludos, spectacula et pompam, sicut supra polliciti fuimus ostendere. Ludi qua causa fuerint instituti Cicero *Legum* primo, etiam Platonis auctoritate, ostendit suntque haec legis verba: 'Ludis publicis, quod sine curriculo et sine corporum certatione fiat, popularem[174] laetitiam cantu et fidibus et tibiis moderanto, eaque cum divino honore iungunto.' Et infra: 'Iam ludi publici cum sint cavea circoque conclusi, sint corporum concertationes cursu et pugillatione luctantium curriculisque equorum usque ad certam victoriam in circo constitutis, cavea cantu, voce et fidibus dummodo ea moderata sint, ut lege praescribitur. Assentiorque Platoni nil tam facile in animos teneros atque molles influere quam varios canendi sonos, quorum vix dici potest quanta sit vis in utranque partem. Nanque et incitat languentes[175] et languefacit excitatos, et tum retrahit animos tum contrahit.' De ludorum veteri ornamento Q. Asconius Pedianus: 'Olim cum in foro ludi populo darentur signis ac tabulis pictis, partim ab amicis, partim e Graecia accommodatis utebantur ad scenae speciem, quia adhuc theatra non erant,' nec amphitheatra. De ludorumque laudibus Cicero *Pro Murena* haec habet: 'Nam quid ego dicam populum ac vulgus imperitum ludis magnopere delectari? Minus est mirandum. Quamquam huic satis est, sunt enim populi ac multitudinis comitia. Quare, si populo ludorum

way of honoring their dead, especially the funeral rites of those accustomed to bear arms or to serve as magistrates, when a band of riders, they themselves and their horses draped in black cloth, has been bidden to escort the funeral cortège. They too like Vergil's riders "circled on horseback and uttered howls."

There remains for me in the sections on religion to describe the 45
games, shows and the procession, as I promised above.[273] Why the games were instituted Cicero shows in Book I of *On the Laws*, following Plato. These are the words of the law: "'At the public games which may happen without chariot races and without physical contest, let them keep the people's delight within bounds by song and by the playing of lyres and flutes. Let them combine these things with honor paid to the gods,'"[274] and, further on, "Now since the public games have been confined to the auditorium and circus, let the physical contests, with the running races, the boxing of wrestlers, the chariot races up to a definite victory be established in the circus, but in the auditorium with song, voice and lyres, provided that these are kept within bounds, as the law prescribes. I agree with Plato: nothing so readily influences young and malleable minds as the diverse sounds of singing, the great power of which in both directions it is scarcely possible to express, for it both stirs up sluggish spirits and calms down excited ones and it both holds them back and checks them."[275] Quintus Asconius Pedianus about the old way of providing adornment for the games: "In time past when games were put on for the people in the Forum, statues and paintings supplied partly by friends, partly from Greece, were used as a backdrop because there were as yet no theaters"[276] or amphitheaters. Cicero in *Defense of Murena* has this about enthusiasm for the games: "Why should I mention that the people and the ignorant crowd take great delight in games? It is hardly surprising. Yet this is enough for our case: for elections are in the hands of the people and the crowd. And so, if the people take pleasure in magnificent games, it is not surprising that this

magnificentia voluptati est, non est mirandum eam[176] L. Murenae apud populum profuisse. Quid tu admiraris de multitudine indocta?[177] L. Otho, vir fortis, equestri ordini restituit non solum dignitatem, sed etiam voluptatem. Itaque lex haec, quae ad ludos pertinet, est omnium gratissima quod honestissimo ordini cum splendore fructus quoque iocunditatis est restitutus.'

46 Quomodo autem ludi fieri possent, quos diis non placere crederetur, *De haruspicum responsis* Cicero docet: 'At si ludus constitit aut tibicen repente conticuit aut puer ille patrimus et matrimus si tela non tenuit aut tensam, si lorum emisit, aut si aedilis verbo aut si nutu aberravit, ludi sunt non recte facti eaque errata expiantur et mentes deorum immortalium ludorum instauratione placantur.' Quomodo autem funesti et perniciosi esse possent ludi, eodem loco infra sic ostenditur. 'Si ludi ab laetitia ad metum traducti sunt, si non intermissi, sed perempti atque sublati sunt, si civitati universae scelere eius, qui ludos ad luctum conferre voluit, funesti extiterunt, dies illi pro festi⟨s⟩ paene funesti.' Ludosque a Romulo rege primum introductos fuisse Livius in primo sic ostendit, cum de Romulo multa dixisset, sic sequitur: 'Ludos ex industria parat Neptuno equestri solemnes, Consualia vocant.' Quibus quidem Consualibus scribit Plutarchus in *Problematibus* consuevisse asinos et equos coronis exornari, quia, cum Neptuno equestri dies festus ageretur et tunc instituta navigatione multa navibus adveherentur, otium et remissio illis animalibus data erat. Tullusque Hostilius secundo loco ludos dedit novendiale sacrum, feriatis novem diebus, quia lapidibus pluisse nunciatum erat. Et Tarquinius Priscus

magnificence advanced Lucius Murena's cause with the people. What is there to be surprised about in the case of the uneducated crowd? Lucius Otho, a worthy man, restored to the equestrian order both their position and their enjoyment. Therefore that law that relates to the games is the most popular of all because there has been restored to this most honorable order, along with its luster, the benefit of pleasure as well."[277]

Cicero in *On the Responses of the Haruspices* tells us what in what ways they could carry out the games with which they believed the gods were not pleased: "If the player stops, or the flute player suddenly falls silent or if that boy with father and mother still living has not kept hold of the weapons or the wagon, if he has let go of the rein, or if the aedile has gone wrong in a word or a nod, then the games have not been performed correctly. These mistakes are expiated and the minds of the immortal gods are pleased by the games being started again (*instauratio*)."[278] How games could be funereal and destructive is demonstrated further on in the same passage, as follows: "If the games have been converted from happiness to fear, if they have been not interrupted, but prevented and stopped, if they have become ill-omened for the whole people by the crime of him who wanted to turn the games to mourning, those days are almost funereal instead of festive."[279] Livy in Book I shows that games were introduced for the first time by King Romulus. After saying a lot about Romulus, he continues like this: "He deliberately made preparations for solemn games in honor of 'equestrian Neptune,' which they call 'Consualia.'"[280] At these Consualia, Plutarch writes in *Problems*, they used to crown donkeys and horses with garlands, because these animals had received the gift of ease and rest, since this holiday was celebrated in honor of "equestrian Neptune," and at that time much was conveyed by ships after sailing was discovered.[281] In second place, Tullus Hostilius put on games, the *novendiale sacrum*,[282] a rite celebrated over nine days, because a rain of stones had been reported.[283] In third 46

rex[178] tertio loco ludos instituit Troianos, de quibus in *Roma instaurata* diffuse descripsimus.[179] Virgilius: 'Troiaque nunc pueri Troianum dicitur agmen.' De quo ludo Suetonius in *Caesaris rebus gestis:* 'Troiam lusit turma duplex maiorum minorumque puerorum.'

47 Quem ludum retinere aetatem nostram pueri nos ipsi vidimus Arimini, munus a Carolo Malatesta, praestanti doctoque principe, datum; non autem pueri, sed viri luserunt nobiles, qui ad nuptias Galaotti[180] Malatestae ex omni Italia invitati erant, numero ad triginta in equis desultoribus velocissimisque singuli arma induti ex corio fabrefacta perpulchre variis ornata coloribus ferreum ensem nequaquam acutum manu gestabant decurrentesque in circuitum galeas in id tumentiores factas et humeros caesim invicem feriebant[181] et proximum prisco ludus nomen retinet pro Troiano agmine torniamen. Primique libera iam Roma ludi fuerunt Capitolini, quos Livius in V datos fuisse dicit, quod Iupiter optimus maximus suam aedem servasset. Anno postea in urbe pestilentissimo scribit Livius in quinto ex libris Sibyllinis 'duumviri sacris faciendis lectisternium in urbe Roma primum fecerunt, per dies octo Apollinem, Latonam, Dianam, Herculem, Mercurium, Neptunum tribus quam amplissimis tum parari poterant, stratis lectis placarunt. Privatim quoque id sacrum celebratum, tota urbe patentibus ianuis promiscuoque usu rerum omnium in propatulo posito, notos ignotosque passim advenas in hospitium[182] ductos ferunt et cum inimicis quoque benigne ac comiter sermones habitos, iurgiis et litibus temperatum, vinctis[183] quoque dempta in eos dies vincula.' Simile nos pueri vidimus[184] accidisse ad annum, unde

place, King Tarquinius Priscus founded the King Trojan Games.[284] We have written about them extensively in *Rome Restored*.[285] Vergil: "Now the boys are called Troy, and the troop is called Trojan."[286] Suetonius in his *Life of Caesar* says about this game: "Two squadrons of older and younger boys played the game called 'Troy.'"[287]

47 I too as a child saw at Rimini that this game survives to our day. The show was put on by Carlo Malatesta, an outstanding and learned prince. The participants were not boys but nobles who had been invited from the whole of Italy to the marriage of Galeotto Malatesta.[288] Up to thirty men were mounted on very fast circus horses, each one dressed in leather armor beautifully decorated in a variety of colors and carrying in their hands blunt iron swords. Parading in a circle they gave each other blows in turn on shoulders and on helmets padded for this purpose. The game still has a name quite close to the one of old, "torniamen" for Trojan troop (*Troianum agmen*).[289] The first games when Rome was by now free were the Capitoline, which Livy says in Book V were put on because Jupiter Best and Greatest had kept his own temple safe.[290] Livy writes in Book V that afterward in a year of severe plague in the city, on the authority of the Sibylline oracles, "the Board of Two for performing rites for the first time put on a banquet for the gods (*lectisternium*) in the City of Rome, and for a period of eight days they sacrificed to Apollo, Latona, Diana, Hercules, Mercury and Neptune by spreading three couches, the most splendid that could be prepared at that time. They say that this rite was also observed by private individuals, with doors thrown open throughout the city and everything laid out in public for common consumption, and everywhere newcomers, whether known or unknown, were welcomed as guests and kind and friendly conversations had with enemies too. They abstained from quarrels and litigation and for that period even prisoners had their chains removed."[291] When I was a boy I saw something similar

quaterdecies a Christi Dei natalibus centenum[185] cum ingenti laborantes peste singularum paene urbium et oppidorum Italiae populi albam et lineam induti vestem catervatim vicinas adirent civitates, ubi publice et privatim hospitio accepti divinam carminibus in id compositis misericordiam implorabant, nullum tunc litigium, nullae fuerunt privatae contentiones, simultates et inimicitiae, quas non populi publico gaudio composuerint.

48 Supradicto etiam V libro scribit Livius: 'Ludiones ex Etruria acciti, ad tibicinis[186] modos saltantes, haud indecoros ⟨motus⟩[187] more Etrusco dabant. Imitari deinde eos iuventus, simul inconditis versibus inter se iocularia fundentes, coepere.' Et paulo post Livius: histriones impletis modis satyras scripto iam[188] ad tibicinem cantu motuque congruenti egisse, Liviumque, qui ab satyris ausus est primus argumento fabulam instruere, carminum auctorem puerum ad canendum ante tibicinem statuisse, inde ad manum cantare histrionibus coeptum, deverbiaque tamen ipsorum voci relicta. Postquam ludus in artem verterat, iuventus, fabellarum actu relicto histrionibus, ipsa inter se more antiquo ridicula intexta versibus recitare coepta, quae exordia postea appellata insertaque fabellis potissimum Atellanis[189] sunt, quod genus ludorum ab Oscis acceptum tenuit iuventus, nec ab histrionibus pollui passa. Et institutum est ut actores Atellanarum nec tribu moverentur et stipendia tamquam expertes artis accipiant. Paulo post sequitur Livius: 'ab sano res initio ad hanc vix opulentis regnis tolerabilem insaniam venit.'

happen in 1399 when there was a severe plague, and people from nearly every single city and town in Italy put on white linen garments and went in bands to nearby cities where they were welcomed as guests on behalf of the public and by individuals. They besought divine mercy with hymns composed for this purpose. At that time there was no litigation, there were no private disagreements, no quarrels and enmities which they did not resolve to the accompaniment of public rejoicing.[292]

Again from Book V Livy writes: "Stage players brought from 48
Etruria, dancing to the measures of a piper, would move gracefully in the Etruscan style. Next the young men began to imitate them, at the same time exchanging a stream of jests in rough verse."[293] A little further on Livy says that the stage players acted "satires" with completed measures in song now written for the pipe and with fitting gestures. Livius was the first to move away from satires and to venture to compose a play with a plot, and, though he composed the songs, he made a slave stand in front of the flute player to sing them. From then on they began the practice of singing to the actors' gestures and yet the dialogue was left to the voices of the actors themselves. After the entertainment had turned into an art, the young men left the performance of plays to the actors, and began to recite among themselves in the old way comic matter composed in verse. These were later called "prologues"[294] and attached especially to the Atellane plays. The young men kept the shows of this kind taken over from the Oscans and did not allow them to be polluted by the actors. And from this it remained the practice that those who performed in the Atellane plays should not be expelled from their tribes and they should perform military service as though they had no connection with the art.[295] A little further on Livy continues: "from a healthy beginning the business has arrived at the present point of unhealthy extravagance barely acceptable in opulent kingdoms."[296]

49 Continuavimus supra tribus in rebus Livii textum in ludionibus, histrionibus et Atellanis, ut eorum vocabulorum originem doceremus. De primis duobus sic habet Valerius Maximus: Ludii, Etruscorum disciplina, qui apud eos histriones, turpes et levissimi, histriones meliore instituto ad scaenica et mutationes. Solusque inter Latinos Festus dicit histriones dictos quod primum ab Histria venerunt. Macrobius autem in *Saturnalibus:* Recitabantur ultra comoedias, mimiambi a mimis et[190] histrionibus, unde Laberius, vir senatorius, a Caesare coactus, quos fecerat, ipse homo sexagenarius mimiambos recitavit et tamen in prohemio suum deploravit infortunium. Is tamen libertate ingenii multa in Caesarem dixit laedoria, quale est in Syri servi persona:[191] 'porro, Quirites, libertatem perdidimus.' Dixit etiam: 'Deceperunt se multi.' 'Frugalitas est miseria rumoris boni.' Quae cantabant histriones et saltabant. Hinc Hylas, Paladis discipulus, cum iam magistrum superaret, id quod eleganter cantaverat a populo coactus est saltare. Histrionesque inter turpes viros non habitos fuisse ostendit Roscii Amerini cum Cicerone amicitia et oratio, in qua populum Romanum reprehendit Cicero, quod Roscio cantante tumultuatus sit, qui scripsit librum in quo histrioniam oratoriae comparavit. Habebant autem histriones mercedem ex publico diurnam mille denarios sine gregalibus. Unde Aesopus ex hoc quaestu filio ducenties sextertium reliquit.

50 Ludorum et eorum, a quibus maiori ex parte edebantur, origine dicta, varias ipsorum aut partis maximae species breviter complectemur. Fuerunt namque, de quibus est dictum, Troiani et Capitolini, fuerunt scaenici, quos Livius in XXIIII[192] primum ab aedilibus

Above I have joined together excerpts dealing with three matters: stage players, actors and Atellanes, so that I might explain the origin of these terms. On the first two Valerius Maximus has as follows: stage players (*ludii*), according to Etruscan lore are those who were called "actors" (*histriones*) among them, the lewd and frivolous *histriones* with a better way of life for stage shows and changing roles.[297] Festus is the only Latin writer who says "that *histriones* were so-called because in the first place they came from Istria."[298] Macrobius however in *Saturnalia*: besides comedies mimic iambics were performed by mime actors and *histriones*. Hence Laberius, a man of senatorial status, was forced by Caesar to perform (as a man in his sixties) the iambic mimes he had composed and yet in his proem he lamented his misfortune. Prompted by his innate candor, however, he uttered much abuse against Caesar, as, for example, in the role of Syrus the slave: "Furthermore, citizens, we have lost our freedom."[299] He said too: "Many have deceived themselves."[300] "Thrift is wretchedness with a good name."[301] Actors also used to dance out the content of their song. Hence when Hylas was already outdoing his master Pylades, he was compelled by the people to dance that which he had sung elegantly.[302] Roscius of Ameria's friendship with Cicero demonstrates that actors were not classed among dishonorable men. So too does the speech in which Cicero rebukes the Roman people because they rioted while Roscius was singing.[303] Roscius wrote a book in which he compared the actor's art to that of the orator.[304] Actors used to get pay of one thousand denarii a day from the public treasury, ordinary members of their troupe excluded. Hence Aesop left his son twenty million sesterces made from this profession.[305] 49

Now that I have spoken of the origin of the games and of those by whom they were for the greater part performed, I shall briefly describe their different kinds, or those of the greatest part of them. There were the Trojan and Capitoline Games that I have spoken about above.[306] There were the theatrical games. Livy in 50

currulibus factos eo anno memoriae proditum dicit, fuerunt Apollinares, de quibus Livius XXV: 'Censuerunt patres Apollini ludos vovendos faciendosque et, quando ludi essent facti, XII milia aeris praetori[193] ad rem divinam et duas hostias maiores dandas. Alterum senatus consultum ut decemviri sacrum Graeco ritu facerent, hisque hostiis: Apollini bove aurato et capris duabus albis auratis, Latone bove femina aurata. Ludos praetor in Circo Maximo cum facturus esset edixit, ut populus, qui eos ludos spectaret, stipem Apollini quantum commodum esset conferret. Haec est origo ludorum Apollinarium, victoriae non valitudinis ergo factos. Populus spectavit coronatus, matronae supplicaverunt, vulgo apertis ianuis in propatulo epulati sunt celeberque dies omni caerimoniarum genere fuit.' Ludi Apollinares Senatus decrevit ut in perpetuum voverentur,[194] quos ad nostram quoque aetatem pervenisse constat. Siquidem hi sunt quos per extremos carnis privii dies in Circo Flaminio, ubi nunc Agonis est appellatio, fieri quotannis videmus. Principio enim mutationis prudenter factae a gentilium superstitione ad ritus Christianos, ut aliquid Apollinarium appellationis ipsi ludo remaneret prope sancti Apollinaris ecclesiam, ea etiam ratione institutam, is locus ludis est retentus, nec multum variat tempus, quando hi sicut et illi ad finem Februarii ut plurimum eduntur[195] et quando hostiae illorum, sicut decuit, sunt omissae, retinet consuetudo aliquod victoriae simulacrum faciendi, sicut eos victoriae ergo incoatos Livius asseruit.

Book XXIV says that the tradition was that they were staged for the first time by the aediles in that year.[307] There were the Apollinarian Games, about which Livy says in Book XXV: "The senators resolved that games should be vowed to Apollo and held in his honor. When the games had been staged, twelve thousand *asses* and two full-grown sacrificial victims should be given to the praetor to perform the ceremony. There was a second decree of the senate, to the effect that the Board of Ten should offer sacrifice according to the Greek rite, and with the following victims: to Apollo an ox with gilded horns and two white nanny goats with gilded horns, to Latona a cow with gilded horns. When the praetor was about to hold the games in the Great Circus he proclaimed that the people who were watching these games should make an offering to Apollo, as much as they pleased. Such is the origin of the Apollinarian Games; they were held because of victory and not good health. The people watched wearing garlands. The married women offered prayers. Everywhere they banqueted in the forecourts with open doors and the day was solemnized with ceremonies of every kind."[308] The senate decreed that Apollinarian Games should be vowed in perpetuity. It is agreed that they survived to our day too, if indeed they are the ones that we see performed every year during the last days of Carnival in the Flaminian Circus (now called "Agone").[309] For at the beginning of the transition wisely made from the Gentiles' false religion to Christian rites, in order that the festival itself might keep something of the name of the Apollinarian Games, the place of the games was kept near the church of St. Apollinare, which had been founded for that reason too.[310] Nor is there a great difference in the time, since the modern ones just like the ancient for the most part are put on at the end of February. In addition, inasmuch as the latter's sacrificial victims have been given up, as was proper, the custom has been maintained of putting on a replica of a victory, in accordance with Livy's claim that the Apollinarian Games were initiated because of victory.[311]

51 Quale proximis diebus fuit spectaculum omnibus nobis gratissimum, qui ecclesiasticae Romanae rei publicae membra curiam sequimur Romanam, cum in eodem Circi Flaminii Agone proelii similitudo quaedam fuit, quod praeclarissimum aeternaque[196] dignum memoria aestate proxima gestum est, ad Danubium qua fluvius influit Savuus cum Maumeth, Turchorum imperator,[197] supra centum milia in exercitu habens ad Bellogradum oppidum, aliquandiu oppugnatum machinisque et bombardis prope solo aequatum, fusus et suis quibusque melioribus ad sexdecim milia occisis fugatus, bombardas et vim paene infinitam machinamentorum ac armorum amni terraque amisit. Laetum quippe nobis et dulcissimum fuit inspicere personatum quendam Iohannem Carvaial, Hispanum Cardinalem sancti Angeli, indumento et ornamentis referentem Christianorum et Romani pontificis exercitui in illam ducendo barbariem[198] praeesse, sed laetius erat videre alia in persona Iohannem Capistraneum,[199] ordinis sancti Francisci fratrem, qui multis continuata annis opinione sanctitatis tanto impleta miraculo milites adduxerit[200] Iesu Christi vexilla secutos, qui celeberrimo Iohanne Conyat Vayuoda Transsilvano duce, pauca hominum milia supradictam in barbaris caedem edidere. Fueruntque ad id Circi Agonis spectaculum ex nostratibus ingenio et doctrina cultiores[201] nonnulli, quibus ea die Romanam rem lacertos adhuc movere, Romanum celebrari nomen apparuit, cum tantas adhuc res adversus Scythas, Tanais olim et Riphaeorum[202] montium accolas, Turchos, maximae partis Asiae et Europae dominatores, sub Romanis signis Romanique legati nomine geri, non magis ob spectaculi quod ante oculos erat ostensionem quam ob recentis victoriae refricatam memoriam videretur. Et quidem his in ludis Apollinaribus suffectis etiam quod habet Livius propemodum servatur, ut

So in recent days there was a spectacle of this kind that pleased all those of us who as members of the ecclesiastical Roman state are attached to the Roman curia, when in the same Agone of the Flaminian Circus a reenactment took place of the celebrated battle,[312] worthy of eternal remembrance, which was waged last summer beside the Danube at its confluence with the river Sava. Then Mehmed, emperor of the Turks,[313] who had above one hundred thousand men in his army, after having besieged the city of Belgrade for some time and almost razed it to the ground with his siege engines and cannon, was routed there, and put to flight. Up to sixteen thousand of his best men were killed, and he lost his cannon and an almost infinite quantity of military engines and weapons on water and land. It gave us joy and much pleasure to watch an actor representing in dress and costume Juan de Carvajal, the Spanish Cardinal of St. Angelo.[314] He was in charge of the army of the Christians and the Roman pontiff being led against that barbarian nation. But it gave more joy to see in another mask Giovanni Capistrano, a Franciscan friar, for whose reputation of sainthood for so many years on end this great miracle was the culmination. He led the soldiers following the banner of Jesus Christ.[315] They, a few thousand men, with the famous János Hunyadi, Voivoda of Hungary,[316] as their general, inflicted on the barbarians the slaughter mentioned above. There were present at that show in the Circus Agone some of our contemporaries, the more intelligent and learned, to whom it was evident on that day that Rome was still flexing her muscles and that the name of Rome was honored, since it seemed that such great deeds were still being accomplished, under Roman standards and in the name of a Roman legate, against the Turks (who are the Scythians, once dwellers in the region of the Tanais and the Rhiphaean mountains),[317] masters of the greater part of Asia and Europe — not so much because of the visual display that was before their eyes, but because memory of the recent victory was refreshed. Indeed in these sub- 51

vulgo apertis ianuis epulentur. Nanque die illa urbaniores quique Romani aut convivia celebrant aut cibaria in id consuetudine introducta vicinis amicisque missitant, cum tamen plebs[203] infima ad tabernas vinarias in propatulo comedant isque cibus est pulte, caseo aromatibusque confectus.

52 Ludi etiam fuerunt Saeculares quos Festus dicit centesimo quoque anno fieri solitos, unde miror Plinium dicere Stephanionem primum togatum[204] saltare in illis instituisse et utrisque sui temporis saltavisse. Et Suetonius scribit Domitianum fecisse ludos Saeculares computata ratione temporum ab iis[205] quos Augustus dederat. Fuerunt et ludi Romani, de quibus Livius X: 'Coronati primum ob res bene gestas bello ludos Romanos spectaverunt palmaeque tunc primum[206] translato ex more regio victoribus datae.' Et libro XXV: 'Ludi Romani pro temporis illius copiis magnifice facti et diem unum instaurati et congii olei in vicos singulos dati.' Ludos Plebeios scribit Q. Asconius Pedianus *secunda actione in Verrem* exactis regibus pro plebis libertate datos fuisse[207] aut pro reconciliatione plebis post secessionem[208] in Aventinum, quos postea L. Sulla post victoriam instituerit. Et Livius in XXVII: 'Aediles plebis ex multaticio argento signa aenea ad aedem Cereris dedere et ludos pro temporis eius copia magnifici apparatus fecerunt.'

53 Circenses ludos describere aggressum subiit animum recordatio ipsos et alios quosdam commodius ostendi posse, si ludos simul et spectacula prout saepenumero dabantur ostendemus. Specum au-

stitute Apollinarian Games even what Livy says as to their banqueting everywhere with open doors is more or less preserved. On that day all the more cultivated Romans either hold dinner parties or send to their friends and neighbors the foodstuffs which had become customary for this, while the humblest of the common people eat at wine taverns in the open air. This food is made from porridge, cheese and spices.

There were also the Secular Games, which Festus says usually 52
took place every one hundred years.[318] For this reason I am surprised that Pliny says that Stephanio initiated the practice of dancing in a toga in them, and that he danced in both the Secular Games of his time.[319] Suetonius writes that Domitian held Secular Games calculating the time period from those put on by Augustus.[320] There were also the Roman Games about which Livy says in Book X: "For the first time they wore wreaths celebrating victory in war to watch the Roman Games, and then the victors were first awarded palms, according to a royal practice that was taken over."[321] And in Book XXV: "The Roman Games were put on magnificently, for the resources of those times, and were repeated on one day. Measures of oil were distributed to each locality."[322] Quintus Asconius Pedianus writes on the Second Action of the *Verrine Orations* that the Plebeian Games were put on after the expulsion of the kings to celebrate the liberation of the people or in honor of the reconciliation of the plebeians after their seccession to the Aventine. Later Lucius Sulla established them after his victory.[323] And Livy in Book XXVII says: "The plebeian aediles donated to the Temple of Ceres bronze statues paid for out of fines and they put on games of magnificent splendor for the resources of the time."[324]

I had begun to describe the circus games, when it occurred to 53
me that they and certain others could be more conveniently described if I were to explain the circus games at the same time as the stage shows, as they were very often put on with them. Plu-

tem Plutarchus in *Problematibus* dicit locum esse unde[209] despicitur et inde spectacula esse dicta. Ut itaque a promiscuis incipiamus, Cicero Galvisio: 'Circenses erant quo genere spectaculi ne levissime quidem teneor:[210] nihil novum, nihil varium, nihil quod non semel spectasse sufficiat, quo magis miror tot[211] milia virorum currentes equos, insistentes curribus[212] homines videre.' Et ad Marcum Marium Cicero: 'Omnino, si quaeris ludi apparatissimi, sed non tui stomachi; deliciae vero tuae, noster Aesopus, eiusmodi fuit, ut ei desinere per omnes homines liceret, is iurare cum coepisset vox eum defecit in illo loco "si sciens fallo." Nec id quidem leporis habuerunt, quod solent mediocres ioci; apparatus enim spectatio tollebat omnem hilaritatem. Quid enim delectationis habent sexcenti muli in Clytaemnestra aut in Equo Troiano creterrarum[213] tria milia, aut armatura varia peditatus et equitatus in aliqua pugna? Quae popularem admirationem habuerunt, delectationem tibi nullam attulissent. Non enim te credo Graecos aut[214] Oscos ludos desiderare. Reliquae sunt venationes binae per singulos dies, magnificae nemo negat, sed quae potest esse homini polito[215] delectatio, cum aut homo imbecillus a valentissima bestia laniatur aut praeclara bestia venabulo transverberatur? Extremus elephantorum dies fuit, in quo admiratio magna vulgi atque turbae, delectatio nulla extitit; quin etiam misericordia quaedam consecuta est atque opinio huiusmodi esse quandam illi beluae cum genere humano societatem.'

54 Sive autem Plinius ab hac Ciceronis epistula, sive aliunde sumpsit de elephantis haec diffusius scribit, quae simul cum plurimis ab eo afferemus. Elephantes in circo pugnarunt Claudii Pulchri aedilitate curruli adversus tauros. Pompei altero consulatu

tarch in *Problems* says a *specus* (conduit) is a place from which one looks down, and *spectacula* (shows) derive their name from this.[325] Therefore to begin with them all together, Cicero to Calvisius: "The circus games were on, a type of spectacle (*spectaculum*) that does not attract me in the slightest. There is nothing new, nothing different, nothing that is not enough after it has been seen once. So I am all the more amazed that so many thousands of men watch horses running and men driving chariots."[326] And Cicero to Marcus Marius: "The games, if you ask, were on the whole splendidly furnished, but you would not have liked them. My friend Aesop, your delight, was in such form that everyone would give him permission to leave off. When he had begun to swear the oath, his voice failed him in that passage 'if I knowingly deceive.' The ordinary jokes did not have even their usual charm. The sight of the costly furnishings removed all enjoyment. What pleasure is to be had from six hundred mules in *Clytemnestra*, or three thousand mixing bowls in *Trojan Horse* or the variegated equipment of foot soldiers and cavalry in some fight? That which won the people's admiration would have brought you no pleasure. I trust you do not have a wish for Greek or Oscan games. There remain the hunts, two a day, magnificent, no one denies—but what pleasure can there be for a refined[327] man when a poor weak man is savaged by a powerful animal, or a splendid animal is transfixed by a hunting spear? The last day was that of the elephants. From it arose great admiration on the part of the common people and the crowd, but no pleasure. Rather what resulted was even a feeling of pity and a thought of this kind, that that animal has some affinity with the human race."[328]

Whether Pliny's source on elephants was this letter of Cicero's 54
or something else, he has the following rather extensive remarks which I shall excerpt from him, along with much else. Elephants fought against bulls in the Circus during Claudius Pulcher's curule aedileship.[329] In Pompey's second consulship, at the

dedicatione templi Veneris Victricis in circo viginti Gaetulis ex adverso iaculantibus mirabili unius dimicatione, qui pedibus confossis repsit genibus in catervas arrepta scuta iaciens in sublime. Universi eruptionem tentavere non sine vexatione populi circunductis clastris ferreis. Qua de causa Caesar dictator simile edens spectaculum principiis arenam circundedit. Nero autem equitatum disposuit, sed Pompeiani, omissa spe eruptionis, supplicavere populo inenarrabili habitu oris, sese quadam lamentatione complorantes, tanto populi dolore, ut oblitus imperatoris ac munificentiae honori suo exquisitae flens universus consurgeret, dirasque deneganti Pompeio poenas, quas brevi habuit, imprecaretur. Pugnavere et Caesari dictatori tertio consulatu viginti contra pedites quingentos, iterumque totidem turriti cum sexagenis propugnatoribus eodem, quo priore, numero peditum et pari equitum ex adverso dimicante.

55 Leonum simul pugnam Romae primus dedit Scaevola praefectus in curruli aedilitate. Pompeius Magnus in circo iubatis CCCXV, Caesar dictator CCCC. Senatus consultum fuit vetus ne liceret Africanas pantheras in Italiam traducere. Contra hoc tulit ad plebem Gn. Naufidius tribunus plebis permisitque circensium gratia importari. Scaurus aedilitate sua varias misit CL, Pompeius deinde CCCCX, Augustus CCCCXX. Idem postea in theatro Romae ostendit mansuefactam tigrim[216] in cavea. Claudius Nero quattuor pariter mansuefactas. Camelum, equo similem[217] collo, pedibus et manibus bovi, camelo capite, albis maculis rutilum[218]

dedication of the Temple of Venus the Victorious, twenty fought in the Circus against Gaetulians who cast spears against them. One put up a wonderful struggle, for though its feet had been pierced through, it crawled on its knees into the troops of men, grabbing shields and tossing them up in the air.[330] They attempted a mass breakout, causing distress among the crowd, though there was an enclosure of iron barriers. (This is why Caesar, when he was dictator and was putting on a similar show, surrounded the arena with frontline soldiers. Nero on the other hand stationed cavalry.) Pompey's elephants, losing hope of making a breakout, besought the people with an indescribable expression as if they were bewailing their fate. They caused the people so much grief that they forgot the general and the exquisite munificence devised in their honor, and rose up in a body weeping. When Pompey refused them, they called down terrible punishment upon him, which he shortly received.[331] When Caesar was dictator and in his third consulship, twenty fought against five hundred foot soldiers. Again, the same number of castled elephants with sixty élite troops, with the same number of foot soldiers as before and an equal number of cavalry fighting on the other side.[332]

In his curule aedileship Scaevola (when prefect) was the first to 55
put on a fight with lions. Pompey the Great in the Circus 315 maned lions, and Caesar when dictator 400.[333] There was an old decree of the senate that prohibited importing African panthers into Italy. Gnaeus Aufidius, a tribune of the plebs, proposed a bill against this to the plebeians, and allowed them to be imported for games in the Circus. Scaurus in his aedileship exhibited 150 female leopards, next Gnaeus Pompeius 400, Augustus 420.[334] The same Augustus later on exhibited a tame tiger in the pit in his theater at Rome, Claudius Nero 4 equally tame.[335] Caesar was the first to exhibit a giraffe at the circus games. It has a neck like that of a horse, feet and legs like those of an ox, a head like a camel's,

colorem distinguentibus Caesar ludis circensibus primum dedit. Pompeius ludis ostendit primum chaum, quem colliraffas[219] vocabant, effigie lupi, pardorum manibus. Idem cephas ex Aethiopia, quarum[220] pedes posteriores humanis[221] cruribus, priores manibus fuere similes. Hippo⟨po⟩tamum et cocodrillos quatuor M. Scaurus aedilitate sua temporario theatro dedit. Domitius Aenobarbus aedilis curulis ursos Numidicos centum et totidem venatores Aethiopas[222] in circo. Fuerunt quoque in spectaculis ludisque plurima, quae infinitum et simul superfluum fuerit hic referre.

56 Sed pauca quaedam non solum spectacula, sed ob ipsa diversis edita temporibus praedictis addere non piget. Lentulus Spinter primus in theatro vela superinduxit Apollinaribus ludis. Caesar dictator totum forum Romanum et viam Sacram intexit[223] et clivum Capitolinum in munere gladiatorio. Marcellus, sorore Augusti Octavia natus, pariter in avunculi aedilitate Kalendis Augusti ut litigantes in umbra essent. Caesar, postea dictator, in aedilitate[224] munere patris funebri omni apparatu arenae argenteo[225] usus est. Nero Pompeii theatrum operuit auro in unum diem, quo Tiridiati regi Armeniorum ostenderet. Claudius Pulcher scaenam prius varietate colorum adornavit, G. Antonius argento, Petreius auro, Catulus ebore et auro. De Caesare autem in dictatura scribit Suetonius: 'Edidit spectacula varii generis: munus gladiatorium, ludos etiam regionatim urbe tota et quidem per omnium linguarum histriones, item circenses athletas naumachiam. In foro depugnavit Furius Leptinius, stirpe praetoria, et Q. Calperius senator quondam actorque causarum. Pyrrichiam saltaverunt et Asiae Bithiniaeque principum liberi cum ludiis. Venationes editae per

and white spots setting off its tawny color.[336] Pompey was the first to exhibit a lynx at the games. They call it "calliraphius."[337] It has the appearance of a wolf and a leopard's hands. The same man brought "cephae" from Aethiopia, whose hind feet are like human legs, their forefeet like hands.[338] Marcus Scaurus in his aedileship exhibited a hippopotamus and 4 crocodiles in his temporary theater;[339] Domitius Ahenobarbus as curule aedile displayed 100 Numidian bears and the same number of Aethiopian hunters in the Circus.[340] There was also a great number of things in the shows and games that it would take for ever and at the same time be superfluous to recount here.

But I am not reluctant to add a few things—not only shows— 56
to those already mentioned because they were put on at different times. Lentulus Spinther, at the Apollinarian Games, was the first to cover the theater with awnings. Caesar too, when dictator, shaded the whole Roman Forum, the Sacred Way and the Capitoline Rise, for a gladiatorial show.[341] Marcellus, Augustus' sister Octavia's son, did likewise from August 1, in his uncle's aedileship, so that litigants would be in the shade.[342] Caesar, who was later dictator, in his aedileship, at the gladiatorial games for his father's death had all the equipment used in the arena made of silver.[343] Nero had Pompey's theater covered with gold for the one day to show it to Tiridates, king of Armenia.[344] Claudius Pulcher first decorated the backdrop with a variety of colors, Gaius Antonius with silver, Petreius with gold, Catulus with ivory and gold.[345] Suetonius writes the following about Caesar in his dictatorship: "He put on shows of various kinds: a gladiatorial show, games by districts throughout the city and performed by actors of all languages, again, circus games, athletic contests, a sea battle. Furius Leptinus, of a praetorian family, fought to the finish in the Forum, as did Quintus Calpenus, once a senator and a pleader of causes. Sons of the princes of Asia and Bithynia danced a Pyrrhic dance with stage players. Wild-beast hunts were put on for five days and

quinque dies, ac novissime pugna divisa in duos acies,[226] quingenis[227] peditibus, elephantis vicenis, tricenis[228] equitibus, hinc et inde immissis. Nam quo latius dimicaretur sublatae metae, inque earum locum bina ex adverso constituta erant repagula. Athletae stadio ad tempus extructo in regione Campi Martii cucurrerunt per triduum. Navali proelio in monte Caelio defosso lacu, biremes ac triremes quadriremesque Tyriae et Aegyptiae classis magno pugnantium numero conflixerunt, ad quae spectacula tantum undique confluxit hominum, ut plerique advenae inter vias tabernaculis positis manerent, ac saepe prae turba elisi exanimatique sint plurimi et in his duo senatores.'

57 De Augusto autem Suetonius: 'Spectaculorum assiduitate et magnificentia omnes antecessit. Fecit nonnumquam vicatim; athletas quoque extructis in campo sedibus ligneis, navale proelium circa Tiberim. Ad scaenicas quoque et gladiatorias operas et equitibus Romanis aliquando usus est. Spectandi confusiorem morem correxit, ut, quotiens quid spectaculi ubique ederetur, primus subselliorum ordo vacaret senatoribus, Romae legatos liberarum sociarumque gentium vetuit in orchestra considere, cum quosdam etiam libertini generis inibi deprehendisset; militem secrevit a populo, multis e plebe prius ordinem assignavit, praetextatis cuneum suum et proximum paedagogis. Feminis ne gladiatores quidem, quos promiscue spectare solemne fuerat, nisi ex superiore loco spectare concessit. Solis virginibus Vestalibus locum in theatro separatum contra praetoris tribunal dedit. Athletarum spectaculo

last of all there was a battle between two opposing lines, with five hundred foot soldiers each, twenty elephants and thirty cavalry having been sent in on each side. To make more space for the combat, the turning posts were removed and in their place two barriers were set up opposite each other. For three successive days athletes ran races in a stadium temporarily erected for this in the region of the Field of Mars. For the naval battle a lake was excavated on the Caelian Hill,[346] in which there was a contest of ships of two, three and four banks of oars belonging to the Tyrian and Egyptian fleets, manned by a large number of fighting men. Such a great number of people flocked from everywhere to these shows that many visitors had to lodge in tents pitched in the streets and often the crowd was such that many people were crushed and killed, among them two senators.[347]

About Augustus Suetonius says: "By the frequency and mag- 57
nificence of his public shows he surpassed all. Sometimes he had them put on in the districts. He put on athletic contests, erecting wooden stands in the Field of Mars, a naval battle beside the Tiber. He sometimes employed even Roman knights for theatrical performances and gladiatorial shows as well."[348] "He reformed the rather indiscriminate fashion of viewing the games, so that whenever a show was put on anywhere, the first row of benches should be reserved for the senators. At Rome he did not allow the ambassadors of free and allied nations to sit in the orchestra, since he had come to know that some of the freedman class were among them. He kept the soldiery apart from the people. He first assigned a row to many from the plebeians, to the young boys their own block and the adjacent one to their tutors. He would not allow women to view even gladiators, except from the upper seats, though it had been customary for them to watch them together with the other spectators. He assigned a separate place in the theater for the Vestal Virgins alone, facing the praetor's tribunal. He

muliebrem sexum omnem semovit. Ipse, cum spectaret, nihil agebat, Caesaris reprehensionem timens, qui solitus fuerit epistulas lectitare et scribere et rescribere. Spectavit studiosissime pugiles et maxime Latinos, non legitimos atque ordinarios modo, quos etiam commiscere cum Graecis solebat, sed et catervarios oppidanos inter angustias viarum pugnantes temere ac sine arte. Athletis confirmavit privilegia et ampliavit, histrionum licentiam adeo compescuit, ut Stephanionem togatarium, cum in puerilem habitum ei circum tonsam matronam ministrare comperisset, per trina theatra virgis caesum relegaverit.'

58 Et de Gallicula Suetonius: 'Scaenicos ludos et assidue et varii generis ac multifariam fecit, quosdam nocturnos accensis tota urbe luminibus.' 'Mirmillionem e ludo rudibus secum battuentem et sponte prostratum confodit ferrea sica[229] ac more victorum cum palma discurrit.' Et Claudius: 'Circo Maximo marmoreis carceribus auratisque metis, quae utraque et tofina[230] et lignea fuerant, exculto, propria senatoribus constituit loca promiscue spectare solitis, ac supra quadrigarium certamen Troiae lusit. Exhibuit Thessalos equites, qui feros tauros per spatia circi agebant insiliebantque defessos et ad terram cornibus detrahebant.' 'Germanorum legatis in orchestra sedere permisit, simplicitate eorum et fiducia commotus, qui in popularia deducti, cum animadvertissent Parthos et Armenios sedentes in senatu, ad eadem loca sponte transierunt, nihilo deteriorem virtutem aut conditionem suam praedicantes.' 'Ad athletarum spectaculum invitavit et virgines Vestales quia

kept the entire female sex away from the athletic shows."[349] "When he himself was a spectator, he did no business, fearing the censure that had been directed at Caesar, who used to read, write and reply to letters. He was a very keen spectator of boxers, especially those from Latium, not only the professional and regular ones, whom he used to combine even with the Greek ones, but also those belonging to city gangs fighting casually and without training in the narrow streets. He confirmed the athletes' privileges and increased them. He was so severe in curbing the actors' lawlessness that when he learned that a married woman with hair cut short like a boy's was serving Stephanio, an actor in plays in Roman dress, he had him whipped with rods through the three theaters and banished him."[350]

Suetonius on Caligula: "He put on theatrical games regularly, 58
of different kinds and in many places, some at night, when the whole city was lit up by lights."[351] "When a *murmillo* from the school was fencing with him with a wooden sword and voluntarily fell to the ground, he stabbed him with a steel dagger and ran to and fro with the palm, in the fashion of a victor."[352] And Claudius "improved the Great Circus with marble starting gates and gilded turning posts, both of which had been made of tufa and wood. He established special places for the senators, who were used to watching among the other spectators. In addition, he put on the four-horse contest of Troy.[353] He exhibited Thessalian riders who drove wild bulls all over the circus, leaped on them when they were tired out and pulled them down to the ground by their horns."[354] "He allowed the Germans' ambassadors to sit in the orchestra, touched by their simplicity and confidence. They had been escorted into the common people's seats, but, when they noticed Parthians and Armenians sitting among the senate, of their own accord they moved to the same place, proclaiming that their worth and rank were in no way inferior."[355] "He [Nero] invited even Vestal Virgins to the athletic shows, because the priestesses of Ceres were allowed

Olimpiae quoque Cereris sacerdotibus spectare licet.' Titus Vespasianus, princeps optimus 'amphiteatro, quod nunc Colosseum, appellant, dedicato thermisque iuxta celebriter extructis—in quibus nunc sunt vineae fratrum sanctae Mariae Novae—munus edidit apparatissimum largissimumque et navale proelium in Naumachia Veteri—quam fuisse docuimus prope ecclesiam sancti Petri, ubi depressus est locus post sancti Michaelis ecclesiam—et gladiatores atque uno die quinque milia omnis generis ferarum.' Domitianusque eius frater: 'spectacula magnifica assidue et sumptuosa edidit, non in amphiteatro modo, verum et in circo, ubi, praeter[231] solemnes bigarum quadrigarumque cursus, proelium etiam duplex equestre et pedestre commisit, ac in amphiteatro navale quoque venationes gladiatoresque et noctibus ad lychnucos,[232] nec virorum modo pugnas, sed et feminarum. Navalis pugna[233] paene iustarum classium, effosso et circunstructo circa Tiberim lacu,' ubi nunc circa sancti Silvestri monasterium et viam Flaminiam depresso in loco vineas esse hortosque videmus.

59 Nunc, quia Aelius Spartianus Hadrianum scribit fabulas omnis generis more antiquo in theatro dedisse, verba libet aliqua, quod supra a nobis desideratum fuisse non dubitamus. Scaenam, orchestram, mirmilliones, panthomimos declarat Placidus grammaticus non incelebris. 'Scaenam esse dicit cameram hinc inde compositam, quae in umbrae locum in theatro erat, in quo ludi actitabantur. Item scaenam dici arborum in se incubantium quasi concameratam densationem ut subterpositos tegere possit. Item scaenam vocari compositionem alicuius criminis, quae digna sit agi in theatro exclamationibus tragicis.' Ulpianus autem iureconsultus titulo de iis qui notentur infamia scribit: 'Scaena est, ut Labeo

to watch at Olympia too."[356] Titus Vespasianus, an excellent emperor, "at the dedication of the amphitheater" (now called the Colosseum)[357] "and when the baths had been built quickly nearby" (where the vineyards of the friars of St. Mary the New are now),[358] "put on a very sumptuous and lavish gladiatorial show, and a mock naval battle in the Old Naumachia" (which I have shown was near the church of St. Peter where there is a depression behind the church of St. Michael)[359] "and gladiatorial shows and on one day five thousand wild beasts of every kind."[360] His brother Domitian "frequently gave magnificent and costly shows not only in the amphitheater, but also in the Circus, where, apart from the usual races of two-horse and four-horse chariots, he also held a double battle, of both cavalry and infantry, and a mock naval battle also in the amphitheater, wild-beast hunts, and gladiatorial shows even at night by lamplight, and fights not only between men but also between women. The naval battle was of fleets that were almost full-size, a lake having been excavated and an edifice constructed around it near the Tiber"[361] (where we see there are now vineyards and gardens in a depression in the neighborhood of the monastery of St. Silvester and the Flaminian Way).

Now, because Aelius Spartianus writes that Hadrian had plays 59
of every kind put on in the theater in the old way,[362] I want to add some definition of terms, something that I am sure has been found lacking in what I have said above. Placidus, a renowned grammarian, explains the *scaena,* the *orchestra, murmillones* and pantomimes. He says "the *scaena* is a room joined on both sides which was in the shaded place in the theater where the plays were usually acted. A clump of trees hanging over each other like an arch so as to form a roof over those beneath is likewise called a "scaena." Likewise called a "scaena" is the composition of some crime which is fit to be put on in the theater with tragic declamation."[363] The jurist Ulpian writes in the section on those who are tainted with civic disgrace and disqualification: "The *scaena* in Labeo's

diffinit, quae ludorum faciendorum causa quolibet loco, ubi quis consistat moveaturque spectaculum sui praebiturus, posita sit in publico privatoque vel in vico, quo tamen loco passim homines spectandi causa admittantur.' Nosque a Cassiodoro in *Roma* ostendimus *instaurata* theatrum Graeca appellatione visorium interpretari, quod turba conveniens eminus videatur et videat, et scaenam theatri frontem binis pluribusve contignationibus constratam, in quibus histriones recitabant, mimique mirmilliones et ceteri ludii varios de quibus supra est dictum ludos gesticulationesque edebant. In scaena autem, cum emicicli formam haberet, gradus sediliaque fuere, de quibus primarii magistratus honoratioresque spectarent eorumque sedilium pars intima orchestra est dicta. Quando autem theatra primum facta sint et in praedicta diximus *instauratione urbis* et infra in rei publicae partibus dicturi sumus.

60 Mirmillones[234] erant pugiles se ad duellum, sed semiludicrum provocantes, quos quid fuerint Festus Pompeius sic edocet: 'Retiario pugnanti adversus mirmillonem[235] cantatur "non te peto, piscem peto, quid me fugis Galle," quia mirmillioneum genus armature Gallicum est, ipsique mirmillones[236] ante Galli appellabantur, in quorum galeis piscis effigies inerat, quod genus pugnae institutum est a Pithaco, uno ex sapientibus septem' Graeciae. Pantomimi autem ab omnium varietate ludorum, in quos se ingerebant appellati sunt. Nam scaenae servientes omnes edocti ludos erant.

61 Sed ad principem Hadrianum revertamur. Is, cum doctissimus esset, fabularum recitationem omnis generis in theatro, ad scaenam scilicet et orchestram dedit, histriones aulicos publicavit, in

definition is that which has been set up for the purpose of putting on shows in any place, where anyone who is going to display himself may stand and move, be it in public, in private or on the street, provided that people are admitted to this place without restriction in order to watch."[364] I have shown in *Rome Restored* from Cassiodorus that "theater" is a Greek term meaning "a seeing place" (*visorium*) because the assembled crowd is watched and watches at a distance.[365] The *scaena,* the forepart of the theater,[366] was made with two or more floors.[367] The actors performed on it and mimes and *murmillones* and all the other stage players displayed a variety of games, about which I have spoken above, and movements. Since the *scaena* had the shape of a hemicycle, in it there were tiers and seats from which the chief magistrates and the more distinguished people watched, and the innermost part of these seats was called the "orchestra."[368] But as to the time when theaters were first constructed, I have both spoken of this in the aforementioned *Rome Restored,* and I shall discuss it below in the sections on government.[369]

Murmillones were boxers who challenged each other to battle, but half in sport. Festus Pompeius explains them as follows: "When the net fighter is fighting against the *murmillo* the chant goes 'I am not trying to catch you, I am trying to catch a fish. Why do you run away from me, Gaul?' Because the kind of equipment the *murmillo* has is Gallic, the *murmillones* themselves were previously called Gauls. On their helmets was the image of a fish. This type of fight was instituted by Pittacus, one of the Seven Sages" of Greece.[370] Pantomimes got their name from all the different kinds of games in which they took part.[371] For those working in the theater were taught all the games. 60

But let us return to the emperor Hadrian. Since he was very well educated, "he put on performances of plays of all kinds in the theater," that is, for the stage and orchestra. "He let the court actors be heard in public. In the circus he had many wild beasts 61

circo multas feras et saepe cunctos leones interfecit. Antoninus autem Pius, etsi modestissimus fuit princeps, munera dedit, 'in quibus elephanti, crococtae, rhinocerontes,[237] cocodrilli atque hippo⟨po⟩thomi et omnia ex omni orbe terrarum animalia, etiam tigres fuere. Centum etiam boves una missione dati.' 'Temperavit autem scaenicas donationes, ut quinos aureos scaenici acciperent, ita tamen quod nullus editor decem aureos supergrederetur.' 'Spectacula mirifica fecit. In munere autem publico tam magnanimus fuit, ut centum leones una missione simul exhiberet ⟨et⟩ sagittis interfectos.' Commodus autem Antoninus, qui proprie est appellatus omnibus incommodus, huiusmodi spectaculorum insaniam per habitus gestationem melius quam ceteri omnes ante se principes declaravit, qui 'paenulatos iussit spectatores non togatos ad munus convenire, quod funeribus solebat. Funebris enim vestis est paenula; ipse pariter in pullis vestimentis praesidens.' Gordianus vero, cum esset ditissimus, clausam indigentibus probis viris per summam sordidamque avaritiam, liberalitatem suam exhibendis ferarum muneribus patefecit. 'Aedilitatis enim suae tempore duodecim populo Romano spectacula per singulos XII dies dedit, ita ut gladiatorum nonnumquam quingenta paria et numquam[238] minus centum quinquaginta, feras Libycas uno die quandoque mille ediderit. Erat ei silva, in qua habuit cervos ducentos, Britannos equos feros XXX, oves feras mille albas, decem aureas capras, quas scilicet ipse inaurari fecerat, structiones Mauros miniatos trecentos, onagros XXX, apros CL, ibices CC, damas CC, haec omnia populo diripienda concessit die muneris, quod sextum edebat.' Et Philippus ipse Arabs primus Romanorum principum, cui desuper ingens datus est munus ut fieret Christianus, cum millesimus annus ab urbe condita suo et filii consulatu incidisset, Saeculares ludos et munera edidit circensia, in quibus ferae

killed, and often all the lions."[372] Antoninus Pius, even though he was a very restrained emperor, put on shows, "in which there were elephants, hyenas, rhinoceroses, crocodiles and hippopotamuses and all the animals from the whole world. There were also tigers. A hundred head of cattle were presented and released at the one time."[373] "He [Marcus Aurelius] restricted the cost of the stage shows, so that the players would receive five gold coins each, yet in such a way that no exhibitor went beyond ten gold coins."[374] "He held wonderful shows. In his public games he was so generous that he showed a hundred lions, turned loose all at the one time and killed with arrows."[375] Commodus Antoninus, who has more aptly been called "unpleasant (*incommodus*) to all,"[376] has, better than all the emperors before him, made manifest the disgrace of shows of this kind through the clothes worn at them. "For he gave orders that the spectators assemble for the show wearing cloaks (*paenulati*) not togas, which was the practice at funerals. For the *paenula* was funeral garb. He himself presided dressed in dark-colored clothes in the same way."[377] Though Gordian was very rich, he kept his liberality closed to good but poor men by the utmost miserly avarice, but displayed it by putting on wild beast shows.[378] "During his aedileship, he put on for the Roman people twelve shows on twelve separate days, such that he offered sometimes 500 pairs of gladiators and never less than 150, sometimes 1,000 wild beasts from Libya on one day. He had a wood in which he kept 200 stags, 30 wild horses from Britain, 100 white wild sheep, 10 nanny goats with gilded horns, which he himself had had gilded, 300 Mauritanian ostriches with reddened feathers, 30 wild asses, 150 wild boars, 200 ibexes, 200 gazelles. All these he handed over to the people to be torn apart, on the day of the sixth show he gave."[379] Philip, the first Roman emperor who was an Arab[380]—who received in addition the huge gift of becoming a Christian[381]—since it happened that the thousandth anniversary of the foundation of the City fell when he and his son were

sunt datae, quas Gordianus in triumphum Persicum paraverat: elephanti duo et triginta, tigres XX, leones mansueti LX, leopardi mansueti triginta, belbi[239] hyeneae X, gladiatores fiscales paria mille, rinorocerus unus, aracleontes X, carmilopardi X, equi feri XL.

62 Quando autem ludos omnes et spectacula quo fierent modo magis particulariter quam supra est factum describere, nec possibile est neque etiam expedit, aliqua de utrisque ex Cassiodoro afferemus, cui ultimo omnium vati contigit, ut ea inspiceret et scriberet. Is detestabilem actum certamenque infelix sicut debuit detestatus, quod homines cum feris vellent contendere, quas fortiores se non dubitarent invenire, solam habuisse eos in praesumptione spem dicit et unicum in deceptione solacium, qui feram si non effugissent, nec sepulturam interdum poterant invenire, cum adhuc superstite homine periret corpus et antequam cadaver efficeretur, truculentissime absumeretur. Ex paucisque huiusmodi spectaculis, quibus referendis contentus fuit, hoc primum est. Expositus in theatrum amphitheatrumve, sanguinem habens venalem, infelicissime avarus quispiam unica, quod cum redemptoribus erat pactus, flexibili pertica armabatur. Dumque populus plenis desuper spectans sedilibus, qua temeritate infelix ille leonem aut ursum fame in id maceratum pertica a se abigere confideret, invicem disputant, emissa derepente fera in eum praeceps fertur, qui, cum pari cursu in illam delatus esset, hianti ore imminentem, non quidem pertica, prout spectantes credebant, aut caesim aut punctim ferire aggrediebatur, sed flexibili adminiculo ligni innixus saltu bestiam trasvolabat, quae, tamquam pudore quodam superata, victorem suum ultra impetere negligebat. Isque, parietibus adhaerens

consul,[382] put on the Secular Games and races in the circus. In these games were shown the wild beasts that Gordian had collected for his triumph over Persia: 32 elephants, 20 tigers, 60 tame lions, 30 tame leopards, 10 *belbi,* that is, hyenas, 1,000 pairs of gladiators maintained by the emperor's private purse, 1 rhinoceros, 10 wild lions, 10 giraffes, 40 wild horses.[383]

Since it is neither possible nor even useful to describe in more 62
detail than has already been done above how all the games and shows were performed, I shall present some excerpts from Cassiodorus that bear on both, since he happens to be the last of all the prophets to observe and write about them.[384] Loathing as he should the abominable performance and ill-starred contest that men were willing to wage with wild beasts which were surely much stronger than they, he says they had their only hope in boldness and their sole relief in trickery. If they did not escape the wild beast, they were unable sometimes to find burial, since the man's body was destroyed while he was still alive and before he could be turned into a corpse he was most cruelly consumed.[385] From among the few shows of this kind he was content to relate this is the first. In the theater or amphitheater there was displayed a man who was most unhappy in his greed, who was offering his life blood for sale. As was stipulated with those who had bought his debts he was armed with a single flexible pole. While the crowd of spectators packed into the seats were looking down and discussing among themselves the foolhardiness of the unfortunate man in relying on the pole to drive away a lion or bear starved for the fight, the wild beast was suddenly released and charged him. Charging it at the same speed, he did not begin to strike it as it threatened him with gaping maw, cutting or stabbing with the pole as the spectators thought he would, but relying on the support of the flexible pole, he leaped over the beast, which, as though overcome by a sense of shame, made no further attempt to attack its defeater. He hugged the walls of the theater and begged the people

theatri, maestum et suae indolentem saluti populum, ut educeretur, orabat. Alius, pugnae cum bestiis committendae scutum[240] fragile cannis contextum deferre pactus, in spectaculum laetus prodiit, sed cavea emissam voracem bestiam, cum prope mordicus apprehensuram expectasset, illico in terram prostratus cannarumque involucro tectus deterruit, quae et ultra contingere non est ausa. Sicque, quod ait Cassiodorus, haud secus quam spinae ericium in orbe collectum, debilis cannarum munitio hunc servabat.

63 Tertium descripturi spectaculum verbi expositionem praemittere cogimur, quod, licet Romana plebs nunc eo passim utatur, paucis alibi etiam doctissimis notum esse vidimus: cancellum id est crates rarior[241] lineolis compacta ligneis altrinsecus superpositis, inter quas semipedalia ut plurimum foramina relinquantur[242] servatque usus eiusmodi claustra vineis pro valvis foribusque apponi. Itaque cancello oblongiore, trinis aperto portis pariter inter se distantibus, in patenti area amphitheatri posito, erant qui constituta mercede ursum ibi[243] leonemve expectarent, quem irruentem evasurus ab uno ad aliud hostiolum se vertebat. Sicque cancellosis, ut ait Cassiodorus, se postibus occulens modoque faciem, modo terga bestiis monstrans, inter leonum dentes unguesque volitabat. Alius, 'labenti rota' feris occurrens, illas irruentes motus celeritate fallebat. Sunt vero haec spectacula ex iis,[244] quae M. Cicero ad Marcum Marium, quod supra diximus, scribit: 'Sed quae potuit esse homini polito[245] delectatio, cum aut homo imbecillus a valentissima bestia laniatur, aut praeclara bestia venabulo transverberatur?' Quam Ciceronis sententiam secutus Seneca

who were sad and sorry for his plight to have him taken out of the arena.[386] Another, who had agreed to carry a fragile shield of wickerwork into his fight with the wild animals, came forward happily into the arena, waiting until the moment when the ravening beast had been released in the pit and was about to seize him with its teeth. At that moment he flung himself down onto the ground and frightened it off by covering himself with the shelter of the rushes. The beast did not dare come any closer and thus the rushes' feeble protection saved him just as a hedgehog rolled into a ball is protected by his spikes, as Cassiodorus says.[387]

Before I describe the third show I am compelled to explain the 63
meaning of a word first. Though the common people of Rome now use this word freely, we see that elsewhere it is known only to a few educated people. The word is *cancellus,* that is, fairly open lattice put together from wooden strips, one superimposed over the other.[388] Between them gaps of six inches at the most are left. It is still the custom that gates of this kind are put on sheds in place of double doors. So when an oblong shaped screen (*cancellus*) pierced by three equidistant doors was set up in the open space of the amphitheater there were some who for an agreed price waited there for a bear or a lion. To escape the animal when it charged him, the man would go from one little doorway to another, and so "concealing himself," as Cassiodorus says, "by the doors of the *cancellus,*" now showing his face to the animals, now his back, he skipped between the lions' teeth and claws.[389] Another went against the wild animals "on a descending wheel," and evaded them as they charged by the speed with which he moved.[390] These shows are of the same sort as those about which Marcus Cicero writes to Marcus Marius (quoted above): "But what pleasure can there be for a refined man when a poor weak man is rent by a powerful animal, or a splendid animal is transfixed by a spear?"[391] Seneca in agreement with Cicero's opinion and

eaque spectacula detestatus sic subiungit: 'Nuper in ludo bestiariorum unus e Germanis, cum ad matutina spectacula pararetur, secessit ad exonerandum ventrem — nullum enim aliud illi dabatur sine custode secretum — ibi lignum illud, quod ad emundandum obscena, adhaerens spongiae positum est, totum in gulam farsit et ibi praeclusis faucibus spiritum elisit.' Et infra: 'Cum adveheretur nuper quidam inter custodias ad matutinum spectaculum missus, tamquam somno premente nutaret, caput eo usque dimisit donec radiis insereret et tam diu in sedili se tenuit, donec cervicem circumactu rotae frangeret.' 'Secundo naumachio spectaculo unus e barbaris lanceam, quam in adversarios acceperat, totam iugulo suo mersit.'

64 Satis iam supraque ludis et spectaculis ostendendis immorati sumus; supplicationes, tensas pompamque ultimas religionis partes simul explicemus, sicut eas saepenumero simul habitas fuisse videmus. Fueruntque his similes, quas nos letanias processionesque appellamus. Supplicationes vero, referendis gesta re aliqua gratiis ad deorum templa et sacra omnia loca institutas, prius quam pompas incohasse constat. Livius V: 'Captis Veiis a Camillo, senatus in quatriduum, quot dierum nullo ante bello, supplicationem decrevit.' Forma autem supplicationis, quae fuerit, Livii verbis ex XXVII apparet. Post victoriam de Hasdrubale nunciatam 'discursum inde ab aliis circa templa, ut diis gratias agerent. Senatus quod M. Livius, G. Claudius incolumi exercitu ducem hostiumque

abhorring these shows adds as follows: "Recently in the training school of those who fight wild animals, one of the Germans was getting ready for the morning show. He went apart to relieve himself, for he was allowed no other act of privacy without the presence of a guard. There he stuffed into his gullet the entire stick that was placed there with a sponge attached for cleaning the private parts, blocked his throat and suffocated himself."[392] Further on: "Recently when a certain man dispatched for the morning show was being taken under guard in a carriage, he let his head nod as though he was being overcome by sleep, and dropped it to the point where he might insert it between the spokes, keeping himself in the seat long enough for the wheel to break his neck as it turned round."[393] "In the second event of a mock naval battle, one of the barbarians sank into his throat the entire spear which he had been given to use against the opposition."[394]

Now I have lingered more than enough in describing games and 64
shows. Let us explain all together the remaining topics in religion: public thanksgivings (*supplicationes*), carriages of the gods (*tensae*) and the procession, as we see that very often they were held at the same time. These were similar to those ceremonies that we call litanies and processions. It is agreed that public thanksgivings were instituted to render thanks at the gods' temples and all sacred places for some deed that had been accomplished, before the processions began. Livy in Book V: After the capture of Veii by Camillus "the senate decreed a solemn thanksgiving lasting for four consecutive days, longer than in any previous war."[395] How a thanksgiving was performed is clear from Livy's words in Book XXVI: After the news of the victory over Hasdrubal was announced, "some then went in haste from one temple to another to render thanks to the gods. The senate decreed a thanksgiving for three consecutive days because Marcus Livius and Gaius Claudius

legiones cecidissent, supplicationem in triduum decrevit. Omnia templa per totum triduum aequalem turbam habuere, matronae cum amplissima veste cum liberis, perinde ac si debellatum foret, omni solutae metu diis immortalibus gratias egerunt.' Et infra libro XXX: 'Praetor extemplo edixit ut aeditui aedes sacras tota urbe aperirent, circumeundi salutandique deos agendique gratias per totum diem populo potestas fieret, decretumque ut quinque dies circa omnia pulvinaria supplicaretur[246] victimaeque maiores immolarentur CXX.' Posteris vero florentis rei publicae temporibus eam vim habuit supplicatio ut, cui ea decerneretur rem bellicam administranti, is brevi post imperator appellaretur. Cicero *Philippicorum* XIII: 'Etenim cui his viginti annis supplicatio decreta est, ut non imperator appellaretur, aut minimis rebus gestis aut plerunque nullis?' Et ad triumphum facilius obtinendum valuisse impetratam supplicationem Cicero M. Cathoni scribens sic innuit: 'Quod si triumphi praerogativam putas supplicationem.' Quo in praestantissimo senatus et populi Romani viris clarissimis decreto honore idem Cicero summum nactus est decus, cui, privato, XX dierum pro sua reductione supplicatio praeter consuetudinem decreta fuit, de qua idem tertia oratione *In L. Catilinam* sic dicit: quod meo nomine supplicationem decrevistis, qui honos togato habitus est ante me memini. Et ad M. Catonem: 'Tu idem mihi supplicationem decrevisti togato.'

65 Sed ad tensam veniendum est, quam Festus Pompeius esse dicit 'vehiculum argenteum, quo exuviae deorum ludis circensibus in circum ad pulvinar vehebantur.' Et Asconius Pedianus *actione in*

had cut to pieces the general and legions of the enemy, while the army remained safe. All the temples for the whole period of three days had crowds of the same size, while the married women in their richest dress, with their children, freed from all fear, gave thanks to the immortal gods just as if the war had been brought to an end."[396] And further on in Book XXX: "Right away the praetor made a public proclamation that the sacristans should open the consecrated temples throughout the city and for the whole day the people were to be given the opportunity to go round and pay their respects to the gods and render thanks"[397] "and it was voted that there would be supplications for five days at all the couches of the gods (*pulvinaria*) and 120 fully-grown victims sacrificed."[398] In later times, at the height of the republic, the import of a thanksgiving was such that whoever had one decreed to him for conducting a military affair was shortly afterward given the title *imperator*. Cicero in *Philippics* Book XIII: "To whom in the last twenty years was a thanksgiving voted without his being given the title *imperator* either for slight achievements or very often for none at all?"[399] In a letter to Marcus Cato Cicero implies that the award of a thanksgiving had the effect of making it easier to obtain a triumph: "But if you suppose a thanksgiving a sure sign of a triumph."[400] By which outstanding honor voted by the most distinguished men of the senate and Roman people the same Cicero obtained this supreme glory: in his honor, even though he was a private citizen, a thanksgiving of twenty days was voted for his return from exile, contrary to custom. He speaks about this in his third oration *Against Catiline* as follows: Because you voted a thanksgiving on my account, an honor never won by a civilian before me,[401] and to Marcus Cato: "You yourself voted a thanksgiving to me as a civilian."[402]

But we must come to the carriage of the gods (*tensa*), which 65
Festus Pompeius says is "a silver chariot on which the accouterments of the gods were carried at the circus games into the Circus to the shrine for the gods (*pulvinar*)."[403] And Asconius Pedianus on

Verrem secunda: 'Tensae sunt sacra vehicula, pompa ordinum et officiorum. Tensas alii a divinitate dici putant, alii quod ante eas lintea tenduntur, quae gaudent manu tenere et tangere qui deducunt.' Et tertia *In Verrem* Cicero: 'Quam tu nunc tensarum atque pompae eiusmodi curam exegisti.' Et quinta actione: 'Qui religiones deorum immortalium retinere vult, ei, qui[247] fana spoliare omnia, qui ex tensarum orbitis praedari sit ausus.' Et septima: 'Omnesque dii qui vehiculis tensarum solemnes coetus ludorum ire iussistis.' Et *De haruspicum responsis* oratione Cicero, Lentulum appellans pontificem maximum: 'Te appello, Lentule, cuius sacerdotii sunt tensae, curricula, praecentio, ludi, libationes.'

66 Quod itaque hic Cicero dicit sacerdotii esse pontificis maximi tensas et ludos causam praebet nobis ostendendi quod supradiximus supplicationes, pompam et tensas et insuper ludos uno eodemque actu fuisse coniunctos. Primum enim quantum ad tensarum ornamentum spectat Livius nono: Triumpho L. Papirii dictatoris de Samnitibus 'longe maximam speciem captiva arma praebuere, tantum magnificentiae in his, ut aurata scuta dominis argentariorum ad forum ornandum dividerentur. Inde natum initium fori ornandi ab aedilibus cum tensae ducerentur,' quas inter alios sacerdotes Salii in primis praecedebant eosque a Numa institutos duodenario numero scribit Livius, quibus 'tunicas pictas

the Second Action of the *Verrine Orations*: "*Tensae* are sacred carriages, the procession is of companies and officials. Some think *tensae* are so-called from the sphere of the gods, and others because in front of them are stretched (*tendere*) linen straps which those who are escorting them rejoice to hold (*tenere*) and touch with the hand."[404] And Cicero's third action against Verres: "The care you have now taken of the sacred carriages and of this kind of procession."[405] And in the fifth action: "He who wishes to uphold the observances of all the immortal gods, [how can he not be the enemy] of a man who dared to despoil all their shrines, and to turn the wheels of the sacred carriages into booty?"[406] And in the seventh: "All you gods who have ordered the regular festival gatherings of the games to go in your sacred carriages."[407] And in the speech *On the Responses of the Haruspices* Cicero calling on Lentulus, the Chief Pontiff: "I call on you, Lentulus, to whose priesthood belong the sacred carriages, the chariots, the singing before the sacrifice, the games, the drink offerings."[408]

Therefore because Cicero says here the sacred carriages and the games belong to the priesthood of the Chief Pontiff, this gives us a reason for demonstrating that the public thanksgivings, the procession and the sacred carriages and moreover the games were combined in one and the same event, as I said above. First, as far as decoration of the sacred carriages is concerned, Livy in Book IX: In the dictator Lucius Papirius' triumph over the Samnites "the weapons of the defeated provided by far the greatest show. They were so magnificent that the gilded shields were distributed among the masters of the bankers to decorate the Forum. From this came the origin of the aediles' custom of adorning the Forum whenever the sacred carriages were led in procession through it."[409] Among the other priests that went before the sacred carriages the Salii were the chief. Livy writes that they were set up by Numa, twelve in number. He decided on "the distinction of an 66

insigne decrevit et super tunicam aeneum pectori tegmen caelestiaque arma, quae ancilia vocantur deferre ac per urbem ire cantantes carmina cum tripudiis solemnique saltu iussit.' Et M. Varro Salios a saltando appellatos dicit. Macrobiusque scribit Appium Claudium, qui inter Salios vir triumphalis consenuit, pro gloria dicere solitum, quod collegas saltando excelleret. Haec de supplicationibus tensisque.

67 Pauca de pompis dicenda sunt, quae tamen supradictis duobus aliquando fuere communia. Festus Pompeius: 'ciceria dicit appellata⟨m⟩ fuisse effigiem quandam argutam et loquacem ridiculi gratia, quae in pompa vehi solita sit. Cato in M. Caecilium: "Quid ego cum illo dissertem amplius, quem ego denique credo in pompa vectitatum[248] ire ludis pro ciceria, atque cum spectatoribus sermocinatum."' Et infra Festus: 'Manduci effigies in pompa antiquorum inter ceteras ridiculas formidolosas ire solebat, magnis malis ac late dehiscens et ingentem dentibus sonitum faciens, de qua Plautus ait: "Quid si ad ludos me pro manduco locem? Quapropter? Clare[249] crepito dentibus."' 'Petreia[250] autem appellabatur, quae pompam praecedens imitabatur anum ebriam, ab agri vitio scilicet petra abundantis appellatam.'[251] Fuit autem ducendae pompae gravitas servata. Nam, cum circensium die pompa duceretur ad placandum propter pestem deos, puer superne spectans sacrorum ritus vidit et patri narravit, quare constitutum, ut viae tegerentur velis per quas pompa esset ducenda. Unde Caesarem dicit Suetonius voluisse in primis 'statuam inter regias, suggestum in orchestra,

embroidered tunic for them with a bronze breastplate over the tunic and he laid it down that they bear the arms from heaven which are called "ancilia" and go through the city singing hymns with a solemn religious dance."[410] Marcus Varro says that the Salii got their name from dancing (*saltare*).[411] Macrobius writes that Appius Claudius, a man who had celebrated a triumph, was still one of the Salii in old age and used to say as a point of honor that he outdid his colleagues in dancing.[412] So much about public thanksgivings and sacred carriages.

A little must be said about the processions, though they at times share features with the two things mentioned above. Festus Pompeius says "that *ciceria* was the name for a certain witty and talkative puppet which was carried in the procession to make people laugh. Cato in his speech against Marcus Caecilius: 'Why should I deal with him at more length? To sum up I think he goes carried in the procession at the games as a *citeria* and would banter with the spectators.'"[413] Festus further on: "A manikin of a Manducus used to go in the ancients' procession along with the other amusing ogres. He had big jaws gaping wide open and made a huge racket with his teeth. Plautus says about this: 'What if I were to hire myself out as a Manducus at the games? How so? My teeth are chattering out loud.'"[414] "She who went in front of the procession imitating a drunk old woman, was called 'Petreia,' the name coming from the spoiling of the land, that is, when it is full of stones."[415] Dignity was maintained in the conduct of the procession. For, when on the day of the circus games a procession was being held to appease the gods on account of a plague, a boy looked down from above and saw the ritual sacred objects. He told his father, and so it was decided that the streets through which the procession was to be led should be covered with awnings.[416] For this reason Suetonius says that Caesar especially wanted "a statue among those of the kings, a raised seat in the orchestra, a sacred carriage and a litter in the procession at the Circus."[417] Augustus 67

tensam et ferculum, circensi pompa.' Et Augustum, cum accidisset votivis circensibus ut correptus valitudine lectica cubaret, tensas manu dedicasse. Pompam unam Livius XXVII talem describit: 'Tacta de caelo aedes in Aventino Iunonis reginae prodigiumque id ad matronas pertinere aruspices cum respondissent donoque divam placandam esse aedilium currulium edicto in Capitolium convocatae, quibus in urbe Roma intraque decimum lapidem ab urbe domicilia essent, ipsae inter se quinque et viginti delegerunt, ad quas ex dotibus stipem conferrent. Inde donum pelvis aurea facta, lataque in Aventinum pureque et caste a matronis sacrificatum. Confestim ad aliud sacrificium eidem divae ab decemviris edicta ⟨dies⟩, cuius talis ordo fuit: ab aede Apollinis boves feminae albae duae porta Carmentali in urbem ductae. Post eas duo signa cupressea Iunonis reginae portabantur. Tum septem et viginti virgines, longam indutae vestem, carmen in Iunonem reginam canentes ibant, illa tempestate forsitan laudabile rudibus ingeniis, nunc abhorrens et inconditum si referatur, virginum ordinem sequabantur decemviri coronati laurea praetextatique. A porta Iugario vico in forum iverunt, in foro pompa constitit et per manus reste data virgines sonum vocis pulsu pedum modulantes incesserunt.'

68 Elegantiorem vero pompam Galienos duos principes duxisse Iulius refert Capitolinus: 'Convocatis patribus Decennia[252] celebravit, magno genere ludorum, nova specie pomparum, exquisito genere voluptatum. Iam primum inter togatos patres et equestrem ordinem albatos milites et[253] omni populo praeeunte, servis etiam

dedicated the sacred carriages by hand when he happened to be ill at the time of the circus games performed in fulfillment of his vow and was lying in a litter.[418] Livy in Book XXVII describes one such procession: "The Temple of Queen Juno on the Aventine was hit by lightning. When the soothsayers advised that this prodigy related to the married women, and the goddess had to be appeased by a gift, the married women who resided in the City of Rome and no further than ten miles from the city were summoned to the Capitol by an edict of the curule aediles. They chose twenty-five from among themselves, to whom they might contribute a donation from their dowries. Out of that a golden bowl was made as a gift. It was taken to the Aventine and after due purification a sacrifice was made by the married women. Speedily a day was set by the Board of Ten for another sacrifice to the same goddess. Its order was as follows. From the Temple of Apollo two white cows were brought into the city by the Carmental Gate. After them were carried two statues of Queen Juno made of cypress wood. Then there went twenty-seven maidens in long dresses singing a hymn to Queen Juno. The hymn was perhaps praiseworthy given the ignorance of the times but would be unsuitable and uncouth if it were repeated now. Following the file of maidens were the members of the Board of Ten garlanded with bay and wearing the purple-bordered toga. They entered the Forum from the gate by way of the Jugarian quarter. The procession came to a halt in the Forum, and, with a rope passed from hand to hand, the maidens moved on, accompanying their singing by beating time with their feet."[419]

A more elegant procession was the one that the two emperors 68
Gallieni held, as Julius Capitolinus relates: "He summoned the senate and celebrated the Decennalia, with a great variety of games,[420] new sorts of processions, pleasures of the most choice kinds. First of all, he went to the Capitol, surrounded by senators in their togas and the equestrian order, soldiers dressed in white,

prope omnium et mulieribus cum cereis facibus[254] etiam praecedentibus Capitolium petit. Praecesserunt[255] etiam altrinsecus centum albi boves cornuis[256] auro iugatis et dorsualibus siriceis discoloribus praefulgentes; agnae candentes ab utraque parte ducentae praecesserunt et decem elefanti, qui tunc erant Romae. Mille ducenti gladiatores pompaliter ornati cum auratis vestibus matronarum, mansuetae ferae diversi generis ducentae ornatuque maxime affectae, carpenta cum mimis et omni genere histrionum, pugiles flacculis[257] non veritate pugnantes. Ciclopes etiam luserunt. Omnes viae ludis strepituque plausibus resonabant. Ipse medius cum picta toga et tunica palmata inter patres, ut diximus, omnibus sacerdotibus praetextatis Capitolium petit. Hastae auratae altrinsecus quingenae,[258] vexilla centena praeter ea, quae collegiorum erant, dracones et signa templorum omniumque legionum ibant. Ibant praeterea gentes simulatae, ut Getae, Sarmatae, Tracae, Persae ut non minus quam ducenti globis singulis ducerentur.' Sed iam de religione satis multa, ad alia transeundum est. Religionis Romanorum *Triumphantis Romae* liber II explicitus.[259]

and with the whole populace leading the way, the slaves too of nearly everyone and women with wax candles preceding them. One hundred white oxen with horns bound with gold and gleaming with multicolored silken saddle cloths also went in front on both sides. Two hundred snow-white lambs went in front on each side, and ten elephants, which were in Rome at that time. Twelve hundred gladiators, decked out for a parade, married women in gold-embroidered garments, two hundred tamed wild beasts of various kinds, particularly splendidly adorned, wagons carrying mime players and all kinds of actors, boxers who fought with soft gloves, not for real. The Cyclopes played too. All the streets echoed with jollity and with shouts and applause. In the middle he himself made his way to the Capitol in triumphal toga and a tunic embroidered with palm leaves, surrounded by the senators, as I said, with all the priests in purple-bordered togas. There were five hundred gilded spears on each side, one hundred banners besides those belonging to the associations, the standards of cohorts and the statues from the sanctuaries and of all the legions. Moreover there marched men costumed to represent foreign nations, such as Getans, Sarmatians, Thracians, Persians, each individual group being no fewer than two hundred."[421] But this is now quite enough on religion. We must go on to other matters. The end of Book II of *Rome in Triumph* on the religion of the Romans.

Note on the Text

Roma triumphans survives in about twenty known manuscripts. Though the *Censimento dei manoscritti delle opere di Biondo Flavio,* carried out under the sponsorship of the Edizione Nazionale delle opere di Flavio Biondo contains twenty-eight entries listing witnesses of *Roma triumphans,*[1] for some of the ones taken from the records of Cranz' *Inventories,*[2] a match cannot be found in modern catalogs; it is quite likely that in some cases the same manuscript may appear in the inventories of several libraries, having moved from one to another over the course of time.

In order to ensure the reliability of the present edition, M. Agata Pincelli has collated twelve manuscripts of the first book of the work;[3] on the basis of this she has identified three witnesses on which to constitute the text, and she has constantly consulted in the process the *editio princeps* of 1473,[4] for which the siglum *ed.* is used. De Micheli's printing establishment received financial support from the Marquis Ludovico Gonzaga, who was also willing to lend manuscripts from his own library as exemplars for printed books.[5] It is probable that De Micheli used for the *editio princeps* the manuscript of *Roma triumphans* that Biondo sent to the prince of Mantua in 1461. This no longer survives, but it must have been copied at about the same time as our other witnesses. All the printed editions descend from the *editio princeps,* but in some cases corrections were introduced by a later editor.

The three witnesses that have been selected are the following:

Chis. Città del Vaticano, Biblioteca Apostolica Vaticana, Chis. I.VIII.290. The manuscript bears the stemma of Pius II and is therefore the dedication copy presented to the pope. It was produced in the Roman environment and can be dated to a time close to the completion of the work, and in any case not later than the early 1460s.

V Roma, Biblioteca Nazionale Centrale, Vittorio Emanuele 509. It is richly decorated and dates to 1460–62.

O Città del Vaticano, Biblioteca Apostolica Vaticana, Ottob. lat. 1917. The manuscript has the note of possession "Ego Paulus Blondus S.D.N. secretarius" and contains interesting marginal textual corrections written in a hand different from that of the scribe of the text.

The author himself provides an important piece of evidence on the manuscript tradition of *Roma triumphans:* in a letter to Ludovico Gonzaga, Marquis of Mantua, written from Rome on December 26, 1461, Biondo describes how the task of copying the work was entrusted to twelve *librarii,* who worked at the same time under his direct supervision.[6] Biondo's statement is confirmed by the results of the collation: *Roma triumphans* is transmitted mainly by a group of manuscripts among which no relationships of dependence can be established and which differ from each other by banal copying errors alone.[7] The dedication copy to Pius II (MS Chis. I.VIII.290) presents a slightly different case in that it differs from the other witnesses by containing authorial stylistic changes. These, however, are almost exclusively confined to word order. MS Ottob. lat. 1917, on the other hand, is distinguished by having marginal corrections added in a different hand from that of the scribe who copied the text. Seeing that the manuscript remained in the author's family, these probably consist of interventions on the part of one of Biondo's sons, perhaps made through comparison with another manuscript. MS Vittorio Emanuele 509 has proved to be the best of the manuscripts that can be attributed to the first phase of the dissemination of the work, which took place under the author's supervision. Furthermore this witness stands out thanks to the presence of certain spellings characteristic of Biondo that point to a relationship of close dependence upon the original: from these may be singled out the form *silicet* for *scilicet,* which is also found in the autograph of *Borsus.*[8] *Borsus* itself, it is worth noting, is a very important witness for the passages on *iurisprudentia* and *militia* contained in *Roma triumphans* Books 4 and 6, seeing that, in this little treatise dedicated to Borso d'Este, duke of Ferrara, Biondo recycled without significant changes entire passages of the larger work.

Unlike *Italia illustrata* and the *Decades, Roma triumphans* did not go through multiple redactions: the work was composed within a relatively short span of time and then published by the author with a dedication to Pius II.[9] It appears that subsequently Biondo did not go back to retouch it. Indeed, the fact that the text of *Borsus,* brought to completion at Mantua on January 16, 1460 — and therefore almost two years before the letter to Gonzaga — coincides, in its recycled passages, with the text of the manuscripts that we believe were prepared in the course of the copying campaign directed by the author is a further element of proof that the text of *Roma triumphans* was essentially finalized at that point. Therefore, the text in this present edition is the one Biondo considered finished and ready for publication. Furthermore, it is the first complete edition, since a later volume will contain the long passage of Book 7 omitted from all the printed editions and first published by Capra in 1977.[10]

A word on the quotations from ancient authors. In the manuscript tradition of the work and in the *princeps* these are often corrupt, partly owing to the state of the manuscripts Biondo was using. Since it is not possible to go back to these, we have thought it best to correct the text where there is a blatant error. We do this as little as possible, always recording the manuscript readings in the apparatus. Other corrections are signaled in the Notes to the Translation. Similarly, in the case of proper names, some incorrect forms (and these forms may sometimes fluctuate in the tradition of *Roma triumphans* itself) have been corrected in the text to the commonly accepted forms. In any case, all proper names are presented in the translation in the forms found in standard modern texts. Errors in naming are sometimes also corrected in the Notes to the Translation. In the Notes to the Text and the Notes to the Translation, we have pointed out those cases of clear slips made by the author in his attributions of the ancient sources. Errors of this kind were caused partly by Biondo's habit of citing from memory[11] and partly by his working method: he collected his sources together by topic, and thus the risk of confusion was very high.

In conformity with the policy of this I Tatti series, the spelling of the text has been lightly modernized and diphthongs used. Capitalization and punctuation follow modern norms. As has already been done in the

edition of *Italia illustrata* and in accordance with the practice of Biondo himself, poetic quotations are treated as prose. The translation follows the text as we have edited it except where, in the case of the corrupt quotations of ancient authors, some adjustment was necessary for the sake of intelligibility.

In the text we use angle brackets to indicate additions and square brackets for deletions; in the translation we indicate editorial additions by square brackets. Quotation marks have been used in the translation to indicate material closely quoted from the ancient sources.

NOTES

1. See http://www.isime.it/index.php/attivita-scientifica/progetti/edizione-nazionale-delle-opere-di-flavio-biondo.

2. F. Edward Cranz, *A Microfilm Corpus of Unpublished Inventories of Latin Manuscripts through 1600* A.D., 341 microfilm reels with typed Guide (New London, CT, 1988).

3. Bruxelles, Bibliothèque Royale de Belgique, MS. II 1416; Città del Vaticano, Biblioteca Apostolica Vaticana, Chis. I.VIII.290; Città del Vaticano, Biblioteca Apostolica Vaticana, Ottob. lat. 1917; Ferrara, Biblioteca Comunale Ariostea, MS. II 186; Madrid, Biblioteca Nacional de España, MS. 8578; München, Universitätsbibliothek, MS. 681; Padova, Biblioteca del Seminario Vescovile, MS. 13; Paris, Bibliothèque de l'Arsenal, MS. 1017; Roma, Biblioteca Nazionale Centrale, MS. Vittorio Emanuele 509; San Daniele del Friuli, Biblioteca Guarneriana, MS. 15; Trento, Biblioteca Comunale, MS. W 3388; Valladolid, Colegio Mayor Universitario de Santa Cruz, MS. 105.

4. [Mantua: Petrus Adam de Michaelibus, around 1473] = ISTC ib00703000.

5. Compare G. Schizzerotto, *Libri stampati a Mantova nel Quattrocento*, Catalogo della mostra (Mantova 1972) (Mantua: Biblioteca comunale, 1972), pp. 11–12.

6. Nogara, *Scritti*, pp. 207–8.

7. On this matter, see L. Capra, "Un tratto di *Roma triumphans* omesso dagli stampatori," *Italia medioevale e umanistica* 20 (1977): 313.

8. Compare Blondus Flavius, *Borsus*, ed. Maria Agata Pincelli (Roma: Istituto Storico Italiano per il Medio Evo, 2009), pp. xxxiv–xxxv.

9. See the Introduction.

10. Capra, "Un tratto di *Roma triumphans* omesso dagli stampatori."

11. "Et ipsum Ciceronem qui numquam dives inter Romanos cives sit habitus, licet per calumniam Salustius id obiiciat, duodeviginti habuisse villas, nos curis aliquando liberiores in epistolis ad *Ad Atticum* collegisse meminimus, sed eas quae nunc memoriae occurrerint referemus" (Cicero himself, who was never considered wealthy among the citizens of Rome [though this was a false accusation Sallust cast against him], had twenty-two villas. I recall that once when I had little to occupy me I collected the ones in the *Letters to Atticus*, but I shall mention the ones that now are fresh in my memory): *R.T.*, p. 191c, and see *Borsus*, p. xxiii.

Notes to the Text

❧

PROEM

1. *corrected*: effecta *MSS*

2. adita *Livy*

BOOK I

1. BLONDI FLAVII FORLIVIENSIS TRIUMPHANTIS ROMAE LIBER PRIMUS INCIPIT FELICISSIME *MSS*

2. mansuetam *Cicero*

3. haberi *Cicero*

4. non *omitted in Cicero*

5. infernae *O ed.*: *inferna Chis. V*

6. thamasim *MSS*: themasim *ed.*: thymiasin *George of Trebizond*

7. Soli caelesti *Chis. V*

8. uxore *corrected to* sorore *in O*

9. *See the Notes to the Translation.*

10. Helius Lampridius *MSS; here and subsequently the spelling has been regularized to* Aelius Lampridius.

11. Helius Sparcianus *MSS; here and subsequently the spelling has been regularized to* Aelius Spartianus.

12. Carretiis *O ed.*: Chareciis *Chis. V*: Carrenis *S.H.A.*

13. Api *O*: Iside *Chis. V*

14. *corrected*: Tolpia *MSS*

15. Alcmena *O*: Damnae *Chis. V*

16. sic *O*

17. traducta *V*: reducta *Chis. O*

18. appellant *V O*

19. *corrected*: reginae *MSS*: regimen *ed.*

20. Voposcus *MSS; here and subsequently the spelling has been regularized to* Vopiscus.

21. Orpheus *ed. and marginal correction in O*: Oetius *Chis. V*

22. Omadio *correction in O V*: Omachio *Chis.*

23. Alicharnasseus *MSS; the spelling has been regularized to* Halicarnasseus.

24. Argeos *O*: Argivos *Chis. V*

25. *corrected*: quod *MSS*

26. *so Cicero*: rei publicae *MSS*

27. *so Cicero*: abessit *Chis. O*

28. *corrected*: incepissent *MSS and ed.*

29. Prema *correction in O*: Premia *Chis. V*

30. mattuosum *Chis.*

31. *so Augustine*: plastellis *MSS*: plaustellis *ed.*

32. *corrected*: Farracalia *MSS*

33. *corrected*: -que *MSS*

34. *corrected*: Fartuacalia *MSS*

35. *so Paulus Festus*: Iuvenili *MSS ed.*

36. *so Paulus Festus*: flaminia *MSS*

37. *so Paulus Festus*: tutellum *MSS*

38. Iohanni *ed. and correction in O*: Iohannis *Chis. V*

39. *so Paulus Festus*: perfericulum *MSS*

40. *so Paulus Festus*: fulcimenta *MSS*

41. anclabris *O*: andabris *V Chis. ed.*

42. cum sigillis ac simulacris deorum *Cicero*

43. simpulum *O ed.*: simplum *Chis. V*

44. eiectae *ed.*: eiecta *MSS*

45. pulsusque Italia ignobili atque inhonesta morte temere nocte ingressus Argos occubuit *Livy*

46. praefectum *marginal correction in O*

47. *so Ulpian*: imposterum *MSS*: in posterum *ed.*

48. Solitaurilia *correction in O, Paulus Festus*: Solida utilia *MSS*

49. purus *Pliny*

50. poparum *Suetonius*

51. *so Cicero*: probatis *MSS*

52. muger *correction in O, Paulus Festus*: mucor *MSS*

53. *so Paulus Festus*: tusum *MSS*

54. *corrected from Paulus Festus*: redimi *MSS*

55. Dici O *Paulus Festus*: dicit *Chis. V*

56. *so Livy*: Carulius *MSS*

57. Veturi *marginal correction in O*: Etrusci *Chis. V*

58. Veturi *marginal correction in O*: Etrusci *Chis. V ed.*

59. praemii *O V*: primum *Chis.*

60. ad maiorem rerum *ed.*: ad tanti rerum involucri *MSS*

61. Herculis *Augustine*

62. *so Ovid: omitted in MSS*

63. exsectis *O V*: ex ictis *Chis.*

64. posimirium *Paulus Festus*: postmurium *Chis. V*: postmurum *O corrected in the margin to* mirium

65. *so Varro*: actuemur *MSS*

66. idest intuemur *V*: idem intuemur *Chis. O*

67. *corrected: sedere MSS*

68. *corrected*: intentissimi *MSS*

69. *so Cicero*: efflata *MSS*

70. Auspicium . . . appellabantur: *omitted in ed., which reads* Auspicium ab aspiciendis avibus dictum est. Ex avibus illae appellabantur funebres quae in auguriis aliquid fieri prohibebant.

71. *so Paulus Festus*: buteos *MSS*

72. *so Paulus Festus*: anqualis *MSS*

73. *so Paulus Festus*: unde musimulus *MSS*

74. *so Paulus Festus*: vultur *MSS*

75. inepte *correction in V*

76. *so Paulus Festus*: terripiucium *MSS*: terripurium *ed.*

77. *so Paulus Festus*: purire *MSS ed.*

78. solistima *correction in* O: solistina *Chis. V*

79. *so Livy*: hoc cecinerit *MSS ed.*

80. *so Pliny*: Tulonis *MSS*

81. *so Pliny*: Theotonas *MSS*

82. de scripto *Pliny*: scripto *Chis. V*: scripto *corrected to* scriptor *in* O

83. ominis *correction in* O: hominis *Chis. V*

84. *corrected*: nuncupabatur *MSS ed.*

85. peperit *ed.*: pepererit *MSS*

86. *so Livy*: celum *MSS*

BOOK II

1. Blondi Flavii Forliviensis Triumphantis Romae liber secundus incipit.

2. creanda O

3. creanda O

4. furida *MSS*: Furina *Varro*

5. feriae O *V*: furiae *Chis.*

6. Numam Pompilium *Chis.*

7. XXV *V*

8. nec iurare ei fas erat *V*

9. qui *Chis.*: qui *corrected to* quorum *in* O

10. ex quibus *corrected to* quod ex illis *in* O

11. uxores *Chis.*

12. quod *added after* alterum *in* O

13. *so Cicero*: statuto anniversari *Chis.*: statuto anniversaria *V*: statuto loco anniversari O

14. *so Tacitus*: augustalem *MSS*

15. contendissent] studissent *corrected to* contempsissent *in* O

16. eum O

17. quia O

18. prexit O

19. istis *corrected to* iustis *in* O

20. eximis O

21. consecrari *Chis.*

22. in numerum deorum *Chis.*

23. senatum O *V*: senatus *Chis.*

24. urbem O

25. coaptum O

26. ferre *corrected to* fere *in V*

27. Salutati *V*

28. reditu O

29. quas *V*

30. plurimis O

31. populo *corrected to* epulo *in* O

32. excreverant *Chis.*

33. videbant *Chis.*

34. administrare *Chis.*

35. habuerunt O

36. modum *Chis.*

37. memoriariam *Chis.*: in memoriam *V*

38. autem *Chis.*

39. casiam O *Tibullus*: cassia *Chis. V*

40. mixta O

41. furit O: fugit *corrected to* furit *in V*

42. *so Vergil*: discunt *MSS*

43. eis O

44. erat *Chis.*

45. emittebaturque O

46. et artibus *omitted in* O

47. *omitted in Chis.*

48. reddebantur *corrected to* reddebatur *in Chis.*

49. que *Chis.* O

50. mirra *corrected to* mica *in* O, mirra *in Chis. V*

51. negligentes multabantur O, *corrected to* negligens *in V*

52. consueverint *V*

53. captas *Chis.*

54. Clivicinae O

55. deleretur O

56. *so Ovid*: ha *MSS*

57. leni *Chis.*

58. clui *Chis.*

59. Anna O

60. pro *added before* impetranda *in* O

61. Caristia *marginal correction in* O: Carissima *MSS*

62. Caristiis *marginal correction in* O: Carissimis *MSS*

63. sint *Chis.*

64. Equriam *corrected to* Equiriam *in* O: Equriam *in Chis. V*

65. *corrected*: Equria *MSS*

66. *corrected*: Equria *MSS*

67. *omitted in Chis. O*

68. armate *Chis.*

69. eaque *V O*

70. quibus *marginal correction in O*: cui *MSS*

71. *corrected*: plateae *MSS*

72. relique *Chis.*

73. divum *Chis.*

74. postulasse *O*

75. iuncti *V*: vincti *O Chis.*

76. mamam *Chis.*

77. natalitia *V*

78. nudis enim viris *O*

79. aqua *O*

80. *so Livy*: captatas *MSS*

81. huiusce *O Livy*: huius *Chis. V*

82. noluerunt *V*

83. *so Livy*: senatu *MSS*

84. et *V*

85. exclamat *V*

86. variaretur *O*

87. nundinali *corrected to* nundinandi *in O*

88. *so Macrobius*: infestis *MSS*

89. vel *added before* certos *in O*

90. instituto *Chis.*

91. his *V*: hiis *O*

92. nos *Cicero MSS*

93. ollos *Cicero*

94. est *V Cicero*: esset *Chis. O*

95. collocata *O*

96. praecepisset *Chis.*

97. conferrent *V*

98. vicinaque *O*

99. iuxta *O*

100. dici *Chis.*

101. nequiret *O*

102. sandapalia *corrected to* sandapila *in O*, sandapalia *Chis. V*

103. sandapalia *corrected to* sandapila *in O*, sandapalia *Chis. V*

104. praefices *corrected to* praeficae *in O*, praefices *Chis. V*

105. et flendo *V*: eflendo *Chis. O*

106. *corrected*: appellati *Chis.*: appellata *O V*

107. reditque *O*

108. quo *ed.*: quod *MSS*

109. ceciderat *Chis.*

110. igne *O*

111. quin *ed. Pliny*: cum *MSS*

112. iuxta *O*

113. idem *O*

114. Sulpicitius *V*

115. tubicinem *O*

116. eum *O*

117. pervenerint *O*

118. gladiatorum *V*

119. voluerant *Chis.*

120. redemi *O*

121. virorum *V*

122. lemuscatum *Chis.*: palma lemniscata *Cicero*

123. miseratum *ed.*: miseratos *MSS*

124. gladiatores *Chis.*

125. gladiatorium *V*

126. *omitted in V*

127. et *Chis.*

128. iussisset *Chis.*

129. gladiatorium *V*

130. *so Livy*: matris *MSS*

131. consuetudine *V*

132. praeferentibus *Chis.*

133. mutare *Chis.*

134. creatibus *corrected to* cratibus *in V*

135. *so Cicero*: -que *MSS*

136. *omitted in V*

137. ex *omitted in Chis.*

138. quod et *O*

139. descripsit *O*

140. monumenti *corrected to* munimenti *in O,* monumenti *Chis. V*

141. sumptu *Chis.*

142. generalites *corrected to* generaliter *in Chis.*

143. *corrected*: Planco *MSS*

144. Catheline *Chis.*

145. manibus *O in margin*: calathis *Chis. V*

146. incessere *Chis. V*: incedere *marginal correction in O*

147. iis *Chis.*

148. ipsas *V*

149. autem O

150. praeterreri O

151. *omitted in V*

152. transfereretur *V*

153. *so Augustine*: deo Gallos *V O*: deo Galli *Chis.*

154. parentebant *Chis.*

155. *omitted in V Chis.*

156. ingenio *corrected to* genio *in* O

157. travisinae *corrected to* Tarvisinae *in Chis.*

158. Brendulensi *corrected to* Leonicensis *in* O

159. *omitted in V*

160. his *V*

161. quadam O

162. totum *omitted in Chis.*

163. praeficitur *V*

164. vulgos *Chis.*

165. ignes O

166. superinduta O

167. his *V*

168. amovet *Chis.*

169. inferendis *corrected to* referendis O

170. ornantur *Chis.*

171. sedent *V* O

172. iacere *Chis.*

173. amplos *added in V*

174. opulorum *Chis.*

175. languescente *corrected to* languentes *in* O

176. ea *Chis.*

177. indocto *Chis.*

178. *omitted in Chis.*

179. descriptis *corrected to* descripsimus *in V,* descriptis *Chis.*

180. Galeoti *V*

181. cedebant *Chis.,* cedebant *corrected to* feriebant *in O*

182. hospitio *O*

183. *so Livy*: vinetis *MSS*

184. videmus *Chis.*

185. millenum *O V*

186. *so Livy*: tibicinem *MSS*

187. *so Livy*

188. scriptorum *Chis.*

189. *so Livy*: Atellana *MSS*

190. *omitted in O*

191. *corrected*: personam *MSS*

192. XXIX *Chis.*

193. praetorii *V*

194. moverentur *Chis.*

195. educuntur *O*

196. eternamque *corrected to* eternaque *in V*

197. imperatore *Chis.*

198. barbarum *Chis.*: barbariam *O*

199. Capistranum *V*

200. adduxit *Chis.*

201. cultiore *Chis.*

202. modo *before* ripheorum *deleted in V*

203. plebis *V*

204. rogatum *Chis.*

205. his O

206. primo O

207. libertate plebis datos fuisse aut *in margin in V*

208. successionem *corrected to* secessionem *in* O, successionem *Chis. V*

209. ex quo O

210. *so Pliny*: ne levis sim equidem teneor *MSS*

211. so *Pliny*: hoc *MSS*

212. in curribus O

213. *so Cicero*: craterarum *MSS*

214. *so Cicero*: ut *MSS*

215. *so Cicero*: politico *MSS*

216. *added in margin in* O

217. *so Pliny*: similis *MSS*

218. *correction of* nitidum *in* O

219. callirafas O

220. *so Pliny*: quorum *MSS*

221. humanis et *Chis.* O

222. *so Pliny*: Aethipes *MSS*

223. *so Pliny*: intexuit *MSS*

224. *so Pliny*: aedilitatis *MSS see* §38

225. *so Suetonius*: argento *MSS*

226. *so Suetonius*: actus *MSS*

227. *so Suetonius*: quinquagenis *MSS*

228. *so Suetonius*: tricentis *MSS*

229. sita *Chis.*

230. *so Suetonius*: tophoa *MSS*

231. praeter *Suetonius and in the margin in* O: etiam *MSS*

232. *so Suetonius*: lichinos *MSS*

233. pugnas *O V*

234. mirmilliones *Chis.*

235. mirmillionem *Chis.*

236. mirmilliones *Chis.*

237. crococtae, rhinocerontes *in the margin in O*: corocrotreri tribitirotes *MSS*

238. quingenta paria et numquam *in the margin in a second hand in V*

239. belli yeneae *Chis.*

240. secutum *V*

241. ratior *Chis.*

242. reliquntur *O*

243. *omitted in Chis.*

244. his *O V*

245. *so Cicero*: politico *MSS*

246. sacrificaretur *Chis.*

247. so *Cicero*: eisque *MSS*

248. *so Paulus Festus*: usitatum *MSS*

249. so *Paulus Festus*: dire *MSS*

250. Preteia *V*

251. *corrected*: appellata *MSS*: petris, appellatam *Paulus Festus*

252. *so S.H.A.*: Decendia *MSS*

253. *so S.H.A.*: ex *MSS*

254. *so S.H.A.*: fascibus *MSS*

255. praecesseruntque *V*

256. *so S.H.A.*: cornibus *MSS*

257. *so S.H.A.*: flosculis *MSS*: flocculis *Ellis*

258. quingente *Chis.*

259. Religionis Romanorum liber secundus et ultimus finit *V*

Notes to the Translation

ABBREVIATIONS

Borsus	Biondo Flavio, *Borsus,* Maria Agata Pincelli, ed. (Rome: Istituto storico italiano per il Medio Evo, 2009). (Edizione nazionale delle opere di Biondo Flavio, 2.)
Capra	"Un tratto di *Roma triumphans* omesso dagli stampatori," *Italia medioevale e umanistica* 20 (1977): 303–22.
CGL	*Corpus Glossariorum Latinorum,* G. Loewe and G. Goetz, eds., vol. 5 (Leipzig: Teubner, 1894)
CIL	*Corpus inscriptionum latinarum* (Berlin: G. Riemer, 1894–)
DBI	*Dizionario biografico degli Italiani* (Rome: Treccani, 1960–)
Eusebius, *PG*	Eusebius, *Preparation for the Gospel*
GLK	*Grammatici latini,* H. Keil, ed., 8 vols. (Leipzig: Teubner, 1855–80).
I.I.	Biondo Flavio, *Italy Illuminated, Volume 1, Books I–IV; Volume 2, Books V–VIII,* Jeffrey A. White, ed. and tran., 2 vols. (Cambridge, MA: Harvard University Press, 2005–16), cited by region and paragraph number.)
LP	*Liber pontificalis,* L. Duchesne, ed. (Paris: E. de Boccard, 1981)
LTUR	*Lexicon Topographicum Urbis Romae,* E. M. Steinby, ed., 6 vols. (Rome: Quasar, 1993–2000)
LTURS	*Lexicon Topographicum Urbis Romae: Suburbium,* A. La Regina, dir., 4 vols. (Rome: Quasar, 2001–8)

OLD	*Oxford Latin Dictionary*, P. G. W. Glare, ed. (Oxford: Oxford University Press, 1982)
Poggio, *DVF*	Poggio Bracciolini, *De varietate fortunae*, O. Merisalo, ed. (Helsinki: Suomalainen Tiedeakatemia 1993)
R.I.	Flavio Biondo, *Rome Restaureé. Roma Instaurata*, Anne Raffarin, ed., 2 vols. (Paris: Les Belles Lettres, 2005–12), cited by book and paragraph number.
RIS	Rerum Italicarum Scriptores
R.T.	Biondo Flavio, *Roma triumphans* (1531 and 1559) (for Books 1 and 2 we refer to the sections of the present volume; for the later books, to the page numbers and sections of the Basel 1559 edition)
S.H.A.	Scriptores Historiae Augustae

[DEDICATORY LETTER]

1. Pius II (r. August 19, 1458–August 15, 1464). One of Pius II's most serious concerns was the advance of the Ottoman Turks toward central Europe and even Italy. In response he promulgated a crusade bull in October 1458 and called a congress of Christian rulers to meet at Mantua on June 1, 1459. Present as a papal secretary, Biondo completed *R.T.* here in 1460 (Nogara, *Scritti*, pp. cxlix–cli).

2. Leo I (r. 440–461) and Leo II (r. 682–683). *LP* 47.5 refers to Leo I's "many letters" and 47.7 to his "freeing the whole of Italy from the danger of enemies." In *LP* 82.1 Leo II is praised for his eloquence and knowledge of Greek and Latin.

3. Bulgaria and Serbia.

PROEM

1. Quintus Cicero [?], *Handbook of Electioneering*, 54. As elsewhere (*Borsus* §29), Biondo mistakenly gives to Marcus Cicero the *Handbook of Electioneering*, purported to be by his brother Quintus but now widely regarded as spurious. Further, in the context from which Biondo selects his quotation, Rome is depicted as a den of vice and intrigue.

2. Cicero, *Verrine Orations* 2.4.81.

3. The main themes of the Proem have much in common with the proem to Book 1 of Lorenzo Valla's *Elegantiae* (1448) and his *Oratio in Principio Studii* (1455). See *Lorenzo Valla. Orazione per l'inaugurazione dell'anno accademico 1455–1456: Atti di un seminario di filologia umanistica,* ed. Silvia Rizzo (Rome: Roma nel Rinascimento, 1995).

4. Cicero, *Against Catiline* 4.11.

5. Pliny the Elder, *Natural History* 3.41.

6. Compare Pliny the Elder, *Natural History* 3.39.

7. Cicero, *On the Responses of the Haruspices* 19.

8. Livy 9.36, compare *I.I.*, Tuscany §60 (Viterbo). The text Biondo was using was corrupt. The translation follows the modern text.

9. We have not found the source. Biondo discusses the Sabine territory to the northeast of Rome in *I.I.*, Umbria §§19–25. The border between Latium and the Sabine territory was the Anio, which met the Tiber three miles from Rome.

10. The reference may be to the "Litana Silva" somewhere near Bologna and Piacenza (Livy 23.24, 34.22).

11. Perhaps based on Caesar, *Gallic Wars* 6.14.3.

12. The best attended council in north Africa during Augustine's life was the Conference of Carthage of 411, for which the official number of Catholic bishops was 287. See Serge Lancel, *Actes de la Conférence de Carthage de 411* (Paris: Éditions du Cerf, 1972), 1:110–22. We cannot account for the figure "800."

13. "Three Decades on the History of the Romans Beginning with the Decline of Their Empire" (*Historiarum de inclinatione Romani imperii decades III*) (1440–53); "Rome Restored" *(De Roma instaurata libri tres)* (finished 1446); "Italy Illuminated" *(Italia illustrata libri VIII)* (1448–53).

14. Cicero, *On the Laws* 1.10.

15. Varro, *On Agriculture* 1.1.3 (paraphrase).

16. Cicero, *Defense of Plancius* 66.

17. Cicero, *Defense of Murena* 19.

18. In Book 10 St. Augustine's wish is formulated differently to refer to an archetypal Roman triumph: "the form of the triumph as Aurelius Augustine is said to have wished to have seen it before his eyes" (*R.T.* Book 10, p. 212f., see also 205c–d). The wish attributed to St. Augustine is apparently a pseudo-biographical detail that no one has been able to trace earlier than Biondo. It had a long afterlife in this and other formulations, such as, "Quid plura? Augustinus tria videre voluisse dicitur scilicet Romam triumphantem Paulum praedicantem et Christum in carne"; see F. Albertini, *Opusculum de mirabilibus novae et veteris Urbis Romae* (Rome, 1510), sig. Vv (§45 De magnitudine imperii et triumphis). M. Laureys, "'The Grandeur That Was Rome': Scholarly Analysis and Pious Awe in Lipsius' *Admiranda*," in *Recreating Ancient History: Episodes from the Greek and Roman Past in the Arts and Literature of the Early Modern Period*, ed. K. A. E. Enenkel, Jan L. de Jong, and Jeanine De Landtsheer (Leiden: Brill, 2002), pp. 123–46, at 130 and n. 27 suggests that it may come from a medieval commentary on *De civitate Dei*. See also Mazzocco, "*Urbem Romam florentem*."

19. Psalm 95:5 (96:5): *quoniam omnes dii gentium daemonia* (for all the gods of the nations are idols).

BOOK I

1. Nonius Marcellus 378.38M.

2. Plutarch, *Aemilius Paulus* 3.2. The *Life* was translated by Leonardo Bruni (1407–9).

3. Aulus Gellius 4.9.8. The quoted words are Gellius' (compare Cicero, *On the Divination* 3).

4. Macrobius 3.3.8, though there the derivation is from *relinquere* (to leave behind). Cicero, *On the Nature of the Gods* 2.72 (compare Aulus Gellius 4.9.11) derives it from *relegere* (to read over), Lactantius, *Divine Institutes* 4.28.2 (Servius, *Ad Aeneidem* 8.349) from *religare* (to bind).

5. Macrobius 3.3.9, citing Paulus Diaconus, *Epitoma Festi* 289.15M.

6. Eusebius of Caesarea (ca. 260–339 CE) was taught in that city by Pamphilus (martyred 310), whose name he took. The Latin translation of his

Preparation for the Gospel by George of Trebizond (1395–1472/73) was completed in 1448. In the following pages, Biondo uses George's translation, often abridging and paraphrasing.

7. Cicero, *On the Laws* 1.24. Cicero in fact wrote "there is no race so civilized or so savage."

8. Cicero, *On the Responses of the Haruspices* 19.

9. Cicero, *On the Laws* 2.26. Roman religious terms are notoriously difficult to translate. Apart from that, the key terms "pietas" and "religio" have acquired other significances in patristic and medieval theology.

10. Augustine, *City of God* 9.11 (based on Apuleius, *On the God of Socrates* 15.3–4). The last sentence is abridged. *Lares* were tutelar deities; *lemures* and *larvae,* specters or malevolent spirits; and *manes,* souls of the departed or benevolent spirits.

11. Eusebius, *PG* 2.6.11–15.

12. Eusebius, *PG* 2.4.3.

13. Eusebius, *PG* 4.5.1–2.

14. Eusebius, *PG* 5.5.2, citing Empedocles, fr. 115.9–12 Diels-Kranz.

15. Eusebius, *PG* 5.4.2.

16. Eusebius, *PG* 5.9.16.

17. Eusebius, *PG* 5.8.1–3.

18. The phrase is perhaps recalled from Cicero, *On the Laws* 1.24.

19. Eusebius, *PG* 1.9.1–2, 4, 8–9.

20. Macrobius 1.7.15 (paraphrase).

21. In the translation, we have restored the correct forms of the words.

22. Eusebius, *PG* 1.9.9, 11, 13. Compare 1.9.7.

23. "Dionysius" was a common appellation for Dionysus in Biondo's time, but we have not retained it in the translation.

24. Eusebius, *PG* 2.1.2–6. In Eusebius, Saturn marries Rhea. Cybele comes from George of Trebizond. Rhea and Cybele were assimilated in antiquity.

25. In *I.I.* (Romagna §34), Biondo had already given the erroneous information (perhaps based on a corrupt manuscript reading of Jerome's translation of Eusebius, *Chronici canones,* p. 246.6f., or on local tradition, see Nogara, *Scritti,* pp. cxcii–cxciii) that the Roman elegiac poet Gaius Cornelius Gallus (70/69–27/26 BCE) came from Forlì in Italy rather than Forum Julii (Fréjus in southern France). The closest passage of Ammianus Marcellinus, 17.4.2–6 (compare *R.I.* 1.62), says nothing about Gallus' origin and does not specify the nature of his "thefts" from Thebes (Cappelletto, *Recuperi ammianei,* pp. 66–74, with p. 147 n. 90).

26. Eusebius, *PG* 2.1.6. In fact, Eusebius here is using Diodorus Siculus 1.23.4–5.

27. Eusebius, *PG* 2.1.21–22. Compare 2.1.17–18.

28. Eusebius, *PG* 2.1.24–25.

29. This detail about cats comes from a misunderstanding of Eusebius, who said that they were "useful against asps." In Greek, the words for shield and asp are the same. Perhaps George of Trebizond was recalling the story that the Persian king Cambyses protected his army in Egypt by putting the Egyptians' sacred animals in front of it (Polyaenus, *Strategemata* 15.6, 7.9).

30. Eusebius, *PG* 2.1.34–35, 37–40, 42–43, 46–47. "Shaving the head" has been substituted for the "shaving the body" of the source.

31. *S.H.A., Commodus* 9.4 (Lucius Aurelius Commodus Antoninus, 161–192 CE).

32. *S.H.A., Pescennius Niger* 6.8–9 (Gaius Pescennius Niger Iustus, emperor 193–194 CE).

33. *S.H.A., Caracalla* 6.6 (Marcus Aurelius Antoninus, 188–217 CE).

34. *S.H.A., Caracalla* 7.1–4.

35. Eusebius, *PG* 2.1.50.

36. Lampridius = Suetonius, *Titus* 5 (see Cappelletto, *Recuperi ammianei,* pp. 69–70).

37. Jerome, *Letter* 123, *To Ageruchia* 8. Silvina (also called Salvina) was a Christian from Africa who lived in Constantinople. A manu-

script contemporary with Biondo has the title *Epistolae ad Salvinam et Ageruchiam.*

38. Jerome, *Against Jovinianus* 2.7. Antinoöpolis, in Middle Egypt east of the Nile, was founded by the emperor Hadrian in 130 CE.

39. Eusebius, *PG* 1.10.1–2, 4, 6–7.

40. Eusebius, *PG* 1.10.14–15, 16.

41. Eusebius, *PG* 1.10.44, 36–37, 46–48, 50–51 (abridged).

42. The reference is to a bronze serpent standing on a granite column in the Basilica of St. Ambrose in Milan. It is thought to have been brought from Constantinople about the year 1001, by Archbishop Arnolf (Landolphus Senior, *Mediolanensis Historia,* 2.18, in *RIS* IV.2, pp. 51–53). St. Ambrose founded the basilica and dedicated it in 386 CE.

43. Eusebius, *PG* 2.2.1–2, 4–10. The name "Hermione" has displaced the correct "Harmonia." Together with Poggio's translation (completed 1449) of the passage of Diodorus (4.4–5) that Eusebius is using, this would have been an important early source for the Renaissance image of Bacchus (A. Emmerling-Skala, *Bacchus in der Renaissance* [Hildesheim: Georg Olms, 1994], 1:91).

44. Eusebius, *PG* 2.2.17, 20, 34.

45. Eusebius, *PG* 2.2.36–40. The name "Atlas" in "Atlas had daughters too" is a slip for "Coelus."

46. Eusebius, *PG* 2.2.41–42, 44.

47. The Greek word should rather be translated as "arrogance." The error originates with George of Trebizond.

48. Eusebius, *PG* 2.2.46–49, 59–60. George of Trebizond, correctly, has "Themis" as the third of Jupiter's wives.

49. Hesiod, *Works and Days* 252–53 in Eusebius, *PG* 5.36.1–2.

50. In §35?

51. Augustine, *City of God* 5.1, 8, referring to Seneca, *Moral Epistles* 107.11 (quoting from the opening lines of Cleanthes' *Hymn to Zeus*) and Cicero's translation of the passage from Homer (*Odyssey* 18.136–37), preserved only here (Cicero, *On Fate* fr. 3 Ax). The attribution here to *On*

Fate is an inference from the context, not information given by Augustine.

52. Servius Tullius, the sixth king of Rome (conventionally, 578–535 BCE).

53. Plutarch, *Roman Questions* 74. Biondo uses the translation by Gian Pietro d'Avenza (1453). "All-Seeing Fortune" exists but is not named by Plutarch, whose description quoted here is of "Sticky Fortune."

54. Compare Eusebius, *PG* 4.1.8.

55. Eusebius, *PG* 5.32.1.

56. Compare Eusebius, *PG* 4.1.8–9.

57. Eusebius, *PG* 5.20.8–10. Doubt is cast on George's authorship of the hexameter translation of the oracle cited by Biondo by its appearance in a manuscript containing verses of the poet and antiquarian Maffeo Vegio (1407–58): Fabio Della Schiava, "Le *Fabellae* esopiche di Maffeo Vegio: Spigolature da un codice lodigiano poco noto," in *Tradition et créativité dans les formes gnomiques en Italie et en Europe du Nord (XIV–XVII siècles)*, ed. P. Galand, G. Ruozzi, S. Verhulst, and J. Vignes (Brepols: Turnhout, 2011), pp. 133–63, especially 152f.

58. Compare Eusebius, *PG* 4.2.1.

59. We have not found a source for this.

60. We have not found a source for this, though Juvenal 6.555–56 may have given the impression that the oracles had ceased at this time. Compare Eusebius, *PG* 5.1.16. After a decline in the first century CE, the Delphic oracle in fact had a short-lived revival in the reign of Hadrian.

61. *S.H.A., Severus Alexander* 22.4, 43.6–7 (Marcus Aurelius Severus Alexander, emperor 222–235 CE), called the "best of the Roman emperors" in the Preface to *I.I.*

62. *S.H.A., Saturninus* 8.1–4, 6 (Sextus Iulius Saturninus, late 3rd cent. CE). The words "no Christian presbyter" are omitted from the list.

63. Eusebius, *PG* 4.3.7–10 (summarized).

64. Compare *PG* 2.8.6.

65. The "trial of chastity" is an inference from Juvenal 6.50.

66. Eusebius, PG 2.3.31-33. The correct name of the old woman is Baubo, as in George of Trebizond's translation. George, however, calls the drink "cycrona," from which Biondo's "citrona" derives. In the translation we use "ciceon," as the Greek name for the drink was transliterated in the Renaissance.

67. Eusebius, *PG* 2.8.8. Biondo has changed the sense somewhat by making the Phrygians perform the cruel sacrifice, whereas the original reference was to the Roman *Ludi Megalenses*.

68. The Capitoline Hill.

69. Eusebius, *PG* 4.16.1–2, 5–8, 11–12, 14–18 (abridged). Saturn's son is more properly called "Jeiid." The reference to Dionysius of Halicarnassus is in Eusebius. "Juno" is a slip for "Jupiter."

70. Cicero, *On the Responses of the Haruspices* 19.

71. *Periochae* of Livy 47.1. In modern texts the name is Gnaeus Tremellio.

72. Augustine, *City of God* 3.31, incorporating Vergil, *Aeneid* 1.416–17.

73. Literally, "the investigation is armed with three divisions." There is a parallel for the military metaphor in Sicco Polenton, *Scriptorum illustrium latinae linguae libri XVIII*, ed. B. L. Ullman (Rome: American Academy, 1928), pp. 221f., where he speaks of Aulus Gellius' lack of arrangement: "Unlike Valerius Maximus and Frontinus, he assigns nothing to a specific general or standards, but is a soldier at loose."

74. The second and third groups of topics are in Book 2, but there is no section on *lectisternia*.

75. Livy 1.5.1–2 (Evander is the usual founder, as in Livy and §54 below). See T. P. Wiseman, "The God of the Lupercal," *Journal of Roman Studies* 85 (1995): 1–22.

76. Livy 1.7.3.

77. Livy 1.19.4–5.

78. Cicero, *On His Own House* 107.

79. Cicero, *On His Own House* 1.

80. Cicero, *On the Laws* 2.19. The text of Cicero's *On the Laws* is recognized as being particularly corrupt, and Biondo's citations from it are of-

ten hard to make sense of. In the translation we try to strike a balance between intelligibility and fidelity to Biondo's text.

81. Cicero, *On the Laws* 2.27–28.

82. Cicero, *Verrine Orations* 2.5.187. The seven so-called Verrine orations are made up of the "*divinatio*" and two "actions," or hearings, of which the second consists of a mammoth speech in five parts, or books, which was never delivered. Biondo, following the manuscripts of his day, calls each speech an "action."

83. Cicero, *Defense of Murena* 2.

84. Compare Jerome, *To the Galatians II, Preface* 353 (Migne): *Varro, cunctarum antiquitatum diligentissimus perscrutator* and Augustine, *City of God* 6.2–6.

85. Macrobius 3.4.6–8, citing Varro, *Human Antiquities* fr. 8; Nigidius, *On the Gods;* and Vergil, *Aeneid* 3.12. Strangely, Biondo omits the words that make the etymology clear.

86. Ovid, *Fasti* 1.527–28.

87. Plutarch, *Numa* 8.7. This *Life* was translated by Francesco Filelfo circa 1430.

88. Augustine, *City of God* 4.31, citing Varro, *Divine Antiquities* fr. 18.

89. Compare Augustine, *City of God* 7.2.

90. Aulus Gellius 13.23.1. The names in modern texts are: "Luam Saturni, Salaciam Neptuni, Horam Quirini, Virites Quirini, Maiam Volcani, Heriem Iunonis, Moles Martis Nerienemque Martis." The meaning of *comprecatio* is now taken to be "public prayers or supplication." Gellius himself does not imply conjointness.

91. Compare Labeo ap. Augustine, *City of God* 2.11. The Neoplatonist Cornelius Labeo (?second half of 3rd cent. CE) would rather have used Varro. The misunderstanding is Biondo's. The specification of *human* sacrifice has been added.

92. Augustine, *City of God* 7.2; compare Augustine *City of God* 6.9 (Varro begins with Janus).

93. Augustine, *City of God* 7.4.

94. Augustine, *City of God* 6.9.

95. Augustine, *City of God* 6.9. In the rest of this discussion of minor gods the forms of their names are given in the translation as they appear in modern texts of Augustine.

96. This seems to be based on Servius, *Ad Eclogas* 8.29.

97. Augustine, *City of God* 6.9.

98. Augustine, *City of God* 7.2. Biondo conflates two mentions, in the second of which Mena is stepdaughter of Juno Lucina.

99. Augustine, *City of God* 7.2.

100. Augustine, *City of God* 6.9.

101. Augustine, *City of God* 6.9 (elaborated). There is no mention of Cornelius Labeo in the chapter.

102. Augustine, *City of God* 7.2; compare 7.3.

103. Augustine, *City of God* 7.4.

104. Augustine, *City of God* 6.9. "Deverra" (Augustine) means "Sweeper."

105. See Augustine, *City of God* 4.11 (compare 4.21).

106. Aulus Gellius 16.16.1, 4; compare *R.T.* Book 8, p. 163b. The names are "Postverta" and "Prorsa."

107. Culled from Augustine, *City of God* 4.11, though these deities are also mentioned in other chapters of Book 4.

108. Augustine, *City of God* 7.14 (Mercury); *City of God* 4.21 (Mercury and Minerva); *City of God* 18.8 (Minerva).

109. Augustine, *City of God* 4.11, 16.

110. Augustine, *City of God* 4.21.

111. Augustine, *City of God* 4.11.

112. Augustine, *City of God* 4.21.

113. Augustine, *City of God* 4.16. Augustine refers to L. Pomponius of Bononia (fl. 89 BCE), a writer of Atellan farces, two hundred of whose lines survive.

114. Augustine, *City of God* 6.1; compare 4.11.

115. See §§19–20?

116. Paulus Diaconus, *Epitoma Festi* 367.17M.

117. Compare Augustine, *City of God* 6.9; and Paulus Diaconus, *Epitoma Festi* 163.1M.

118. Augustine, *City of God* 7.19.

119. Augustine, *City of God* 4.8.

120. Augustine, *City of God* 4.11.

121. Augustine, *City of God* 4.8.

122. Augustine, *City of God* 4.21.

123. Augustine, *City of God* 4.11. Augustine says, simply, "Liber among the vines."

124. Augustine, *City of God* 18.13.

125. Compare Eusebius, *PG* 2.2.9–10. We cannot find a source for "Brotinus."

126. For a similar apology, see Augustine, *City of God* 7.21; compare 4.8.

127. Biondo's comment recalls one made in *I.I.*, Lazio §20, on the identification of "Civita Indivina" with Lanuvium, on the evidence of an inscription supplied by his patron, Prospero Colonna (d. 1463). Stemming from the powerful Roman Colonna family, Prospero was named cardinal, with the title of St. George in Velabrum, by his uncle Martin V in 1430. See White ad loc. and Martino Filetico, *In corruptores latinitatis*, ed. Maria Agata Pincelli (Rome: Edizioni di storia e letteratura, 2000), pp. 48–50.

128. Augustine, *City of God* 7.21. Augustine, however, sets this in Lavinium (Pratica di Mare), though some of his manuscripts had the name in the same form as Biondo.

129. Augustine, *City of God* 4.8.

130. Placidus, *Glossary*, in CGL, pp. 4.10, 47.5. According to Augustine (7.22), "Salacia" is Neptune's wife.

131. Augustine, *City of God* 7.22.

132. §29.

133. Augustine, *City of God* 4.23, 6.10. In neither place is "Fever" mentioned as deified by Hostilius, but she is associated with "Fright" and "Paleness" at 4.15 and further on in 4.23. Romulus is not among the deifications of Titus Tatius in Augustine. Titus Tatius predeceased him. There may be a confusion with Tacitus, *Histories* 2.95 (see *R.T.* Book 2, n. 31 below).

134. Augustine, *City of God* 18.13, paraphrased and abridged; *inextricabili errore* is a Vergilian phrase (*Aeneid* 6.14) borrowed by Augustine.

135. Ulpian, *Digest* 1.8.9.2–3.

136. Marcian, *Digest* 1.1.8.1.

137. Cicero, *On the Laws* 2.22.

138. Cicero, *On the Response* 13.

139. Paulus Diaconus, *Epitoma Festi* 62.11M. The *curiae* were the ten sections into which the original three tribes were subdivided.

140. Paulus Diaconus, *Epitoma Festi* 93.11M.

141. Plutarch, *Aemilius Paulus* 24.1.

142. Macrobius 1.12.28 (paraphrase).

143. Macrobius 1.16.4.

144. Macrobius 3.3.2, with Vergil, *Aeneid* 3.19, 4.638, 8.84. Here, and in the following extract, Macrobius is quoting from Book 1 of Gaius Trebatius Testa's lost *Religious Observances*. Trebatius was a lawyer of the late Republic and a friend of Cicero.

145. Macrobius 3.3.5–6, with Vergil, *Aeneid* 12.648–49. Trebatius in fact said that "sanctum" was sometimes the same as "sacrum," sometimes the same as "religiosum," sometimes something else.

146. Macrobius 3.3.6.

147. Macrobius 3.4.1.

148. *S.H.A., Hadrian* 22.10.

149. Livy 5.40.9–10.

150. Livy 7.19.6–20.8.

151. Paulus Diaconus, *Epitoma Festi* 44.4M.

152. Pliny the Elder, *Natural History* 18.7–8. Lucius Cassius Hemina wrote history in Latin in the later second century BCE.

153. Nonius Marcellus 52.14M.

154. Paulus Diaconus, *Epitoma Festi* 3.10M.

155. Nonius Marcellus 52.15M.

156. Paulus Diaconus, *Epitoma Festi* 110.5M.

157. Paulus Diaconus, *Epitoma Festi* 140.10M.

158. Macrobius 1.16.3. Biondo uses a slightly corrupted text.

159. Nonius Marcellus 424.19M.

160. Macrobius 3.5.4.

161. Cicero, *On the Laws* 2.21.

162. Varro, *On the Latin Language* 5.130.

163. Paulus Diaconus, *Epitoma Festi* 16.3M.

164. Paulus Diaconus, *Epitoma Festi* 104.12M

165. Paulus Diaconus, *Epitoma Festi* 345.7M.

166. Paulus Diaconus, *Epitoma Festi* 349.16M.

167. Livy 36.35.12–13.

168. Cicero, *On His Own House* 127.

169. Livy 1.20.2, 4.

170. Paulus Diaconus, *Epitoma Festi* 10.12M.

171. Paulus Diaconus, *Epitoma Festi* 92.16M. The reference in Paulus was to the *flammeum*, a flame-colored veil.

172. Paulus Diaconus, *Epitoma Festi* 160.1M.

173. Paulus Diaconus, *Epitoma Festi* 354.7M.

174. Aulus Gellius 10.15.26, 29, 30, 32.

175. Cicero, *On the Laws* 2.45.

176. Pliny the Elder, *Natural History* 35.153, 157, 158 (extracts).

177. Seneca, *Moral Epistles* 31.11; Vergil, *Aeneid* 8.364–65.

178. Persius 2.69–70.

179. Cicero, *On the Laws* 2.45.

180. Plutarch, *Roman Questions* 40. Biondo's methods of excerpting occasionally led to such misattributions.

181. Paulus Diaconus, *Epitoma Festi* 248.9M.

182. Livy 5.46.2–3 (abridged).

183. Not Vergil but Lucan 1.596.

184. Paulus Diaconus, *Epitoma Festi* 312.1M (*Stroppus* . . . "strophion"). There is a mention of a *strophium* at Cicero, *On the Response* 44.

185. Paulus Diaconus, *Vesper Hymn for the Feast of St John the Baptist* 22, *Monumenta Germaniae Historica. Poetae latini aevi Carolini* 1, ed. Ernst Dümmler (Berlin: Weidmann, 1881; rpt. 1997), pp. 83–84.

186. Paulus Diaconus, *Epitoma Festi* 248.11M.

187. Paulus Diaconus, *Epitoma Festi* 248.12M (*patellae*).

188. Paulus Diaconus, *Epitoma Festi* 113.1M.

189. Paulus Diaconus, *Epitoma Festi* 113.18M.

190. Paulus Diaconus, *Epitoma Festi* 18.7M.

191. Paulus Diaconus, *Epitoma Festi* 18.11M *(athanuvium).*

192. Paulus Diaconus, *Epitoma Festi* 11.11M.

193. Paulus Diaconus, *Epitoma Festi* 349.1M.

194. Cicero, *Verrine Orations* 2.4.46.

195. Paulus Diaconus, *Epitoma Festi* 337.10M.

196. Paulus Diaconus, *Epitoma Festi* 346.3M.

197. Paulus Diaconus, *Epitoma Festi* 349.8M.

198. Compare Cicero, *On the Laws* 2.40.

199. Biondo may have in mind Augustine, *City of God* 4.30. The latter's whole chapter on superstition quotes from Cicero, *On the Nature of the Gods* 2.70–72; compare 2.71: "religion has been distinguished from superstition not only by philosophers but also by our ancestors."

200. Compare Cicero, *On the Nature of the Gods* 2.72 (Augustine, *City of God* 4.30). The definition is not found at Gellius 4.9.2.

201. Livy 4.30.9–11. Instead of "souls entrapped by religious dread," Livy has "entrapped by superstition."

202. Livy 29.18.4–6 (abridged). The last sentence is corrupt, and we have translated Livy's text.

203. Cicero, *On His Own House* 121.

204. Livy 9.46.1, 6, 7 (abridged).

205. Livy 10.1.8–9 (abridged). Gaius Iunius Brutus Bubulcus cos. 311 BCE. On the Quirinal Hill, the temple was begun in 306 BCE (*LTUR*, 4:229–30).

206. Livy 23.31.9 (where "Otacilius" is now read). Livy has been misread. It was Q. Marcius Ralla who dedicated the temple to Fortuna Primigenia.

207. Livy 34.53.4–5, 7.

208. Valerius Maximus 5.10.1.

209. This story was told many times in antiquity (see, for example, *Periochae of Livy* 18; *Cicero, On Duties* 1.39, 3.97–115).

210. Paulus Diaconus, *Epitoma Festi* 115.3M.

211. Cicero, *On the Laws* 2.22.

212. For example, Livy 5.6.1, and often in Cicero.

213. The explanation is false, but it is found, for example, in *Commentum Einsidlense in Donati artem minorem*, *GLK*, 8:260.12–14; compare 8:212.34–35.

214. Based on Ovid, *Fasti* 6.213–18; compare Varro, *On the Latin Language*, 5.51, 52, 66; *R.I.* 1.9. Ovid says the temple was dedicated to Sancus by the Sabines. See *LTUR*, 4:263–64.

215. Cicero, *On Duties* 1.36. The military oath is discussed again in *R.T.* Book 6, p. 136f–g, where the source for the Cato anecdote is Plutarch, *Roman Questions* 39.

216. Varro, *On the Latin Language* 5.180.

217. Sulpicius Severus, *Life of St. Martin of Tours* 2.5.

218. Livy 22.58.8, 22.61.4.

219. Livy 31.50.7, 9.

220. The source is hard to determine. Perhaps Paulus Diaconus, *Roman History* 4.17 (compare *Periochae* of Livy 54.1, 55.5, 56.1); Appian, *Numantine Wars* 6.79, 80, 83; Orosius, *History against the Pagans* 5.4.20–21. The same words recur in *R.T.* Book 7 (Capra, p. 320, §26).

221. Suetonius, *Tiberius* 35.1.

222. Cicero, *Defense of Roscius the Comedian* 46.

223. *S.H.A., Caracalla* 1.4. The claim that "elemosina" occurs here is a mistake.

224. Ulpian, *Digest* 50.13.1.3. The point at issue there is whether someone who practices exorcism can be counted as a doctor.

225. Pliny the Elder, *Natural History* 18.8.

226. That is, it occurs several times in Paul's *Epistle to the Romans*.

227. Macrobius 3.11.1–2.

228. Livy 1.3.11.

229. Jerome, *Letter* 123, *To Ageruchia* 8. See above on §13.

230. Livy 36.37.4.

231. Ovid, *Fasti* 4.657–58.

232. *S.H.A., Didius Julianus* 3.9.

233. Jerome, *Against Jovinian* 2.5.

234. Macrobius 3.5.1–3, citing Vergil, *Aeneid* 4.57, 63; 3.5.3; 5.483–84. Macrobius refers to Trebatius, *On Religious Observances* Book 1.

235. Placidus, *Glossary*, in *CGL*, p. 8.15.

236. This could be a paraphrase of Ovid, *Fasti* 1.335–36. We have not found the distinction in Aulus Gellius. See *R.T.* Book 2, §15.

237. Paulus Diaconus, *Epitoma Festi* 126.13M.

238. Paulus Diaconus, *Epitoma Festi* 292.1M.

239. Not Pliny, but Macrobius 3.5.8, citing Vergil, *Aeneid* 2.395, 9.627.

240. Pliny the Elder, *Natural History* 8.183.

241. Pliny the Elder, *Natural History* 8.206, 204; 33.39.

242. Suetonius, *Caligula* 32.3. In the Latin text the words for the people cheated are in the feminine, which seems wrong, as it is hard to see why the victims deserve to be cheated. In sixteenth-century editions, *quas* was dropped and *meritae* became the masculine *meriti*. We translate Suetonius' *poparum*.

243. Cicero, *On the Agrarian Law* 2.93.

244. Paulus Diaconus, *Epitoma Festi* 93.13M. In modern texts it is "to Aternus," a river of Central Italy.

245. Paulus Diaconus, *Epitoma Festi* 159.9, 10M. Biondo accidentally transcribes the previous item, leaving out the appropriate lemma, "Muries" (brine).

246. Paulus Diaconus, *Epitoma Festi* 228.12M.

247. Paulus Diaconus, *Epitoma Festi* 251.13M.

248. Paulus Diaconus, *Epitoma Festi* 349.4M. The text is, rather, "trodden *(calcatae)* grapes . . . winepress."

249. Paulus Diaconus, *Epitoma Festi* 349.9M.

250. Paulus Diaconus, *Epitoma Festi* 220.21M (abridged).

251. Macrobius 1.12.31–33.

252. Macrobius 2.2.4. The reading now is "propter viam."

253. Macrobius 1.12.18.

254. Macrobius 1.12.20.

255. Macrobius 3.11.10.

256. Paulus Diaconus, *Epitoma Festi* 379.11M.

257. Plutarch, *Roman Questions* 32. "Greek man" was added by Biondo, who also seems to have changed Gian Pietro d'Avenza's *imitantes* to *omittentes*. Compare §25.

258. Plutarch, *Aemilius Paulus* 17.10–12 (abridged).

259. *S.H.A., Maximus and Balbinus* 11.4–7 (with omissions). Marcus Clodius Pupienus Maximus and Decius Caelius Calvinus Balbinus were chosen as joint emperors in 238 CE.

260. Macrobius 3.2.6. At 3.2.3–4 Macrobius names his source as Veranius (a Republican antiquarian) citing from Fabius Pictor. (Paulinianus was Jerome's younger brother.) For the Romans, someone was "condemned" to discharge a vow made to a god if the request was granted and remained "guilty of a vow" until it was discharged.

261. Pliny the Elder, *Natural History* 28.25. Pliny said "we turn round the whole body (to the right)." This was a ritual act performed during worship of the gods or divine objects *(adoratio).*

262. Macrobius 3.2.11–15, citing Varro, *Divine Antiquities* 15 (fr. 223); Vergil, *Aeneid* 6.657, *Eclogue* 3.77. Hyllus is otherwise unknown.

263. Macrobius 1.10.20–21.

264. Paulus Diaconus, *Epitoma Festi* 67.15M.

265. Paulus Diaconus, *Epitoma Festi* 106.2–4M.

266. Nonius Marcellus 430.28M.

267. Pliny the Elder, *Natural History* 11.250.

268. *Tesquum* is an uncertain augural term used in association with *templum, OLD* s.v.

269. Varro, *On the Latin Language* 7.13.

270. Pseudo-Asconius Pedianus, *On the Divination* 3 (Stangl p. 187).

271. Varro, *On the Latin Language* 7.10. The text Biondo was using did not allow him to understand fully. Varro's point is that the preponderance at Rome of *aedes* that were also *templa* and inaugurated had wrongly encouraged the view that all *templa* were *sancta.*

272. Macrobius 3.3.3–4, incorporating Vergil, *Aeneid* 6.258, 12.777–79 (abridged).

273. Varro, *On the Latin Language* 7.11. The text is corrupt and we translate *ubi* rather than *ibi.*

274. Macrobius 3.4.2, citing Varro, *Divine Antiquities,* Book 8 (fr. 70). Varro's example is the shrine of Jupiter Stator in the Circus Flaminius (*LTUR,* 3:157–59), now known to have been an open area near the Tiber in the southern part of the Campus Martius. Elsewhere, Biondo identifies the Circus Flaminius with Piazza Navona, see *R.I.* 1.9; 3.30, 38.

275. Macrobius 3.4.4, citing Vergil, *Aeneid* 2.225–26, 248–49.

276. Paulus Diaconus, *Epitoma Festi* 29.10M, 350.6M. The exact location of the Tarentum (*LTUR*, 5:20–22) is not known, but it was probably in the western part of the Campus.

277. Biondo elsewhere (*R.I.* 1.75, 2.40) refers to this altar as "the first," citing Livy Book 1. For the legend of the foundation of the Ara Maxima (*LTUR*, 3:15–17), see also Livy 1.7.3–15, and Vergil, *Aeneid*, 8.184–272. See below, §55.

278. Ovid, *Fasti* 1.551, 581, also cited in *R.I.* 2.55, where Ovid is deemed a "more reliable" source for the origin of the name "Boarium" than the mutilated Tacitus, *Annals* 12.24. The Forum Boarium (*LTUR*, 2:295–97) was an area beside the Tiber, below the Capitoline, Palatine, and Aventine hills and adjacent to the Tiber Island.

279. Macrobius 3.2.7–9, citing Varro, *Divine Antiquities*, Book 5; Vergil, *Aeneid* 4.219–20, 12.201.

280. Plutarch, *Roman Questions* 46. Biondo omits the alternative name "Horta," derived from *hortari*. The goddess is not otherwise known.

281. Plutarch, *Roman Questions* 47. The location of the temple is uncertain.

282. The term *lararium* is found for the first time in literature in the S.H.A., for example, *Aurelian* 3.5; *Tacitus* 17.4.

283. Vergil, *Aeneid* 3.12.

284. Cicero, *On His Own House* 109.

285. Plutarch, *Roman Questions* 51. The phrase "in the Lararium" occurs neither in Plutarch nor in the translation by Gian Pietro d'Avenza. Similarly, it is Biondo who calls these Lares *(praestites)* "Penates."

286. Pliny the Elder, *Natural History* 18.12. Biondo seems to have been led by a corrupt text to suppose Pliny was talking about the Lares, when in fact he had written "coins" *(aes)*.

287. Pseudo-Asconius Pedianus, *On the Second Action of the Verrine Orations* 1.48 (Stangl p. 235).

288. Livy 1.53.2–3. On the Capitol, see *R.I.* 1.74.

289. Livy 2.21.7, 27.5. Above and facing the Circus Maximus, on the slope of the Aventine (*LTUR*, 3:245–47). See *R.I.* 3.27.

290. Livy 2.40.1–12. It was four miles outside Rome on the Via Latina (*LTURS*, 2:272f.).

291. Livy 5.23.7; compare 1.55.3–4. In the Forum Boarium (*LTUR*, 2:281–85), which Biondo sometimes joined to the Aventine. See *R.I.* 1.21.

292. Livy 5.50.5 (the god is "Aius Locutius" in modern texts). At the north corner of the Palatine (*LTUR*, 1:29).

293. Livy 1.55.3–4; compare 5.54.7. *LTUR*, 5:27–28.

294. Livy 7.28.4–5. See *LTUR*, 3:123. Biondo discusses the location on the arx in *R.I.* 1.73–74.

295. Livy 9.43.25 (compare 10.1.9). Compare §40.

296. Livy 10.46.14. Livy says Spurius Carvilius' temple (293 BCE) was near Servius', which was on the right bank of the Tiber outside the city.

297. Cicero, *Cross-examination of Vatinius* 24.

298. Paulus Diaconus, *Epitoma Festi* 272.3M.

299. Livy 1.20.5–6. In Livy it is Numa Marcius, son of Marcus.

300. Cicero, *On the Laws* 2.19. This is hard to understand because of corruptions in Cicero's text and abbreviation by Biondo.

301. Cicero, *On the Laws* 2.20.

302. Cicero, *On the Laws* 2.22.

303. Livy 5.15.4–5, 16.8–9.

304. Livy 5.22.4–7. Biondo summarizes the wars between Rome and Veii in *I.I.*, Tuscany §56. The Temple of Juno on the Aventine was in the neighborhood of the basilica of Santa Sabina (*LTUR*, 3:126–127), compare *R.I.* 1.75.

305. Ovid, *Fasti* 3.373–80.

306. Compare Livy 1.20.4.

307. Paulus Diaconus, *Epitoma Festi* 131.7M. Mamurius Veturius was a legendary sculptor, probably Oscan. We have translated *latius*, the reading favored by Mueller, not *latus*.

308. Cicero, *Philippic Orations* 11.24. In fact, Cicero is referring to the Palladium, a statue of Athena (*LTUR*, 5:128–29). Biondo has a long essay on Pallas and the Palladium in *R.I.* 1.76.

309. Vergil, *Eclogue* 3.60, 7.219.

310. This formula of medieval theology cannot be attributed to any particular source.

311. Vergil, *Georgics* 4.221–22. Vergil does not mean Jupiter but a divine spirit. The lines were well known; see D. S. Wiesen, "Vergil, Minucius Felix and the Bible," *Hermes* 99 (1971): 85–87.

312. Augustine, *City of God* 4.26.

313. Terence, *Eunuch* 584–91; compare Augustine, *City of God* 2.7, 2.12. In Terence, *impluvium* was used for the hole in the roof through which rain fell into a basin beneath, but its meaning later shifted to the rain itself: compare John of Salisbury, *Policraticus* 7.17 §676, *per impluvium auri* (by a shower of gold).

314. In the Middle Ages the Roman courts of civil justice were held by the senate on the Capitol. At *R.I.* 1.73, Biondo refers to a brick palace of Boniface IX, built in 1390 on the ruins of the Tabularium, "for the use of the senator and the lawyers."

315. Augustine, *City of God* 6.7, referring to Varro's *Divine Antiquities*. "Epulones," more commonly applied to members of the college of priests (originally three in number) formed to take care of the Feasts of Jupiter and the other gods (Paulus Diaconus, *Epitoma Festi* 78.11M), is used by Augustine of gods dining with Jupiter, but Biondo confuses the two.

316. Augustine, *City of God* 6.10, citing Seneca, *On Superstition* fr. 35–36 (abridged). In the original context, *perveni* means "come to," but Biondo reads *puduit* in place of *pudebit*.

317. Aulus Gellius 2.10.3–4, citing a reply given by Varro to the jurist Servius Sulpicius; compare Paulus Diaconus, *Epitoma Festi* 88.4M.

318. Plutarch, *Roman Questions* 111 (paraphrase).

319. Plutarch, *Roman Questions* 113.

320. Augustine, *City of God*, 7.24.

321. At *R.I.* 2.56–57, without mentioning Cybele, Biondo argues that the round Temple of Vesta (*LTUR*, 5:125), now rediscovered in the Forum, was the extant one beside the Tiber (this perhaps belonged to a form of Hercules, *LTUR*, 3:19–20). It survived in Biondo's day as St. Stephen "of the carriages." The bridge, also called *Pons senatorius* in the fifteenth century, is the fragmentary Ponte Rotto, see *R.I.* 1.21, 2.56–57.

322. Livy 29.11.7, 14.8–11 (compare *Periochae* 36.2), with Ovid, *Fasti* 4.345–48 (we translate Ovid's text, not Biondo's version of it). On Biondo's presentation of this episode, see M. A. Pincelli, "La *Roma triumphans*," pp. 19–28. In *R.I.* 1.76, Biondo has Scipio escort the goddess from the sea to the Palatine (compare Livy 29.14.14), where the temple referred to here was built (*LTUR*, 3:206–8). Biondo confuses the ancient Porta Capena (*LTUR*, 3:325) with the Porta Appia of the Aurelian Walls. See *R.I.* 1.17–18.

323. Vergil, *Aeneid* 6.784–85.

324. Drum, crown, seat, and Galli are together in Augustine, *City of God* 7.24 (from Varro). On "virgin and mother" see below, note 333.

325. Pliny the Elder, *Natural History* 35.165.

326. Paulus Diaconus, *Epitoma Festi* 95.13M.

327. Livy 37.9.8–9. "Holy" is not in Livy's text and was expunged in the later printed editions of *R.T.*

328. Livy 38.18.9.

329. Augustine, *City of God* 7.24.

330. Augustine, *City of God* 7.26.

331. Augustine, *City of God* 6.8.

332. Compare Augustine, *City of God* 6.7.

333. Augustine, *City of God* 2.4. Augustine is describing the purification ritual *(dies solemnis lavationis)* of a statue that is at the same time both Cybele and Caelestis *(Caelesti virgini et Berecynthiae matri omnium)*.

334. Plutarch, *Roman Questions* 16 and 17. For Ino-Leucothea-Matuta, see Ovid, *Fasti* 6.479–562.

335. This legend was well known by medieval authors, through Isidore, *Etymologies* 1.4.1, 5.39.11.

336. Ovid, *Fasti* 1.477–78.

337. Ovid, *Fasti* 2.423–24

338. Livy 1.5.1–2. Biondo added Romulus as the agent. See above, note 75. On the name of the Palatine Hill, see *R.I.* 1.68 (Livy is not used here).

339. Augustine, *City of God* 18.17 ("Lupercos" not "Lupercalia").

340. Ovid, *Fasti* 2.381–410.

341. Compare Livy 1.4.5, 10.23.12 (*LTUR*, 2:249).

342. Ovid, *Fasti* 2.413, 421–22.

343. The Lupercal lay at the southwestern corner of the Palatine (*LTUR*, 3:198–99). The *Curiosum* and *Notitia* had it in Regio X, Palatine. In *R.I.* Biondo does not mention it (compare 1.76–77).

344. Varro, *On the Latin Language* 5.85; 6.13, 34.

345. We have not found an ancient source for this song.

346. Paulus Diaconus, *Epitoma Festi* 57.2M.

347. For the standard version see Suetonius, *Julius* 79.2; Plutarch, *Antony* 12.1–3. At some point an anecdote about the emperor Elagabalus (Marcus Aurelius Antoninus Augustus, 218–222 CE) from his life in *S.H.A.*, *Heliogabalus* 29, to the effect that he rode naked in a chariot drawn by naked women, has become attached to the Republican figure M. Antonius (Mark Antony), who did not. Pietro Crinito, *Honorable Learning* (1504), 16.10, shows how this may have occurred, for he juxtaposes information about them both yoking lions to chariots and includes, in Elagabulus' case, the women. At about the same time, in J. Britannicus' commentary on Juvenal (Brescia, 1501) ad 2.142, the confused version is imputed to Plutarch in his *Life of Antony*.

348. See above, note 277. Here Biondo is perhaps following Ovid, *Fasti* 6.477–78.

349. On St. George and the Velabrum (*LTUR*, 5:102–8), see *R.I.* 1.74; 2.51–52, 54. The Velabrum is usually thought to be all the low-lying area between the Capitol and the Palatine. For Biondo it was a building on

the ruins of which St. George had been built. T. P. Wiseman argues that it was a "precise toponym . . . roughly where S. Giorgio in Velabro preserves the ancient name," in his article "Rethinking the Triumph," *Journal of Roman Archaeology* 21 (2008): 389–91, at 390.

350. Livy 1.7.3, 15.

351. The omission of Oeonus, the name of Licymnius' son, and the consequent errors are owing to Gian Pietro d'Avenza's translation. In addition Biondo omits Iphicles, the name of Hercules' brother. For "Hippocoontidon" (the sons of Hippocoon), Gian Pietro has *hipochostibus,* which gave rise to Biondo's *Ipothomatibus.*

352. Plutarch, *Roman Questions* 90.

353. Ovid, *Fasti* 1.579–82.

354. Augustine, *City of God* 6.7. Compare Plutarch, *Romulus* 5, *Roman Questions* 35. There is nothing in the sources for this anecdote to connect it with the Ara Maxima.

355. Paulus Diaconus, *Epitoma Festi* 119.1M.

356. Aulus Gellius 7.7.8. Gellius names the jurist Masurius Sabinus' *Memorialia,* Book 1, as his source. The (false) question of the two Larentias is discussed in Plutarch (see above), but in Macrobius (Biondo's main source) they are treated as one; see Robert E. A. Palmer, *The Archaic Community of the Romans* (Cambridge: Cambridge University Press, 1970), pp. 109–15.

357. Varro, *On the Latin Language* 5.85.

358. Macrobius 1.10.15. Valerius is hard to explain. Gellius (7.7.6) refers to Valerius Antias, but for the detail of the will, not the burial.

359. Augustine, *City of God* 4.10, to which is added Persius 2.70, and Augustine, *City of God* 6.7.

360. Temple of Venus Erucina (*LTUR,* 5:114–16). The ruins seen by Biondo may have been those of another temple of Venus Erucina, in the Horti Sallustiani. The same lines from Ovid, *Fasti* 4.871–72, are cited at *R.I.* 1.9.

361. Augustine, *City of God* 2.26.

362. Pliny the Elder, *Natural History* 3.65; Macrobius 1.10.7–8 (Angeronia); Giovanni Boccaccio, *Genealogy of the Pagan Gods, Volume I, Books 1–5*, ed. and trans. Jon Solomon (Cambridge, MA: Harvard University Press, 2011), 4.15. The shrine of Volupia (*LTUR*, 5:213) was on the New Way near where it entered the Velabrum.

363. Information about the antiquity of the grove (*LTUR*, 3:125–26) on the Cispius (Varro, *On the Latin Language* 5.49–50, 74), one of the summits of the Esquiline, may come from Pliny the Elder, *Natural History* 16.235. The temple dates from 375 BCE. Biondo's remark on the grove's extent has no ancient source and seems to be suggested by his otherwise unattested identification of it with the Campus Martius.

364. Compare Livy 2.5.2–3; *R.I.* 2.78. The expulsion of Tarquinius Superbus, by tradition the last king of Rome, is dated 510 BCE.

365. Compare Poggio, *DVF*, p. 95.146–48.

366. Ovid, *Fasti* 2.443–46. Ovid does not in fact say the priest was a member of the Luperci, but it is a legitimate inference from the context.

367. Ovid, *Fasti* 2.449.

368. Ovid, *Fasti* 2.443–46.

369. Juvenal 2.141–42. Juvenal is talking about the uselessness of aids to conception for male brides.

370. Ovid, *Fasti* 6.33–34. In Ovid the reference is to Juno's sharing of the Temple of Jupiter Optimus Maximus on the Capitol. Biondo however may be thinking of the Temple of Juno Moneta (*LTUR*, 3:123). See *R.I.* 1.73–74, citing Livy 7.28.5.

371. Based on Augustine, *City of God* 6.10, citing Seneca, *On Superstition* fr. 35.

372. Varro, *On the Latin Language* 5.67, 69.

373. Cicero, *Defense of Murena* 90.

374. Cicero, *On the Nature of the Gods* 2.70; compare Augustine, *City of God* 4.30.

375. Varro, *On the Latin Language* 5.64.

376. Varro, *On the Latin Language* 5.68.

377. Juvenal 6.443.

378. Plutarch, *Aemilius Paulus* 17.7–9. See §46 above for the same anecdote.

379. Paulus Diaconus, *Epitoma Festi* 368.3M.

380. Ovid, *Fasti* 1.609–12.

381. Cicero, *Brutus* 1.

382. Based on Augustine, *City of God* 3.28. Scaevola died in 82 BCE. Biondo added "Sulla's butchers."

383. We have not been able to find this, but compare Cicero, *On the Laws* 2.31.

384. For the location, see *R.I.* 2.31–32, on the function, 2.60. The *curiae veteres* (Varro, *On the Latin Language* 5.155; *LTUR*, 1:337), a religious building, were on the Palatine. Biondo confuses this with the Senate House and, further, sets his *curia vetus* on the slope of the Esquiline facing the Colosseum, near the ruins of the baths of Titus and Trajan. The reason for this is not clear.

385. Nicholas of Cusa (1401–64), named cardinal by Eugene IV in 1446, was Nicholas V's legate in Germany in the 1450s with a reforming mission. In 1458 he returned to Rome to work for Pius II and was present at the Congress of Mantua. He and Biondo were probably acquainted (E. Meuthen, *Die letzten Jahre des Nikolaus von Kues* [Cologne and Opladern: Westdeutscher Verlag, 1958], p. 307).

386. Paulus Diaconus, *Epitoma Festi* 357.3M.

387. Paulus Diaconus, *Epitoma Festi* 248.15M. We use the manuscript reading, *posimirium*, not Mueller's *posimerium*.

388. Plutarch, *Cicero* 38.7–8. Biondo knew Jacopo Angeli da Scarperia's translation (1400–1401), which he mentions with praise in *I.I.*, Tuscany §33.

389. The story refers to Publius Claudius Pulcher (cos. 249 BCE) defeated at sea by the Carthaginian fleet at Drepana (Cicero, *On the Nature*

of the Gods 2.7; *Periochae* of Livy 19.2, etc.). It was very well known and Biondo is probably relying on his memory.

390. Plutarch, *Cicero* 38.7–8. Titus Labienus (ca. 100–45 BCE) had been Caesar's legate but deserted to Pompey in 49 BCE.

391. Based on Augustine, *City of God* 4.30? Augustine, however, is talking about Cicero. Compare Seneca, *Natural Questions* 2.32.3–4.

392. Extracts from Varro, *On the Latin Language* 7.6–13. Varro says nothing about a *curia vetus*.

393. Livy 1.18.6–7.

394. Valerius Maximus 1.1.5; compare Pliny the Elder, *Natural History* 8.223; Plutarch, *Marcellus* 5.1–7.

395. Compare Livy 1.36.6.

396. Augustine, *City of God* 8.16. Augustine refers to "the same Platonist," that is, Apuleius, *The God of Socrates*.

397. Pliny the Elder, *Natural History* 28.17.

398. Nonius Marcellus 429M.

399. Livy 10.6.6–7, 9.1–2.

400. Livy 27.36.5. His name was Publius Aelius Paetus.

401. Cicero, *On the Laws* 2.20–21. Biondo's text in this and the following extracts is very different from the modern version.

402. Cicero, *On the Laws* 2.31.

403. Cicero, *On the Laws* 2.33.

404. Cicero, *On the Laws* 3.10.

405. Cicero, *On the Laws* 3.27.

406. Cicero, *On the Laws* 3.43.

407. Varro, *On the Latin Language* 6.95.

408. Cicero, *Philippic Orations* 2.4.

409. Paulus Diaconus, *Epitoma Festi* 260.8M.

410. Paulus Diaconus, *Epitoma Festi* 3.5M. The *sanqualis* and *inmusulus* were birds of prey, the first a kind of vulture, according to Pliny the El-

der, *Natural History* 10.20. They were not well understood by the ancients themselves.

411. Paulus Diaconus, *Epitoma Festi* 109.19M.

412. Paulus Diaconus, *Epitoma Festi* 196.1, 3M.

413. Paulus Diaconus, *Epitoma Festi* 304.5M.

414. Paulus Diaconus, *Epitoma Festi* 244.11M.

415. Plutarch, *Roman Questions* 38.

416. Plutarch, *Roman Questions* 72. Biondo's version differs considerably from Gian Pietro d'Avenza's. According to both Plutarch and his translator, the lantern is kept open and the flame visible.

417. Plutarch, *Roman Questions* 93. The corruption of "Herodorus" to "Herodotus" is already in Gian Pietro d'Avenza's version.

418. Plutarch, *Roman Questions* 73.

419. Plutarch, *Roman Questions* 99.

420. Paulus Diaconus, *Epitoma Festi* 64.9M.

421. Paulus Diaconus, *Epitoma Festi* 64.10M.

422. Paulus Diaconus, *Epitoma Festi* 244.19M.

423. Pliny the Elder, *Natural History* 10.30, 33–35.

424. Compare Pliny the Elder, *Natural History* 10.51. The story of the saving of the Capitol from the Gauls (traditionally 390 BCE) is told in Livy 5.47.

425. Pliny the Elder, *Natural History* 10.156.

426. Pliny the Elder, *Natural History* 11.140. "Nigidius" belongs to what follows in the original context.

427. Pliny the Elder, *Natural History* 10.49. *Tripudia solistima* is the technical term for omens derived from the birds' feeding.

428. Livy 6.41.4, 8.

429. Livy 8.30.2, 4, 12–14.

430. Livy 10.40.2, 4, 14.

431. Cicero, *Against Catiline* 3.20.

432. Cicero, *On the Responses of the Haruspices* 18 (the text is very corrupt and is impossible to translate properly). Cicero's point was that the priestly colleges (the pontificate, the augurs and the *haruspices*) relied on writings that had been handed down.

433. *S.H.A., Aurelian* 19.1–3, 6 (the text is very corrupt). Lucius Domitius Aurelianus (ca. 215–275 CE). There was never a temple of Commodus, but Biondo seems to have mistaken the adjectival *commodi* for the name *Commodi*.

434. *S.H.A., Aurelian* 20.1, 3.

435. *S.H.A., Aurelian* 20.4–7.

436. *S.H.A., Aurelian* 24.3–4. Apollonius of Tyana was a Neo-Pythagorean holy man whose fame for prophecy survived his death. Aurelian was said to have spared Tyana, on the request of Apollonius' ghost, during his expedition against the Palmyran queen, Zenobia, in 272 CE. In *S.H.A.* Apollonius says finally, "If you wish to live."

437. Pliny the Elder, *Natural History* 9.55.

438. Pliny the Elder, *Natural History* 10.40–41. The circumstances of Aelius Tubero's portent are not known. Pliny says disaster to the empire was to result from the bird's release, so Tubero killed it and died.

439. Pliny the Elder, *Natural History* 15.136–37 (paraphrase and abbreviation). The point there is that the portent happened before she married Octavian and became "empress" (Pliny says "Augusta").

440. Compare Nonius Marcellus 16.8M.

441. Vergil, *Aeneid* 4.63–64. (See §45.)

442. Augustine, *City of God* 2.24 (Livy 77 fr. 16). The portent belongs to Sulla's march on Rome in 88 BCE. Postumius was Sulla's personal *haruspex*.

443. Suetonius, *Julius* 7.2.

444. Tacitus, *Histories* 2.78.3–4.

445. See §60 and note. We have not traced a source for the further words attributed to Varro.

446. Cicero, *Defense of Cluentius* 194.

447. Another reference to such a sacrifice at Utica is more positive, Sallust, *Jugurtha* 64.

448. Pliny the Elder, *Natural History* 11.189. The absence of the upper part of the liver was considered a bad omen.

449. Pliny the Elder, *Natural History* 11.197. Pyrrhus of Epirus died in 272 BCE, while besieging Argos; see Pseudo-Aurelius Victor, *Deeds of Famous Men* 35.

450. Pliny the Elder, *Natural History* 11.190. This was at an auspication to validate the senate's grant of propraetorian *imperium* made five days earlier.

451. Pliny the Elder, *Natural History* 11.195.

452. See, for example, Cicero, *On Divination* 2.87–100, and Pliny the Elder, *Natural History* 30.1 (where Pliny says he has taken every opportunity in his work so far to expose the emptiness of magic).

453. Livy 1.31.8. Tullus Hostilius, the third king of Rome (conventionally 672–641 BCE), failed to perform correctly the rites of Jupiter Elicius, and thus angered the god, according to Livy.

454. Augustine, *City of God* 8.19.

455. Pliny the Elder, *Natural History* 26.18–19, expounding the system of medicine invented by Asclepiades, a first-century BCE physician. Pliny is being sarcastic, for he himself believed in herbal remedies. Biondo reads *adimere* (remove) in place of *adiuvere* (helped).

456. *S.H.A., Didius Julianus* 7.9–10. Marcus Didius Severus Iulianus lasted as emperor for two months in 193 CE.

457. Suetonius, *Tiberius* 36.

458. Tacitus, *Histories* 1.22.

459. Tacitus, *Histories* 2.62.

460. Livy 22.57.6.

461. Livy 25.1.6–9, 11–12.

462. Pliny the Elder, *Natural History* 28.11. In Pliny the attendant simply "kept watch."

463. Pliny the Elder, *Natural History* 28.11.

464. Pliny the Elder, *Natural History* 28.20.

465. Pliny the Elder, *Natural History* 28.12–13.

466. Pliny the Elder, *Natural History* 28.22.

467. Pliny the Elder, *Natural History* 28.4.

468. Suetonius, *Augustus* 90.

469. Pliny the Elder, *Natural History* 28.21.

470. Pliny the Elder, *Natural History* 28.18.

471. Cicero, *Cross-examination of Vatinius* 20.

472. Pliny the Elder, *Natural History* 15.134.

473. Pliny the Elder, *Natural History* 15.135.

474. Plutarch, *Roman Questions* 4. In abbreviating the story about Antro Curatius, Biondo leaves out some of the steps.

475. Suetonius, *Vespasian* 5.7. Here Biondo, or the manuscript he was using, replaced *praesagia* (presages) with *praestigia* (conjuring tricks, deceptions).

476. Suetonius, *Vespasian* 4.5.

477. Suetonius, *Vespasian* 5.6.

478. Cicero, *On the Laws* 2.21.

479. Nonius Marcellus 44.17M, 430.7M, 436.2M.

480. Livy 7.28.7. The name of the consul was Gaius Marcius Rutilus, and the year 344 BCE.

481. Livy 21.62.6–10 (abridged and corrupt). Biondo's text differs from Livy's, most significantly in putting Jupiter at Lanuvium instead of Juno. On Lanuvium see above, §34.

482. Livy 24.10.6.

483. Livy 24.44.7–8 (abridged).

484. Ulpian, *Digest* 50.16.38.

485. Pliny the Elder, *Natural History* 17.243.

486. Pliny the Elder, *Natural History* 17.244. Instead of "courtyards" Pliny has "altars." Apparently, the annalist L. Piso dated the start of moral decline among the Romans to 154 BCE.

487. Nonius Marcellus 345.27–28M.

488. Paulus Diaconus, *Epitoma Festi* 140.5M.

489. Paulus Diaconus, *Epitoma Festi* 368.2M.

490. *S.H.A., Hadrian* 2.8, citing Vergil, *Aeneid* 6.808–11.

491. Livy 22.1.11.

492. Livy 22.1.19–20.

493. Livy 1.27.7. The college of Salii vowed by Tullus Hostilius is the second, the first being Numa's.

494. Livy 5.21.2. In fact, the tithe was for Pythian Apollo.

495. Livy 2.21.9.

496. For Prospero Colonna, see above, note 127. The town is modern Genzano, near Nemi and its lake; compare Biondo, *I.I.*, Lazio §§46–47. The name *Nemorensis* comes from Suetonius, *Julius* 46.2 (cited by Biondo in *I.I.*, Lazio §46). The connection between the nymph Egeria and the cult of Diana at Nemi is attested in Vergil, *Aeneid* 7.761–64; Ovid, *Fasti* 3.261–64, 275–76; *Metamorphoses* 15.482–90, 547–51.

497. Biondo's account is perhaps based on Ovid, *Fasti* 4.145–50 (Ovid does not mention the role of the priest). How Biondo came to locate Manly Fortune here we cannot say, unless he interpreted the hot water at Ovid, *Fasti* 4.146, not as the baths but as the lake at Nemi. There is little evidence for a temple of Fortuna Virilis at Rome (perhaps Dionysius of Halicarnassus, *Roman Antiquities* 4.27.7; Plutarch, *On the Fortune of the Romans* 5). In any case, it was owing to these passages that Renaissance tradition saw it in the temple near the Pons Aemilius, then converted to the church of St. Mary of Egypt, now the Temple of Portunus (*LTUR*, 4:152–53).

BOOK II

1. Varro, *On the Latin Language* 5.83.

2. Paulus Diaconus, *Epitoma Festi* 126.10M.

3. Livy 22.57.3 and Cicero (*On the Responses of the Haruspices* 12) mention *minores pontifices; maiores* are an inference. Biondo may be thinking of the *flamens*, who also had a distinction of this kind; compare Paulus Diaconus, *Epitoma Festi* 151.3M.

4. *Periochae* of Livy 47.1. In Livy his name is Gnaeus Tremellius.

5. Livy 25.5.2–4 (abbreviated).

6. An inference from Cicero, *On the Agrarian Law* 2.16–18. A special assembly of seventeen of the thirty-five tribes elected the *pontifex maximus*.

7. Suetonius, *Julius* 13.

8. Suetonius, *Titus* 1.1, 9.

9. Varro, *On the Latin Language* 5.84 (slightly shortened and altered). In *On the Latin Language* 6.19, Varro says Furina is an ancient goddess (compare Ennius, *Annals* 116 Sk), knowledge of whom was dying out in his time. She had a grove on the right bank of the Tiber (*LTURS*, 2:278–84). The festival was on July 25.

10. Livy 1.20.2.

11. Livy 27.8.5–6.

12. Asconius Pedianus, *On Cicero's* Defense of Milo, *argumentum*, p. 31 Clark.

13. Cicero, *Defense of Milo* 27.

14. Paulus Diaconus, *Epitoma Festi* 155.11M.

15. Aulus Gellius 10.15.6.

16. Aulus Gellius 10.15.9.

17. Plutarch, *Roman Questions* 44.

18. Plutarch, *Roman Questions* 50. Biondo adds the designation of the wife as *flaminica*.

19. Paulus Diaconus, *Epitoma Festi* 244.5M. This interrupts the information on the *flamen Dialis*.

20. Plutarch, *Roman Questions* 109. Where we have "yeast," Biondo's text has *frumentum* (grain), though the translation by Gian Pietro d'Avenza has *fermentum*.

21. Plutarch, *Roman Questions* 112.

22. Varro, *On the Latin Language* 5.83.

23. Cicero, *On the Agrarian Law* 2.16–18. See on §2 above.

24. Cicero, *On the Agrarian Law* 2.18.

25. Cicero, *On the Responses of the Haruspices* 12. Biondo adapts this passage to suit his purposes. P. Lentulus Spinther (con. 57 BCE) was not pontifex maximus. Names in Cicero without a role designation are omitted, and some of the *praenomina* are incorrect.

26. Biondo's number "five" is incorrect. There were three senior flamens: those of Jupiter, Mars, and Quirinus.

27. Livy 9.29.9.

28. Cicero, *On the Laws* 2.47–48.

29. Cicero, *On the Responses of the Haruspices* 32. Biondo's text of Cicero was corrupt.

30. Tacitus, *Histories* 1.77.

31. Tacitus, *Histories* 2.95. In place of *incessit*, we have translated the modern reading *fecisset*.

32. See §3.

33. Livy 1.20.3.

34. Livy 30.26.10. Biondo's version is a misreading. The son became augur, and it was Servius Sulpicius Galba who had two priesthoods.

35. Suetonius, *Julius* 1.1–3 (paraphrase). When Caesar's friends defended him, Sulla conceded that they could "have him" but warned that he would bring disaster.

36. Cicero, *On the Laws* 2.22. Cicero's text has *famulos* (servants).

37. Cicero, *Defense of Cluentius* 43. Cicero was comparing the numbers of the Martiales to those of the Sicilian Venerii.

38. *S.H.A.*, *Hadrian* 27.2–3; *Antoninus Pius* 5.1–2. In fact the senate had opposed the deification.

39. Suetonius, *Galba* 8.1.

40. *S.H.A.*, *Antoninus Pius* 5.2, 8.1, 13.4.

41. *S.H.A.*, *Marcus Aurelius Antoninus* 18.8, 26.4–9. *S.H.A.* does not mention *satellites*.

42. The Order of the Teutonic Knights was founded in 1190 during the Third Crusade. In the thirteenth century they engaged in the Christianization of Prussia, with which they became associated.

43. The Order of Santiago was founded in 1170, originally to protect pilgrims traveling to the shrine of St. James of Compostella. It rose to considerable wealth, power, and influence in Spain, until it was incorporated to the crown by the Catholic Monarchs in 1493.

44. Cicero, *On the Laws* 2.40.

45. Biondo refers here to annates, the first year's income of an ecclesiastical benefice paid to the papal Curia by the holder.

46. Suetonius, *Claudius* 9. There is no further evidence for such a payment.

47. See below, §13.

48. *CIL* XI 1226, 14. The text differs in several places.

49. *CIL XI* 142. The measurements refer to a zone of protection claimed for the tomb. This second inscription is irrelevant. Its inclusion suggests Biondo was using a sylloge of local inscriptions compiled by himself or another. See on Classis (taken by Luitprand and sacked not later than 725 CE) and Ravenna, *I.I.*, Romagna §§19, 22–25, 32–33. Biondo's hometown, Forlì, is close to Ravenna (§34).

50. *I.I.*, Piceno §18.

51. The college of priests who superintended banquets for the gods.

52. Book 1, §51.

53. Augustine, *City of God* 6.7.

54. Paulus Diaconus, *Epitoma Festi* 78.11M.

55. Livy 9.30.5–10 (abbreviated). Livy says the flute players were banned by the censors.

56. Augustine, *City of God* 8.27. Augustine's mention of feasts leads Biondo to substitute *obsonia* (victuals) for *obsequia* (offerings).

57. Aulus Gellius 1.12.6, 12 (paraphrase).

58. *CIL* VI 1374a. The pyramid (*LTUR*, 4:278–79) was called "sepulchrum Remi," in the medieval tradition (e.g., *Mirabilia Urbis Romae* §2). Poggio, *DVF*, p. 93.78–85, quotes the inscription and criticizes Petrarch by name for making the mistake (in *Familiar Letters* 6.2.5–14).

59. Cicero, *On His Own House*.

60. Tibullus 1.3.58–66.

61. Tibullus 1.3.67–72.

62. Vergil, *Aeneid* 6.638–47.

63. Vergil, *Aeneid* 6.673–75.

64. See *R.I.* 2.31–33, 34, 35. The altar was in the Senate House in the Forum. In *R.I.* Biondo speaks of ruins of the *curia vetus* near St. Peter in Chains. There, however, he confuses the Senate House with the Old Curial Offices *(curiae veteres)* on the Palatine (compare 2.60). See *R.T.* Book 1, §59.

65. Biondo does not usually use the word *paganus*. Here it comes from his fourth-century material (see Alan Cameron, *The Last Pagans of Rome* [Oxford: Oxford University Press, 2011], pp. 14–25).

66. Quintus Aurelius Symmachus (cos. 391 CE) was Prefect of the City of Rome in 384. In this year he conveyed the senate's appeal to the young emperor of the West, Valentinian II (375–392), for the restoration of the Altar of Victory, public subsidies for pagan cults, and the Vestal Virgins' rights of inheritance (see *Relation* 3). He had protested over the same matter to the previous emperor, Gratian, in 382. Ambrose's *Letters* 17 and 18 contain his successful arguments against Symmachus' appeal. For the texts, see Brian Croke and Jill Harries, *Religious Conflict in Fourth-Century*

Rome: A Documentary Study (Sydney: Sydney University Press, 1982), pp. 28–51, and for further discussion, Cameron, *The Last Pagans of Rome*, pp. 39–47.

67. Summarized more than excerpted from Symmachus, *Relation* 3, and Ambrose, *Letter* 18. Arguing for the restoration of funds for state cults, Symmachus stresses the Vestals' poverty and says nothing about charitable distributions on their part in Rome.

68. Ovid, *Fasti* 1.317–32.

69. Ovid, *Fasti* 1.335–36. In Book 1 (§45), using the same words, Biondo wrongly attributes the distinction to Aulus Gellius.

70. Ovid, *Fasti* 1.318. Ovid associates the Agonalia with Janus but not with a specific temple. In *R.I.* 2.46–53, Biondo confuses various temples of Janus and archways (also called Iani). The one referred to here is the fourth-century CE quadrafrons "Arch of Janus," still extant in Via del Velabro (*LTUR*, 3:94). For St. George, see Book 1, §55.

71. Ovid, *Fasti* 2.19–26. Lines 23–24 are a *locus vexatus*, as the corruptions in Biondo's text reflect.

72. Macrobius 1.10.1.

73. Paulus Diaconus, *Epitoma Festi* 224.1M. Here the otherwise unattested word is *pr(a)eciae*.

74. Macrobius 1.16.9–10.

75. Plutarch, *Roman Questions* 5.

76. Pliny, *Natural History* 15.119, 120. Compare *LTUR*, 1:290–91.

77. Ovid, *Fasti* 2.35–42, 45–46.

78. Vergil, *Aeneid* 6.230–31.

79. Cicero, *On the Laws* 2.24.

80. Macrobius 3.1.6–8, citing Vergil, *Aeneid* 2.719; 4.634–35, 512; 6.229–30, 635–36. In place of "bough," Biondo wrote *ianuam* (door).

81. See *R.I.* 1.17–18. The (erroneous) identification is apparently Biondo's own.

82. Ovid, *Fasti* 5.673–90.

83. If Biondo refers to the Parentalia (February 13–21), the last day of which was the Feralia, it is hard to see why he says twelve days (unless he was confused by *Fasti* 2.567–68).

84. For example, Paulus Diaconus, *Epitoma Festi* 85.13M; Augustine, *City of God* 7.7.

85. Ovid, *Fasti* 2.557–58.

86. Ovid, *Fasti* 2.617–22.

87. The word used is *applausu*, from which an appropriate meaning cannot be extracted.

88. There were no "Caprotine Kalends." Biondo is probably following Plutarch, *Romulus* 27.5–29.2, where the death of Romulus is incorrectly linked to the Caprotine Nones (July 7). We have not found the Palus Capreae (see Livy 1.16; Ovid, *Fasti* 2.491; Plutarch, *Romulus* 27.6) in *R.I.*

89. Ovid, *Fasti* 2.679–82.

90. We cannot explain this. St. Sebastian was traditionally martyred on a spot on the Palatine (*Gradus Heliogabuli*), and his catacombs are on the Via Appia.

91. Ovid, *Fasti* 2.667–70.

92. Compare Livy 1.55.4; Augustine, *City of God* 4.29. Varro seems to be an error.

93. On the Mausoleum of Augustus, see *LTUR*, 3:234–37. For the denomination "Augusta," see *R.I.* 1.41, 2.74.

94. *R.I.* 3.33–35. For a discussion of this section and the next, see Muecke, "*Ante oculos ponere*," pp. 288–98.

95. St. Mary in Aquiro.

96. Ovid, *Fasti* 2.857–60.

97. Ovid, *Fasti* 2.858.

98. *R.I.* 2.69–70.

99. *R.I.* 2.76.

100. See *LTUR*, 2:289–95.

101. Ovid, *Fasti* 5.569–70.

102. Ovid, *Fasti* 5.555. Modern texts read "Giants' trophies."

103. Biondo's association with Domenico Capranica (1400–58) can be traced to the latter's governorship of Forlì (1428–30). In the 1450s Capranica, now based in Rome, was an important patron and friend. The Palazzo Capranica (from 1451, built on earlier structures) stands with St. Mary in Aquiro on the present Piazza Capranica.

104. The Temple of the Deified Hadrian, on the Piazza di Pietra (*LTUR*, 3:7–8). The church of St. Stephen has been demolished.

105. Pliny, *Natural History* 7.103. Pliny has "in the Forum of Augustus" *(in foro Augusti)*.

106. Ovid, *Fasti* 5.559–68. We now know that the statues of Aeneas and the "Julian ancestors" were in the portico surrounding the temple.

107. Plutarch, *Pompey* 2.1–4, 6–8. Compare Giovanni Boccaccio, *Famous Women*, ed. and trans. Virginia Brown (Cambridge, MA: Harvard University Press, 2001), chap. 64.

108. Lactantius, *Divine Institutions* 1.20.6–8. There were two temples of Flora, one on the Quirinal and the other on the Aventine. The story of Larentina is told in Book 1 (§55).

109. April 27–May 3; compare Ovid, *Fasti* 4.947; 5.183–90, 277–375. The circus games took place on the last day of the Floralia, in the Circus Maximus. Biondo has perhaps confused the Clivus Publicius on the slope of the Aventine (compare *Fasti* 5.293) with the Clivus Capitolinus (*LTUR*, 1:280f.).

110. Seneca, *Moral Epistles* 97.8.

111. Campo dei Fiori. The story of Flora's house giving the square its name is apocryphal, and long lasting. We have not traced it earlier than Biondo.

112. *R.I.* 2.109–10.

113. In F. Albertini's *Opusculum de mirabilibus novae urbis Romae*, ed. A. Schmarsow (Heilbronn: Henninger, 1886), p. 86b, the builder of the *domus Ursinorum* (now Palazzo dell'Orologio) is Cardinal Francesco Con-

dulmer (d. 1453), a powerful nephew of Eugene IV. On the question of whether he was an enemy of Biondo's, see Nogara, *Scritti*, pp. xii–xiii; Fubini, *DBI* 10 (1968), p. 549; Clavuot, *Biondos Italia Illustrata*, p. 45. His name was removed from *I.I.*

114. Two dates are provided in Ovid, *Fasti* 5.725 (May 23) and 3.849 (March 23). The misnomer "Lustria" for "Tubilustrium" comes from variant readings in the manuscripts of Ovid's *Fasti*.

115. St. George's day (April 23). It was celebrated as a blessing of the standards in Milan at least; see Maria Nadia Covini, *L'esercito del duca: Organizzazione militare e istituzioni al tempo degli Sforza (1450–1480)* (Rome: Istituto storico italiano per il Medio Evo, 1998), pp. 355–56.

116. December 17–23.

117. Seneca, *Moral Epistles* 18.1.

118. From Macrobius (1.4.6), and Augustine (*City of God* 4.9), Biondo could have got the impression that there was a festival called Bacchanalia, but it was not a regular part of the Roman religious calendar. The description appears to be Biondo's own and had a long afterlife (see Muecke, "'*Fama superstes*'?")

119. Augustine, *City of God* 6.9 (who claims to cite from Varro).

120. Livy 39.13.8–13, abridged. "Esoponem" in the Latin text is a corruption in the tradition of the place of origin of the priestess, Paculla Annia.

121. Livy 39.13.14.

122. Livy 39.15.1, 6–9, 10–11.

123. Livy 39.18.8.

124. Plutarch, *Cicero* 18.1–3, compare 10.4–5. The relevance of the comment about the Catilinarian conspiracy (63 BCE), of which Publius Lentulus Cornelius Sura was a member, is hard to discern.

125. Augustine, *City of God* 1.32.

126. Augustine, *City of God* 2.6 (Fugalia); February 24: Ovid, *Fasti* 2.685–710 (Regifugium).

127. Augustine, *City of God* 2.7.

128. Plutarch, *Cicero* 5.

129. *R.I.* 2.103–22.

130. Paulus Diaconus, *Epitoma Festi* 86.7M.

131. Paulus Diaconus, *Epitoma Festi* 85.12M.

132. Macrobius 1.16.32.

133. Macrobius 1.16.30. Macrobius in fact says that Hortensius made them *fastae*, lawful for business.

134. See *R.T.* Book 2, §15; Book 1, §54.

135. Macrobius 1.16.5–8 (abbreviated). Varro, not mentioned by Macrobius in this passage, is one of the latter's sources in his chapter. Biondo has *frugum* (crops) for Macrobius' *fulgurum* (lightning strikes) .

136. Pliny, *Natural History* 18.285.

137. Pliny, *Natural History* 18.286.

138. Pliny, *Natural History* 18.287 (April 23).

139. Pliny, *Natural History* 18.289.

140. Varro, *On the Latin Language* 6.26.

141. See Paulus Diaconus, *Epitoma Festi* 255.3M; Ovid, *Fasti* 2.513–32.

142. Macrobius 1.16.11. The comment about Jewish practice is Biondo's own.

143. Livy 1.20.7.

144. Cicero, *On the Laws* 2.22.

145. Cicero, *On the Laws* 2.59.

146. Paulus Diaconus, *Epitoma Festi* 155.7M. The last clause is altered from the difficult reading in Paulus: "when they had remained in the fast of Ceres."

147. Cicero, *On the Laws* 2.59.

148. Cicero, *On the Laws* 2.59–60.

149. Valerius Maximus 4.4.1.

150. Valerius Maximus 4.4.2.

151. Plutarch, *Fabius* 27.2. This *Life* was translated by Lapo da Castiglionchio in 1436.

152. *Periochae* of Livy 48.9, 11.

153. Biondo's account of the ritual of bewailing seems to be an elaboration of Servius, *Ad Aeneidem* 6.218 (with reference to a lost passage of Pliny, *Natural History*).

154. Paulus Diaconus, *Epitoma Festi* 77.18–78.3M.

155. See Paulus Diaconus, *Epitoma Festi* 63.15M; Pliny, *Natural History* 16.139; Servius, *Ad Aeneidem* 6.216.

156. Compare Paulus Diaconus, *Epitoma Festi* 106.13M.

157. Varro, *On the Latin Language* 7.42.

158. For example, Fulgentius, *Explanation of Obsolete Words* 3.

159. Plutarch, *Roman Questions* 23. The sense has been changed by the misreading of the Latin translator's "fragility" as "frugality."

160. See Paulus Diaconus, *Epitoma Festi* 368.17–69.2M.

161. Suetonius, *Domitian* 17.

162. Paulus Diaconus, *Epitoma Festi* 207.3M.

163. Cicero, *On the Laws* 2.59 (above).

164. Nonius Marcellus 66.27M (paraphrase).

165. Paulus Diaconus, *Epitoma Festi* 163.1M.

166. Paulus Diaconus, *Epitoma Festi* 236.6M.

167. Plutarch, *Roman Questions* 26.

168. Cicero, *On the Laws* 2.56. Compare *R.T.* Book 7, p. 146h.

169. Livy 1.2.6. *Indiges* means "divine ancestor."

170. *Periochae* of Livy 119.5. Pansa was Gaius Pansa.

171. Cicero, *On the Laws* 2.56–57.

172. Pliny, *Natural History* 35.160.

173. Paulus Diaconus, *Epitoma Festi* 148.11M.

174. Pliny, *Natural History* 2.145.

175. Pliny, *Natural History* 7.187 (abridged).

176. Terence, *Andria* 127–31.

177. Pliny, *Natural History* 19.19–20. Pliny is describing a kind of asbestos cloth. He mentions it again at *R.T.* Book 8, p. 178f.

178. Suetonius, *Caligula* 1.2.

179. Macrobius 7.7.5. Macrobius is now identified with Macrobius Ambrosius Theodosius, praetorian prefect in 430 CE. In the Latin-speaking west, inhumation had already replaced cremation by the third century CE. Hadrian was emperor in the early second century.

180. Macrobius 7.7.5.

181. Cicero, *On the Laws* 2.58.

182. Plutarch, *Roman Questions* 79. Publius Valerius Poplicula reputedly in 503 BCE, and Gaius Fabricius Luscinus after 275 BCE.

183. *S.H.A.*, *Antoninus Pius* 12.3.

184. Cicero, *Letters to Friends* 4.12.

185. Plutarch, *Roman Questions* 79. In Plutarch it is the torch that is immediately removed.

186. Cicero, *On the Laws* 2.62.

187. Livy 27.27.12–14.

188. Quintilian, *Institutes* 12.6. In Suetonius, *Julius* 6.1, the reference is to his eulogy of his aunt when he was quaestor.

189. Suetonius, *Tiberius* 6.4.

190. Pliny, *Epistles* 2.1.2, 6.

191. Cicero, *On the Laws* 2.62. The translation takes liberties with the text, which is corrupt.

192. *S.H.A.*, *Maximus and Balbinus* 8.5–7. Compare *R.I.* 3.11.

193. Livy wrote *ex quo lanistis comparare mos est* (from which the trainers usually match pairs). As the beginning of the next section shows, Biondo's understanding of *lanista* was mistaken.

194. Livy 28.21.2–6.

195. Paulus Diaconus, *Epitoma Festi* 115.1M, explains *lemnisci,* ribbons attached to garlands as signs of honor. The *palma lemniscata* (adorned with ribbons) comes from Cicero, *Defense of Roscius of Ameria* 100.

196. Cicero, *Defense of Milo* 92. We have translated Cicero's *hominum* in place of the manuscripts' *omnium.*

197. *Periochae* of Livy 16.6. This was the funeral of Decimus Junius Brutus Pera in 264 BCE.

198. Valerius Maximus 2.4.7. Valerius refers to the same event as "in the consulship of Ap. Claudius and Q. Fulvius" (212 BCE). It was not put on by them.

199. Pliny, *Natural History* 11.144.

200. Pliny, *Natural History* 35.52. Pliny says Gaius Terentius Lucanus began the practice of commissioning paintings of gladiatorial shows (in the late second cent. BCE).

201. Macrobius 2.6.1. Biondo has misunderstood the anecdote. Vatinius was stoned because of the unpopularity of his show and ensured that only fruit would be thrown in future.

202. Suetonius, *Augustus* 45. Suetonius uses the technical term *sine missione,* which means the combatants could not be released without a clear victory. For this Biondo has *sine intermissione* (without an intermission).

203. Suetonius, *Tiberius* 7.1.

204. The *rudis* was a wooden staff given as a sign of freedom. Here it is confused with the *vindicta* (ceremonial rod) of manumission, mistakenly called the praetor's in some sources, for example, Paulus Diaconus, *Epitoma Festi* 381.5M; scholion on Persius 5.175. We cannot explain the unlikely notion of retirement at sixty.

205. Suetonius, *Caligula* 18.1. Both venues were in the Campus Martius. The Amphitheater of Statilius Taurus (compare *R.I.* 3.1) was the first built in stone in Rome (29 BCE, *LTUR,* 1:36–37). Biondo explains the Voting Pens (*LTUR,* 4:228f.) in *R.T.* Book 3, p. 77d.

206. See Pliny, *Natural History* 19.21.

207. Suetonius, *Caligula* 26.5 (elaborated).

208. Suetonius, *Claudius* 21.4.

209. Suetonius, *Claudius* 24.2 (paraphrase). Biondo added the reference to avarice.

210. Suetonius, *Claudius* 34.1–2.

211. *S.H.A., Hadrian* 7.12.

212. *S.H.A., Antoninus Pius* 12.3.

213. *S.H.A., Marcus Aurelius Antoninus* 11.4.

214. See §30.

215. *S.H.A., Maximus and Balbinus* 8.5–7. In fact, gladiatorial shows continued in the Roman west until the fifth century CE.

216. We cannot explain this statement. See V. Fauvinet-Ranson, "Les spectacles traditionnels dans l'Italie ostrogothique: l'attitude de Cassiodore et de Théodoric d'après les *Variae*," in *Les jeux et les spectacles dans l'Empire romain tardif et dans les royaumes barbares*, ed. F. Thélamon and E. Soler (Rouen: Publications des universités de Rouen et du Havre, 2008), pp. 143–60. Flavius Magnus Aurelius Cassiodorus Senator (ca. 490–ca. 585 CE) held various official administrative positions under the Ostrogothic kings, most importantly Theoderic (ruler of Italy 493–526 CE), and left a number of influential works. See I. G. Mastrorosa, "Cassiodoro, Biondo Flavio e la 'memoria' dell'Italia teodericiana," in *Acta Conventus Neo-Latini Upsaliensis*, ed. A. Steiner-Weber et al. (Brill: Leiden, 2012), pp. 661–70.

217. Paulus Diaconus, *Epitoma Festi* 335.5M *(simpludiarea)*.

218. From §43.

219. Livy 23.30.15.

220. Livy 31.50.4.

221. Livy 39.46.2–4.

222. Apparently, this promise is not fulfilled.

223. Compare Servius, *Ad Aeneidem* 6.253; Cicero, *On Duties* 2.55; M. Kajava, "*Visceratio*," *Arctos* 32 (1998): 109–31, p. 110: "*visceratio* simply suggests public distribution of meat which could take place on many different social occasions."

224. In classical Latin, *triclinium* was used both for the arrangement of three couches around a table and for the dining room. Biondo has fallen into error out of a desire to resurrect what he sees as the lost ancient primary sense, called for by the passage of Livy. When he describes houses in Book 9, he uses the word *cenatio* for the dining room. Compare Servius, *Ad Aeneidem* 1.698.

225. Horace, *Satires* 1.4.86–88.

226. Juvenal 5.15–18.

227. Vergil, *Aeneid* 2.2.

228. *R.T.* Book 9, pp. 182h–85a.

229. Livy 39.46.2.

230. Cicero, *On the Laws* 2.55. The "Tarquinius" of Biondo's text is an error.

231. Cicero, *On the Laws* 2.58 (Biondo omits "forum," here a technical term for an area in front of the tomb; Paulus Diaconus, *Epitoma Festi* 84.9M).

232. Cicero, *On the Laws* 2.61.

233. Cicero, *On the Laws* 2.64, 67–68.

234. Cicero, *Philippic Orations* 9.14.

235. Nonius Marcellus 32.18M (from Caesar, *Letters* II [7]).

236. Paulus Diaconus, *Epitoma Festi* 139.6M.

237. *Digest* 11.7.37.1 (Macer, *Law of Death Duties*, Book 1).

238. *Digest* 11.7.42 (Florus, *Institutes*, Book 7).

239. Cicero, *Letters to Atticus* 12.36.1.

240. Pliny the Younger, *Letters* 6.10.2–4 (to Albinus).

241. Pliny the Younger, *Letters* 7.29.1–2.

242. Cicero, *Letters to Friends* 4.12.3.

243. Pliny, *Natural History* 21.10.

244. Cicero, *Defense of Flaccus* 95.

245. Vergil, *Aeneid* 6.882–86.

246. Pliny, *Natural History* 33.53. See *R.I.* 2.124.

247. Macrobius 3.11.6.

248. *S.H.A.*, *Marcus Aurelius Antoninus* 21.5.

249. Cicero, *On the Laws* 2.43–44.

250. Cicero, *On the Laws* 2.68–69 (abbreviated).

251. Cicero, *Against Piso* 46.

252. Cicero, *Philippic Orations* 14.32.

253. Cicero, *Defense of Roscius of Ameria* 67.

254. Cicero, *Cross-examination of Vatinius* 14.

255. Nonius Marcellus 135.13–14M.

256. Paulus Diaconus, *Epitoma Festi* 156.5M. "Gentiles" in the sense of "pagans" (as Biondo uses it) comes from Paulus Diaconus (Paul the Deacon), who epitomized Sextus Pompeius Festus' *On the Meaning of Words* in the eighth century, probably at Monte Cassino.

257. Suetonius, *Caligula* 59.

258. Suetonius, *Nero* 34.

259. Augustine, *City of God* 15.23. We have restored the name of the Gallic sprites, which, in Biondo's text (and possibly his text of Augustine), is obscured by a corruption. The last phrase of the quotation belongs to what follows in its original context.

260. Cicero, *Philippic Orations* 1.13.

261. Plutarch, *Roman Questions* 34 (Cicero, *On the Laws* 2.54), referring to Decimus Junius Brutus Callaicus, consul in 138 BCE.

262. Pliny, *Natural History* 18.118. Compare Plutarch, *Roman Questions* 95.

263. Pliny, *Natural History* 18.119.

264. Marco Barbo, a distant relative of Pope Paul II, was bishop of Treviso from 1455 to 1464. See Nogara, *Scritti*, p. xxxi n. 30; G. Gualdo, *DBI* 6 (1964): 249–52.

265. The humanist teacher Ognibene da Lonigo (from a small city near Vicenza) is mentioned in *I.I.* 378h as a student of Vittorino da Feltre.

From 1453 he lived and worked in Vicenza. His friendship with Marco Barbo is attested elsewhere, see G. Ballisteri, *DBI* 12 (1971): 234–36.

266. The translation follows Herodian. Ognibene's *passim* (everywhere) does not make sense.

267. Biondo and Ognibene have "below" following a corrupt manuscript of Herodian.

268. The anticipation of the eagle here is owing to Ognibene.

269. An error introduced by Biondo, for "in honor of the emperor."

270. Herodian 4.2–3. See D. Gionta, "Storia di una citazione erodiana nella *Roma triumphans:* da Ognibene da Lonigo a Poliziano," in *Vetustatis Indagator. Scritti offerti a Filippo di Benedetto,* ed. V. Fera and A. Guida (Messina: Università degli studi di Messina, 1999): 129–53. Biondo felt free to improve the style of Ognibene's version, clarify it, and add antiquarian detail.

271. Vergil, *Aeneid* 11.182–202.

272. On this section, see Muecke, *"Gentiles nostri,"* pp. 103–5.

273. See §23.

274. Cicero, *On the Laws* 2.22. The modern text is very different from that of the manuscripts here.

275. Cicero, *On the Laws* 2.38. Biondo's version of the text is corrupt. In Cicero, in the last phrase, there is a contrast between releasing and restraining.

276. Pseudo-Asconius Pedianus, *On the Second Action of the Verrine Orations* 1.58 (Stangl p. 238).

277. Cicero, *Defense of Murena* 38–40.

278. Cicero, *On the Responses of the Haruspices* 23. Biondo's text differs at several places from the modern. We have translated Cicero's *ludius* rather than Biondo's *ludus.*

279. Cicero, *On the Responses of the Haruspices* 23.

280. Livy 1.9.6. The Consualia on August 21 were wrongly associated with Neptune Equestris.

281. Plutarch, *Roman Questions* 48.

282. A public rite of purification.

283. Livy 1.31.1–4.

284. Livy 1.35.9 says Tarquinius Priscus instituted the *ludi Romani* or *Magni* (see below).

285. *R.I.* 3.24.

286. Vergil, *Aeneid* 5.602.

287. Suetonius, *Julius* 39.3. Like the reference to Tarquinius Priscus, this citation supplements what had already been said in *R.I.*

288. In November 1395. See A. Falcioni and R. Iotti, eds., *I Malatesti* (Rimini: Banca popolare dell'Emilia Romagna, 2002), p. 121. Carlo Malatesta (1368–1429) was lord of Rimini, and Galeotto Belfiore his younger brother. See A. Falcioni, ed., *La signoria di Carlo Malatesti (1385–1429)* (Rimini: B. Ghigi, 2001).

289. The nonclassical word for tournament is more usually *torneamentum* or *torniamentum*.

290. Livy 5.50.4. The games were held on October 15. Other sources give different accounts of their beginning.

291. Livy 5.13.6–8.

292. For the context, see especially Chapter 3 of Daniel E. Bornstein, *The Bianchi of 1399: Popular Devotion in Late Medieval Italy* (Ithaca: Cornell University Press, 1993).

293. Livy 7.2.4–5. Interpretation of this whole passage remains difficult, partly owing to problems with Livy's text, of which Biondo presents a corrupted version.

294. The reading is now *exodia* (interludes).

295. Livy 7.2.7–12 (abbreviated).

296. Livy 7.2.13.

297. Valerius Maximus 2.4.4? Translation is difficult.

298. Paulus Diaconus, *Epitoma Festi* 101.1M.

299. This is largely paraphrase of Macrobius 2.7.1–4. It is important for the anecdote that Laberius was a Roman knight (as Laberius says in his prologue, quoted there), not a senator.

300. The source cannot be found.

301. Publilius Syrus, *Maxims* (F 28M) from Macrobius 2.7.11, and mistakenly attributed to Laberius here.

302. Macrobius 2.7.12–19. Biondo has a corrupt version of Pylades' name and has misunderstood the anecdote. Both Hylas and Pylades were dancing the same *canticum*, not singing, Pylades doing his own version of the one performed by Hylas.

303. Macrobius 3.14.11–12. Biondo has confused Quintus Roscius the actor with Sextus Roscius of Ameria, as at *R.I.* 2.115 and *I.I.*, Umbria §17. Cicero wrote speeches in defense of them both, rediscovered by Poggio Bracciolini in 1415 and 1417, respectively. The speech for Roscius the actor, which Biondo appears to have known (see Book 1, §42), is incomplete.

304. Macrobius 3.14.12; compare *R.I.* 2.116.

305. Macrobius 3.14.13–14; compare *R.I.* 2.117.

306. See §46.

307. Livy 24.43.7. In 214 BCE the number of days for theatrical shows at the *ludi Romani* was fixed at four.

308. Livy 25.12.12–14; compare *R.I.* 3.38–39, there citing Livy from Macrobius 1.17.27–30.

309. See *R.I.* 3.38. *Agone* (or *Circus Agonalis*) was the name for the modern Piazza Navona, on the site of the stadium of Domitian, not for the Flaminian Circus.

310. The Basilica of St. Apollinare is close to Piazza Navona. Because of the confusion with the Flaminian Circus, near where a temple of Apollo was located, Biondo is able to suggest in *R.I.* 3.39–40 that the church was intended to preserve the memory of the name of the temple. There is nothing in *LP* to support this.

311. Biondo had already made this suggestion about the Carnival *feste* in *R.I.* 3.38–39. It entailed ignoring the dates of the Apollinarian Games (July 6–13: Livy 27.23.5–7, 37.4.4) and the fact that they were held in the Circus Maximus (Livy 25.12).

312. The celebration took place in March 1457, the significant victory over the Turks at Belgrade on July 21–22, 1456. See Muecke, *"Ante oculos ponere"*, pp. 275–98; Giuseppe Marcellino, "Lo studio delle antichità romane."

313. The Ottoman Sultan Mehmed II (r. 1451–81), conqueror of Constantinople.

314. At the time of the battle (at which he was not present), Juan de Carvajal was Calixtus III's legate in Hungary. L. Gomez Canedo, *Un español al servicio de la Santa Sede. Don Juan de Carvajal, cardinal de Sant'Angelo, legado en Alemania y Hungria (?1399–1469)* (Madrid: Instituto Jerónimo Zurita, 1947), pp. 153–85.

315. Giovanni da Capestrano (1386–1456) was a much-traveled preacher and, after 1453, propagandist for the anti-Turk cause in Germany and Transylvania. In 1456 he collected an army to support Hunyadi at Belgrade. He died in October of the same year. Biondo knew him and admired him for his sanctity (*I.I.* 338f and 396e). See H. Angiolini, *DBI* 55 (2000): 744–59.

316. János Hunyadi (ca. 1400–56), governor of Hungary from 1446 and leader of Hungary's wars against the Turks, achieving some brilliant victories. He died shortly after the battle (*R.T.* Book 7, pp. 150h–51a).

317. On the identification of the Ottomans with the ancient Scythians, see M. Meserve, "Medieval Sources for Renaissance Theories on the Origins of the Ottoman Turks," in *Europa und die Türken in der Renaissance,* ed. B. Guthmüller and W. Kühlmann (Tübingen: M. Niemeyer, 2000), pp. 409–36. The river Tanais (the Don) and the mythical northern Rhiphaean mountains, for ancient authors, marked the Scythians' dwelling place.

318. Paulus Diaconus, *Epitoma Festi* 328.3M.

319. Pliny, *Natural History* 7.159. Pliny professes himself "not surprised," because there was an interval of sixty-three years between Augustus' (17 BCE) and Claudius' games (47 CE).

320. Suetonius, *Domitian* 4.3 (in 88 CE). That is, he ignored the Claudian games.

321. Livy 10.47.3. The Roman Games (celebrated in September) are the oldest; they had become annual by 366 BCE. In Livy the practice was not "royal," but "from Greece."

322. Livy 25.2.8.

323. Pseudo-Asconius Pedianus, *On the First Action of the Verrine Orations* 1.31 (Stangl p. 217). Celebrated in November, the date of the Plebeian Games' establishment is unknown. For Cicero they were the oldest of all (*Verrine Orations* 2.5.36).

324. Livy 27.6.19.

325. Ulpian, *Digest* 43.21.1.4.

326. Pliny the Younger, *Letters* 9.6.1–2.

327. Some manuscripts of Cicero read *politico* (a political man), and this was standard in the fifteenth century.

328. Cicero, *Letters to Friends* 7.1.2–3 (abbreviated).

329. Pliny, *Natural History* 8.19.

330. Pliny, *Natural History* 8.20.

331. Pliny, *Natural History* 8.21. Instead of Pliny's *euripis* (water channels), Biondo's manuscripts have *principiis*.

332. Pliny, *Natural History* 8.22.

333. Pliny, *Natural History* 8.53. "Prefect" is an error arising from a misreading of the abbreviation *P. f.* (*Publii filius*, son of Publius).

334. Pliny, *Natural History* 8.64.

335. Pliny, *Natural History* 8.65 (the paraphrase here is slightly inaccurate).

336. Pliny, *Natural History* 8.69. Pliny also calls the giraffe *nabun*.

337. Modern texts read "the Gauls call it *rufius*."

338. Pliny, *Natural History* 8.70.

339. Pliny, *Natural History* 8.96. Here Pliny is again talking about a temporary moat (*euripus*), but Biondo confuses it with Scaurus' theater, described in *R.I.* 2.106.

340. Pliny, *Natural History* 8.132.

341. Pliny, *Natural History* 19.23–24. See *R.I.* 2.124.

342. Pliny, *Natural History* 19.24. Pliny specifies that it was the Forum that was shaded and not during games.

343. Pliny, *Natural History* 33.53. See above, §38, and *R.I.* 2.124.

344. Pliny, *Natural History* 33.54. See *R.I.* 2.108, 124.

345. Valerius Maximus 2.4.6. See *R.I.* 2.124.

346. Modern texts have "in the lesser Codeta" (Turnebus' emendation). This was a swampy place in the Campus Martius (Cassius Dio 43.23.4). Compare Paulus Diaconus, *Epitoma Festi* 38.17, 58.4M.

347. Suetonius, *Julius* 39.1, 3.

348. Suetonius, *Augustus* 43.1, 3.

349. Suetonius, *Augustus* 44.1–3.

350. Suetonius, *Augustus* 45.1–4 (abbreviated).

351. Suetonius, *Caligula* 18.1–2.

352. Suetonius, *Caligula* 32.2. The *murmillo* was a type of gladiator with a distinctive fish-crowned helmet. His opponent was usually armed with a net. See below, §60.

353. Suetonius said, "in addition to the four-horse chariot races he put on the game of Troy."

354. Suetonius, *Claudius* 21.3.

355. Suetonius, *Claudius* 25.4.

356. Suetonius, *Nero* 12.4.

357. See *R.I.* 3.2, 5.

358. See *R.I.* 2.11, 3.3. St. Mary the New (now St. Frances of Rome) is on the north side of the Via Sacra of the Roman Forum. Biondo identi-

fied the adjacent ruins of the Temple of Venus and Rome as the baths of Titus (which were at the base of the Esquiline Hill, *LTUR*, 3:260)—as well as the Temple of Peace (3.2).

359. Biondo discusses the site of the Vatican Naumachia (perhaps Trajan's) in *R.I.* 1.44. See *LTUR*, 3:337f. Sts. Michael and Magnus is perched on the northern edge of the Janiculum.

360. Suetonius, *Titus* 7.3. We have translated *celeriter* (quickly), the emendation of *celebriter*, which does not make good sense.

361. Suetonius, *Domitian* 4.1–2. See *R.I.* 2.12–13, 3.13. The site of this building is not securely known. The ruins beneath St. Silvester in Capite are those of the Aurelian Temple of Sol Invictus. See *LTUR*, 4:333.

362. *S.H.A.*, *Hadrian* 19.6.

363. Placidus, *Glossary*, in *CGL*, pp. 41.9, 98.3, 148.5. See Mary H. Marshall, "Theater in the Middle Ages: Evidence from Dictionaries and Glosses," *Symposium: A Quarterly Journal in Modern Literatures* 4.1 (1950): 1–39. For "crime," modern texts have "poem."

364. Ulpian, *Digest* 3.2.2.5, citing M. Antistius Labeo (d. 22 CE).

365. *R.I.* 2.103, citing Cassiodorus, *Variae* 4.51.5.

366. Cassiodorus, *Variae* 4.51.6.

367. Compare *R.I.* 2.104, 118.

368. Compare *R.I.* 2.105.

369. *R.I.* 2.108. The topic does not reappear.

370. Paulus Diaconus, *Epitoma Festi* 284.2M.

371. Compare *R.I.* 2.122; Cassiodorus, *Variae* 4.51.9.

372. *S.H.A.*, *Hadrian* 19.6–7.

373. *S.H.A.*, *Antoninus Pius* 10.9. For "cattle," modern texts have "lions."

374. *S.H.A.*, *Marcus Aurelius Antoninus* 11.4.

375. *S.H.A.*, *Marcus Aurelius Antoninus* 17.7.

376. Orosius 7.16.4.

377. *S.H.A.*, *Commodus* 16.6.

378. This comment on his avarice has no basis in S.H.A., where the first Gordian is "worthy of respect" (7.1).

379. S.H.A., *The Three Gordians* 3.5–8 (abbreviated). The *venatio* involved the planting of a wood in the amphitheater, and the S.H.A. author claims a painting of it with the animals was extant. The names of some of the animals are corrupt.

380. Marcus Iulius Philippus (r. 244–249 CE). Compare S.H.A., *The Three Gordians* 29–30.

381. Orosius 7.20.2; Eusebius, *Ecclesiastical History* 6.34. R.T. Book 7, pp. 150e–f. See Hans A. Pohlsander, "Philip the Arab and Christianity," *Historia* 29 (1980): 463–73.

382. 247 CE. Orosius 7.20.2–3. Philip and his son were not "consuls" but "consortes" (joint emperors).

383. S.H.A., *The Three Gordians* 33.1–3.

384. Flavius Magnus Aurelius Cassiodorus Senator (ca. 490 CE–ca. 585) held various official positions under the Ostrogothic kings and left a number of influential works.

385. Cassiodorus, *Variae* 5.42.1–2 (abbreviated). The same letter is cited at greater length and with more fidelity in R.I. 3.9.

386. Compare Cassiodorus, *Variae* 5.42.6. Biondo greatly elaborates.

387. Compare Cassiodorus, *Variae* 5.42.8.

388. Compare R.T. Book 9, p. 181h.

389. Compare Cassiodorus, *Variae* 5.42.9.

390. Compare Cassiodorus, *Variae* 5.42.10.

391. Cicero, *Letters to Friends* 7.1.2. See §53.

392. Seneca, *Moral Epistles* 70.20.

393. Seneca, *Moral Epistles* 70.23.

394. Seneca, *Moral Epistles* 70.26.

395. Livy 5.23.3.

396. Livy 27.51.7–10 (abbreviated).

397. Livy 30.17.6.

398. Livy 30.21.10.

399. Cicero, *Philippic Orations* 14.11.

400. Cicero, *Letters to Friends* 15.5.

401. Cicero, *Against Catiline* 3.15.

402. Cicero, *Letters to Friends* 15.4.11.

403. Paulus Diaconus, *Epitoma Festi* 365M. *Tensae* were specific to the procession belonging to the circus games.

404. Pseudo-Asconius Pedianus, *On the Second Action of the Verrine Orations* 1.154 (Stangl p. 255).

405. Cicero, *Verrine Orations* 2.1.154.

406. Cicero, *Verrine Orations* 2.3.6.

407. Cicero, *Verrine Orations* 2.5.186.

408. Cicero, *On the Responses of the Haruspices* 21.

409. Livy 9.40.5.

410. Livy 1.20.4. Biondo has explained the *ancilia* in Book 1, §49.

411. Varro, *On the Latin Language* 5.34.

412. Macrobius 3.14.14.

413. Paulus Diaconus, *Epitoma Festi* 59.20–60.2M. On *citeria*, see H. S. Versnel, *Triumphus: An Inquiry into the Origin, Development and Meaning of the Roman Triumph* (Leiden, 1970), pp. 264–66. See *R.T.* Book 10, pp. 215b–c.

414. Paulus Diaconus, *Epitoma Festi* 128.12M, citing Plautus, *Rudens* 535–36.

415. Paulus Diaconus, *Epitoma Festi* 243.5M.

416. Macrobius 1.6.15 (paraphrase). What the boy saw were *secreta sacrorum* (secret sacred objects). We have translated freely.

417. Suetonius, *Julius* 76.1 (abbreviated).

418. Suetonius, *Augustus* 43.5.

419. Livy 27.37.7–14.

420. We have taken a slight liberty with the translation here.

421. *S.H.A., The Two Gallieni* 7.4, 8.1–7. Among the textual alterations note that *S.H.A.* referred to an act of clowns called "the Cyclops" and that "Thracians" has replaced "Franks."

Bibliography

EDITIONS OF THE LATIN TEXT

[Mantua: Petrus Adam de Michaelibus, about 1473] (See Note on the Text.)

Brescia: Bartholomaeus Vercellensis, 1482.

Brescia: Angelus Britannicus, 1503.

Venice: Philippus Pincius, 1511.

Basel: *In officina Frobeniana*, 1531.

Paris: Simon Colinaeus, 1533.

Basel: Hieronymus Frobenius and Nicholas Episcopius, 1559.

ITALIAN TRANSLATION

An (abbreviated) translation/paraphrase entitled *Roma trionfante di Biondo da Forlì* by "Lucio Fauno" (i.e., Giovanni Tarcagnota) was issued in the following printings:

Venice: Michele Tramezzino, 1544; reprinted in 1548, and 1549.

STUDIES

Cappelletto, Rita. "*Italia illustrata* di Biondo Flavio." In *Letteratura Italiana: Le opere*. Vol. 1: *Dalle origini al Cinquecento*, a cura di Alberto Asor Rosa, pp. 681–712. Turin: Einaudi, 1992.

——. *Recuperi ammianei da Biondo Flavio*. Rome: Storia e letteratura, 1983. (Note e discussioni erudite, 18.)

Capra, Luciano. "Un tratto di *Roma triumphans* omesso dagli stampatori." *Italia medioevale e umanistica* 20 (1977): 303–22.

Clavuot, Ottavio. *Biondos "Italia illustrata": Summa oder Neuschöpfung: über die Arbeitsmethoden eines Humanisten*. Tübingen: M. Niemeyer, 1990. (Bibliothek des Deutschen Historischen Instituts in Rom, Band 69.)

Fubini, Riccardo. "Biondo Flavio." In *Dizionario biografico degli italiani*, 10:536–59. Rome: Treccani, 1968.

———. *Storiografia dell'umanesimo in Italia da Leonardo Bruni ad Annio da Viterbo*. Rome: Storia e letteratura, 2003.

Hay, Denys. "Flavio Biondo and the Middle Ages." *Proceedings of the British Academy* 45 (1959): 97–128.

Marcellino, Giuseppe. "Lo studio delle antichità romane e la propaganda antiturca nella *Roma triumphans* di Biondo Flavio." *Studi Classici e Orientali* 60 (2014): 163–86.

Masius, Alfred. *Flavio Biondo, Sein Leben und Seine Werke*. Leipzig: Teubner, 1897.

Mastrorosa, Ida Gilda. "Paganesimo e Cristianesimo nella *Roma Triumphans* di Biondo Flavio." In *Roma pagana e Roma cristiana nel Rinascimento. Atti del XXIV Convegno Internazionale (Chianciano Terme—Pienza, 19–21 luglio 2012)*, edited by L. Secchi Tarugi, pp. 217–30. Florence: Franco Cesati, 2014.

Mazzocco, Angelo. "Biondo Flavio and the Antiquarian Tradition." In *Acta Conventus Neo-Latini Bononiensis: Proceedings of the Fourth International Congress of Neo-Latin Studies*, edited by R. J. Schoeck, pp. 123–36. Binghamton, NY: Medieval and Renaissance Texts and Studies, 1985.

———. "Decline and Rebirth in Bruni and Biondo." In *Umanesimo a Roma nel Quattrocento*. Atti del convegno, New York 1–4 dicembre 1981, edited by P. Brezzi and M. de Panizza Lorch, pp. 249–66. Rome: Istituto di Studi Romani, and New York: Barnard College, 1984.

———. "Rome and the Humanists: the case of Biondo Flavio." In *Rome in the Renaissance: The City and the Myth*, edited by P. A. Ramsey, pp. 185–95. Binghamton, NY: Medieval and Renaissance Texts and Studies, 1982.

———. "Some Philological Aspects of Biondo Flavio's *Roma Triumphans*." *Humanistica Lovaniensia* 28 (1979): 1–26.

———. "*Urbem Romam florentem ac qualem beatus Aurelius Augustinus triumphantem videre desideravit*: A Thorny Problem in Biondo Flavio's *Roma triumphans*." *Studi Umanistici Piceni* 30 (2010): 133–41.

Miller, Anthony. *Roman Triumphs and Early Modern English Culture*. London: Palgrave, 2001.

Muecke, Frances. "*Ante oculos ponere:* Vision and Imagination in Flavio Biondo's *Roma triumphans.*" *Papers of the British School at Rome* 79 (2011): 275–98.

———. "*Fama superstes?* Soundings in the Reception of Biondo Flavio's *Roma triumphans*" In *A New Sense of the Past: The Scholarship of Biondo Flavio (1392–1463)*, edited by Angelo Mazzocco and Marc Laureys. Leuven: Leuven University Press, 2016. (Supplementa Humanistica Lovaniensia, XXXIX).

———. "From Francesco Barbaro to Angelo Poliziano: Plutarch's *Roman Questions* in the Fifteenth Century" (forthcoming).

———. "*Gentiles nostri:* Roman Religion and Roman Identity in Biondo Flavio's *Roma triumphans.*" *Journal of the Warburg and Courtauld Institutes* 75 (2012): 93–110.

Nogara, Bartolomeo. *Scritti inediti e rari di Biondo Flavio.* Vatican City: Tipografia Poliglotta Vaticana, 1927. (Studi e Testi 48.)

Nuovo, Isabella. "*De civitate Dei—Roma Triumphans.* Teologia della storia e storiografia umanistica." In *L'Umanesimo di Sant'Agostino*, edited by Matteo Fabris, pp. 573–87. Bari: Levante, 1988.

Pincelli, Maria Agata. "La *Roma triumphans* e la nascita dell'antiquaria: Biondo Flavio e Andrea Mantegna." *Studiolo. Revue d'histoire de l'art de l'Académie de France à Rome* 5 (2007): 19–28. Reprinted in *Mantegna e Roma. L'artista davanti all'antico*, edited by T. Calvano, C. Cieri Via e L. Ventura, pp. 79–97. Rome: Bulzoni, 2010.

Tomassini, Marina. "Per una lettura della *Roma triumphans* di Biondo Flavio." In *Tra Romagna ed Emilia nell'Umanesimo: Biondo e Cornazzano*, edited by Marina Tomassini and Claudia Bonavigo, pp. 9–80. Bologna: CLUEB, 1985.

Index

Entries are by book and paragraph number; Ep = Dedicatory Letter; Pr = Proem.